CONTENT

Introduction

Index

Abbreviations used in footnotes:

OBC *Oxford Bible Commentary* Eds. J.Barton and J. Muddiman   OUP 2001

PGM D. O. Wilhelm *Preaching the Gospel of Mark* Westminster John Knox 2008

RTF R. T. France *The Gospel of Matthew* Eerdmans NICNT 2007

TGJ J. Ramsey Michaels - *The Gospel of John* - Eerdmans NICNT 2010

TGL Michael Mullins *The Gospel of Luke* Columba Press 2010

TGM R. H. Lightfoot *The Gospel Message of Mark* Oxford, Clarendon 1950

TLC *The Lectionary Commentary - Third Readings* Ed. R. E. Van Harn   William B. Eerdmans 2001

UFG John Ashton *Understanding the Fourth Gospel* Oxford (2nd Edition) 2007

INTRODUCTION

Motivation

This work began due to the combination of a number of factors: my early experience of retirement, an invitation to address *The Northamptonshire Theological Society* and a sense of unease with some of the current dominant ideologies which influence much of church life and ministry, but which seem contrary to the spirit and sometimes the letter of the New Testament Gospels.

When I retired from full-time Baptist ministry I thought I would focus on and enjoy the kind of wider reading which the demands of my job had largely prevented. For about a year I read intensively and very widely, novels, poetry, plays and some of the Bible in French translation - formerly only enjoyed as a holiday diversion. To be honest, apart from reading the French Bible the other reading left me with a sense of "incompleteness". I had to acknowledge that after forty years of pastoral ministry and related theological study, theology was the diet to which my soul had become accustomed. The new diet was not making me feel satisfied - or healthy. Other writings were very enjoyable as a side-dish, but not as the main course.

It so happened that this realisation coincided with an invitation to speak to the local theological society on a subject of my choice. I needed no second invitation to get back to some serious theology. I settled on the rather grand title: *A Gospel-Shaped Church - Gospel Bases for Corporate and Individual Discipleship*. My intention was to produce a relatively short paper based on the study of the four New Testament gospels to offer some basic guidelines for personal Christian living and for a church.

In recent years, not least in my experience of British Baptist denominational life, but also in other denominations and countries, there have been repeated calls for "A Mission-Shaped Church"[1] and for "A Gospel-Shaped Mission"[2]. I believed, and still do, that it might be helpful to lose what I consider this particularly unhelpful kind of promotion of *Mission*. It is often associated with a church growth agenda which judges success by increases in the numbers attending a particular church. On such a basis Jesus at his death was a miserable failure. I am not suggesting that churches should not be engaged in mission. Jesus certainly was. But it should not be some special addition to, or focus for church life requiring extra time, increased effort and tailor-made "programmes". Time-consuming programmes are a way of justifying management systems and may give a sense of achieving "goals", but

---

[1] e.g. *Mission Shaped Church* Church House Publishing 2004
[2] e.g. *'Gospel-shaped mission of a Mission-shaped Church'* James Bell - Bishop of Knaresborough 16th Paulinus Lecture 2008

what is important *"... is not how much we do, but how much love we put into the doing - a lifelong sharing of love with others"*[3]. If the whole life of a church or an individual is Gospel shaped, in other words if our lives have at their heart good news for others, this will naturally produce features of our lives which might be identified as mission. But this will primarily arise out of what we believe about God as embodied in Jesus, not out of what we think we ought to be doing, or what we have decided others should believe. Furthermore, I do not believe you can separate one aspect of following Jesus for special treatment as Gospel-shaped. It is a case of all or nothing. The DNA of a church or any Christian should be, as it was for Jesus, the gospel as good news for living and sharing.

So my original aim was to offer some of the shaping principles which are to be found in the four New Testament gospels telling the life of the one whom Paul described as *"the head of the church, his body, of which he is the Saviour"*. Paul went on to say *"Now as the church submits to Christ..."* (Ephesians 5:23-24a). Paul took it as a basic expectation that a church will honour Jesus Christ by the way it functions in all its several parts embodying his spirit. Many churches today may need to change their priorities in order to meet this expectation. The churches' task is not to preserve and propagate a religion, but faithfully and humbly to act in response to what we learn from Jesus; with an ever open invitation for others to be part of both our learning and of what we do as a consequence.

> *"Therefore everyone who hears these words of mine and puts them into practice is like a wise man who built his house on the rock"* (Matthew 7:24)

I soon realised that my aim for the theological society lecture was impossible in the time available. Looking solely at Matthew with a view to identifying principles for the life of a church was taking far longer than I had anticipated. I decided to concentrate just on Matthew, to see what this particular gospel writer had to offer. Although I instinctively knew it before, this reinforced for me just how distinctive is Matthew's gospel - and how satisfying it was to listen to Matthew as much as I could without "other voices" blurring what he has to say. Furthermore, I think this brought out what I already knew: the same would be true for each gospel. I realised I would thoroughly enjoy trying to allow each gospel to speak its own message to me, what I would call a *"monoptic"* approach to the four New Testament gospels. My work became much less looking at the gospels to share with others what they might say to a church; and much more re-searching the gospels to see what each one had to say to me. The result of such study is what follows in this book. I still hope some of what I have discerned may be instructive for the life of a church, and at times comments and the selection of subjects for reflection may make this obvious, but it ceased to be the major concern. Perhaps the questions which I

---

[3] Mother Teresa *Words to Love By* 1983 p.75

regularly ask in preparation for preaching ought always to be a prerequisite for attempting to encourage or help others to ask the same question, "What does this scripture say to me?"

Re-reading the gospels for this study in this *monoptic* way has been like music to my ears - and even though the discordant notes are often of particular interest, as the old chorus puts it, "*In my heart there rings a melody ... with heaven's harmony .... of love*"[4].

Personal Considerations and Perspectives

All writing comes out of a personal (and/or group) history and a particular culture. This is patently true of this work. It might therefore be helpful to share a little of the personal and cultural history which lies behind it. I was born in 1942 mid-way through the Second World War, and raised in a conservative evangelical Baptist Church in London's East End before studying in Yorkshire and Lancashire for Baptist Ministry. Like many others of my generation I have been influenced over the years by writers and commentators on the Gospels and theologians as varied as G. Campbell Morgan, Denis Nineham, F.F. Bruce, C. H. Dodd, Paul Tillich, William Barclay, John Robinson, John Vincent, Anthony Thiselton, contributors to IBRA daily Bible Readings or The Expository Times, ministers whose sermons I have been privileged to hear, and countless others whose sharing of the fruits of their studies and experience has nourished my mind and spirit. I have tried when preparing this work to read the gospels as deliberately as possible seeking to hear what the Gospels themselves actually say, rather than what centuries of interpretation suggest they might be saying; but I am aware that many subconscious voices will not have been completely silenced. It is also difficult to read one of the Gospels and then to read another without noticing similarities and differences. Even though this has some benefits, this in itself inhibits the ability to give each Gospel its own unique voice. But just as I firmly believe it is beneficial to read Genesis 2-3 without the works of Augustine and Milton, or even Paul exercising undue influence, trying to look at each of the Gospels with fresh eyes is equally worthwhile.

I have not set out to write an academic work. For example, I have deliberately not reflected on the subject of genre[5]. The academic's main task is rightly to contribute

---

[4] Written by Eleton Roth 1924
[5] For those wishing to look at the subject of genre, Richard Burridge,) provides a scholarly and extensive treatment. Burridge concludes, "*The genre of the four canonical gospels is to be found in βίος literature. (What are the Gospels?* Second edition Eerdmans 2004 p.246). This understanding of the genre of the gospels as "biographies" reflects my approach to them in the present work: and Jesus as their subject is the major key for their interpretation (See Burridge p.248).

to the machinations of the academy, whereas I have only ever engaged in postgraduate study as a means to critically examine, refine and improve my contribution to ministry and church life. Whilst taking every opportunity to use "the academy" as a proving ground for my praxis and highly valuing the work of those who are engaged in academic studies of the highest order, throughout my ministry, and in this work I have consciously tried not to express my own thoughts in academic language. I think that is actually following the example of Jesus who interacted with the academics of his day, but did not teach like them. He spoke in ways which were open to the non-intelligentsia - which, of course, is not at all the same as "unintelligent"[6]. I hope this work will have something to offer to others engaged in ministry and to lay people who are prepared to engage in what might be for them a different approach to thinking about the gospels.

Brief periods ministering in France and Jamaica have been important for me, but England has been the cultural context of ninety-five per-cent of my life, ministry and study. This limits my perceptions. For example, I had always seen the story of Jesus' disciples' unwashed hands in Mark 7 as strictly related to religious ritual, or even religious preciousness, until an African pastor opened my eyes to another way of seeing it. He pointed out that in his African community the washing of hands before eating is not an optional nicety. When people use their hands to eat, if they neglect basic hygiene, it can be a matter of life and death. Whilst it should be recognised that in Jesus' day the concept of germs was unknown, the notion of "uncleanness" was important[7]. It is hard to imagine that hands unwashed after possibly being used for toilet purposes would not cause offence. MacCulloch points out that much traditional African culture includes genealogies and "spirits". Africans were often delighted to discover confrontation with "evil spirits" in the Bible, and confidently expected them to be as much part of their churches' lives as in their communities; whereas many in Western countries have found them difficult, even embarrassing[8]. A missionary working with impoverished children in Kolkata tells how when the children arrive for school they have a shower and put on a clean school uniform. This is not "empty ritual". These children have a deep sense of being accorded dignity and of belonging because the "norm" in their lives is isolation and marginalisation[9]. Their experience can provide new insights into the treatment of the Prodigal son by his father in Luke 15. No single perspective is enough on its own; but each may have a valuable contribution to make, including the predominantly English one which is offered here.

---

[6] Cf. Acts 4:13

[7] Job 17:9 and Psalm 24:4 can be interpreted as promoting physically as well as morally clean hands

[8] D. MacCulloch *A History of Christianity* 2010 p.882

[9] Sara Stone reporting on the work of the *Good News Children's Education Mission* in Kolkata. "Engage" Sprng 2014 Pub. BMS World Mission.

However, if one perspective is allowed to dominate interpretation, that can be unhelpful. For example, Dawn Wilhelm seems to have adopted the view that Mark's Gospel is ALL about a supernatural, apocalyptic battle between the forces of evil (demons, evil spirits, etc.) and the force of good (Jesus, God, and the Holy Spirit). For example, "*The successful exorcism of the demon in the synagogue at Capernaum* (Mark 1:21-28) *assures us of God's ultimate success in the apocalyptic showdown between the powers of God and the destructive forces of evil*"[10]. Actually the story is about Jesus helping a person who has a serious problem, but Wilhelm never says so, because the overlay of a heavy, pre-determined framework has obscured the detail. I would go so far as to say it has taken the humanity, the immediacy and all practical value out of it. In looking at the Gospels I have tried to allow the details to speak for themselves whilst at the same time recognising repeated or emphasised themes; and acknowledging that the details are part of a "whole" story. I have also engaged a "personal" reading of each gospel does not mean a failure to engage in a critical evaluation of what I believe the gospel has to offer.

Most will be familiar with the saying, "*Not seeing the wood for the trees*". This is always a possibility when gospels are dissected into verses or even individual words which are commented on one by one. Although I have always regarded it as a great privilege to have been part of a class which Professor Zunz of Manchester University took through Mark's Gospel in Greek one word at a time, the gospels also need to be read, at least sometimes, as complete works with overall aims and intentions. So this work may at times offer comments on individual verses or passages, but always bearing in mind possible underlying or overarching themes which may emerge from the wider context of the particular gospel. Take for example, Jesus' beatitudes. In Matthew (Matt.5:3-10) they are separated by a considerable distance from Jesus' woes (Matt.23:13-32). This is entirely in keeping with Matthew's major emphasis on Jesus as a teacher; whereas Luke places Jesus' woes (Lk.6:24-26) immediately after the blessings (Lk.6:20-22) in keeping with Luke's focus on the great reversal inaugurated by Jesus' presence in the world. Taking each gospel as a discreet entity leads to four very different works, not the homogeneous picture which can deprive the authors of their individuality and potentially unique impact on their readers or listeners.

Ashton says, "*Broadly speaking then, an exegete is entitled to take the text in its entirety. Certain caveats, however, are in order. There is no virtue in the kind of pure unsullied approach sponsored long ago by the so-called New Critics and subsequently by the Postmodernists, too high minded to look outside and behind the text for alternative sources of illumination*"[11]. On this basis Ashton to my mind

---

[10] PGM 2008 p.25
[11] UFG p.306

often allows the sources he discerns *outside and behind the text* to override a more reasonable interpretation of the current "received" text. I was once told that a thesis I had submitted was a postmodernist thesis, whereas I believed I had written a thesis within the discipline of Pastoral Theology. Perhaps the unpredictable nature of "serious, contemporary, pastoral engagement" inculcates a measure of post-modernity however unwittingly. But to approach a text within such a work ethic is by no means indicative of being "high-minded". Indeed it is perhaps the very opposite in its determination not to impose pre-determined frameworks on any text or story. As the Old Testament scholar Brevard Childs so ably argued, source criticism can become an end in itself. But the outcomes of vigorous full-hearted, open-minded engagement with the text as received have their own validity. This is not "*The swampland of ... epistemological relativism, whereby one set of beliefs is as true as any other, and there is no way to adjudicate the difference*" which Braaten decries[12]. It is recognition that "*any proposed outline of the gospel is imposed by the interpreter, not dictated by the author, and is therefore open to discussion*"[13].

Whilst my original aim to use the gospels as a basis for a pattern for church life has been replaced with an attempt to let the gospels speak for themselves, nonetheless as a minister for forty years it was impossible to read the gospels without relating on church life as I have shared in it, to some extent shaped it, and now experience it in semi-retirement. This is quite deliberate in my commentary on Matthew, but from time to time it will also be apparent in critical comments arising out of my reading of the other gospels and in my final reflections.

I am not writing as the consummate practitioner. Nor am I offering a made-to-measure outfit for a church based on my experience. Rather I hope to offer reflections to support my contention that material taken from the Gospels could create an individually (or personally?) tailored mantle or set of principles for a body of believers. Very Baptist!

I have an unashamed Baptist perspective on church life. For Baptists true to their inherited identity Church tradition is important, but never mandatory. Rather, Scripture enlightened by the working of the Holy Spirit, in tandem with the local church meeting's discernment of the spirit of God's contemporary movement, are the two *sine qua non* for all decisions affecting church life. Each local gathered company of believers has a duty to seek to know God's will and purpose for its life at this moment in time - and possibly in the future. But only the future in so far as a church should always be open to God's leading and redirection. So the manner and

---

[12] Carl E. Braaten *That they may believe - A theology of the Gospel and the mission of the church* Eerdmans - Grand Rapids 2008 p.150. For Brevard Childs see *Biblical Theology in Crisis* (1970) and *The New Testament as Canon: An Introduction* (1985)
[13] RTF p. 2.

direction of its life may at any time be altered radically by what we hear God saying to us through the scriptures, our common life and the life of the world! Of course, we Baptists don't achieve this high standard; sometimes because it is attitudes more than structures or plans that need to be changed, but I can honestly say it has been my consistent aim for over 40 years - and it has been an exciting adventure - like all discipleship inevitably shot through with blessing oft times in the form of failure.

Approaches to the Bible

It is probably helpful to give a brief introduction to how I relate to the Bible in general, and the Gospels in particular. I offer two comments (a + b) and some additional thoughts (1-4).

a) I am frustrated that I cannot remember either the author or the exact wording; but the gist of what he or she wrote has stayed in my mind, reflecting my own belief: *"We should not be so concerned to understand the Bible, as ready to stand under it"*. Reading and studying the Bible in any sense as the Word of God will not be an exercise in mastery, but a practice in humility.

b) Christian humility is not subservience. It is recognising godly authority or wisdom, and then living in continuous interaction with it and response to it. Julia O'Brien said, *"Rather than simply obeying the Bible, we should engage with it"*. Kenneth Wilson sees the Bible as *"a key part of God's great conversation with us"*[14]. Some live constrained by the Bible; others, whilst finding direction through the Bible, find a fuller life and freedom in God as a result. I grew up in the former camp, but with joy discovered and have embraced the latter possibility.

1) I find it bracing to consider the parable of The Prodigal Son as Jesus' autobiography. In his reflections on the parable of the Prodigal Son Henri Nouwen offers a different but possibly related challenge. He says that when we reflect on the story we are invited to imagine ourselves into it as any one of the characters. When this is encouraged, most often we are expected to identify with the Prodigal Son, less often the older brother, and rarely with the servants which should possibly be our most natural role as Christians. But Nouwen asks if we have ever heard or preached a sermon in which we were invited to put ourselves in the place of the loving, forgiving Father - which Nouwen suggests is probably the most likely lesson Jesus or the Gospel writer Luke intended to give. Maybe we imagine ourselves as the pleading son rather than the forgiving father because we have an inbuilt tendency toward dependency rather than responsibility, toward receiving

---

[14] "Methodist Theology" T & T Clark 2011 - reviewed by Richard Clutterbuck in Expository Times Feb. 2012

rather than giving. Certainly our individual personalities and predilections, as well as the societies in which we function, shape our reading of any text, including the Bible. But these are *false limits* which the hymn writer suggests *God will not own*[15].

But the reverse can also be true. The Bible as a living Word of God can be, and is intended to be the instrument whereby that Word which is of God comes alive in us, to re-shape us, individually and corporately. In Genesis 1, John 1, the birth narratives and genealogies of Matthew and Luke the word of God gives shape, meaning and purpose to life, including the ongoing human story. All life at its best is appreciated as, and motivated by God's dynamic and creative spirit. The Bible is not a closed world, it is an open door through which we can see the world and all its people as God's, and we are invited to enjoy and love what God has given.

2) I aim to give the New Testament Gospels the crucial role in interpreting the Bible. Tiemeyer expresses very well much of my own thinking:

> *I shall read the text, maintaining that all Scripture is inspired by God and therefore profitable in the life of believers (2 Tim.3:16). Moreover I shall hold on to the plain literal sense of the text set in its historical context; and I shall maintain that this 'plain' reading has something to tell us as Christians today .... The view that all Scripture is authoritative allows for the view that some parts of Scripture are more authoritative than others .... In Christian interpretation this role of guiding star is normally assigned to the New Testament."*[16]

I have, however, taken this one step further in selecting the Gospels as "the" *guiding star*. An obvious question is why give the Gospels more significance than any other part of Scripture. My answer is that in doing so I believe priority is given to being a "Christian", rather than being a follower of church teaching. Church teaching includes that which is given in the rest of the New Testament by Paul and others. I know this can be a false distinction, for the gospels to some extent were almost certainly written by "the church" as teaching for "the church". But churches in my experience often seem to give priority to the letters in the New Testament. The focus is then on "in-house" church life, and a cerebral appreciation or personal moral response is encouraged, and perhaps inevitable. This is in contrast to the Gospels which are narratival, lived, an invitation to share a life, to abide or remain

---

[15] Frederick W. Faber, Oratory Hymns, 1854

[16] L-S. Tiemeier Expository Times 121:10 July 2010 p482f. It should be noted that unlike Martin Luther, neither Tiemeier nor I use this principle to regard other parts of Scripture as inferior.

Introduction

in Jesus who challenged institutional life and predominantly ministered in, and deliberately died for the world, "out there".

Braaten says, "*The gospel that Jesus preached (Mk.1:14) and the gospel preached by Paul about Jesus (Rom.1:1 and 2 Cor.11:7) are together the gospel of the God who elected Israel*"[17]. I disagree. The four Gospels are the only extended attempts in the New Testament to tell the story of Jesus and in this way to encapsulate his spirit which as "Christians" we are called to share. The natural or root meaning of the word Christian is *ian*/follower, combined with *Christ*/Jesus. It is the Gospels which give the primary pictures of the life, teaching and spirit of Jesus Christ who is to be taken to heart and followed. There have been those who have suggested that the Gospels were written later than Paul's writings and therefore should be treated as secondary, but Baukham has argued:-

> "*The essential ingredient in the making of the Gospels - John as well as Synoptic - is the testimony of eyewitnesses ... they are simply firsthand observers of the events*" (and) "*Understanding the Gospels as testimony, we can recognise theological meaning ... not as an arbitrary imposition on the objective facts, but as the eyewitnesses perceived the history ... observable event and perceptible meaning.. Testimony... is where history and theology meet*"[18].

Baukham's thesis might be open to question, but he provides substantial arguments to support it[19], and it accords with my own long held practice of treating gospels as the primary witness to, and resource for, the faithful following of Jesus. Furthermore André Resner Jnr. refers to the tradition which says, "*Mark is actually Peter's story related to Mark in Rome. If so...*"[20] In other words, this thesis need

---

[17] Carl E. Braaten *That they may believe - A theology of the Gospel and the mission of the church* Eerdmans - Grand Rapids 2008 p.10

[18] R. Baukham *Jesus and the Eyewitnesses* 2006.117 - Cited by John Collins *Re-thinking 'Eyewitness' in the Light of 'Servants of the Word' (Luke 1:2)* Expository Times June 2010 No.9 p.447.

[19] Op Cit. p.5 *We need to recover the sense in which the gospels are testimony. This does not mean they are testimony rather than history. It means that the kind of historiography they are is testimony. Trusting testimony is not an irrational act of faith that leaves critical rationality aside; it is the rationally appropriate way of responding to authentic testimony... the way the witnesses perceived the history [was] in an inextricable coinherence of observable events* (fact) *and inherent meaning* (or interpretation cf. p.411). Crucial to Baukham's thesis is that, "*The gospels were written within living memory of the events they recount*" (p.7). Baukham points out that John's Gospel internally makes the claim to have been written by an eyewitness (John 21:24f) (p.328)

[20] TLC 2001.p.236

Introduction

not be ruled out, and if the primacy of Mark in the Synoptic Gospels is accepted, there is even more good reason to treat the Gospels as the primary resource for discovering and following the way of Jesus[21].

I recognise that the selection of the four New Testament Gospels is itself part of church tradition. This is a challenge for Baptists and other evangelicals who claim to put the Bible not tradition first. Every position has its inherent weaknesses. This is one of mine! However, I believe on balance it is less of a weakness in attempting to follow Jesus than any other available choice. The bottom line is that the Gospels must have been produced by people in the churches, perhaps intended to some degree for the churches' internal consumption (as with Matthew? & John?), or to be used by churches to share with others the story of Jesus (as with Luke? & Mark?). But all four are written to inspire faith which bears fruit for the Kingdom. We are told in The Acts of the Apostles about new believers: "*They devoted themselves to the apostles teaching*" (Acts 2:42) - this could not have been the letters or thoughts of Paul! It has to be acknowledged that unlike the genuinely Pauline epistles the Gospels are probably not the direct teaching of an apostle, but they are the closest we are ever likely to get to the first disciples-cum-apostles' accounts of the story of Jesus.

3) Foundational for this work is my conviction that each of the four gospels has different emphases. It is theologically naive always to conflate them. But what they have in common is that they were written so that the story or the good news of Jesus as God's agent of salvation would continue to be told, heard and believed. That is fundamentally what a church should be for people – the herald of Good News rooted in the story of Jesus. So often in its history it has been anything but good news. A reasonable yardstick to use when considering the churches of which we are a part is to ask, "Are we sharing the story of Jesus? And is it good news?"

4) The gospels are full of symbols and lessons from life and earlier scriptures. A gospel-shaped church will be likewise. Sadly, as mentioned above, churches in addressing the un-churched have often taken the "in-house" New Testament letters of Paul to believers and other "ministers" as its primary resource. All the gospels, including John's, are stories to be told. But churches too often turn the imaginative, inclusive, living and potentially life-giving Word of God into a deadly dull, excluding set of facts, morals and dogma. The Bible as God's mind-blowing Word is not best served by those who take it literally. Indeed, "literalism" is a sign of not taking the scriptures seriously enough. Once, when being interviewed by a church's deacons with a view to the pastorate I was asked, "*Do you believe that*

---

[21] See also Mullins on "eyewitness" and "ministers of the word" (TGL pp.103-104: Columba Press)

Genesis Chapter one is literally true?" To which I replied spontaneously, *"Oh. It is much more important and inspiring than that".*

I wonder sometimes when a Bible passage is read and there is no chance for reflection, or alternatively when it is read and followed by a 20-30 minute exposition or even worse an *excursus,* how many people remember anything of the Bible passage itself. Has the Bible itself spoken to them or had a reasonable chance to do so? When preaching I have regularly encouraged people to have a Bible in front of them, to feel free to ignore what I am saying and to let the Bible speak for itself. Jesus' charge against the religious of his day was, *"So, for the sake of your tradition, you have made void the word of God"* (Matt.15:6). Traditions, including our own, are not always helpful. We should heed the warning. It should go without saying that I hope readers of this "commentary" will have Bibles open to test what is offered here.

Method

In order to arrive at a comparable balanced picture of each of the gospels I adopted a particular framework of discipline for this study. The first requirement was to read each Gospel straight through a number of times in its entirety: to "feel" the work as a continuous and complete story; to get an overview of the particular evangelist's work. Next, to read that Gospel recording my own reflections as to what the individual Gospel seemed to be conveying in its several parts and as a complete work. Eric Franklin says, *"Any serious student of the Gospels will regard a synopsis as an indispensable tool, for comparison of Luke's episodes with their parallels in Matthew and Mark allows the contours of Luke's Gospel to be clearly seen"*[22]. I respect but reject that point of view. A synopsis can be a useful tool at times, but I dispute that it is "indispensable" for either being "serious" or for discerning contours when reading one of the gospels. Indeed, synopsis can be unhelpful. Kiefer, for instance, often reads John as though John was a commentary on Mark. I believe in doing this he loses the uniqueness of John's recounting of the feeding of a multitude and the teaching associated with it[23]. Mullins' interpretation of Luke often seems dependent on the use of Matthew or Mark. He also makes regular reference to the Book of the Acts of the Apostles. As helpful as this may be, I believe strongly that something is lost when the Gospels are treated as though they do not have an essential independence and individuality. There are scholars who concur that each gospel has quite distinct contributions to make to thinking about Jesus. France says: *"From the point of view of an exegetical commentary it is more responsible to read Matthew's story on its own terms, and in its own literary context, than to look for its meaning primarily in terms of how it differs from*

---

[22] OBC p.924
[23] cf. Kiefer on John 6:1-71 *OBC* p. 971

Luke's[24]. Mullins cites Strelan's belief (for example) that Luke should be allowed to "*stand on his own two feet and to be seen, heard, and understood for himself as ... (an) independent thinker and author*"[25]. Mullins does not always put France's or Strelan's beliefs into practice. I have tried to do so.

A useful and telling example of how failure to read the gospels as separate witnesses can lead to error is given by Richard Burridge. He recounts how Luke's unnamed "sinful" woman who washed Jesus' feet with her tears and dried them with her hair before anointing them (Luke 7:36-38) was linked in the early church people's imagination with both John's Mary of Bethany who anointed Jesus' feet in her own home (John 12:1-8)[26], and the account in Matthew and Mark of the anointing of Jesus' head by a woman at Bethany in the house of Simon the leper (Matt:26:6ff. & Mk: 14.3ff.). Possibly added somewhere into this mix was the fact that another Mary, Mary Magdalene was cleansed of seven demons (Mark 16:9; Luke 8:2). So we finish up with Mary Magdalene as a sinful woman: for which there is no evidence. Being possessed by demons is a sign of sickness not sin. Burridge says, "*It is important, therefore, when preaching on this passage* (John 12:1-8) *to study what John actually says very carefully - and to expound that, rather than the popular amalgam*"[27]. Michaels gives a scholarly basis for this separate treatment of John in preference to interpretation based on synopsis. "*While there are exceptions, most interpreters today view the Gospel of John as independent of the other written gospels (even Mark), yet familiar with many of the unwritten traditions behind them*"[28]. Contrast Ashton, "*The easiest way of explaining the formal similarities between the Synoptics and the Fourth Gospel is that John was acquainted with at least one of the others*"[29]. To interpret one Gospel by using another is fraught with danger, whereas judicious comparison and contrast based on the independent appreciation of each gospel can prove beneficial. My attempts to engage in judicious comparison can be found in the chapter "Reflections" which follows the consideration of each of the four gospels as an individual voice. I recognise that the subjects chosen for reflection might be considered eclectic, even unbalanced, but they are in keeping with the

---

[24] RTF p. 821

[25] TGL p.26

[26] Ottermann recounts how women in northern Brazil were horrified to find that in contrast to John the woman in Luke is described as "a sinner"; which they understood to mean a prostitute and carrying with it all the negativity and demeaning stereotyping which many of the women in Brazil had unjustly experienced. (*"How Could He Ever Do That to Her?!" Or, How the Woman Who Anointed Jesus Became a Victim of Luke's Redactional and Theological Principles* in Gerald West *Reading Other-wise: Socially Engaged Scholars Reading with Their Local Communities* Pub.Society of Biblical Literature 2007:105)

[27] Richard Burridge *TLC* p.538

[28] TGJ p. 29

[29] John Ashton UFG 2007 p.24

acknowledged approach of this work. That is they are a personal selection arising out of reading the gospels rather than a list of subjects which have some "academic" justification.

Looking at each Gospel separately, as an independent text, can also have other benefits. For example, their dissimilar records of the way Jesus' first disciples began following him leads to a number of quite different possibilities how this might happen today (see Chapter 6). If the stories are blended into one, then one understanding tends to dominate, even to become the norm. This can have disastrous consequences as people are manipulated to fit into one single way of responding to their sense of calling to follow the way of Jesus. Martin Dibelius recognised that the divinisation of the historical Jesus required separate answers for Paul, the Synoptists and John "*for they all reached their positions independently*"[30].

Truth which is inclusive rather than exclusive, open-hearted and not narrow-minded, as is surely the case of the truth which Jesus lived, is bigger than any one set of facts, or any one story. For this reason I have tried my best to let each Gospel speak for itself as an independent witness to the greater truth which even four Gospels cannot comprehensively cover. John's Gospel itself acknowledges this:

> "*There are also many other things which Jesus did; were every one of them to be written, I suppose the world itself could not contain the books that would be written* " (John 21:25).

There are no extant manuscripts of the "original" Gospels, and even if such things existed they were not written in English. Even the process of writing included the translation of the vernacular into literary genre. We know that in any translation and in many transmissions something is lost as well as possibly gained. Even when using the most ancient manuscripts of the gospels there are still possible variant readings. This should caution us against dogmatism with regard to what scripture "says". Sadly, from my point of views, the tendency to think that a particular translation can be "accurate", conveying exactly what was originally intended, is widespread; often assumed without any reflection, but sometimes championed as a matter of principle. This has been particularly so with the "Authorised Version" (KJV). For many years the Gideon Society, funded and dominated by American fundamentalists, would only distribute the KJV, because in spite of its title page it was not seen as "authorised/monitored" by a king with a political as well as an ecclesiological agenda, but by God (plus, of course, their "Founding Fathers").

---

[30] Martin Dibelius *From Tradition to Gospel* James Clark & Co. 1971

To read a translation of the Bible in any other modern language immediately throws any assumptions of a definitive text into question. Take for example the story of Abram and Isaac. In English translations we normally read something like, *"So they went both of them together"* (RSV Genesis 22:8). However the Hebrew word יחדו rendered "together" in English is usually translated as *"ensemble"* in French Bibles. "Together" and "ensemble" do not have exactly the same meaning or nuances. As far as I am aware, there is not a French word which exactly parallels the English word "together", just as there is not an English word which exactly parallels the Greek "λόγος" (Logos) or the Hebrew "דָּבָר" (Dabar). Neither the French nor English words carry all the connotations of prohibition which the Hebrew attaches to "together". Words are specific to the language world in which they are generated and used. Any translation is at best an approximation. As Nicholas Wood put it, *"There is no such thing as a literal translation. We are always looking for equivalences"*[31]. A good measure of humility in making any claims as to what the Bible says is appropriate. The evangelists themselves were presumably translating the language used by Jesus and his Jewish contemporaries in Judaea and Galilee (Hebrew or Aramaic) into Greek[32]. Nonetheless we must do our best to be true to their witness in what is a two-part practice. *"We should let each and every part of the Bible .....determine what its central themes are, and let them inform each other mutually"*[33].

For this study the main version used has been the NIV (UK), often in conjunction with other versions (RSV, NRSV, GNB, etc.) and the Greek text[34]. I hope in this way to have got as close as I can to the oldest manuscripts as well as the best contemporary English translations. But I have also used secondary resources. In refining my thoughts *The Oxford Bible Commentary* [35] has been a valuable tool. It includes a succinct, scholarly commentary on each Gospel by a leading expositor, who in turn has drawn upon the wisdom of other noteworthy commentators. As someone who has used scripture so often in the context of preparation for worship, I enjoyed using the sermons/expositions from various authors in *The Lectionary*

---

[31] Dr. Nicholas Wood: Northampton University's Chaplaincy Autumn Lecture 2011 on *William Carey*

[32] Dr. Lena-Sofia Tiemeier *Expository Times* vol.21:10 July 2010 p.483. Note: There are those who would claim that in fact at least the Synoptics were originally written in Hebrew. But they probably remain a very small minority for good reasons. cf. some of David Bivin's work issuing from the Jerusalem School of Synoptic research; or Guido Baltes *Hebräisches Evangelium und synoptische Überlieferung. Untersuchungen zum hebräischen Hintergrund der Evangelien* Pub: Tubingen: Mohr Siebeck 2011

[33] *The Gospel of John - A Commentary* F.D. Bruner Eerdmans 2011

[34] British & Foreign Bible Society Greek Text 1962 - a collaborative work of Erwin Nestle (Wurttemberg) and G.D. Kilpatrick (Oxford)

[35] OBC 2001. A slightly more conservative one-volume Bible commentary is *Eeerdman's Commentary on the Bible* Eds. Dunn & Rogerson 2003

Commentary on the Gospels[36]. In addition to these I have used at least one more recent commentary on each Gospel. This has been a way of checking that what I have gleaned through reading the Gospels is not patently refutable on the basis of what other and more able contemporary scholars have discerned. In some senses I have entered into a very one-sided conversation with them[37]. I am deeply indebted to all these "other voices" for their inspiration, guidance and at times correction, whilst still feeling at liberty to work out my own faith and understanding of the gospels in "fear and trembling" – as is proper if in any way these texts communicate the living God[38]. Bruner largely bases his excellent commentary on John's Gospel on the classical commentaries of the likes of Augustine and Aquinas[39]. There is clearly no singular right or wrong way to plumb the depths of a gospel text; for on the other hand France (in spite of a thirty-five page bibliography) says: "*My intention has always been to make this a commentary on Matthew, not a commentary on other commentaries*".[40] Whilst making no claim to France's erudition, I believe his intention to be of great worth and have attempted to do something similar on a far smaller scale for each of the four New Testament gospels.

There will be those who turning to a commentary on the four gospels will look for a consistency in presentation or format. The reader will not find that in what follows. It would, I believe, demonstrate that the four gospels can in some sense be fitted into a common mould. It is avowedly my conviction that they should not be treated in such a way. There are not four different "Jesuses", but the one Jesus evoked innumerable and vastly different personal responses in those who met him "in the flesh" and those who recorded his life and death in the form of gospels. The New Testament offers four of these. It has been my privilege to grapple with such distinct testimonies. This work invites you to do the same.

I hope I will be forgiven for what might seem an *ad hoc* mixture of tenses used in looking at the gospels. For example, sometimes it seemed right to say, "Jesus said", at other times, "Jesus says". I can only offer in my defence the words of Diarmaid MacCulloch: "*In the gospels, events in historic time astonishingly fuse with events beyond time; it is often impossible to define a distinction between the two*"[41]. That is the experience the following pages do their best to share.

---

[36] *The Lectionary Commentary* on the Gospels edited by Gunton & Burridge (2001)

[37] e.g. PGM; or TGJ

[38] Cf. Philippians 2:12

[39] Cited in UFG p.4

[40] RTF p.xix

[41] Diarmaid MacCulloch *A History of Christianity* p.77f. Pub. Penguin 2010

My special thanks to Simon Woodman who lectured in New Testament studies at South Wales Baptist College as well as being an honorary lecturer at Cardiff University and an author specialising in the Book of Revelation[42]. He took time out of his current work as co-minister at Bloomsbury Central Baptist Church to read through a draft of this work offering encouragement, useful criticism and suggestions for additional reading.

[42] Simon Woodman *The Book of Revelation* SCM Core Press 2008

Chapter One
MATTHEW - A NEW DECALOGUE FOR CHURCHES

Introduction

As may be apparent at times, this chapter on Matthew in its original form was written to be given as a lecture. The intention was to look at all four gospels in order to arrive at a gospel-basis for church life. Matthew is the only Gospel to mention the church (Matt.16:18 & 18:17), so it seemed the best Gospel with which to begin. As mentioned in my general introduction, the intention to look at all four gospels in this way was altered partly because of time factors, but also I recognised that Matthew offers a singular voice which does not benefit from being subsumed in a wider testimony. Matthew's gospel narrative deserves to be, and is here considered in its own right.

Whilst I contend that there are more subtle, yet equally important substrata from which can be derived a "Matthean message", the strongest element in my view is what I have called a New Decalogue. After some thoughts based on the earliest chapters of Matthew we shall look at a proposed content for such a Decalogue; but to get a feel for the gospel as a whole it may be helpful to offer a summary outline. I shall not do this for the other gospels, but the manner in which Matthew has constructed his gospel might itself be considered a template for church life - i.e. a balance of action and reflection[1].

(N = narrative/story/action   D = discourse/commentary)

Chapters
1-4 N Main characters introduced - *Genealogy, Birth & death threat, John the Baptizer/Baptism, temptation, first ministry and first disciples*
5-7 D Jesus' greater demands on Israel *- The Sermon on the Mount - the embryonic new community is called to a higher righteousness - the way of life for citizens of the Kingdom of Heaven/God*
8-9 N Jesus' deeds within and for Israel *- a ministry of healing*
10 D The sending of the twelve *- extension of ministry through words and deeds of others - the new community will encounter hostility - principles for evangelism*
11-12   N   Negative responses *– Herod imprisons John the Baptizer – Jesus is subjected to constant criticism*

---

[1] France notes that there are parts of Matthew's Gospel which appear to have little structure - e.g. 11:2 - 16:20 which appears to be a miscellany of Jesus' words and deeds, possibly based in Judaea, but for which there was no natural place in the rest of the story as Matthew tells it with just a single visit South (RTF p.137).

13   D   Reflections on negative responses - *the Parable of the Sower and other parables - the new community uses both old and new in its teaching - the (sometimes hidden or latent) presence of God's Kingdom*

14-17 N   Founding of a new community
Death of John the Baptist, feeding of multitudes, Peter's confession, Jesus' prediction, The Transfiguration

18-20 D   Instructions to the new community in church and social matters - *the new community practices forgiveness   and reconciliation - relationships in the Kingdom of Heaven/God*

21-23 N   Commencement of the passion
Entry to Jerusalem, cleansing of the Temple, questions - conflict - the 7 "woes"

24-25 D   The future: judgement and salvation - *teaching on "the end times", two parables, the final judgement - the new community prepares itself for the coming of the Son of Man - the future of the Kingdom of Heaven/God*

26-8 N   Conclusion: the passion and resurrection
Anointing, Passover meal, betrayal/desertion/denial by disciples, trials/abuse, death/burial, resurrection, the great declaration and commission [2].

We shall look later at what I suggest is a Matthean Decalogue, given its fullest literary summary in chapters 5-7 (The Sermon on the Mount). But Matthew provides a backdrop to the Sermon through the chapters which precede it (Matt. 1-4). It is to these first four chapters we now turn.

A Historical Background

Matthew's gospel begins with a genealogy (Ch.1) in which Jesus is presented as the apogee of the God-structured-history of an entire nation called to be "God's people". Jesus was part of "a bigger story", a nation's story; yet the genealogy notes and values the lives and roles of individuals. Each one of them, including specifically named gentiles and females, is included in a purpose which embraces yet surpasses individual or national history, is wider than their own location in time and space. This radically inclusive and expansive story and all who have a place in it are part of God's purposes in which Jesus plays a crucially significant role. Though those named may be regarded legitimately as representative characters, in some sense their individual lives as much as the life of their tribe or nation find their full meaning through what God does in Jesus. Matthew will end his gospel

---

[2] I am indebted to Dale Allison Jr. for much of this outline (OBC p.847). It is commendable and generally helpful although the divisions are necessarily over simplified.

(Matt.28:19-20) with an indication that individuals in every time and place can similarly find their fulfilment by relating to Jesus.

Many of the individuals named in this and other Biblical genealogies did no more than what we might call the ordinary things of life - including just struggling to survive. Some of them, especially perhaps the four women who are named, did very down-to-earth things, some of which can challenge modern religious sensitivities. France calls the four women *four embarrassing mothers*[3]. The life of many churches, and of individuals within them, could benefit from this down to earth and inclusive perspective. There is little support here and a notable challenge for those who believe that orthodoxy, moral rectitude, signs and wonders, selective recruitment, and personality cults are important or essential factors in the working out of God's purposes[4]. The church magnifies "Saints" – God loves "sinners".

We will learn elsewhere in Matthew that people who draw attention to themselves, or who think they are spiritually rich are outside of a kingdom which is for the humble and the poor in spirit - that is, people like Jesus and his spiritual ancestors[5]. Jesus wanted people to see signs not miracles and contrary to the ambition of so many in twenty-first century culture did all he could to avoid being "famous" or "sought after" in any glamorizing sense. Jesus' experience that miracles were not effective in producing the desired outcome of repentance led to a series of "Woes" directed at towns where miracles had been performed (Matt.11:20f). But how rarely are repentance and miracles directly connected today? If anyone or any group boast of performing miracles Jesus advised caution as to their worth (Matt.7:22-23) and their provenance (Matt.24:24). No one in any of Jesus' parables of judgement is ever asked, *"How many miracles did you perform?"* The question is consistently, *"How well did you serve your master and your neighbour?"* - And master and neighbour may at times be indistinguishable (cf. Matt 25:31-46). If God was at work in Jesus, Jesus stood within a truly remarkable and extremely varied succession of God's "servants".

---

[3] RTF p.37

[4] Matthew's inclusive understanding of God's purposes, especially of non-Jews is made quite explicit in the account of the healing of the gentile centurion's servant, which elicits the comment *Many will come from the east and west and join Abraham, Isaac and Jacob at the feast in the Kingdom of Heaven* (8:11). France commenting on this passage says it is *entirely in accord with the consistent NT hermeneutic which understands the nationalistic and territorial promises of the OT in terms of a new supranational people of God* (RTF p.318). France also notes the likelihood that Matthew's second account of a mass feeding (15:32-38) is *to be interpreted as a Gentile counterpart to the Jewish feeding in 14:13-21.* And the whole of 15:21-38 might be seen as a ministry to Gentiles which parallels Jesus ministry to the Jews (RTF p.597).

[5] E.g. Moses is described as *a very humble man, more humble than anyone else on the face of the earth* (Numbers 12:3)

The Work and Worth of Jesus

The Gospels are full of Christological nuances in addition to some quite direct statements, even within a story format. For example, right up front Matthew offered the first indication of the work of Jesus - to save. "*She will bear a son, and you shall call his name Jesus, because he will save his people from their sins*" (Matt 1:21). Such statements, however, are not self-explanatory. They are an invitation to engage in reflection – for example, who are "*his people?*" and what are "*their sins*"? It is not my intention here to reflect at length on the concept of sin, but suffice it to say it is to do with "missing the mark", being misguided, being lost, being less than God intends us to be; all of which may include a moral dimension, but it is so much more than that. So is Jesus' work: and so should be the work of churches. People's morality should not be our first concern, because it was not Jesus's. Their "lostness" or "brokenness" was. Perhaps Jesus makes this more explicit when he says his ministry is not to the (self) righteous, but to sinners (Matt 9:13).

As has already been said, only Matthew's Gospel has any mention of "The Church"[6]. It is probably significant that one of the two chapters in which it appears is about broken relationships, about dealing with this "sin", and it leads into the parable of the unforgiving servant (Matt.18:21-35). One of the attractive features of the gospels is how often particular teaching given early in the story then echoes on through the rest of the Gospel. Matthew 1:21 feeds into Matthew 18.

But to continue with the early part of Matthew's Gospel; we find that Matthew contrasts the story of the unwise, fearful and fearsome King Herod with the story of wise men. In this way Matthew impresses on his readers a proper response to Jesus, even Jesus as a child. The powers of this world will want to destroy Jesus. What do wise people do? They take the trouble to discover where Jesus is to be found; they fall down in humble worship (not just bow); they offer gifts which relate to the work of God's kingdom and they continue to listen for God's counsels of wisdom. This is a very simple template for churches willing to recognise and use it. France says,

> *For these foreign dignitaries* (who could gain an audience with "King" Herod) *to prostrate themselves in homage before a child in an ordinary house in Bethlehem is a remarkable illustration of the reversal of the world's*

---

[6] To some this is obviously an anachronism. But it is worth taking into account France's view that in Matthew from the call of the first disciples onward Jesus is seen to be very deliberately establishing his "church", an *ekklesia* - not a hierarchical or physical structure, but a *messianic community* (RTF p.145). Matthew 16:18 might usefully be read with this in mind.

values which will become such a prominent feature of the Messianic proclamation of the kingdom of heaven (Matt.11:25f; 18:1-5; 20:25-28; etc.)[7].

We might to advantage set alongside this story which comes at the beginning of the Gospel one near the end, the story of the anointing of Jesus' head with expensive perfume by an unnamed woman in which a gift is made of such a kind and in such a way that Jesus' messiah-ship is acknowledged - generosity and appropriateness hand-in-hand (Matt 26:6-12). There will be others in Matthew's gospel who feel it appropriate to bow down, to adopt the stance of a worshipper in Jesus' presence, including his disciples when they acknowledged Jesus to be the Son of God (Matt.14:33) and the Canaanite woman (Matt.15:25) who is the only person in Matthew's gospel to be told by Jesus that she has demonstrated *great faith* (Matt.15:28).

Baptism

Matthew tells the story of John the Baptizer who recognised his need of Jesus' ministry (Matt.3:14). In Matthew John the Baptizer's story begins with John as an adult exercising a prophetic ministry of word and sacrament designed to prepare people to receive Jesus. I have never heard his ministry used as a basis for the induction or ordination of a minister of the gospel, yet it is surely a most relevant, even archetypal story. John's message is a call for people who are missing the mark (*amartano*), to turn their lives around and to testify to their repentance (*metanoia*) by Baptism. Of course for Baptists like myself, this story is music to our ears, because from Matthew we know Jesus was baptised as an adult believing it to be in accordance with God's will (Matt 3:15). We are told, "*he came up out of the water*" (Matt.3:16), so we Baptists and others with some justification see "total immersion of believers" as a logical exposition and outworking of this account of Jesus' baptism. "*The language of Baptism speaks of immersion, of being saturated and snowed under in the life of God*"[8].

However true this may be, it has to be recognised that in Matthew's Gospel, apart from Jesus' commission to his disciples at the end of the gospel (Matt.28:19) baptism plays no role whatsoever in the ministry of Jesus or of his disciples. It is not Jesus, but John whose ministry includes baptism. Indeed when Jesus questions the chief priests and elders about the nature of John's baptism, he makes no

---

[7] RTF p.75. For a far more complicated, yet possibly more rewarding perspective on Matt.2:1-12, see Elaine Wainwright's "*Place, Power and Potentiality - Reading Matthew 2:1-12 Ecologically*". But for this work I am reading it ecclesialogically.

[8] W. J. Abraham TLC p. 166

reference to any such ministry of his own (Matt.21:25)[9]. France in his commentary on Matthew's gospel says that Jesus, like John the Baptizer, probably did include baptism as part of his ministry. He says of John that we cannot be certain how John baptized people, but the basic meaning of the verb "baptize" probably indicates immersion. However, he goes on to say,

> *We need not assume that the actual method was always the same, nor that John's method was necessarily the same as that of later Christian practice, especially when the latter took place away from a major river such as the Jordan* [10].

One of the challenges which arises out of a sensitive and imaginative reading of a gospel is to know whether in reading the stories I am invited to learn about Jesus with the aim that I might try to become more like him - or should I be focused on what he taught the disciples so that, like them, I can also be a disciple? Or are the two aims identical? I think not! But it helps to know which choice I am making. In Matthew I believe we have a clear case of Jesus being portrayed as the example to be followed. "*A student is not above his teacher, nor a servant above his master. It is enough for the student to be like his teacher, and the servant like his master*" (Matt.10:24f). If we would live in the manner of Jesus, his story, including his baptism, can offer guidance.

The Scriptures

Jesus' sense of calling, or his commissioning (Matt.3:17) is followed by a story of his temptation (Matt.4:1-11). All Jesus' temptations are set in "challenging places": stony desert, temple and high mountain. It is noteworthy that Deuteronomy provided teaching against temptation for Israel in comparable challenging situations - high mountains and desert[11]. Because he knew the appropriate scriptures, Jesus was able to use them as a defence against the propositions put to him by the devil. That may be to state the obvious, but I suspect that less and less

---

[9] According to John's Gospel Jesus himself never baptised anyone, only his disciples did that - and we don't know how they did it.

[10] RTF p.109. It is interesting that in the story of Philip and the Ethiopian Eunuch the availability of "water" leads to the invitation to be baptized; and *they both went down into the water* and like Jesus *came up out of the water* (Acts 8:38f). This might suggest a continuing pattern which was accepted as the norm. France also remarks that the order of the participles in Matthew 28:19-20 suggests baptism as an initiation or enrolment ceremony which precedes a life-long learning process, rather than Baptism as the result of having arrived at a certain level of understanding (RTF p.1116).

[11] Deuteronomy 6 & 8

church people in England know their scriptures[12]. Why? I would like to suggest some answers. Sadly these answers do not provide solutions to the problem of widespread biblical illiteracy, but if the points are taken seriously they may offer pointers as to what may need to be done.

First, and contrary to the spirit of Deuteronomy 6:7, the great stories of the Bible are not told to most children - even children who come to church. I found the editors of all-age Sunday worship resources very resistant to the idea that sometimes they might move away from slavishly following the Sunday lectionary and include more of the great stories from the Bible - especially for use with children[13]. Churches do not use the Bible as a book of stories in a way that fires imaginations and creates memorable mental pictures. It is commonly used instead as a study guide, an intellectual exercise, in an often vain effort to promote the remembering of data or stimulate a predetermined response. I am immensely grateful to those people who when I was a child loved the most graphic stories in the Bible, and shared them with me.

Second, the Bible is no longer repeated in memorable choruses. Seventy years on I still have in my heart such choruses as, *"Only a boy called David, only a babbling brook"*, or *"The wise man built his house upon a rock"*. In addition, nowadays the connection between scripture and hymns is rarely highlighted. Many older hymn books had a verse of scripture written against each hymn. Some of the supposed connections were questionable, but it was preferable to the absence of any obvious connection which typifies many modern hymn books. In passing I would mention that the use of OHP for singing hymns, usually displayed one verse at a time, perhaps as an aid to singing yet another new hymn or "worship song", adds to the difficulty of seeing how a hymn as a whole might convey a biblical story or biblical messages. In my experience projection inhibits reflection and connection.

Third, translations of the Bible which were once poetic and memorable have been replaced by easily forgettable prose. In addition we have multiple versions of the Bible so there is no common or shared text: acceptably post-modern; but certainly

---

[12] Research conducted for the Bible Society in 2014 supports this view. The report says: 1 in 5 children (20%) did not choose Noah's Ark when asked to select from a list the stories they think are from the Bible. A similar proportion (19%) did not choose Adam & Eve. Almost one in three (29%) did not select The Nativity as a part of the Bible, rising to 36% for The Good Samaritan, 41% for David & Goliath and well over half, 59%, for Samson & Delilah and Jonah & The Whale.

[13] I do not wish to denigrate particular individuals who work for particular publishers. They provide valuable resources for teaching children in church. But in my correspondence with the major providers I have found a reluctance to balance the widespread use of lectionaries by churches with the need for children's imaginations to be fed with the most exciting (non-lectionary) stories from the Bible.

no help in producing "community memories". It was fascinating during my time in Jamaica where the KJV was still widely used to listen as preachers would recite half a verse of scripture and leave the congregation to recite the rest. There was no problem for these people to use their scriptures in testing times. It therefore gave me very mixed feelings to see the NIV as the pew Bible in a large Kingston church. On the one hand I welcomed the potential move away from much uncritical use of the Bible as an "authoritative" and therefore unquestionable word. On the other hand I could sense that inevitably the then current shared knowledge and use of what is in the Bible by people ranging from the highly academic to the illiterate in time would be lost.

Fourth, in England in my childhood days of the 1940s for most people there was a common diet of information and entertainment via the radio which included daily acts of worship and other frequent quotations from the Bible (KJV). This, along with many other symbols of a shared identity, has changed to individualised, private, multiple-choice media within a multi-faith, multi-cultural society. I welcome much of this change and have a long standing and deeply satisfying involvement with Northampton Interfaith Forum as well as years ministering amongst an increasingly ethnically rich diversity of people. But for the majority there is a consequent loss of the Bible as a well known, oft-recited resource – compounded by the demise of "Scripture Lessons" in schools. The primary task of churches to share the gospel in word as well as deed is no longer a shared or devolved task. If we do not in some way assist the scriptures to enter into people's minds and hearts, it will not be done.

Fifth, multiple interpretations of Scripture is the accepted and welcome norm in many churches. But it has the unintended result that people no longer feel able to use it in the kind of direct and confident way Jesus used it in the story of his temptation. It is worth reiterating the important insight that it is less important to understand scripture than it is to stand under it – and similarly being able to recite it is secondary to being willing to find fullness of life through it. But if the word is not "*hidden in my heart* ...." (Ps.119:11)

There are other reasons why the scriptures have been lost as a spiritual resource for the majority of church people. Pressured lives, for example, may make setting aside time for daily devotions and Bible reading more difficult. Therefore the pressing Gospel challenge for all of us is first to think through how we encourage and enable as many as possible to regularly engage with the scriptures at a personal level. The current proliferation of Bible-related apps is one example of realistic attempts being made to engage with people whose lives seldom include lengthy periods of time for reflection. The second step is to help people to see the Bible as an available resource which can be used with confidence in a way that helps our commitment to worship God alone - to give God priority over all other calls upon our time and attention. That is the essence and outcome of the story of Jesus' trials in the wilderness, overcoming the temptations with the witness and purpose of the scriptures in mind[14].

Jesus' Early Teaching Ministry

Having demonstrated his obedience in the waters of baptism and in his acceptance of scriptural priorities[15], Jesus ...

> "... *began to preach, saying, 'Repent, for the kingdom of heaven is at hand.'* (Matt.4:17... And) *he went about all Galilee, teaching in their synagogues preaching the gospel of the kingdom and healing every disease and every infirmity among the people*" (Matt.4:23)[16].

Healing was an important part of Jesus' public ministry; but Matthew tells us, "*Seeing the crowds, he went up on the mountain, and when he sat down his disciples came to him. And he opened his mouth and taught them*" (Matt.5:1-2). At this time in Matthew's gospel we only know of four disciples; but a disciple is always one who is taught. Matthew (7:28) might seem to suggest there was no separation of the disciples from the crowds when Jesus was teaching: but the crowds, typical of the Middle East, should probably be pictured as listening-in to the teaching Jesus addressed primarily to his disciples. In fact, in other places Matthew makes it quite clear that Jesus separated disciple-teaching from his general ministry: the whole of chapter 10 leads to: "*When Jesus had finished instructing his twelve disciples, he went on from there to teach and preach in their cities*" (Matt.11:1). In Matthew, what we call the Sermon on the Mount, which includes the Beatitudes, is not meant for Jill and Joe public to consume[17]. If a person has no eschatological vision of the ultimate reversal of the present order of things, nor a vision of the Kingdom of Heaven breaking into the here and now, nor an ongoing relationship with Jesus whose death will make sense of and redeem all

---

[14] Almost the entirety of the Qur'an is a call to obedience, to give Allah's will absolute priority - and it is interesting to note the efforts of Islamic scholars to see that the Qur'an remains a book which is recited and remembered in its Arabic poetic musicality. The message is in the medium.

[15] France suggests that the story of Jesus' temptations is *not concerned with his messianic agenda, but with his own relationship with his Father* (RTF p.560), but I cannot see how the two can be separated. Indeed, since the story so clearly acts as an introit leading immediately into Jesus' preaching and calling his first disciples, his agenda might be regarded as the prime message of the temptation story.

[16] *Kingdom of God* is used 4 times by Matthew and in other Gospels as well: but *Kingdom of Heaven* is used 32 times and is peculiar to Matthew; as is his use of the word Kingdom without either *of heaven* or *of God*.

[17] Unlike the teaching on the plain in Luke 6:17ff.

suffering and death, how could anyone possibly understand or accept that they are blessed when they mourn, or blessed when someone persecutes them for doing the right thing? When Jesus said, *"Don't cast your pearls before swine"* (Matt.7:6), it wasn't an insult to swine, it was inappropriate for them, and for the pearls! Churches need to feed people appropriately - which makes for considerable difficulty in public worship when committed disciples and unbelievers may share worship, word and sacrament together.

Ministers might especially take note of this for funeral services and other rites of passage with predominantly un-churched congregations. Typical "Church-based" ritual, language and faith-understandings, suitable for those familiar with such things are regularly used in contexts where they are at best ineffective as a means of ministry and at worst harmful confirmations of the opinion that churches have a private language and are only concerned with themselves[18]. Between 1960 and 1980 the practice of many Baptist churches to separate the ordinance of the Lord's Supper from public worship was abandoned. The desire to be more inclusive was commendable, but something significant was also lost. Other denominations maintain segregation with regard to some sacraments, but rarely for "the word" - perhaps the one thing in which Jesus practised discrimination more than any other [19].

The Sermon on the Mount

There can be no single interpretation of the Sermon the Mount, but looked at from the point of view of guidance for churches, a key point seems to be that Kingdom values have to be more than froth, more than surface appearance; more than a

---

[18] For more on appropriate ritual for funerals see *Help I've been asked to conduct a funeral* Ted Hale (2013) available via the Baptist Union website resources
http://www.baptist.org.uk/Groups/220878/Guidelines_and_Support.aspx
[19] Consideration might also be given to Matthew's account of Jesus' teaching in which only Jesus can choose who will understand his words and who will not (11:25-27). Jesus in the spirit of Isaiah says he teaches in parables precisely so that ONLY disciples will understand (13:10-13 - not in the Sunday lectionary!). But all 4 gospels testify that they, the disciples, did not! Even Jesus' private explanations did not always seem to lead to real understanding. France helpfully notes that Jesus' use of parables often served to divide people into those who understood and those who did not. Indeed the parables in chapter 13 all involve division; good and bad soil, good grain and weeds, good fish and bad: or the exceptional; the seeker after the pearl of great price or hidden treasure, and the householder who can produce new as well as old. The modern reader may think of parables as helpful illustrative stories, but in fact they are "hidden things". *In this way the medium (parables) is itself integral to the message it conveys (the secrets of the kingdom of heaven). A "parabole" is an utterance which does not carry its meaning on the surface ... it demands thought and perception - entering into an interactive process to which the hearer must contribute - if the hearer is to benefit from it* (RTF pp.500, 502).

Sunday habit! Definitely more than slavish observance of rules and rituals. Saying, *"Lord, Lord"* is not enough (Matt.7:21); nor is just *"hearing the word"*. Whatever Luther and his interpreters might have made of Galatians and Romans prioritising of faith, Jesus' teaching is quite clear (cf. Matt:7:21-7, 21:28-32). Hearing must be accompanied by doing, but equally important what is done must be a response to what God is saying. Many churches fixated on exorcisms and miraculous healings might do well to heed Jesus' caution that casting out demons and performing miracles may be anathema to God (Matt.7:22f). Hearing and not doing is unacceptable to Jesus, but equally so is doing without having first listened.

Kingdom values require a willingness to listen, then to act, and to act generously; to *go the extra mile - to turn the other cheek - to forgive the unforgiving* - and so on (Matt 5:38-41). But this comes from within, and comes most of all from our personal times of devotion. Knocking on heaven's door, asking for heaven's benediction, and seeking to know God's purposes (Matt.7:7) are all intended to shape the way we look at the world and how we live in it. The way the world is filtered into our souls is crucial to evoking a truly God-given way of life.

> *"The eye is the lamp of the body. So, if your eye is sound, your whole body will be full of light; but if your eye is not sound, your whole body will be full of darkness. If then the light in you is darkness, how great is the darkness! "No one can serve two masters; for either he will hate the one and love the other, or he will be devoted to the one and despise the other. You cannot serve God and mammon."* (Matt.6:22-4).

There is a depth and singularity of commitment required for "kingdom life" which is rooted in our soul (*Psyche*), our inmost being, the most influential motivator of all we think, say or do. As Jesus put it, *"What good will it be for someone to gain the whole world, yet forfeit their soul? Or what can anyone give in exchange for their soul?"* (Matt.16:26). Heart and soul seem to be interchangeable terms for Matthew. Today we might well say, "Her heart is not in it" to express the same lack of inner commitment. Elsewhere in Matthew's Gospel the theme recurs and is expressed precisely in such terms. *"Out of the overflow of the heart the mouth speaks. The good man out of his good treasure brings forth good, and the evil man out of his evil treasure brings forth evil"* (Matt.12:34-5.). Perhaps to emphasise the importance of this message, Matthew records a further conversation about what comes from inside a person's heart, in contrast to what comes from their stomach (Matt.15:10-19)[20].

---

[20] The "heart" in the Bible is usually considered to be the source of deepest thoughts, leading to words or actions which are often unconsciously motivated. So in Jesus' teaching lust - an internal process - is as dangerous and damnworthy as adultery - an overt act. Jesus' teaching *promotes an "inward" concern with motive and attitude above the "outward" focus on the visible and quantifiable observance of rules and regulations* (RTF p.197). *We need*

Chapter 1 - Matthew

It is apparent that for Jesus the *how or why* something is done (i.e. the attitude/intention) is as important as *what* is done (see above on Matt.7:21-3). As Dr. Andrew Morton suggested in a recent sermon, the greatest reversal invited by the New Testament is to turn our focus from our own *virtue* to a focus on *God's grace*. The generous or gracious love of God in which we trust needs to be reflected in our lives. I reject the notion that we cannot be commanded to love. Love when it is agape, even if motivated by gratitude, is primarily a duty not an affection - *"Above all be concerned with the Kingdom of God and with what he requires of you"* (Matt.6:33). In this sense we don't have to like someone to love them - though in loving them we may come to like them. Furthermore love is visible, it bears fruit.

The work of the churches in relation to committed disciples is to help one another to interiorise Kingdom values. The Sermon on the Mount (especially chapter 6) gives guidance as to how this is done. J. P. Meier speaks of *Jesus' demand as a radical interiorization, a total obedience, and a complete self-giving to neighbour that carries the ethical thrust of the Law of God to its God-willed conclusion* [21]. For Matthew Jesus is the new Moses. Like Moses Jesus was threatened by a murderous king's decree at birth. He passed through the waters and went up the Mountain to declare the new Decalogue, ten "words" describing life which has God's blessing because it accords with the kingdom of heaven which Jesus embodied. R. T. France says of the kingdom of heaven, or Kingdom of God:

> *The phrase the kingdom of God in both its Hebrew and Greek forms denotes the dynamic concept of "God ruling". It represents, in other words, a sentence of which the subject is not "kingdom", but "God". This dynamic sense is now better conveyed by an abstract noun such as "kingship" or "sovereignty" rather than by "kingdom", which has become in general usage a concrete noun. Matthew's summary of John's and Jesus' declaration that the kingdom of heaven has arrived, might thus be paraphrased as "God's promised reign is beginning" or "God is now taking control". The traditional portrayal of Peter as porter at the pearly gates*

---

to remind ourselves that Jesus' aim is not to establish a new and more demanding set of rules to supplant those of the scribes and Pharisees. It is to establish a "greater righteousness", a different understanding of how we should live as the people of God, an alternative set of values (RTF p.217f.) *The rhetorical questions of 5:46-47 therefore sum up the thrust of all these examples of greater righteousness: it is to live on a level above that of ordinary decent people, to draw your standards of conduct not from what everyone else is doing, but from your heavenly Father* (RTF p.224).
[21] cited in France - RTF p.190

> *depends on misunderstanding "the kingdom of heaven" as a designation of the afterlife rather than denoting God's rule among his people on earth.*[22]

Disciples are called to live each and every day seeking to know and do God's will for them - for God to reign over and in them. This is an immediate and constant aim as opposed to living with some vague eschatological expectation of a future situation when "one day" God will reign. Jesus' message is that God already reigns. The task of disciples is to accept this and behave accordingly. Jesus' life is manifestly a life in which God's control is constantly acknowledged. His teaching makes explicit how this can be so for others.

Lots of older churches had the Exodus Decalogue on their walls. They might have done better to have displayed the Sermon on the Mount. The teaching of Jesus may appear at times to be general ethical teaching, given in the third or second person plural, but Matthew consistently and typically presents it in a way which invites the reader to consider the personal application of the teaching (cf. Matt.5:23-6, 29-30, 36, 39-42; 6:2-4, 6, 17-18, 21-23). Although in Matthew Jesus does not come to abolish the Laws of Moses - (see Matt 5:17-20 & 19:16-30) - he does come to give it a Kingdom of Heaven connotation - and in this sense to fulfil it. Followers of Jesus are required to recognise the written records of the Law and the Prophets as God's word to them, but rather than using them as a basis for literal interpretation and regulatory observance the disciple's task is to use the scriptures as an aid to discerning the will or intention of God which lies behind the written word. France says of Matthew's own use of the scriptures: *This is not simple proof-texting, but the product of long and creative engagement with scripture which delights to draw connections between passages and to trace in the details as well as in the basic meaning of the text the pattern of God's fulfilment of his prophetically declared agenda.*[23]

Using the Sermon on the Mount as a basis, with cross referencing to other parts of Mathew's Gospel I believe it is possible to offer a quick check list for a Gospel-based church and personal life. This should inevitably raise the question, "*Does the church of which I am a part encourage and help me to know and to live in the light of the teaching of Jesus?*" I am suggesting ten things to consider, Some will occupy less attention than others, but all have in common a calling to live as God's people, mirroring God's very self. (Matt.5:48).

---

[22] Ibid. pp.102, 151, 625
[23] Ibid. 1043-4

13

Ten Words of Jesus from Matthew's Gospel

1. Almsgiving (See Matt.6:2-4)
Almsgiving, giving to the poor, as with all life in the kingdom which Jesus proclaimed, should be done in such a way that attention is not drawn to oneself (Matt.6:2). The beatitude *"Blessed are those who are meek"* (Matt.5:5) provides the ground rule which underlies such sayings as, *"Be careful not to do your 'acts of righteousness' before men to be seen of them"* (Matt.6:1). Meek people are not weak; they are the opposite of self-publicists – figuratively speaking they do not even let their right hand know what their left hand is doing (Matt.6:3).

Almsgiving was encouraged by Jesus in his teaching: *"Give to the one who asks you"* (Matt.5:42): and it would seem almsgiving was practiced by Jesus and his disciples. When the disciples were angry because a woman lavished expensive perfume on Jesus' head, they said, *"This perfume could have been sold for a large amount and the money given to the poor"* (Matt.26:9). Clearly Jesus felt that in the particular circumstances of his imminent death the act of generosity toward himself was not out of place, but the poor are not forgotten either. *"The poor you will always have with you"* (Matt.26:11).

Jesus, whom Matthew records as having neither house nor home (Matt.8:21), said to the wealthy young man, *"If you want to be perfect, go, sell your possessions and give to the poor, and you will have treasure in heaven. Then come, follow me"* (Matt.19:21). For this person sacrificial giving to the poor was an essential requirement if he was to enter into life as intended by God. He was surely not unique. Do churches tend to encourage their members to be generous toward their church - that is themselves - instead of generous toward the poor? And if we are able to say we give to both, which has the priority? And why?

I am aware that directly giving money to people who beg on the streets in twenty-first century Britain can be ill-advised. There are often better ways to provide help. It is also true that for all its imperfections, we live in a country with a welfare system which means we are somewhat removed from the harsh realities of poverty in first century Palestine. But another difference is that we more obviously live as participants in a global economy within which the same harsh realities of poverty do persist. Whilst radically new economic structures may be needed to significantly tackle this at international level, the giving of alms for the benefit of those who are poor is still a way to follow Jesus' teaching and example. Through Christian Aid, CAFOD and other agencies almsgiving is not difficult.

Giving to those in need is a crucial criterion in Jesus' parable of the final judgement (Matt.25:35,42): but for many Christians the most important motivation for almsgiving would be accepting the principle enjoined by Jesus,

"Freely you have received, freely give" (Matt.10:8).

2. Praying (see Matt.6:5-13)

Not a lot of words are needed, wanted, or always appropriate in the kind of trusting relationship which Jesus believed should undergird prayer. Although there may be occasional spontaneous outbursts of feelings such as joy, gratitude, frustration or anger, I suspect these need never be long-winded. Jesus said, *"Don't go babbling on like pagans who think they will be heard because of their many words"* (Matt.6:7). The Lord's Prayer assumes a relationship of trust and is a model of brevity! Brevity does not mean that persistence may not be needed at times, but the belief Jesus shared with his disciples is that if they asked their heavenly Father for what they needed, their requests would not be denied (Matt.7:7; 21:22).

France helpfully notes that the prayers Jesus offered in Gethsemane resonated with the Lord's Prayer as given by Jesus to his disciples.[24] Jesus lived his own teaching. It is hard to imagine his prayers went "babbling on" or that he made any kind of public display of praying (see above on Almsgiving and Matt.6:1).

Prayer as taught and practiced by Jesus is primarily a private matter. I have been to many meetings where public prayer has seemed to be an opportunity for someone to demonstrate how good they think they are at praying. That is always a danger; as is the prospect of a "prayer" actually being a mini-sermon which is about God not to God.

It would probably come as a shock to many Christians, but Jesus never called a prayer meeting. Instead he encouraged prayer to be offered in a private space: *"But when you pray, go into your room, close the door and pray to your Father, who is unseen"* (Matt.6:6). Matthew tells us that at one time Jesus recognised the need for more "reapers" (Matt.9:38). This is precisely the kind of situation in which many churches would call a prayer meeting. Jesus did not. He encouraged his disciples to ask God for what was required, presumably in the quietness and privacy of their own devotions. France says, *"Gatherings for prayer together were a regular feature of the life of Jesus' disciples from the beginning"*[25]. This may have been true after Jesus' ascension, but France offers no evidence that it was a feature of the life of Jesus with his disciples as recorded in the gospels. There is none. To the contrary, their request to Jesus to teach them to pray suggests they were not engaged in a corporate activity which could be called prayer.

---

[24] Ibid. p.1006
[25] Ibid. p.239

In Gethsemane we are told that Jesus separated himself from his disciples for his time of prayer (Matt.26:39). Matthew also tells his readers that Jesus made his disciples get into a boat and go ahead of him, and he sent the crowds away, and then *"went up into the hills by himself to pray"* (Matt.14:22-23).

Jesus' teaching about the efficacy of prayer made in the context of belief, or practical trust in God, is to his disciples (plural), but nothing in the text suggests that the prayers are to be offered communally (Matt.21:21f). I am not suggesting abandoning prayers in public worship in which one person voices those prayers which may be in the hearts and minds of the majority of those who gather for worship. The obvious example of this is the aptly named "collect". But if public or community expressions of the prayers of God's people are not echoes of their private prayers and devotions one has to ask if they have any practical value. One caveat is that there will be others like me whose personal prayer life was originally encouraged in part by participation in times of public prayer, but I would maintain this was not me praying, it was me learning to pray. The few examples we have of Jesus' prayer life suggest praying is the personally committed business of being attentive to, or waiting upon God in readiness to do God's will. One of the lessons the parable of the wise and foolish girls can teach is that *"spiritual preparedness is not something that others can provide for you: each needs to provide their own oil"*[26].

Significantly in Matthew the cleansing of the Temple comes as a climax to Jesus' public ministry, and it is connected with prayer in a public space, though never as a public spectacle. Jesus challenged the "authorities" to return the Temple to its proper function as a "house of prayer". This is the kind of reasoning which led one church where I ministered to add a small room for prayer at the front of its multi-purpose building, and another to add a small separate chapel to its suite of community buildings. These chapels were intended to be always open, a quiet place to be used as a house of prayer. I have heard it said many times that buildings are not necessary because wherever two or three are gathered in the name of Jesus the presence of Christ is made real (Matt.18:20) - or, " *I can pray anywhere*". The former argument has been the rationale for many churches' *modus operandi* (e.g. house-churches). This may be alright for committed people, those who can meet in the name of Jesus, or those who want to "belong" to a group; but there are many who do not want to belong, and who may not relate to Jesus, but who value a place which is especially provided and set apart for them to pray - seeking to relate to the "mind" of that which is beyond human imagining. I have never forgotten the hurt which was caused, or understood what was in the mind of a priest when he refused to open the church building he controlled, so that a woman whose son had died could offer her prayers there.

---

[26] Ibid. p.949 on Matt.25:7-9

Ted Noff established his first wayside chapel, a place for prayer in a city high street, in Sidney, Australia in 1964. In my early days as a church minister I was greatly influenced by Noff's book *Wayside Chapel*. Set this time in New York in the later 1960s, it made the case for "prayer spaces" very well [27]. If churches do not provide people with places for prayer, who else will? This is not to champion the maintenance, or worse still the selfish possession of massive buildings unused for more than a few hours a week. It is to suggest that church buildings should have space for one of their primary functions as places to "seek God in prayer" and make every effort to be "user friendly". For some people it is essential that churches provide a place for prayer, and not simply or even mostly as part of public worship. It is heartening to see the increased collaboration of churches, inter faith groups and even secular organisations in the provision of prayer spaces in public arenas such as airports and shopping centres.

An example of what I consider good practice, and what I hope bodes well for the newly planned major shopping centre in Northampton, was the provision made by an inter-church group in Northampton around Good Friday in 2008 offering an un-let small retail unit in the Peacock Place shopping centre as:

> *THE SPACE FOR HOPE*
> *THE SPACE FOR QUIET*
> *THE SPACE FOR PRAYER*
> *THE SPACE FOR GOD*

3. Forgiveness (see Matt.6:12-14)

Jesus recognised that forgiveness usually needs to be at least a two-way process, and sometimes it becomes impossible for one party to resolve it, even with help (Matt.18:15-17). But in Matthew the imperative of forgiveness as part of Jesus' own ministry and in the lives of his disciples is clear; though the concept is complex.

Matthew's first comment about Jesus is that Jesus will save "his people" from their sins - their broken lives and relationships with each other and with God. Potentially there is a national dimension in this work of Jesus. However, in the pages of Matthew's gospel it is worked out predominantly in personal terms. For example, forgiveness as the essence of being made whole in the story of the healing of the paralytic is made explicit (Matt.9:1-8).

---

[27] Ted Noff's *Wayside Chapel*. Collins 1969

Forgiveness is a constant for Jesus. France points out that Jesus' ministry began with a call to repentance from sin (Matt.3:2, 6; 4:17); he asserted his authority on earth to forgive sins (Matt.9:6): and "*His mission will culminate in his death 'as a ransom for many*'" (Matt.20:28), or a covenant "*for the forgiveness of sins*" (Matt.26:28)[28].

Just as his life and death were marked by forgiveness so Jesus encouraged the same spirit in his followers. Forgiveness was the first petition that Jesus picked up and emphasised at the end of the "Lord's Prayer" (Matt.6:14). The relationship between the heavenly Father and the one who prays is such that in Jesus' understanding if we ask we will receive God's forgiveness. But the corollary is that those who would ask for and receive God's forgiveness must in like manner be ready to forgive anyone who they believe has wronged them (Matt.6:14f; 18:35). This teaching is emphasised in what is sometimes called the ecclesiological discourse. Peter asked how many times he should forgive his brother or sister. Jesus told him to forgive "*seventy times seven*" - that is, beyond all reasonable human expectation (Matt.18:22). Furthermore, this is not to be a token forgiveness, but as with all responses to Jesus' teaching, it is to be "*from the heart*" (Matt.18:35).

Jesus' blood (the cup) was "*poured out for many for the forgiveness of sins*" (Matt.26:28). Stevenson goes so far as to claim that the central aim in celebrating the Eucharist, remembering the last supper, is "*to remember Christ's forgiveness*"[29]; but he also points out that the concept of Christ's forgiveness has a corresponding idea of *responsibility*. You can only receive forgiveness if you are also willing to give it. The teaching is transparent:

> "*For if you forgive other people when they sin against you, your heavenly Father will also forgive you. But if you do not forgive others their sins, your Father will not forgive your sins*" (Matt.6:14f. See also 18:35).

> "*There is something inevitably reciprocal about forgiveness. Those who ask for forgiveness must be forgiving people. Only the forgiving will be forgiven.*"[30]

France commenting on the place of forgiveness in the story of the healing of the paralysed man (Matt.9:1-8) cautions against seeing Jesus words, "*The son of man has authority on earth to forgive sins*" (as being a) "*blanket authorisation for human beings in general* (or churches) *to dispense God's forgiveness* (because this) *would detract from Jesus' unique authority*". France may have in mind the

---

[28] RTF p.54

[29] Kenneth Stevenson *Take, Eat: Reflections on the Eucharist* 2008

[30] RTF p.348

unfortunate history of some sections of the church in which forgiveness became a commodity for sale - an indulgence. But malpractice should not outlaw good practice. Jesus' disciples are expected to freely offer forgiveness, even when to do so is costly to the forgiver. As said above a precondition of the disciples receiving forgiveness is that they must forgive others (Matt.6:14). Furthermore in Matthew Jesus quite clearly gives his authority to his disciples for their ministry (Matt.10:1) and their mission (Matt.28:18ff.). He is pained when his disciples cannot exercise that authority (Matt.17:14-17). Jesus' authority is impotent without faith, a faith which includes forgiveness received and given.

Closely allied to forgiveness is a non-judgemental attitude. "*Do not judge or you too will be judged. For in the same way you judge others you will be judged, and with the measure you use it will be measured to you*" (Matt.7:1-2). This leads to what has been described as The Golden Rule, "*Do for others what you want them to do for you*" (Matt.7:12)[31].

Also noteworthy in this connection is that Hosea 6:6 is quoted twice by Jesus in Matthew: "*It is kindness that I want, not animal sacrifices*" (Matt.9:13 & 12:7). The stories of Jesus' physical contact with a woman with a haemorrhage and a dead girl, both of whom would be considered "ritually unclean", and therefore untouchable, are obvious examples of Jesus demonstrating that for him prejudice was unacceptable; and mercy was far more important than ritual or regulation (Matt.9:13, 18-26; cf.12:7). Dr. Leslie Milton commented, *In the history of the church so much has been done that has not been loving or true ... through the belief that somehow God has made the church judge, without subjecting it to judgement* [32].

4. Fasting (see Matt.6:16-18)

As with almsgiving and prayer, fasting is a spiritual discipline to be exercised or offered as part of one's personal relationship to God. As Matthew records Jesus' teaching, fasting was even more something not to be publicly paraded. Indeed, all possible steps should be taken so that no one else would know (Matt.6:16-18).

---

[31] It is given this name because there are parallels in the scriptures of all the world's major religions to Matthew 7:12. Viz:- Buddhism: *Hurt not others with that which hurts yourself* (Udana 5:16). Hindusim: *Never do to others what would pain you* (Panchatantra 3:104). Islam: *Do unto all people as you would they should do to you* (Mishkat-el-Masabih). Judaism: *What is hateful to you do not do to your neighbour* (Talmud, Shabat 31a). Sikhism: *Treat others as you would be treated yourself* (Adi Granth). Baha'i: *Desire not for anyone the things you would not desire for yourself* (Baha'Ullah 66).
[32] Expository Times. Feb 2010

A question posed by John the Baptizer's disciples was why Jesus' disciples "*do not fast at all*" (Matt.9:14). Jesus replied that there are times when it would be unseemly to fast, but his expectation was that his disciples would fast (Matt.6:16). In the exercise of discipleship as I know it today fasting is a much neglected yet, if Jesus is to be taken as an example, potentially a highly beneficial practice; and perhaps the most obvious example of a discipline that can be practiced in private. So, for example, when Jesus was led into the wilderness to be tested, the first part of his response was to fast for forty days and nights (Matt.4:1-2). In the light of this experience Jesus could say with conviction, "*Blessed are those who hunger and thirst after righteousness*" (Matt.5:6). It is so easy and so unhelpful not to take this blessing literally!!

After the last supper Jesus made it plain he would observe abstinence for the time which had to pass before the reunion of master and disciples in "*my father's kingdom*" (Matt.26.9). Like the days of Jesus' temptation, the days of Jesus' passion would be a time of testing for Jesus. But they would also test his disciples, demanding a depth of mental or spiritual application which could be aided by a physical discipline.

The normal meaning of "fasting" is to go without food for a period of time. A good friend pointed out that if people with certain levels of diabetes or other illnesses go without food they risk their lives or potentially make themselves a burden to others. Clearly in such circumstances this kind of "fasting" would be foolhardy, but other forms of self-deprivation or discipline, such as no television, or no conversation might serve a similar purpose.

In days of Bulimia and other eating disorders promoting fasting has to be done sensitively, and balanced with a gospel encouragement to feast when that is appropriate. But fasting should not be abandoned. At the very least, as Islam can teach us, fasting is a way of identifying with our brothers and sisters who go without food through no choice of their own. It might also indicate the kind of trust in God which means we are not worrying about what we will eat and drink (Matt.6:31), but instead are consciously focussed on doing "*what God requires*", which France helpfully suggests is the best English translation of the word "*righteousness*"[33].

---

[33] RTF p.14 n.15; 167. France points out that after Jesus' fasting in the wilderness there is no evidence that he ever did so again (RTF p.254). However, the story told in John 4 (31-34) suggests that Jesus may well have physically fasted at other times and lived out his conviction that man does not live by bread alone.

5. Wealth and Possessions (see Matt.6:19-24)

Jesus told a parable which at least in part was about the different kinds of reception his message received. Amongst the unsuccessful "sowing of the word" is the case of one who hears the word, "*but the worries of this life and the deceitfulness of wealth choke it, making it unfruitful*" (Matt.13:22). For a certain rich young man his wealth meant that the word never even began to take root (Matt.19:22). Indeed the narrative of the rich young man and the Jesus/disciples dialogue/reflection on it (Matt.19:16-30) serve as an excellent commentary on Jesus' words from the Sermon on the Mount. "*Where your treasure is there will you heart be also.*" *(*Matt.6:21) and, "*You cannot serve both God and 'Mammon'*" (Matt.6:24). Jesus summed up the situation by saying, "*How hard it is for a rich man to enter the Kingdom of Heaven ... easier for a camel to go through the eye of a needle*" (Matt.19:23f).

This is not to say that a person cannot be both rich and a disciple. Joseph of Arimathea is described as both (Matt.27:57). But the idea that at the same time one can be both rich and as a true disciple denying oneself, is clearly a challenging proposition since the two conditions do not seem easily reconcilable. In addition it should be said that seeing the whole world as nothing in comparison to the saving of one's soul (Matt.16:26) is not easy for rich or poor. Poverty which does not involve self sacrifice is no guarantee that someone is not seeking after worldly wealth but rather seeks to know and do God's will. Jesus' closest disciples could say to him, "*We have left everything to follow you*" (Matt.19:27). Probably few of us can say the same. Commenting on Matt.6:24 France puts it succinctly, *Discipleship and the pursuit of wealth are fundamentally incompatible*[34]. Many people might want to say that the creation of wealth is not necessarily the same thing at all as the pursuit of wealth; but it can be.

France also throws a simple yet profound light on Jesus' words, "*For to him who has will more be given; and he will have abundance; but from him who has not, even what he has will be taken away*" (Matt.13:12). France makes the perhaps obvious, yet frequently overlooked point that this verse, like every other, should be read in context [35]. It therefore refers to those "*to whom it has been given to know the secrets of the kingdom of heaven*" and to those to whom "*it has not been given*" (Matt.13:11). This is not about possessions, but about those gifts which can only be received by faith, and which, when they are received in faith, bring abundant life - true and imperishable wealth.

Of course, the ultimate living parable of someone's preference for money to the teaching of Jesus is Judas Iscariot. He betrayed Jesus into the hands of the chief

---

[34] Ibid p.730
[35] Ibid p.512

priests for thirty pieces of silver (Matt.27:15f) – an action with consequences he later regretted so deeply that he hanged himself (Matt.27:3-5). In so many different ways prizing money above God's kingdom can prove fatal.

6. Trusting in God (see Matt.6:25-34)

The petition in the Lord's Prayer, *Give us this day our daily bread* (Matt.6:11) is followed shortly afterward in the Sermon on the Mount with Jesus' caution against the human tendency to worry (Matt.6:25-34)[36]. Those who worry about their basic needs being met are described by Jesus as *"Ye of little faith"* (ὀλιγόπιστοι - Matt.6:30)[37]. The faith of which Jesus spoke appears to find expression in two ways. The first is an overriding commitment to the things that really matter, his Father's Kingdom and righteousness (Matt.6:33). The second is faith as trust that God will act in response to the prayers of God's people to provide for them:

> *"Seek first his Kingdom and his righteousness, and all these things will be given to you as well"* (Matt.6:33).

> *"Ask, and it will be given you; seek, and you will find; knock, and it will be opened to you. For every one who asks receives, and he who seeks finds, and to him who knocks it will be opened. If you who are evil know how to give good gifts to your children, how much more will your Father who is in heaven give good things to those who ask him"* (Matt.7:7-11).

In marked contrast to much church praxis, in the gospels faith is not belief in a creed or dogma, but trust and hope in God. Such humble faith, which is not too proud to ask, is the precondition which seems to have been ordained for many of God's actions in the world (cf. Matt.21:22). There is a story told of an old Rabbi who said, "In olden days there were men who saw the face of God." A young student asked, "Why don't they any more?" And the wise old rabbi replied, "Because, nowadays no one stoops so low". The sequence of events in the story of the centurion who asked for Jesus' help for his servant is a paradigm, a living parable demonstrating humble faith. The centurion came *asking for help* (Matt.8:5). He deemed himself unworthy to have Jesus *come under my roof* (Matt.8:8). He was recognised by Jesus as possessing *such great faith* (Matt.8:10).

---

[36] *"Worry (merimna) is the antithesis of the practical trust in God which is the essential meaning of faith (pistis) in this gospel (Matt. 8:10; 9:2, 22, 29; 15:28; 17:20; 21:21.)* RTF p.266.

[37] France notes that the disciples may be described as *oligopistoi*, of little faith, but only those who reject Jesus are called *apistia*, faith-less, or unbelieving. RTF p.550.

He was told by Jesus, "*It will be done just as you believed it would*" – and *his petition was answered in keeping with Jesus' word* (Matt.8:13).

The centurion came for the sake of his servant, not himself - which may in no small part be why Jesus found the man's faith so impressive. It is important to stress that the outcome of all the disciplines outlined above is never intended to be a sense of personal righteousness nor personal reward: nor even a special private relationship with God. I have long understood this to be the underlying sense of the words of Jesus, "*Blest are those who know they are spiritually poor*" (Matt.5:3). Storing up treasures in heaven (Matt.6:20) is surely not an alternative form of self-aggrandisement, but the corollary of a life which is devoid of self-interest since it puts God's will first. (Matt.10:39).

The first four of the ten instructions which form the Decalogue in Exodus and Deuteronomy provide a disciplined attitude toward God which is intended to be the basis or wellspring of a life which relies on, and then channels the goodness and grace of God into relationships with our neighbours and our world. So in Matthew personal piety is not an end in itself, but the basis for a life marked by commitment and service of our neighbours with authority and compassion. It is to these that we now turn our attention.

7. Commitment (see Matt.8:18-22)

The depth of commitment invited by Jesus is unequivocal and demanding. The English word "wholehearted" perhaps captures a little of the attitude Jesus invites from would-be followers. The required depth of commitment is expressed in the parables of the pearl of great price and the treasure in the field (Matt.13:44-6), but made more explicit in Jesus' challenging words:

> "*Anyone who loves his father or mother more than me is not worthy of me; anyone who loves his son or daughter more than me is not worthy of me; and anyone who does not take his cross and follow me is not worthy of me*". *Whoever finds his life will lose it, and whoever loses his life for my sake will find it* (Matt.10:37-9; 16:24).

France points out that a modern reader of the word "cross" will not experience the "shudder" this would have caused in a time and place where crucifixions, and the sight of condemned people carrying their cross pieces were common place[38]. A calling which embraces martyrdom is no easy requirement. But this demanding commitment to Jesus and his Father, as with personal piety (see above), is not an end in itself. We referred earlier to the only Old Testament verse quoted three

---

[38] Ibid p.410

times in Matthew, "the golden rule", "*love your neighbour as yourself*" (Leviticus 19:18 in Matt.5:43; 19:19; 22:39). In his first citation of Lev.19:18 Jesus was at pains to say that love of neighbour did not preclude love of one's enemies - quite the reverse. On the second occasion this enjoinder to love our neighbour, along with other commandments, is a precursor to an invitation to give sacrificially to the poor. Finally, Jesus set Lev.19:18 alongside the total dedication enjoined in Deut.6:5 with its repeated "all": "*Love the LORD your God with all your heart and with all your soul and with all your strength*". In the conjunction of love of God and love of neighbour Jesus creates what has been called "the great commandment" in which ethics and theology are undivided - as of course they are in the original Decalogue. As Jesus says, "*All the Law and Prophets hang on these two commandments*" (Matt.22:40).

The parable of the sheep and goats, or final judgement makes it clear that love of God and service of one's neighbour are not separable, they are two sides of the same coin (Matt.25:31-46). And we do well to set alongside this the parable of the talents. In this parable it would seem that in the judgement of the real owner of the talents the one who was unprepared to take a risk in order to preserve what they had was a loser – the essential commitment for service was absent. Probably my most consistent criticism of churches is that so often we have been more interested in preserving our own ritual and devotion - our own life - than in giving it away. However imperfectly, within the churches of which I have been a part I have tried to encourage this kind of self-examination: "Is what we are doing, or what we propose to do, first and foremost for our benefit? For example, is our worship designed to turn us inward, or to send us out? Are our Bible studies intended to make us feel better "educated" or are they an encouragement to share Christ's path of humble service? Are the activities in which we engage primarily "for our benefit" or for the sake of others? If the former, we are essentially being selfish and therefore un-Christ-like. Commitment to our own good has no place in the life of any people claiming to be his body.

Churches usually have plenty of crosses on their walls, and even on their graves, but the self-giving cross-marked life may be far less evident. Yet Jesus says explicitly and unconditionally, "*He who does not take up his cross and follow me is not worthy of me*" (cf. Matt 10:38-9 //s 16:24-5). The way of life is the way of the cross. The cross is not optional for followers of Jesus. Because it is the way Jesus has already taken there is not an alternative route (Matt.7:13f.). To be a "Christian" is literally to follow the path which Jesus trod, to follow in his footsteps. All other definitions of "Christian" are deficient and belie the crucial commitment.

8. Service (see Matt.8:5-13)

Being a disciple of Jesus is a call to learn and live with a "servant mentality", no longer living for oneself, but living for the sake of, or in the service of others; or even, like little children or slaves, in submission to others. Being submissive is something I have struggled with for most of my life – and struggled to see it in the way Jesus lived. I have not been helped by commentators who present Jesus as the Master of every situation – even in his hours of crucifixion, where without doubt he submitted to the will of malicious people. But I can find no other reasonable interpretation of Jesus call for his followers to be like servants/slaves or children. In first century Palestine these were subordinates – and slaves in particular existed solely to serve and meet the demands of others. Jesus' followers are called to be salt and light, entities in the life of the world which give flavour and illumination - but in doing so both lose their present existence (Matt.5:13-16). The candle, or oil, and the salt are consumed in the process of giving. Following Jesus is not a path to self preservation let alone self-promotion.

Many of Jesus' parables of the kingdom included servants or the service of others, and where there may be an element of personal satisfaction others are drawn in to share the celebration. Modern Western individualism encourages us to think of Jesus calling us to be individual lights, whereas for Jesus it would be like a city set on a hill (Matt.5:14) the "*collective light of a whole community*" which would "*draw the attention of a watching world*"[39]. Earlier we noted how Jesus sent his disciples out in twos. In the ancient world a solo witness was seldom sufficient evidence for determination of the truth. Whilst there have been notable examples of individuals whose lives have been a convincing testimony to their faith (often for co-believers) it is the lives of Christian communities which carry the main burden of witness. To sing *Shine, Jesus shine* (on ME!) is very popular in England today. It makes me feel uncomfortable. Partly because I can find no Biblical justification for such a prayer. Actually the Biblical imperative is for Christians to shine with the light of Christ through their corporate as well as individual life of service for the benefit of others.

Another thought to set alongside this is the example and call of Jesus to engage in *the witness of public exposure*, rather than the pursuit of *personal private holiness*[40]. The parable to explain all Jesus' parables, the sowing of the seed (Matt.13:1-23) leads to other parables. Matthew juxtaposes these other parables with real-life situations, and further teaching mediated both through Jesus' acts of service to others and his trenchant criticism of those who used religion to justify, enrich, or glorify themselves[41]. The best examples of this are the "seven woes" in

---

[39] Ibid p.171

[40] Ibid p.176

[41] Most notably in the mass feedings - but also in a ministry of healing

Matthew 23. All of this led up to Jesus' last spoken parable in Matthew, the final or ultimate basis for judging people's lives. The "last judgement" is based on the blunt question, *Did you or did you not serve the needs of others?* (Matt.25:31-46). There is rich irony in the words of Jesus' mockers, *"He saved others, but he can't save himself"* (Matt.27:42): for the mission of Jesus was not to save himself but precisely to save or to serve others. Hence my intense suspicion of the question, *"Have you been saved?"* Jesus is only my saviour if I am sharing his work of serving and possibly saving others.

In addition to the weight of evidence of Jesus' parables, other teaching, and examples of service as part of the essence of discipleship, there are important lessons from two stories. One is about Jesus and Peter, the other concerns James and John. These are the ones who in Matthew would seem to be Jesus' three closest disciples.

1) Peter who has become such a "key figure" for some churches is given the keys not to the church, but to the Kingdom (Matt.16:19). But Peter as a servant in the Kingdom of Heaven needs confession, commission and admonition. He needs to know his place, which is that of a servant in the cause of his master. The servant must not try to control, or personally profit from the household, the field of crops, the vineyard, the fishing business, the financial affairs or any other aspect of the business of the master whom they serve. Peter, like all disciples, must learn that the way of self-denial is the way to fulfil God's will for Jesus and all his true followers (16:24). When Peter opposed Jesus way of sacrificial self-giving Jesus' called Peter Satan (16:23), words which are powerfully echoed in the parable of the sheep and the goats. Those who fail to serve the needs of others are consigned to a place for *"the devil and his angels"* (25:41)[42].

2) The context of the story in which James' and John's mother asks for the best places for her sons in Jesus' kingdom is instructive (Matt.20: 20ff). The mother's request for preferential treatment immediately follows two things. First, Jesus told a Kingdom of Heaven parable in which labourers make claims for greater rewards as just recompense for greater work. Second, Jesus' foretold of his death in Jerusalem. Their request, which demonstrates their failure to learn from either the parable or Jesus' prediction, is followed by this crystal clear teaching:

---

[42] If Peter is to be accorded any special status, he is probably best regarded as the founding patriarch of the church // Abraham & Israel - i.e. he is a foundation stone, not a feature or "personality" or specific role/function which is to be repeated. cf. Isaiah 51:1b-2a *Think of the rock from which you came, the quarry from which you were dug. Think of your ancestor Abraham.* France commenting on 16:18 says: *It is Simon Peter himself, in his historical role, who is the foundation rock. Any link between Peter and the subsequent papacy is a matter of later ecclesiology, not of exegesis of this passage* (RTF p.622).

Whoever will be great among you must be your servant; and whoever will be first among you must be your slave; even as the Son of Man came not to be served, but to serve, and to give his life as a ransom for many (Matt.20:27-28).

This teaching was repeated and emphasised in light of the self-promotion or mutual-elevation practised by the Scribes and Pharisees; wearing religious regalia and paraphernalia, or having titles like *Rabbi, father* or *leader*. Although churches have consistently ignored his clear teaching, significantly Jesus offered a "three-fold warning" against adopting titles such as Rabbi, Father or Teacher (Matt. 23:8-10). This strong prohibition accords with Jesus' *sine qua non* for life in God's kingdom: *"The greatest among you will be your servant. For whoever exalts himself will be humbled, and whoever humbles himself will be exalted."* (Matt.23:5-11). In effect, in God's kingdom there will be a reversal of the normal human expectations and assumptions about status and rewards: *"The last shall be first and the first shall be last"* (Matt.20:16) [43].

This, of course, is not just spoken teaching, it is a lived lesson! In a mind-blowing way the supreme moment of Jesus making manifest his Father's kingdom was his death on the cross. At that moment the places on his right and his left were taken by criminals sharing his fate of crucifixion, not by willing disciples who have made great sacrifices, but by two men who without doubt accompanied him unwillingly. Typically Jesus' ministry flourishes amongst those who have a socially reinforced sense of unworthiness, of humility, even of failure. They are open to the possibility of being "saved", or served. The longest quote from the OT in Matthew is from Isaiah. It begins, *"Here is my servant ..."* (Matt.12:18-21). The life of Jesus is deliberately a life of humble service, which in "this life" received no reward other than knowing that he was doing his Father's will. Any reward in God's kingdom

---

[43] Whilst I have chosen to focus here on the significance of this teaching with regard to a taboo on self-elevation for disciples of Jesus; the teaching also relates to the unique function of Jesus as teacher and leader and of his Father as the only Father. Even when the disciples are instructed to teach (28:20) there is no suggestion they are to be addressed as "teacher", and the teaching they are to convey is under the authority of Jesus. It is Jesus' teaching which is to be conveyed, not their own. In most churches today this teaching of Jesus is ignored and a hierarchical structure, with religious and academic titles, and assumptions of superior knowledge abound. In my own denomination, the Baptist Union, whilst the title "Father" has been eschewed, the title "leader" has been actively promoted for at least the past twenty-five years. Those who promote it refuse to accept that it is in direct contradiction to Jesus' teaching.

will be the free gift of a gracious master (God/Father 6:4), not the earned achievement of the servant, and it may be reserved for heaven (Matt.5:12)[44].

Yet the life of a servant of God is a life lived with ...

9. Authority (see 7:28f.)

The Greek word *exousia* (ἐξουσία), usually rendered as "authority" (though sometimes as "power"), is a notoriously difficult word to translate. It defies precise definition. However, given all that has gone before, the gift of *exousia* in no way can justify an exercise of power which inaugurates or sustains an authoritarian relationship or regime, or legitimizes an elevated, specially privileged person or group, in church organisation - or even in wider society. The guiding image Jesus used of his disciples as helpless "*sheep amongst wolves*" cautions against any notions of power over others as a feature of individual discipleship or church structures (Matt.10:16). When the mother of James and John asked Jesus for elevated positions for her sons in his kingdom, he said to them, "*You know that the rulers of the Gentiles lord it over them. And their high officials exercise authority over them*". Then added the important dictum, "*It shall not be so with you*" (Matt.20:25f). I am dismayed that there are many churches in which one person, or a group of people sometimes called "elders" or "leaders", control the corporate and sometimes even the individual life of members. Claims to authority which are in effect claims to power over others are anathema to the spirit of Jesus [45].

It cannot be over emphasised that in Matthew's gospel Jesus is the exemplar as well as the oral teacher. His teaching in the Sermon on the Mount Chs. 5-7 in which he said, "*You have heard it said, but I say unto you ....*", concludes with the telling comment, "*He wasn't like the teachers of the Law; instead he taught with authority*" (Matt.7:28). On the surface this is a strange comment, because the teachers of the Law doubtless believed they taught with authority, the authority of the scriptures as God's word, and the authority of their sacred traditions and their own professional standing. Jesus' way of teaching, however, was typified by the words, "*but I say unto you*". Unlike his contemporary rabbis Jesus did not cite other "experts" to provide legitimacy for his teaching. The authority of Jesus' teaching was his personal trusting relationship with God as his heavenly Father; and his teaching was legitimised by the life of service which was its companion. It

---

[44] .cf. Ephesians 3:8-9, *"being found in appearance as a man, he humbled himself and became obedient to death—even death on a cross! Therefore God exalted him to the highest place ".*

[45] For France Jesus' personal claim to authority rests in Jesus' self-understanding: "Jesus sets his own status alongside that of the highest authority figures in the OT, David the king, the priests in the temple, Jonah the prophet, and Solomon the wise man and.....claims that *something greater* has now superseded those recognised authorities (RTF p.452, 493).

is because Jesus' words are accompanied by or lead to actions which confirm his belief in, and his own commitment to his teaching, that they have the stamp of authority. Literally, he is not a hypocrite, an actor speaking other people's words; his words and works are a unity. Whilst we may fall short of Jesus' achievements in this regard I would suggest the only legitimate "authority" a Christian can have is inspired by, and results from words and actions given for the sake of others which are rooted in a humble trust in God.

The words of the Sermon on the Mount (chapters 5-7) preceded Jesus giving himself in a ministry of service for others in a variety of ways (chapters 8-9). France highlights the story of the healing of the centurion's servant (Matt.8:5-13) as a case in which Jesus' authority is clearly recognised by a man who is himself able to exercise a certain kind of authority within a chain of command: "*I also am a man under authority, with soldiers under me*" (Matt.8:9)[46]. But the centurion knew Jesus had that very different kind of authority which can bring healing. The story of the Centurion's servant is accompanied by two stories. The story of the authoritative rebuking of wind and waves (Matt.8:26), physically bringing salvation for the disciples; and the story of the Gadarene demoniacs whose demons reluctantly but unavoidably accepted Jesus' authority because it is the authority of God's true servant (Matt.8:29). In all manner of ways Jesus ministry produced calm or peace after or within turmoil and distress (see also Matt.9:32-3; 12:22; 15:21-28; 17:14-20).

The message of the Sermon on the Mount is expressed in both words and action. It is the same notion of authority that informs both. Furthermore, having demonstrated both, Jesus then sent his disciples out to do the same. The disciples were given "*authority over unclean spirits to cast them out; and to heal every disease and every infirmity*" (Matt.10:1-4). I have found this to be one of the most difficult elements of the gospel to translate into my life and into church life. I firmly believe this is not about impressive signs and wonders which often draw attention to the person supposedly exercising authority in the name of Jesus. It is about having confidence in the power of God's spirit as demonstrated in Jesus to bring about health and wholeness - what the OT calls Shalom and the NT hints at with *eirene*. I have seen this authority used crudely (and even so sometimes effectively). For example, I well remember watching a Jamaican pastor pacifying a disturbed and agitated man who was disrupting a meeting. He laid his hands on the man's head and began with the words, "*In the name of Jesus I say to you*". But I have much more often seen Jesus' call to authoritative discipleship ignored.

---

[46] RTF p.309ff. *This pericope is not about defining Jesus' Christological status, but about the recognition of his unquestioned authority*

I would suggest the authority grounded in Jesus-like love and trust is an inner, God-authenticated authority which is prepared to be bold for the welfare of others. Examples of Jesus being forthright abound. The exorcism to cure the boy who had seizures (Matt.17:18) and the healing of the two blind men outside Jericho (Matt.20:29-34) are prime examples. However, this was not a special gift to be exercised by a few. It was the calling given to all Jesus' disciples-cum-apostles [47]. When in the spirit of Jesus' ministry people are loved enough, remarkably good things do happen; but this may be more like the action of yeast and the buried seed - working and growing quietly without ostentation – than the product of a meeting called to facilitate "signs and wonders".

It needs to be emphasised that any authority which Jesus commended was never an authority of one of his followers over another. Jesus would have no truck with authoritarian church "leaders" who expect to be followed. Disciples are called to serve and feed and accompany, not lead or command. France calls Matt.18:1-19:2 "The discourse on relationships". He rejects the idea that this is a manual for church leaders. Even the community aspect of the discourse is not primarily about corporate action, but is a guide for the individual member on how they should relate to other members. The discourse begins with a question about status, "*Who is the greatest in the kingdom of heaven*"? Jesus response is to take a child, an individual with no social status, no legal power, one who is dependent on others, who is literally socially and physically a "little one". Jesus says that to be great in the kingdom of heaven we must *humble* ourselves, become a "little one". That is how all disciples of Jesus should regard themselves. In fact, as France says,

> There are no great ones in the kingdom of heaven. The portrait of the church which emerges (from Matthew 18 &19) is an attractive one. Status consciousness and formally constituted authority have no place. The focus is on the relationship and mutual responsibility of all members of the community, each of whom matters, and yet all of whom must regard themselves as "little ones". The resultant pastoral concern and action is not the preserve of a select few, but is the responsibility of each individual disciple, and where necessary, of the whole group together. The structure is informal, but the sense of community is intense. And overarching it all is the consciousness of the presence of Jesus and of the forgiveness and pastoral concern of "your Father in heaven" [48].

It was interesting to find in correspondence with a Baptist minister in Norway that Baptists in that country have no professional ministers, and certainly no individual is regarded in any sense as having superior status or authority. The work of the

---

[47] Cf. Matt.28:18-20 which should be read in conjunction with 10:1
[48] RTF p.674f

church is a collaborative exercise in which all members are equal and interdependent. One or more members might be able to make a significant theological input, or have a recognised ability to preach, but others will, for example, be exercising an equally valuable pastoral ministry. Matthew and Jesus would have recognised this as a company of people who are faithful to the teaching of Jesus. The absence of ministers paid by their churches is probably also significant. Financial pressures may see a welcome increase in such "tent making" ministry in England in the not too distant future.

Jesus' use of a child to deflate his disciples' desire for status, as mentioned earlier, was reinforced with a triple denunciation of the kind of titles which the scribes and Pharisees used, and the telling conclusion, *Whoever exalts himself will be humbled, and whoever humbles himself will be exalted* (Matt.23:8-12). Sadly the titles are still used in most of today's churches as a basis for authority. Jesus subversively, prophetically and meekly, rides a donkey, not a warhorse into Jerusalem. The popular notion of Jesus as the "servant-king" is a convenient way to avoid the choice he actually made between the two and thereby to avoid the choice we too must make about both Jesus and our self-perception. The crowd, and many in churches today, may want him to be an earthly king, but Jesus in absolute contrast is always a heavenly servant.

I enjoy the chorus, *"Be bold, be strong, for the Lord our God is with you"*. It is a thoroughly Biblical concept and a Gospel one too. But discerning the boundaries between an authority which elevates others and authority which is self-serving arrogance, control, or manipulation of others is not always easy. Jesus said, *"I have been given all authority in heaven and on earth"* (Matt.28:18) - but this is the kind of authority which derives its legitimacy by way of the cross - and stands in total opposition to the "authority" which the devil offered in the wilderness. When Jesus said to his disciples *"go and make disciples ... and teach them to obey"* Jesus completed the commission with the words *"everything I have commanded you"*. "Our" own obedience, our own submission to Christ-like authority is an essential prerequisite for inviting others to take on board the loving, peace-giving, uplifting and healing authority of God as seen in Jesus.

10. Compassion (see 5:43-45)

To show mercy or compassion is a recurring theme throughout Matthew's gospel. *"Have mercy"* is the cry of others to Jesus (Matt.9:27; 15:22; 17:15; 20:30); and showing mercy a regular response of Jesus (Matt.9:36; 14:14; 15:32; 20:24). It is part of the guidance Jesus gives to others: *"Blessed are the merciful, for they will be shown mercy"* (Matt.5:7. See also 9:13; 12:7; 18:33; 23:23). Whilst mercy, as in the parable of the unforgiving servant (18:23-35) includes the notion of forgiveness, it is often better understood in Jesus' ministry and teaching as the capacity for, and the valuing and prioritising of compassion (Matt.9:13; 14:14; 15:32; 20:34). The works of Jesus as recorded in Matthew 8-9 have been specifically called the compassion miracles, perhaps because Jesus' ministry seems to be dominated by his capacity to heal. It cannot be overemphasised that Jesus' ministry was targeted toward those who might be described as "damaged". The image used of God's servant as one who would not reject the bent reed or the smoking wick - both damaged goods and effectively useless - is of particular significance. In Matthew 8-9 Jesus' ministry is directed largely to people who were "outsiders" in Jewish religious and social terms - a leper - a Roman soldier - a tax collector - a woman with a haemorrhage - a dead child - a blind man - all perhaps brought together in the words; "*As Jesus saw the crowds his heart was filled with compassion*" (9:36. See also 20:30-34). The Greek word used here is *splanchnizthe* (σπλαγχνισθε). France reflects on the related verb *Splanchnizomai:-*

> *No single English term does justice to it: compassion, pity, sympathy and fellow feeling all convey part of it, but "his heart went out" perhaps represents more fully the emotional force of the underlying metaphor of a "gut response". A further feature of this verb appears through a comparison with its other uses in Matthew (Matt.14:14; 15:32; 18:27; 20:34). In each case there is not only sympathy with a person's need, but also a practical response which meets that need; emotion results in caring and effective action. Splanchnizomai is a verb which describes the Jesus of the gospel stories in a nutshell [49].*

Compassion is not the same as pity, condescension, revulsion or despair. It means literally being alongside people in suffering and need, but being there with strength, support, faith and hope; believing in potential through God's creative, redeeming and loving spirit at work. The parable of the sheep and the goats lists examples of the needs of people and commends or condemns according to the compassion people have or have not shown. The response of the master in the parable of the unforgiving servant is variously translated (Matt.18:27), but the crucial words are "*σπλαγχνισθεις δε ο κυριος του δουλου*", "the master's *heart went out* for his servant". This compassion, being alongside, sharing the load is exemplified by Jesus' invitation (which is not just for existing disciples!):

> *"Come to me, all you who are weary and burdened, and I will give you rest. Take my yoke upon you and learn from me, for I am gentle and humble in heart, and you will find rest for your souls. For my yoke is easy and my burden is light"* (Matt.11:25-6. See also 14:14; 15:32; 20:34).

---

[49] RTF p.373

Time and again Jesus had compassion. Hence his words: "*Jerusalem, Jerusalem, how many times have I wanted to put my arms around all your people?*" But the verse goes on to say, "*but you would not let me*" (Matt.23:37). Matthew makes it plain that the desire to be of compassionate service will often lead to rejection and even provoke hostility and persecution (Chapters 11-12). But Com - passion is "suffering with" people, having a passion for people: perhaps suffering - maybe even dying - *because* of them, but always *for* them.

The relationship of Jesus to the people of Jerusalem is difficult to relate to the concept that he died *for them*. Jesus died for the whole world, including Jerusalem. But the people of Jerusalem, both its leaders and its crowds, engineered his death and accepted responsibility for it. The parable of the vineyard suggests that when the son was sent it was the tenants' last chance to accept the vineyard owner's invitation to return the fruits of the vineyard to their rightful owner. When they killed the son the vineyard was taken away from the tenants and given to others (Matt.21:33-41). Jesus directly applies this: Jerusalem is the vineyard, the chief priests and Pharisees are the tenants (21:43). In consequence Jesus forecast the destruction of Jerusalem (Matt.23:38) and the temple (Matt.24:2). If this really was the last chance for the Jews of Jerusalem, then not only are Christian Zionists compelled to overlook this teaching if they would maintain their position, but it would seem the death of Jesus is only efficacious for those who have faith in him. Jesus becomes "the stone that crushes" for those who do not (Matt.21:44). With few exceptions, Jesus' prophecy to his opponents, "*You will not see me again until you say 'Blessed is he who comes in the name of the Lord'* "(Matt.23:39) seems to have been the expression of an unfulfilled hope[50].

Dying because of "them" and for "them" is the final lived parable of Jesus in Matthew's Gospel. Jesus made his self-offering, and in the process of giving up his life, as he predicted (Matt.16:21; 17:22-23; 20:18-19), he suffered rejection, vilification and pain, shame and death. Matthew precedes Jesus' sacrifice with a record of a Passover meal (Matt.26:17-30). This meal includes what has often been described as the four-fold action of the Eucharist. Bread was taken: thanks were given: the bread was broken: the bread was shared (Matt.26:26). But the actions

---

[50] France points out that contrary to some commentators who see this as a positive prediction, the use of εως αv with the subjunctive gives Jesus' words the sense of, "*If you do this*". Jesus' words set a real condition which was not met (RTF p.885). In fact the destruction of Jerusalem and the temple was the vindication of Jesus' claims with regard to his own place in God's purposes. Oddly, given France's recognition of the Jews being given a last chance, which they did not take, he is still convinced that *Jesus nowhere revokes the mission to Israel... the Gentile mission extends the mission to Israel* (RTF p.1115). From Matthew's account of the relationship between Jesus and the Jews I find this difficult to accept: although other New Testament writers make it clear that the mission to the Jews did in fact continue and even at times had priority.

was accompanied by Jesus' words, Take and eat, *this is my body*. It is Jesus himself, whose life has been a gift from his Father, who is to be received with gratitude, but also to be shared in self sacrifice by the recipients. Through the bread Jesus invited his disciples to take his example, his pattern of living as a template for their own. It should be noted that in Matthew what has been described as the four-fold action of the Eucharist has been demonstrated twice before in the feeding of five thousand men (Matt.14:19) and of four thousand men (Matt.15:36). The action at the last supper is neither the inauguration of Jesus self-giving symbolised by the taking, blessing, breaking and sharing of bread, nor the primary model for doing what Jesus did. It was primarily when the disciples shared with others bread which Jesus had blessed that they discovered there was more than enough for themselves as well.

> *The "Eucharistic" wording of the miracle in 15:36 is as clear and detailed as in 14:19, thus reinforcing the message of 8:11-12 that Gentiles are to share with Jews in the messianic banquet. The Lord's Supper which anticipates that banquet is thus for people of all races and backgrounds who share the Canaanite woman's faith that there is also bread for the dogs* (Matt.15:27) [51].

In the last supper the breaking of bread is followed by a parallel action with the cup. The cup, unlike the bread, is manifestly associated with the forgiveness of sins as well as the advent of the Kingdom. In this way Matthew brings us full circle. Jesus was to be born to "*save his people from their sins*" (Matt.1:21), and his ministry was announced with the words, "*The Kingdom of Heaven is near*" (Matt.3:2; 4:17).

It is an inexplicable and for me inexcusable oversight that the major lectionaries of readings for Sundays only include a Gospel account of Jesus' death once every three years - and it is Luke's account. Matthew chapters 26-27 are never read on a Sunday in churches who follow the lectionary. What does that say about the shaping of the churches?

The child who was born under the shadow of Rome's puppet king to save people from their sin, and who escaped Herod's slaughter of the innocents, became the man who died at the hands of a Roman Governor for the same saving purpose. The whole Matthew story of Jesus is a timeless one about suffering humanity living in the context of military, political and religious oppression, conspiracy, confrontation, jealousy, power seeking, misunderstanding, controversy, death and dishonour. This is still the world as we know it and as countless people still experience it. But the Matthean story of Jesus is also of a spirit-filled life of humble obedience to a heavenly calling with a pattern for living which turned the

---

[51] Ibid. p.601

world's values upside down and inside out. In its own peculiar way it is simply glorious. Matthew gives us the good news that when a church is true to its founder's teaching it too is glorious - by which I mean it glorifies God as God has been made known to us in Jesus. Matthew provides the practical guidelines which indicate how this can be done.

Chapter Two.
MARK'S GOSPEL QUESTION
Who is this?

The Question

As soon as we begin to read Mark's Gospel critically, the very first verse invites us to tackle an important question. Does Chapter 1 verse 1 include, or does it not include, the description of Jesus as *The Son of God*? Some of the ancient manuscripts include these words *"The Son of God"*, others do not[1]. I am amongst those who feel it is more likely that copyists have added these words, since it is difficult to think of a reason why anyone would have deleted them. The balance of probability lies with those who see it as a later addition to the text of the Gospel: not part of Mark's original recounting of the story of Jesus. This issue is not being raised because it is of academic interest, but because by making the change and including such a definitive statement I believe those later copyists undermined the essence of Mark's very special way of inviting his listeners or readers to think about or to "meet" Jesus.

Those same or other copyists also present us with a similar choice almost at the end of Mark's Gospel (Mk.15:39). The centurion present at the crucifixion is sometimes recorded as saying, *"Truly this man was The Son of God"*. But other versions of Mark record the centurion's words as *"...a son of God"*. The 1952 RSV indicates in a footnote that the ancient authorities differ on this point. It is worth noting here that the ascription *Son of God* would not mean the same to a Roman as it would to a Jew. Furthermore, contrary to what many Christians today might automatically think, in Judaism the meanings attached to "God's son" varied (The Messiah, the king, Israel) but there was no intimation of divinity; whereas in Roman religion gods could have many sons, some of whom were deemed to be divine, but quite clearly not within the monotheistic tradition which can give the title "son of God" its distinctive sense in Christianity[2]. This means that even if the Roman centurion said *The Son of God*, it is highly improbable that he would be ascribing the same kind of divinity to Jesus which many Christians have done. We are, of course, still faced with a choice. Should we read and evaluate the intention of these words as those of a Roman soldier, or as those of the Gospel writer? If we opt for the gospel writer, we are then faced with a decision as to which manuscripts to count as authoritative. For the same reasons as given in connection with 1:1 the

---

[1] I find it strange that most commentators on Mark do not take this point into account at all. For example, Craig Evans: *Mark's Christology is focussed on Jesus as Son of God. This is clear from the gospel's incipit "The beginning of the good news of Jesus Christ the Son of God" (1:1) And from the dramatic confession of the Roman centurion, "Truly this man was the Son of God"* (Word Bible Commentaries Vol.34b *Mark 8:27-16:20* lxxix 2001).
[2] RTF p. 1084

balance of probability has to lie with the less specific "*a son of God*" being the earlier text, and therefore closer to the original version – assuming such a thing ever existed.

The absence in the Greek of the definite article in 15:39 has been described as *a grammatical ambiguity*[3]. To grammatical ambiguity one can add *theological ambiguity* with good reason. For many readers of Mark there is a deeply significant difference between *The Son of God* and *a son of God*. The former designation could legitimately be read as an affirmation of divinity in line with what became traditional mainstream Christian orthodoxy, whereas the latter, because the article is "indefinite", implies a lack of uniqueness and need be interpreted as no more than a cry of admiration, respect and possibly compassion for someone who, like everyone else, is a child of God. If *"The" Son of God* was in Mark's original opening, and if the same title is used in 15:39 then Mark begins and ends his gospel with a very clear statement as to who he believes, and who his readers should believe Jesus is. But if these verses should be read with the indefinite article, as I would contend, the question, *"How exactly are we to describe Jesus?"* or more succinctly, *"Who is this?"* remains to be answered. In fact, I believe , *"Who is this?"* is the fundamental question constantly posed by Mark's Gospel and provides the key to reading Mark[4].

The conversation between Jesus and his disciples at Caesarea Philip (Mk.8:27-30) has rightly been called the watershed of Mark's Gospel, for the crucial question, *"But who do you say that I am?"* gives a precise focus to the oft repeated questioning which it both precedes[5] and follows[6]. Mark's gospel invites its readers to respond to that specific question, *"But who do you say that I am?"* Those copyists who introduced their own theological convictions into the text at the beginning and end of Mark's gospel (even more so those who added endings) did a great disservice in foreclosing what Mark intended to be an open exploration of this potentially life-giving question.

---

[3] A complicating factor in determining whether "the Son of God" or "a son of God" is the better translation is that Aramaic often uses the definite article in contexts where Greek would use the indefinite article. See Ashton UFG p. 227 [78]

[4] Robert Guelich holds that the major thrust of the various approaches to Markan theology have fallen into one of three categories: a) eschatology, b) Christology and c) discipleship and paraenesis. He contends, *to single out one of these themes as primary .. distorts Mark's gospel* (Word Bible Commentaries Vol.34A *Mark 1 – 8:26*xi 2001). Contrary to Guelich, I believe my focus on "Christology" brings out the central purpose of Mark's Gospel by paying particular attention to its central character, Jesus.

[5] e.g. 15:2-5 Pilate's questioning of Jesus

[6] e.g. 4:41 The disciples after Jesus' calming of the storm

In many different ways throughout the entire Gospel, sometimes directly, but sometimes in different guises, the perplexing question is constantly raised concerning Jesus, *Who is this?* (In addition to Mk.8:27ff - the watershed referred to earlier - see Mk.1:22, 24, 34; 2:7; 3:22; 4:11; 5:15; 6:2; 10:32; 11:9, 28; 15:29, 39; 16:6, 14). This question could be the subtitle for the whole Gospel. The second gospel's many "answers" to this question permeate the text. In Mark's Gospel descriptions of Jesus are many and varied. A discerning reader is compelled *to look and perhaps decide for oneself who this Jesus is, rather than what Jesus is.* The former implies a relationship which can grow in depth of understanding; the latter can so easily but inappropriately become a closure of identification by description or nomenclature. After all, even the name Jesus, or Joshua was not unique. It was one of the most common Jewish names in the first century.

On the basis that Mark's gospel invites it's hearers or readers to grapple with the question, *Who is this?*, and that there is no single answer to the question, what follows is an attempt to set out some of the rich variety of hints Mark offers as ways of contemplating the question and more important the person who is the subject of the question.

By what name or title?

It is sometimes possible to gain insights into a person's role in life, or even their character by the description others have applied to them. Titles, names or descriptions relating to Jesus come both from reports of how his contemporaries addressed him or spoke about him, as well as sometimes more obviously from the gospel writer. We shall look at some titles or names from both sources.

Son of God?

Tuckett, on the basis that he believes 1:1 is best translated as *The Son of God* , follows this through and makes the centurion's confession in 15:39 the climax of the entire Gospel. Tuckett says, *"For Mark, it seems certain that he intends the centurion to make the ultimate Christological confession: Jesus is the Son of God"* [definite article and capital S][7]. Were this the case I believe Mark would logically have continued his story, following up this confession of faith with resurrection appearances and the ascension. Mark does not do this. Instead Mark has a conclusion which is anything but full of certainty. Contrary to Tuckett's view I would maintain that a lack of clarity or certainty in what is being ascribed to Jesus is in keeping with the whole of Mark's Gospel. For example, John the Baptizer (Mk.1:7-8) offers a description of Jesus, *"He who is mightier than I"*, on which Abrahams comments:

---

[7] OBC p. 2001:920

"These descriptions are deliberately opaque and open ended. They are more formal than material, leaving a lot to be filled in by the one who comes. They work precisely because they provide enough to kindle the imagination in anticipation, but not enough to satisfy the intellect as they stand. They propel one to look for oneself ....."[8]

Martin Hengel in his study, *Son of God*, concludes that this title was primarily used by the earliest Christians as a Messianic ascription. In keeping with contemporary establishment Judaism it was neither a divine appellation, nor implied metaphysical union[9]. It was commonly understood as a synonym for Israel, or Israel's king. It is interesting to note that as Mark nears the end of his gospel, in chapter 15 the title "King of the Jews" is used to describe Jesus five times; in questions by Pilate (Mk.15:2, 9, 12), in mockery (Mk.15:18), and in an inscription of the charge against him (Mk.15:26). In similar vein Jesus' enemies, speaking as Jews, mockingly accord him the title, "*The Christ, the King of Israel*" (Mk.15:32); but none of this necessarily implies divine status. Many modern readers of Mark's gospel have a predisposition to regard Jesus as divine and to interpret every description of him as an amplification of this basic understanding. For Mark Jesus may have been the "new Israel", and in this sense the Son of God, but this again would not imply some quasi-physical relationship. Intriguingly, and I believe deliberately, Mark chooses to have Jesus unambiguously addressed as *The Son of God* almost exclusively by unclean or evil spirits. But such recognition issued in the command that they are not to make him known as such (Mk.3:11f)[10]. The Gerasene man with an unclean spirit is perhaps an exception. He addresses Jesus as "*Jesus, Son of the Most High God*" (Mk.5:7) which does not elicit exactly the same command to say nothing to anyone from Jesus. But the one who has been healed is instructed to share with a limited number of people what God had done for him rather than repeating the words prompted by his evil spirit (Mk.5:19).

For internal evidence of Mark's view of Jesus as a son, or even The Son, the parable of the wicked husbandmen may be instructive (Mk.12:1-11). In this parable the beloved or only son is commissioned in the same way as all the envoys who preceded him[11]. In the parable the son carries the authority, plenipotentiary powers, from his Father which a son can uniquely possess. On this basis, to welcome the son is tantamount to welcoming his Father (Mk.9:27), but there is no hint of his being equal to, or the same as his Father. Jesus calls God 'Father' only once in Mark (Mk.14:36), and at least on one occasion encouraged others to think

---

[8] W. J. Abraham   TLC p.162
[9] See also Ashton UFG p. 220
[10] RTF p. 815
[11] 1:25 has *Holy One of God*, but the same response by Jesus

in the same way (Mk.11:25; see also 13:32). Jesus only knows what his Father reveals to him, and that is not everything. For example, only the Father knows *the day* and *the hour* (Mk.13:32); and significantly when the son returns it will be *in his Father's glory* (Mk.8:38).

With regard to Jesus as The Son of God Ashton's thoughts reflect my own:-

> *"It is not part of my purpose to establish that the historical Jesus knew God as Father in a way that no one else has ever done in fact or ever could do in principle. Such an extreme claim can neither be verified nor disproved. All I wish to insist upon is that there is reason to believe Jesus really did have an unusually deep awareness of God's transcendent majesty and of his all-embracing regard for humankind"*[12].

But I would wish to add to Ashton's comment about *God's transcendent majesty*, that some of those who met Jesus were aware that there was something, perhaps indefinably majestic, even transcendent, about Jesus. So it is worth taking time to look at some of the "titles" or "descriptions" of Jesus by means of which Mark encourages us to be filled with the respect and wonderment experienced by some of Jesus' contemporaries.

Teacher?

Jesus was called "*teacher*" on numerous occasions. Although Mark's gospel includes very little of Jesus' actual teaching, references are scattered throughout the gospel saying that a regular activity of Jesus was teaching. For example, "*He taught them many things in parables*" (Mk.4:2), "*Crowds of people came to him and, as was his custom, he taught them*" (Mk.10:1), "*As he taught* (in Jerusalem) *Jesus said* ..." (Mk.12:38). Indeed, in the story of the feeding of four thousand Jesus tells his disciples that the people had already been with him three days (Mk.8:2), which if the previous feeding account is taken for guidance (Mk.6:34) would have been time spent teaching. Furthermore, Mark tells us early in his gospel that Jesus was unlike other teachers. Jesus' teaching had an impressive kind of authority (Mk.1:22). This "authority" produced both positive and negative responses to his teaching.

The disciples *in extremis* in the face of a storm called to Jesus not as Master, which occurs only four times in the gospel: by Peter (Mk.9:5; 11:21); a blind man (Mk.10:51); and Judas Iscariot (Mk.14:45). Nor do they call him Lord; a title by which Jesus is addressed only once (Mk.7:28 - the Syrophoenician woman). They

---

[12] The terms 'beloved' and 'only' are interchangeable in Septuagint Greek - see UFG p. 223 n 66

cried out to him as "Teacher" (Mk.4:38 see also 9:38; 10:35; 13:1). The circumstances would suggest this was the most natural or instinctive way for his disciples to address Jesus.

Jesus' opponents used this title, teacher, probably with sarcasm (Mk.12:14, 19): but then others use the title who are not opposed to Jesus, and definitely not mocking. Unnamed people from Jairus' house (Mk.5:35), a man whose son had a "dumb spirit" (Mk.9:17), the rich man whom Jesus saw and loved (Mk.10:17, 20), and a friendly scribe (Mk.12:33) all called Jesus teacher. Perhaps of greatest interest, though not necessarily intentional on Mark's part, is that the last reference in Mark's gospel to Jesus as "teacher" is by Jesus of himself. He used it when he sent his disciples to book a room for the Passover meal (Mk.14:14).

However, the title "teacher" which was used by others about Jesus was in common use. Therefore whilst it may give us some insight into how others saw Jesus, and even a glimpse into how he saw himself, it remains a far from well-defined title, and leaves a great deal of leeway in how it was specifically applied to Jesus and how it was understood by Mark or those whose words he conveys. This is not to detract from the perhaps obvious lesson in Mark's gospel that we too might think of Jesus as our teacher; but as a teacher who is like no other - incomparable. Just in looking at this one title it may be evident that in looking at Jesus descriptions or titles may need to be stretched beyond their normal use.

Prince of Demons?

Another possible example of a name or title given to Jesus and inviting contemplation is to be found in Mk.3:22. According to the scribes who came from Jerusalem, Jesus was in league with, and effectively was *the Prince of demons.* This is an intriguing accusation-cum-title, for Mark begins his gospel with Jesus' baptism and then what we may reasonably assume was an overcoming of Satan's powers of temptation (Mk.1:13). Mark goes on to recount many instances of Jesus having (princely?) authority to command demons, or unclean spirits (Mk.1:23-5, 32; 3:11f; 5:1-14; 7:26ff). Noticeably in 5:1-20 (RSV) "unclean/evil spirits" and "demons" are explicitly equated: and NIV consistently prefers the term "*demon possessed*" to "*having an unclean spirit*". We know that sometimes enemies of Jesus are used in the Gospels to express truths which they doubt, but of which the reader should have no doubt. In this sense Mark may be telling us that Jesus may indeed merit the title "Prince of - or over - Demons", though not in a way his enemies understood or accepted. One of the older endings of Mark sees authority over demons as one of the hallmarks of those who put their trust in Jesus (Mk.16:17).

Probably the most graphic example of Jesus confronting an evil or unclean spirit (Mk.5:2), or as we subsequently discover, many evil spirits (Mk.5:9) is the story of Jesus and the man who calls himself Legion, *"for we are many"*. This story is of a man whom Jesus helps find freedom from the many "demons" which have tormented him as well as from the physical chains which have bound him and the ostracism which has socially crippled him. The man's choice of name, Legion, also invites a reader to reflect on the wider malevolent power which oppressed the entire region: namely, the legions of the Roman Empire. Did this individual express in his aberrant behaviour the hell in which his whole community lived, but which they and many others were frightened to see disturbed? If so, the film *One Flew Over the Cuckoo's Nest*, with its juxtaposition of sanity and insanity might be seen as a commentary on the story of Legion. The political reading of Mark which informs the commentary by the Mennonite theologian Ched Myers, *Binding the Strong Man*, specifically addresses this issue, not just for the story in Mark 5, but as a key to understanding the whole of Mark's Gospel. Whilst I have chosen a different key, Myers' thesis is well argued and worthy of consideration.

Is Jesus the Prince of Demons? And just who or what are these demons? For answers to such questions the reader of Mark must legitimately imagine beyond the text: what is currently called *thinking outside of the box*. We probably need to do a lot of that if we are to stand any chance of coming closer to knowing who Jesus might be.

The Christ/Messiah?

The word Messiah in my experience is rarely used of Jesus amongst Christians today; though this word, rather than Christ would have been the more common term amongst Jesus' Aramaic speaking or Hebrew educated contemporaries. However, Mark's gospel uses both. In most Christian circles Jesus is regularly referred to as Jesus (the) Christ, with the definite article omitted. This in effect makes Christ part of Jesus' name rather than a description of him. In this way the necessary and legitimate grappling with what it means to call Jesus "The Christ" is generally avoided.

After the calming of a storm at sea which precedes the story of Legion, Jesus' disciples asked one another, *"Who is this?"* (Mk.4:41). Later in the region of Caesarea Philippi Jesus invited them to answer that question; first by way of how others were describing him; but then as a direct challenge to the disciples concerning their own thinking on the matter: *"Who do you say I am?"* This drew the response from Peter, *"You are the Christ (Messiah)"* (Mk.8:27-31), but as the subsequent conversation makes plain Peter did not understand what this really meant. The acceptance by Jesus of the appellation "Messiah", rather than clarifying who he was, opened up many more questions concerning Jesus' self-understanding and his interpretation of his Messiah-ship. Only at a superficial level can the question *"Who do you say I am?"* seem to require or to have a simple or self-explanatory answer.

Messiah-ship was never a simple matter, as Jesus' exchange with the High Priest demonstrates (Mk.14:61f). At Jesus' trial before the Sanhedrin the High Priest asked Jesus, *"Are you the Christ, the Son of the Blessed One?"* To which, in keeping with Mark's opening description of Jesus as the Christ (Mk.1:1), Jesus replied, *"I am"*[13]. But Jesus undermines this singular descriptive classification by immediately referring to himself as *"The Son of Man (*who will sit) *at the right hand of Power"*. It is highly unlikely that Mark's first readers were able to draw clear Christological conclusions from this dialogue with the High Priest. I suspect all subsequent unprejudiced readers who consider what it means to call Jesus "the Messiah" or "the Christ" will be left with further questions rather than one satisfying answer to the question, *Who is this?*

Son of David?

Blind Bartimaeus insistently called Jesus, *"Son of David"*. For those who believe there is only one way to relate to Jesus it is salutary to see that this blind man came to Jesus on the basis of this faith (that Jesus was the Son of David) and he found healing (Mk.10:47-8). The crowds took up Bartimaeus' accolade. They praised Jesus, believing that he ushered in the *Kingdom of our Father David*, and possibly going further, giving messianic status to Jesus in their proclamation, *"Blessed is he who comes in the name of the Lord!"* (Mk.11:9). However, in Jerusalem Jesus invited the crowds to think more deeply about the relationship between himself or the Messiah and David, *"How is it that the teachers of the law say that the Messiah is the son of David?"* (Mk.12:35). Using a Psalm (Ps.110:1) in a literal way which many today might find questionable, Jesus seems to reject this relationship of David as Father and himself as David's son. It seems that Mark, as at Caesarea Philippi, offers a title for Jesus thereafter to deliberately question how it is to be understood. The challenge or invitation for deeper thinking is consistently presented.

James Montgomery provides a poetic reflection and something of a possible response to both Jesus' Messiah-ship and his relationship to David in his magnificent nineteenth century hymn: *"Hail to the Lord's anointed, great David's greater son ... Kings shall bow down before him ... His praise all peoples sing"*.

---

[13] Jesus gives the same response, *I am (ego eimi)* to the fearful disciples in a storm on the lake when Jesus walks on water, but I am unconvinced by those commentators who see every use by Jesus of *"I am"*, (or *"It is I"* RSV 6:50) as claims to divinity.

The Nazarene?

Right at the end of Mark's Gospel dressed in white the young man in the tomb used the description *Jesus the Nazarene* (Mk.16:6). Nazareth is the original home of Jesus in Mark's account of Jesus' life: "*In those days Jesus came from Nazareth in Galilee*" (Mk.1:9). The description *Jesus of Nazareth* is confirmed by the man with an evil spirit (Mk.1:24) who adds that Jesus is "*the Holy One of God*". But Jesus' Nazarene connection is mentioned only once more, in the story of blind Bartimaeus (Mk.10:47), until Peter's denial (Mk.14:67) and in the message from the tomb. *Jesus the Nazarene* would seem a very strange title to use given the post-resurrection context if it were not for the fact that it is so typical of Mark. The resurrection introduces no novel or grand Christological titles to enthuse or satisfy Mark's readers. He offers instead a simple reminder of who had been placed in the tomb and where he was to be found - not in Jerusalem, not on some high mountain, but back in his and the disciples' own back yard, Galilee. There is a lesson here perhaps for all those who look for the risen Christ, or for any other evidence of God's presence in so many special places yet fail to find him in their own home patch.

The Beloved Son?

At his baptism the voice from heaven declared to Jesus, "*Thou art my beloved Son*" (Mk.1:11). This found an echo for the disciples at the transfiguration: "*This is my Son, whom I love". Listen to him*!" (Mk.9:7). But in neither case is there any expansion of this affirmation of sonship, nor does it lead to further use of the title other than within the parable of the tenants in the vineyard in which the *beloved son* is killed (Mk.12:6-8). For Mark being a son who is loved by a father, God, does not issue in the normal expectations of such a relationship.

Although I find the relationship unattractive, the best parallel I can imagine for Jesus as a son beloved of his father is that of a family with a long military tradition. In such a family the father might well love a son with every ounce of his being, but that would not inhibit his blessing of his son going off to war and possible death. In such a family, whilst the son might follow the path of his father and be equally of even more "successful", the Father/Son relationship would never be one of complete equality. The Father, as long as he lived, would be the head and inspiration for the family. In the same way the words *Beloved son* are most unlikely to imply some kind of divine equality for Jesus with his Father. In fact, though a son might with permission exercise authority on behalf of his father, the relationship of father and son would never naturally imply equality. The response of Jesus to the rich would-be follower is probably indicative of how Mark viewed the relationship between Jesus and God. Jesus asked, "*Why do you call me good?*

No one is good but God alone" (Mk.10:18 my underlining). According to Mark, is Jesus God's son? Yes. But is Jesus the same as or equal to God? No[14]

Son of Man?[15]

The most prevalent title or description of Jesus in Mark is not Son of God (which occurs just three times and which Jesus never used of himself), but *Son of Man* (fourteen times). No one speaking to Jesus ever used this description, but Jesus used it regularly as a self-referent. He used this title when he predicted his death (Mk.8:31, 9:12, 31; 10:33), when he predicted his resurrection (Mk.9:9) and in connection with his final return:

> *"If anyone is ashamed of me and my words in this adulterous and sinful generation, the Son of Man will be ashamed of him when he comes in his Father's glory with the holy angels. At that time men will see the Son of Man coming in clouds with great power and glory"* (Mk.8:38; 13:26).

In keeping with the association Jesus made between Son of man and death and suffering, the same self-description, was used by Jesus at the last supper in connection with the actions and fate of his betrayer (Mk.14:21), and yet again when he addressed the High Priest at his trial (Mk.14:62)[16]. Nowhere does Mark give any indication as to why he, or Jesus, used this title, but its frequent repetition and the associations given for it, for example - *Lord of the Sabbath* (Mk.2:28) - *Coming in clouds.* (Mk.13:26), *etc.* suggest its importance in Mark.

Son of Man is used a number of times in the Old Testament (Ps.80:17; Daniel 7:13; 8:19; and 93 times in Ezekiel), but usually without the Messianic or apocalyptic connotation which Mark assigns to it. André Resner Jnr. suggests that Jesus preferred this term because *"It was a way to reveal his identity and mission free of the ideological baggage that the term 'Messiah' brought with it"*[17]. Mullins believes

---

[14] The terms 'beloved' and 'only' are interchangeable in Septuagint Greek - see UFG p. 223 n 66

[15] For a much fuller treatment of this subject see Douglas Hare *The Son of Man Tradition* Fortress Press 1990 – or Craig Evans summary of many points of view, including Hare's (Word Bible Commentaries Vol.34b *Mark 8:27-16:20* lxiii-lxviii 2001).

[16] See also 2:10, 28, 10:45, 14:41 for other instances of this title in Mark

[17] TLC. p.233. It should be noted that a number of scholars have suggested "Son of Man" is a Messianic title. E.g. Heikki Räisänen *The Messianic Secret in Mark* T&T Clark 1990

Jesus' use of *Son of Man* in reference to himself "*is often used as a corrective to misplaced messianic expectations*"[18]. France says:

> "*It seems the reason Jesus found this title convenient is that, having no ready-made titular connotations in current usage, it could be applied across the whole range of his uniquely paradoxical mission of humiliation and vindication, of death and glory, which could not be fitted into any pre-existing model*"[19].

None of these scholars seem to me to take sufficiently into account that in the first century the title "Son of Man" would be familiar to Jesus' Jewish listeners from its use in Psalm 80, Daniel's two references and Ezekiel's frequent use. It was hardly likely to be unburdened with expectations. The context of foreign occupation would probably fill up the title Son of Man with both political and theological content. Nonetheless, it was almost certainly less well defined in the popular imagination than the term Messiah. Hence France is probably right to suggests that at Caesarea Philippi Jesus used the self-description "Son of Man" because "*The open-ended and puzzling nature of this designation as used by Jesus during his ministry, as a title invites the question 'Who?' The title alone does not provide an answer*".[20]

The relationship between *Son of Man* and *Son of God* is complex. Ashton points out that whereas the title "Son of God" actually carried no divine connotations, "Son of Man" pointed to a figure whose true home is in heaven - although even this does not necessarily, nor even probably, imply divinity[21]. Raymond Bailey suggests that the popular concept of Messiah in Jesus' day was *based on Daniel 7 and the apocryphal book of Enoch* (which) *anticipated a figure who could bring judgement and punishment on the unrighteous and vindication of the righteous*"[22]. Certainly Daniel 7:13 could be in Mark's mind; "*In my vision at night I looked, and there before me was one like a son of man, coming with the clouds of heaven*" (See also Daniel 8:17). However, although the text actually refers to "*one like a son of man*", if there were those who understood Daniel 7 as a description of the Messiah,

[18] TGL p.194

[19] RTF p.327

[20] Ibid p.615

[21] UFG p.240. Note: Canon Dr. Mark Harris commenting on the Jesus/Nathanael encounter notes that to Nathanael's appellations of Jesus as "Son of God" and "King of Israel" Jesus replied that Nathaniel would see "greater things" because he would see the "Son of Man". (Expository Times: December 2011 p.120). Harris makes no comment about this elevation of Son of Man over Son of God, other than to say that the Son of Man is *the bridge between heaven and earth* - surely a function which most Christians would ascribe to Jesus as the incarnate "Son of God".

[22] TLC p.237

Jesus' use of this title would not deflect all his hearers from considering him as a messianic claimant[23].

Given that the ascription 'Son of Man' appears only twice in Daniel (and once in Psalms), but ninety three times in Ezekiel, it is possible that although many commentators seem to focus on Daniel as Mark's (or Jesus') inspiration, Mark might also, or even more, have had its use in Ezekiel in mind. This would be appropriate. For example, "*Son of man, I have made you a watchman for the house of Israel; so hear the word I speak and give them warning from me*" (Mk.3:17. cf. 33:7). Or, "*And you, son of man, they will tie with ropes; you will be bound so that you cannot go out among the people*" (Ezekiel 3:25). Or "*Son of man, set your face against the mountains of Israel; prophesy against them*" (Ezekiel 6:2). All of these prophecies seem highly relevant to the life and ministry of Jesus, and to Jesus' understanding of his ministry and his "fate".

It will be interesting to take further this use of the prophets in searching for some of Mark's answers to the question of who Jesus is, but before moving on to pursue the notion of Jesus as the embodied fulfilment of prophecies, or indeed as himself a prophet, it is worth pausing to make three important points which arise out of the above sample of the rich variety of titles used by or of Jesus.

1. Lord - or Son of Man?

The major titles for Jesus which present-day churches tend to use, and sometimes use as though they are self-explanatory and definitive, such as *The Son of God*, are certainly not the dominant ones in Mark's Gospel. Even more intriguing, given its great popularity in many church circles today, *Lord Jesus*, as a way of talking about Jesus is not in Mark at all, unless the additional endings are taken into account (Mk.16:19). In Mark, if the additional endings of Mark's Gospel are discounted, Jesus possibly refers to himself as *Lord* only once - and even here the word might be applied to Jesus, but just as plausibly to God (Mk.11:3). When Jesus says to the demoniac, "*Go home to your family and tell them how much the Lord has done for you*" it is unlikely that *Lord* is a self-reference by Jesus

---

[23] Ashton UFG p.272f notes two complementary works offering theories as to how the term *Son of Man* may have become associated with Jesus' passion and resurrection: Morna Hooker's *The Son of Man in Mark* - London 1967; and John Bowker *Religious Imagination* pp.139-169. Both use Daniel as a primary and important source, but Ashton is not totally convinced. Ashton further notes that the "original" Hebrew words of Daniel, *like a man*, somehow and inexplicably in translation became *the Son of Man* (UFG p.240f). France commends Carson who "*provides a useful brief survey of discussion of the issue up to about 1980; it is doubtful whether much of substance has been added since*" (RTF p. 326 n14 re D. A. Carson "Matthew" in F. E. Gaebelein (ed.) The Expositor's Bible Commentary. vol. 8. Grand Rapids 1984 209-213).

(Mk.5:19). To add to the complexity of understanding any lordship which might be ascribed to Jesus, Jesus as *The son of man* is *Lord of the Sabbath* (Mk.2:28); but to extract from this combination a general use of the term *Lord* for Jesus hardly seems justified. On only one occasion was the title *Lord* used by others of Jesus: by a Syrophoenician woman (Mk.7:28), and we have no way of knowing with what meanings she endowed the term. John the Baptizer may also be included if his use of "Lord" taken from Isaiah 40:3 is referring to Jesus (Mk.1:3). Whether or not that is so remains an open question. The crowd who shouted as Jesus approached Jerusalem did not welcome Jesus as Lord, but as *"he who comes in the name of the Lord"* - and it is *"the Kingdom of our father David"* that is coming (Mk.11:9f). A church influenced at all by Mark's Gospel might need to rethink the way it so often speaks or sings that Jesus is Lord - and why we use so rarely the much more common gospel title of Son of Man. It might be that we prefer to think of Jesus as being like God, the Lord, rather than like us, *one like a son of man.*

2. No Instant Naming?

The number of different titles or descriptions Mark uses for Jesus should act as a caution against any presumption that we can summarise who Jesus is by using one or two traditional Christian titles - what we might call "instant labelling". Jesus is a much bigger, deeper, mysterious and challenging person than our narrow use of language often acknowledges or can embrace. W. J. Abraham says: *"In coming to see who Jesus is, we all need time and space to ponder what is before us. The urge to move in for immediate decision must be tempered with adequate reflection..."*[24].

I have no research data to support this contention, but I sense that modern hymns or songs are generally speaking less expansive and inclusive in their descriptions of Jesus than was once the case. This may be allied to the modern tendency to prize "5-minute personalities" rather than to value people whose appeal exists only for those who take the trouble and time to really get to know them. Patrick Appleford's, *"Jesus our Lord, our King and our God - humblest of priests - suffering servant - shepherd - prophet of God - the way the truth and the life - our God"* is the kind of hymn which does invite a mature, deeper contemplation rather than childish instant gratification.[25]

3. A Name for Personal Interpretation?

I believe Mark's Gospel, accurately reflecting Jesus' own practice, deliberately makes extensive use of the term *Son of Man* precisely because it is a term which is open to wide interpretation. In the final analysis, perhaps Mark does not want to

---

[24] W. J. Abraham TLC p.164
[25] 100 Hymns for Today (No.49) 1969

give his readers a title or descriptive term which would imply there is a ready-made, comprehensive answer to the question about Jesus, *"Who is this?"* Mark wants his readers to search for answers to the question for themselves - and people may legitimately come to different answers according to their needs and experience, because often the names given are closely linked to the roles which Jesus fulfils in people's lives such as healer, prophet, exorcist, teacher, and so on. I have known people who perhaps like Legion needed Jesus to be *Prince of (over) Demons.* Others like Bartimaeus might need him to be the *Son of David.* Ultimately the question for each of us is the one posed by Jesus to his disciples at Caesarea Philippi, *Who do you say that I am?* Churches making dogmatic assertions may well either prevent this question from being asked, or hinder it from being answered in the most helpful way. This is not to deny the value of corporate or shared understandings, but it is to say that within the body of a church there should be a healthy reticence toward imposing any single description of Jesus as essential dogma for every individual.

> *"The ... evangelists... incorporated their insights into a bios Iesou ...largely through Christological titles, chief among which were Son of God, Messiah (Christ), Lord, Son of Man, Saviour, Prophet, Son of David and King. These titles do not function independently, but help to interpret one another, and in so doing correct misunderstandings and false expectations that had grown up around the various titles".[26]*

André Resner Jnr. rightly points out:
> *"The Gospels have an ongoing iconoclastic function in the church's theological and ecclesial imagination, challenging the static formulations and abstractions of his identity and personhood which are devoid of narrative envelope... Who is Jesus? And what is the nature of HIS Messiah-ship? can only be answered by the narratives (Matthew, Mark, Luke & John) ... which concretely display for us Jesus' own life, words and action".[27]*

France puts it succinctly:
> *The title "the son of man" came with an air of enigma, challenging the hearer to think new thoughts rather than slot Jesus into a ready-made pigeonhole. The very mysteriousness of the title "the Son of Man" indicates an element of enigma.[28]*

As a small footnote to the descriptive ways in which Mark invites us to think about Jesus, it may be noteworthy that when a woman came and anointed Jesus' head,

---

[26] TGL p.60
[27] TLC p.234
[28] RTF pp. 327, 484

which might have been seen as recognition of kingship or Messiah-ship, Jesus interpreted it in terms of his death. And in referring to himself in this context he used no titles, but simply said, "*She has done a beautiful thing to __me__*" (Mk.14:6 my underlining). Perhaps this unnamed woman had plumbed the depths of Jesus' true nature and identity; discovered the truth of Jesus for her in a way which inspired true respect and devotion, and needed no titles. An exemplary case of actions speaking louder than words?

Jesus the Prophet

We must return to the texts from Ezekiel cited earlier; "*Son of man, I have made you a watchman for the house of Israel; so hear the word I speak and give them warning from me*"; (Ezekiel 3:17 // Ez.33:7) and "*Son of man, set your face against the mountains of Israel; prophesy against them*" (Ezekiel 6:2). Mark's Gospel does not directly use these verses, but as we have seen it repeatedly uses the term *Son of Man* (thirteen times). It would also seem that Mark deliberately and closely identifies Jesus with the wider prophetic tradition of his people. Although he may be other things (e.g. 12:6-8 where he is the son and heir), in Mark's Gospel Jesus is identified as a prophet, and set in the context of prophecy from almost the very first words of the gospel (Mk.1:2 quotes from Isaiah the prophet).

Jesus asked, "*Who are my mother and my brothers?*" He answered the question himself, "*Whoever does the will of God is my brother, and sister, and mother*" (Mk.3:33-34). In the context of Mark's Gospel this identification of "*whoever does the will of God*" as Jesus' true family is highly significant. Mark's Gospel does not begin with or include a genealogy, or birth narratives. Mark does not set Jesus' entry into the world in a specific family or in a national or universal history. For Mark, the story of Jesus begins and is rooted in the prophecies of Isaiah, Malachi and Exodus. These are all his family, his kinsmen. Jesus' ministry is prefaced by the prophetic ministry of John the Baptizer (Mk.1:1-8). It is legitimized through participation in John's prophetic ministry of a "baptism of repentance" (Mk.1:9-11). It is tested by a prophet's experience of 40 days fasting and temptation in the wilderness. As Moses fasted for 40 days (Exodus 34:28), and Elijah was in the wilderness and hungry (1 Kings 19:4-7) so it is with Jesus. And the highly probable connections continue: for example, the call of the first disciples has similarities with Elijah's call of Elisha (1 Kgs.19:19-20a), and Jesus' experience of being isolated and abandoned by God (and by his "friends") has parallels with Elijah (1 Kings 19:4, 10, 14).

According to Herod and to his disciples Jesus was thought predominantly by others to be either *John the Baptizer* (returned to life), or "*Elijah or one of the prophets*" (Mk.6:14-16, 8:28). This was not just the opinion of the ill-informed or of other people. When Jesus was rejected in his "own country" he used this description of himself: "*Jesus said to them, 'Only in his hometown, among his relatives and in his own house is a prophet without honour'* " (Mk.6:4). Of course, it may be argued that Jesus is simply referring to his specific role in that situation. Even so it is part of his self-identification. In the story of the transfiguration when Jesus is seen by three of his disciples in company with the two great prophets, Moses and Elijah, a voice from the cloud gives Jesus pre-eminence as *my beloved Son* and the other prophets disappear (Mk.9:7-8). But the event resonates with Daniel 7:9 and is immediately followed in Mark by a discussion about the significance of Elijah (Mk.9:11-13). Through the thoughts of some bystanders Elijah again becomes part of Mark's story of Jesus at the crucifixion (Mk.15:35-6). As the transfiguration supremely symbolises, the spiritual presence of the prophets is never far away from Jesus' life and ministry - he is in conversation with them.

In days when positive interfaith relationships seem essential for peace in the world and its many communities, and when claims for the divinity of Jesus can be a stumbling block, it is worth remembering that Jesus can with warrant from the Christian scriptures as well as the Qur'an be described as a prophet. This is a perspective which might be shared easily with people of faiths other than Christianity, and a resource not to be lightly rejected.

Furthermore, even within a church's own life a focus on Jesus' divine status can easily distract a church from the challenges which Jesus poses when his prophetic function is taken seriously. Herod and others were right to see Jesus' ministry as full of the spirit of the prophet John the Baptizer, Elijah and Isaiah. Jesus also demands the *straight paths*, the repentance and the calls for justice which alone make it possible to share in God's coming Kingdom (Mk.1:3; 12:14).

Prophetic status for Jesus is no small claim. It in no way diminishes or undermines him. The role and work of a prophet as we have noted above from Ezekiel and Daniel can be simultaneously contemporary and apocalyptic. Prophets are called to challenge ungodly authority or abuse, wherever they may be found - even in the palace and the temple. In consequence prophets often pay a heavy price for making such challenges. Mark alerts his readers to this by referring to John the Baptizer's imprisonment very early in the story (Mk.1:14), and later through Jesus' parable of the tenants in the vineyard (Mk.12:1-8).

Although in Mark there is no suggestion of a genetic relationship between John the Baptizer and Jesus, there is a close identity in their ministries. They are both challenging. *"Beware of the leaven of the Pharisees and the leaven of Herod"*, says Jesus (Mk.8:15), a combination of interests which conspired against him (Mk.3:6); whilst *the leaven of Herod* had literally brought about the murder of John the Baptizer (Mk.6:16). Jesus' clearing of the temple traders, was a challenge to the authority of the chief priests and scribes. The conspiracy to do away with him was the unsurprising result (Mk.11:15-18). Tuckett persuasively sees Mark's sandwiching of the Temple episode between the two parts of the fig tree cursing (Mk.11:12-26) as indicative that Mark sees Jesus' actions and words in the temple as a prophetic cursing of the temple [36]. If Tuckett is correct, then subsequent events have a measure of inevitability. Jesus' refusals to kowtow to the high priest, or to defend himself before Pilate, were equally challenging to the assumed authority of those who would judge him: and equally dangerous.

There are many fine examples of Christians who follow or have followed the prophetic path of Jesus, and who also often paid with their lives. But the church as a whole has far too often been on the side of, or at least uncritical of those whose use of power is primarily for their own benefit. It is in effect an abuse of those who in worldly terms are weak, or "*the poor*". Sometimes we are even with the disciples admiring the architecture instead of seeing their inevitable transience and focussing on what really matters (Mk.13:1). Para-church movements such as the Jubilee Debt campaign, Amnesty International and Christian Aid help redress the balance; but the fact that many Christians withdrew their support for Christian Aid when it openly criticised apartheid in South Africa and became "involved in politics" is one indicator of how far removed from the prophetic spirit of Jesus some of his followers can be. I find it interesting that a parallel charitable organisation for overseas aid, Tear Fund, which was set up at that time to be "non-political" after a number of years realised the necessity of a political voice. Honestly facing up to the injustice which is the root cause of much poverty has compelled it to include a prophetic ministry.

A Gospel-shaped church will own Jesus as prophet. Following Jesus will mean that a church must have a prophetic role to play in the world. Playing it safe, self-preservation, always trying to be acceptable, are not the hallmarks of prophets, or of a church full of, and ennobled by the spirit of John the Baptizer or Jesus. Perhaps the greatest support for thinking of Jesus as a prophet is that he shared their not uncommon fate (Mk.12:5; 14:1).

Do Not Tell Anyone - It is a Secret

Those familiar with Mark's Gospel and commentaries on it will be aware of what is sometimes called *The Messianic Secret*. I believe the Messianic secret is crucial in appreciating Mark's gospel. It is not just an interesting diversion for scholars to debate; it is at the very core of Mark's telling of Jesus' story, a vital key to understanding the gospel's purpose and Jesus' method[29]. Like many of the best

---

[29] W. Wrede in *Das Messiasgeheimnis in den Evangelien* (1901) wrote that the motif of the Messianic Secret dominated the whole of Mark's presentation of Jesus; but Wrede saw this as Mark accounting for an historical situation in which Jesus was considered to be the Messiah by his disciples only after his resurrection and ascension.

mysteries, this "secret" is an invitation into an ever deepening exploration which can be totally absorbing and transforming.

Mark makes it evident that Jesus did not want to draw attention to himself as primarily a worker of signs and wonders[30] ; sometimes even trying to hide himself (Mk.7:24). Jesus tried to persuade the newly healed "demoniac" to share the good news of what the Lord (God?) had done for him only with his friends at home (Mk.5:19). Similarly, the blind man healed at Bethsaida is told to go home and not go into the village (Mk.8:26). The experience of many suggests that one's home can be the most difficult place to share something of the gospel, and often requires a faithful, intimate kind of sharing rather than indiscriminate broadcasting. The parable of the farmer and the seed and soil might be used to suggest an indiscriminate sharing of the word, but in a land where sometimes scrub and stony ground could be more easily found than fertile soil, it is a parable which might equally be intended to encourage discrimination as to where the precious seed/word is "sown" (Mk.4:1-12).

There will be times when the way of the cross will include not being ashamed of Jesus' words (Mk.8:34-38): but there is ample evidence that Jesus did not want to be publicised willy-nilly. So in other places in Mark Jesus told, or strongly urged people not to broadcast what he had done at all; although his intentions were often frustrated because his request was ignored: "*The more he charged them to tell no one, the more zealously they proclaimed it*" (Mk.7:36; cp. 1:43; 6:31-34; 7:36). Jesus ordered unclean spirits not to identify him (Mk.1:34, 3:12). He even told his disciples not to tell anyone what they had understood about him (Mk.8:30) or what they had witnessed of his glory "*until the Son of Man should have risen from the dead*" (Mk.9:9). If we exclude the additional endings of Mark's Gospel, the story of Jesus ends with his readers being told that the women who had visited the tomb "*said nothing to anyone*" (Mk.16:8). All of this is in keeping with the view that Jesus believed people needed to find out for themselves who he was; not to receive it second-hand. Mark is true to this principle throughout the construction of his gospel.

In Mark the parable to explain all Jesus' parables is the parable of the farmer sowing seed. It has an accompanying conversation or explanation (Mk.4:3-20). Jesus said to his disciples, "*Don't you understand this parable? How will you understand any parable*" (Mk.4:13). Jesus says that his use of parables is consonant with what had been prophesied,

---

[30] Contrast this with Jesus' words in John, "*believe because of the works themselves*" - John 10:38; 14:11

"Go and tell this people: be ever hearing, but never understanding; be ever seeing, but never perceiving. Make the heart of this people calloused; make their ears dull and close their eyes. Otherwise they might see with their eyes, hear with their ears, understand with their hearts, and turn and be healed." (Isa.6:9-10. cp. Ez.12:2).

Tuckett sees this as an intrusion by Mark and he would deny Jesus this use of Isaiah, because Tuckett maintains that *"Jesus himself (it is usually assumed) used parables to enable understanding, not prevent it"*[31]. But Tucket overlooks the likelihood that parables were an integral part of the consistent "method of secrecy" Jesus used to sift the genuine seeker after truth from those who wanted instant gratification - *"who have no root in themselves"* and who will *"prove unfruitful"* (Mk.4:17, 19).

Mark adds to the parable of The Sower two further parables about seeds (Mk.4:26-32). These are preceded and followed by further explanation. Firstly Jesus says that what is now secret will eventually come to light - or have light shone upon it (Mk.4:21-22). Secondly Mark tells us that Jesus always spoke to the crowds through parables, *"as they were able to hear it"*, but privately explained everything to his own disciples (Mk.4:33-35; cp.10:10). I would add that, contrary to many sermons I have heard and read, the meaning of the parables as originally given, that is, without the context of the wider story as we know it, would be far from self-evident. Mark's gospel is not only aware of this but sees it as entirely in keeping with the challenging nature of Jesus' self-disclosure. Jesus may be God's gift, but he is a gift not to be received lightly.

Churches so often believe they have to make it as easy as possible for everyone to accept the teaching of Jesus, or to follow Jesus. My considerable reservations about this stance is why I am instinctively nervous about such things as Alpha courses when they seem to suggest an easy method for understanding what taking Jesus seriously means - for getting to know Jesus. It seems out of kilter with Jesus' way. Our methods of evangelism should at least take into account the fact that Jesus seemed to have intentionally made it hard for people to understand his message, which was intimately bound up with his true identity. The kind of truth which Jesus came to share was to be lived. As George McLeod insightfully put it, *"The faith is an experience, not an exposition. Christians are explorers, not map makers"*[32]. What is required is something deeper than a quick and easily digestible acceptance of some facts or data, which regrettably are often confused with some notion called "truth". The foundation of the true way of living which Jesus embodied is a commitment to the way of the cross. Even the disciples with their

---

[31] OBC p.895
[32] Daily readings with George McLeod 1991 Fount Paperbacks

private explanations of the parables, were not able to understand this prior to Jesus' crucifixion (Mk.9:32). In my experience of church life churches have often been full on Palm Sunday and even fuller on Easter Sunday, but a comparatively small number have engaged with Good Friday. Excuses may be made, but if contemplating the cross is avoided - indeed if it is not central to our thinking - then we are likely to be sharing that *cheap grace* which Dietrich Bonhoeffer rightly decried.[33]

There are some Christian denominations who never observe The Lord's Supper. This is in keeping with Mark's Gospel which gives no justification for the ritualisation or repeated remembrance of the Passover meal, or last supper, which Jesus shared with his disciples. Mark has no record of Jesus saying, "*Do this in remembrance of me*".

As a London Baptist I was raised in the 1950's to "observe the Lord's Supper" once a month. It was an add-on to the main service, reserved for members only. This is not the place to discuss at length the pros and cons of an open or closed "Lord's Table", but at my instigation in the Baptist churches where I have served as minister The Lord's Supper (Holy Communion, Eucharist) has been celebrated almost every week, because it ensured that a reminder of the sacrifice, or death of Jesus had a regular and significant place in the worship of a church. The elements have been available to all who in faith wish to receive them; although matzos and grapes have also been available at times to allow participation by young children or some adults who do not yet feel ready for the invitation "*take it, this is my body*" and the offer of the cup which " *is my blood*" (Mk.14:22, 24). I am sorry that some churches who observe the Lord's Supper every week (even every day) have made it so predictable and so mechanical that the gift of Jesus of himself in bread and wine can be lost in ritual and verbosity, or in mystical incantations; but it may be preferable that something is there which speaks of Jesus' death, even if it is poorly enacted, than for it not to be there at all. At its best the sharing of bread and wine will always include the dimension of mystery, the acknowledgement of death, and the sense that what is on offer is a foretaste of the joy that can be known whenever and wherever God's kingdom comes - a secret or mystery to inform and inspire our daily lives, yet still to be un-earthed.

A Gospel shaped church will find ways to ensure the cross is at the centre of its work and worship. This is not an easily understood, much less easily embodied focus or lived-out reality. The identity of the Messiah is a secret, or a mystery, in the sense that it is only discovered or entered into by earnest, faithful seeking,

---

[33] Paul wrote to the church at Corinth, "*When I came to you I did not come proclaiming to you the testimony of God in lofty words or wisdom. For I decided to know nothing among you except Jesus Christ and him crucified*" (1 Cor. 2:1-2). Mark's Gospel in its original form has a similar focus, a kindred spirit, which churches would do well to imbibe.

prayerful asking, humble learning, forgiving and generous self-giving of the kind which led Jesus to the cross (Mk.cf.11:24f). Ultimately it is not that Jesus wanted his identity kept secret, but rather that his true identity was so bound up with the way of the cross that only in the light of the cross can who Jesus really is begin to be perceived or appropriated [34]. Jesus did not want anyone to say who he was until after his death, because without his death his identity was incomplete. Tucket makes the point: "*That Jesus' identity can only be truly perceived in the light of the cross is the best solution to the 'Messianic Secret' debate.*" [35]

One further important consideration is that Jesus' desire not to draw attention to himself was because his true purpose was to draw attention to God. Tuckett notes that the sole occurrence in Mark of the words "*who believe in me*" (Mk.9:42) are not in all manuscripts of the Gospel[36]. If they are words of Jesus they would not only be unique in Mark but also in the Synoptics which characteristically present Jesus as pointing away from himself and toward God. Only when Jesus as a physical presence is out of the picture - post resurrection/ascension - can his role as harbinger of the Holy Spirit and inaugurator of God's Kingdom be properly understood and shared. The question of Jesus, "*Why do you call me good? No one is good but God alone.*" (Mk.10:18) is not a cryptic clue or false modesty. It reflects the respect, humble obedience and prayerful worship which Jesus offered to his heavenly Father. To regard Jesus as God's equal, or as divine, is not justified by a plain reading of Mark's witness to Jesus. Consistently at least part of the answer to the question, "*Who am I?*" is, "*I am the one who points beyond myself*" [37]
[38]

---

[34] W. Wrede in *Das Messiasgeheimnis in den Evangelien* (1901) proposed a similar view that Jesus deliberately obscured understanding of himself as the Messiah, and (in spite of Peter's confession in Mk.8:29) Wrede believed no one thought of Jesus as the Messiah prior to his crucifixion and resurrection.

[35] See Tucket in OBC p.890: "*That Jesus identity can only be truly perceived in the light of the cross*" is the best solution to the "Messianic Secret" debate. See further on this in Tucket *The Messianic Secret* SPCK 1983 and Raisanen The *Messianic Secret in Mark's Gospel* 1990 T. & T. Clark.

[36] OBC p.906. These words in Mark are also in Matt.18:6 in the same context.

[37] This gives an interesting nuance to the Johannine testimony of Jesus, "*If you really knew me, you would know my Father as well. From now on you will know him*" (John 14:7). That is, following on from Jesus death there will be a new relationship between the disciples and the Father.

[38] The question has been raised as to whether or not there is in Mark a "secret" which legitimately can be related to the concept of "mystery" as understood in the context of apocalyptic literature, "*A secret once hidden and now revealed is the essence of apocalyptic*" (Ashton UFG p.311). Mark 13 is sometimes referred to as *the little apocalypse*. If this chapter is regarded as crucial to understanding the whole of Mark's gospel (and perhaps related to the Son of Man references in the gospel), then it offers a possible rationale for the

Chapter 2 - Mark

What Would Jesus Do?

What a person chooses to do is often a guide to their character or spirit. I believe that tackling the question, "What did Jesus do?" is an important part of finding clues to his identity. In keeping with the tenor of the whole of Mark's Gospel, the answer to this question was never going to be given on a plate, but principles which should inform our answers are there to be discovered. The bigger challenge is how to convert an appreciation of what Jesus did into the choices for action which we make. Not just to ask the past-tense question, "What did Jesus do?", but also to contemporise it, "What would Jesus do here and now?" and to use what must often be tentative answers as guiding principles for our own lives. This is part of living by faith as Christians.

Whatever title we may think most appropriate for Jesus, in his ministry he responded not just to the shortcomings and injustices of the religious (and secular?) authorities of his day, but to un-wholeness, disease or want in whatever form it confronted him. Such challenges exist no less for today's church.

Mark records several instances of Jesus healing specific, sometimes named individuals who suffered from paralysis or blindness or other types of physical illness. Mark also records that at times there were crowds who came to him when many received healing (Mk.1:29-45; 3:1-12; 5:21-43; 7:24-37; 8:22-26; 10:46-52). Although the accounts of healing are diverse enough not to provide any kind of template for such a ministry, there are common elements amongst the stories. One factor is that of faith recognised by Jesus on the part of the person who is being healed (Mk.5:34; 10:52) or in others who act on behalf of their friends or family (Mk.2:5). Where the prerequisite faith was absent the possibility of miracles and healing was much reduced (Mk.6:5-6). The touching of the hem of Jesus' garment is a most graphic symbol of someone acting in faith, and in such instances there was not always verbal interaction between healer and healed prior to the healing (Mk.3:10; 5:27-28). The spiritual resource which makes contact with Jesus a healing process is predicated on Jesus' own commitment to prayer, his spiritual discipline, his faith; but it is an interaction in which faith responds to faith (cf. Mk.8:11-12; 9:24, 29). Tuckett goes so far as to say, "*Faith for Mark can never be based on miracles; miracles can only occur in the context of already existing faith and commitment*" [39]. This seems to hold true even when there are elements of unwillingness to be healed (Mk.1:34; 5:7).

Messianic Secret. Whilst accepting the logic of this notion, I reject it on the grounds that I do not see Mark 13 as providing the overriding motif for the whole gospel.
[39] Tuckett: OBC p.920

Fewer instances are recorded by Mark of exorcisms, the casting out of demons or unclean spirits (Mk.1:23-39; 3:7-12; 5:1-20). These are noticeably confined to the first half of Mark's Gospel. When the twelve are chosen it is for this ministry rather than healing of the sick that Jesus calls them to be with him (Mk.3:15) and commissions them (Mk.6:7); although their mission did include healing of the sick and preaching as well as casting out demons. However, later in Jesus' ministry his disciples were unable to deal with a boy with a dumb and violent spirit (Mk.9:18), whilst others, not of the twelve, and to their consternation, were able to successfully engage in this kind of ministry in Jesus' name (Mk.9:38-40).

Though the two may be interconnected at times, it is helpful to make a distinction between the cases of individuals who were released from the power of an evil spirit which essentially involved self-harm, and the greater corporate evil of false and oppressive religious systems and temporal powers which imposed harm on others and demeaned or shackled whole societies. Jesus was concerned with and confronted both, but the former required healing, the second needed criticism, opposition and reform or, in the light of non-repentance, the destruction which God would bring to pass[40]. The parabolic story of Legion demonstrates that what appears to be the expulsion of demons from an individual can have significant social implications. The story may also imply that some demonic forces need to be destroyed completely.

Because these two distinct aspects of Jesus' ministry, the individual and the corporate, have sometimes been conflated, there are those who have seen in Mark's recording of exorcisms by Jesus evidence of a supernatural battle in which Jesus was engaged against universal powers of evil which are ranged against God and personified in the figure of Satan. But there seems little warrant for such a meta-narrative. Braaten believes that today there is an under-emphasis on the work of Satan and this is part of the de-mythologizing process of the last century. He suggests that if the reality of Satan is removed from the context of Jesus' ministry, *"God the redeemer loses much of his identity through the abolition of his opposition, his satanic antithesis"*[41]. But an emphasis on some supposed overarching supernatural context for both Jesus' ministry and ours can easily subvert us from paying the necessary attention to either the individual sickness or corporate evil, or both, which need our attention in the here and now. Often people need saving from themselves or from oppressive systems and regimes not from some imagined external or internal disembodied force. But to return to exorcisms, people with "evil spirits", spirits which harm them, are sick, just as much as people

---

[40] For the notion of destroying evil regimes see Jeremiah 18:7-12. Countless other examples of verses from the Old Testament could be given, but the entire histories of Israel and Judah witness to this as part of God's working.

[41] Carl E. Braaten *That they may believe - A theology of the Gospel and the mission of the church* Eerdmans - Grand Rapids 2008 p.124

with physical ailments. Jesus was concerned to respond in the here-and-now to all kinds of sickness; *"Those who are well have no need of a physician, but those who are sick. I came not to call the righteous, but sinners"* (Mk.2:17).

This comment about the "sick" and "sinners" is placed by Mark after three pericopes: the healing of the paralysed man in which the relationship between sin and suffering is questioned by Jesus (Mk.2:1-12), the call of Levi, a tax collector (Mk.2:12-13), and a description of the company Jesus kept in his own house at his table, *"tax collectors and sinners"* (Mk.2:15-16). Jesus came to change the way people were regarded and treated as well as the way they chose to live. The two are often interconnected. Those who work to lift the street children of Brazil out of poverty and prostitution, to give social standing to Dalits in India, or champion dignified treatment for prisoners in England seem to me to be doing what Jesus would do in the same circumstances. In the story of the paralytic where the paralysed man's friends tore open the roof of Jesus' house the relationship between forgiveness of sins and physical healing is by no means clear, but it is there, and it follows naturally on from Jesus' very first proclamation of the Gospel which included a call both to repentance and to faith in the good news (Mk.1:15). A church at its best is good news for those who most need some - including the many who need to be told and to realise that what others, and perhaps they themselves would see as their imperfect condition is neither an insuperable nor a supernatural impediment to them being made whole by God's love.

Graydon Snyder says the direct connection between sin and suffering was taken for granted in the Hebrew tradition, *"whereas in the Jesus tradition illness and disability may simply have happened"*[42]. He suggests that Jesus' challenge to the idea that personal suffering was always related to the sin of an individual was revolutionary. There is undoubtedly truth in Snyder's claim, but the nexus in Mark of sin, suffering, evil spirits or demons, forgiveness, healing and exorcisms does not allow for certainty in explanations. Like much in Mark readers must either make their own decision, or perhaps be prepared to live with uncertainty.

At the heart of the conflict over sin and suffering may be the difference between Jesus understanding of "sin" and that of his critics. Jesus seemed to regard sin as most of all a matter of someone being "lost" and therefore in need of being graciously "found" or "saved". His opponents thought of "sin" as either to do with ritual and moral incorrectness which required "legal remedy"; or as God's will and therefore beyond human intervention. In later teaching Jesus suggested a willingness to forgive other people was an essential prerequisite for prayer requests to be answered (Mk.11:25). For Jesus sin is relational as well as personal, as are its

---

[42] TLC p.186f. The book of Job's challenge to the belief that suffering is always the result of sin seems to play no part in the thinking of Jesus' contemporaries.

consequences. Its abrogation lies in the sharing of a gracious and generous spirit; which is what Jesus did. Church "discipline" in particular and life in general would be exercised better, more redemptive, and more wholesome if practised with this in mind.

One further example of what Jesus did must be mentioned. Mark has two accounts of multiple feedings: five thousand men (Mk.6:30-44) and four thousand people (Mk.8:1-9). The first feeding account has no separate commentary in Mark, but the second feeding story is followed by a conversation with his disciples which refers to both stories and specifically to the number of baskets of leftovers which the disciples were able to gather - twelve and seven respectively (Mk.8:14-21). Jesus seemed surprised that the disciples did not see the significance of this and equates the disciples to the crowd who lack perception and understanding, have eyes but do not see and ears but do not hear (Isa.6:9-10, Ez.12:2). Some commentators have attempted to draw lessons from the disparity of the numbers used in the two accounts, and the two different Greek words used for "baskets". One difference of possible significance in the two feeding stories is the location. The first (Mk.6:34-44) appears to be in a Galilean/Jewish setting, whereas the second (Mk.8:1-10) is probably in predominantly Gentile territory. The number twelve has obvious connections with Judaism, whereas Revelation 1:20 gives an example of how the number seven might be applicable to the wider/gentile world. It is possible that Jesus' disciples failed to see the widening of the scope of Jesus' ministry, but honesty may compel us to admit that in common with the first disciples we also do not know the significance of the numbers of either the crowds or of the baskets of leftovers.

It is helpful to acknowledge that being a disciple, or church member, does not mean that we always have a better understanding than others. It is not a case of, "We know. They do not know. Therefore we shall tell them what they need to know", which seems to be the assumption underlying a number of popular introductory courses to the Christian faith. As Wilhelm points out, there is even a case for saying that in Mark's Gospel a number of non-disciples appear to have a better grasp of Jesus' nature than the disciples[43]: for example, the woman with the haemorrhages (Mk.5:25-34), the Syrophoenician woman (Mk.7:24-30) and the father of the Epileptic boy (Mk.9:24). There is no basis in Mark's Gospel for the claims some make to superior knowledge of or about Jesus. Quite the reverse; we all need at all times to come as humble learners with a common need to know more, and a common teacher, the Holy Spirit. The notion of a common journey is captured in the story of Jairus. Many people were called to follow Jesus, but in the story of Jairus, who falls at Jesus' feet with a humble plea, significantly Jesus "*went with him*" (Mk.5:24) - presumably because in this instance Jairus knew the way.

---

[43] PGM p.76

In my contacts with thousands of "non-church" people through funeral ministry I have met countless people who pray daily, who go out of their way to help others, who are generous beyond measure, who are faithful and sacrificially loving in their relationships, and who in so many other ways reflect the life of Jesus. I also see this in many within the churches I know; though by no means all! Churches have a distinctive calling to do what Jesus would do, but no monopoly or supremacy in the embodiment of Jesus' spirit and its manifestations.

There are common elements in the feeding stories from which present day churches might learn (Mk.6:30-44; 8:1-9). In both stories we are told that Jesus had compassion on the crowd (Mk.6:34; 8:2). I believe that is only possible when crowds are not regarded as homogenous. In chapter 6 Jesus' compassion leads first of all to teaching and the feeding of five thousand is a by-product of this. In chapter 8 the crowd of four thousand had been with Jesus for three days, had run out of food, and Jesus' compassion led directly to a feeding. There is no justification in Mark's cryptic recounting of Jesus' temptation for ignoring the physical needs of multitudes who hunger and thirst in our generation. The stories of mass feedings tell us that Christ-like compassion will lead to us doing all we can to meet the physical needs of those who hunger or experience physical poverty in other ways - and there will be enough left over to meet the needs of those who share with others.

In both stories Jesus was teaching crowds of people who came to hear him. We have no record of the content or the outcomes of this teaching on this occasion. We shall consider this further in a while, but here it may be important to recognise that a teaching ministry for willing listeners provides the backdrop for the sharing of food in a miraculous manner.

In both stories Jesus took the elements, bread and fish, and blessed them. In this instance "blessed" probably means that Jesus gave thanks for them as good gifts from God, dedicated to God, and to be used in God's service. Then Jesus broke them and gave them to the disciples to distribute to the hungry crowd. To "*take, thank, break and share*" has become known as the four-fold action of the Eucharist, what a church does around the Lord's Table or at the Altar. Certainly that same four-fold action is in Mark's account of the last supper (Mk.14:22), but what Jesus did in the upper room (a sanctuary?) with his disciples just before his death was a reflection of what he had done in the world. It derived its meaning from the parallels in Jesus' wider self-giving ministry. Jesus could not possibly be celebrating the Eucharist, or re-enacting the last supper when he fed the multitudes. At this time self-evidently there had been no last supper. In fact without Jesus' ministry of compassion for the world the last supper would have been an isolated and to some extent a private event of minimal significance. As is discussed at greater length elsewhere in this work, to "*take, thank, break and share*" is a pattern intended for sacrificial living, not for inward-looking ritual.

Sadly, many churches have regularly put the feeding of the multitudes very much into second place. It easily becomes more important that the Eucharist is celebrated in the sanctuary than that the hungry in the world are fed. Some churches have a legal obligation to celebrate the Eucharist every day, but no such obligation to feed the poor every day. In this way the compassion which motivated Jesus' life and ministry to and for the multitudes has been relegated to secondary status. The churches' self-feeding rituals are considered to be more important. A church living in the spirit of Jesus would value the work of the local soup kitchen or food bank and the world-wide work of Christian Aid or CAFOD above its own in-house, and too often self-serving ministry. A survey of all the churches in the Baptist Union of Great Britain some years ago found that a significant number of churches were unable to cite a single example of something they did for anyone other than themselves. I know the situation has improved dramatically. The Cinnamon Network[44], for instance, offers many examples of ground-breaking community involvement by churches. So, of course, I recognise that there are many churches of all denominations or affiliation who do not fit the above negative description, but there are enough who still do to make pleas for the revised priorities which are necessary if what Jesus did is to be our guiding light.

The question, "What would Jesus do?" (WWJD) became a catchphrase for some churches in the two decades marking the turn of the 20th/21st centuries C.E. This "sloganising" of the question may have devalued it in some people's eyes, but it seems an inescapable and fundamental question for anyone claiming to be a follower of Jesus - even if simplistic answers are to be eschewed. The above examples of healing, exorcism, and feeding provide answers to the question which may appear simple, but are far from easy to reflect in our own lives. My contention has been that the simplest and most obvious way to answer the question "What would Jesus do?" is by looking at what Jesus did! Using Mark's gospel to identify what Jesus did, five further pointers can be discerned.

1.   Jesus encountered a man with a withered hand (Mk.3:1ff). The Pharisees watched him to see what he would do; whether his impulse to heal would be greater than his commitment to observe the Sabbath law. Jesus' words to his critical observers implied that to do nothing would be tantamount to doing evil, whereas to heal would be to do good (Mk.3:4). With hindsight and distance from the particular situation it might seem obvious which priority Jesus would choose. In reality churches are always confronted with this choice, but do not always follow his

---

[44] www.cinnamonnetwork.co.uk/

example, or adopt the priorities of Jesus. Jesus said to the scribes and Pharisees, *"You have a fine way of rejecting the commandment of God in order to keep your traditions!"*(Mk.7:9). Of course, his critics could rightly respond that Sabbath observance was a command of God, and Jesus was the one rejecting God's law as given in the scriptures. Let us be clear. Jesus did reject what was a legitimate, scripturally justified point of his opponents. This needs to be taken on board whenever scriptural warrant is claimed in order to deny those in need the compassion and help they require. In Jesus' life active compassion had priority, not Scripture. When churches are truly following the way of Jesus, their life is directed much less to preserving their own traditions, including their understanding and use of scripture, and much more toward meeting the physical, mental, spiritual and social needs of others.

When The Abbey Centre was built in 1996 as the new premises for the local Baptist Church, a leaflet was delivered to every house in the new and expanding district of Hunsbury, Northampton. A local lay preacher wrote to the Baptist Union to complain that the leaflet placed more emphasis on how the Abbey Centre was designed to serve the social or community needs of the local population than it did on inviting people to come to the church or receive the gospel. Perhaps he found the strapline we used irksome, *"Serving Social and Spiritual Needs in South Northampton"*. I find it almost incredible that anyone could not see this as replicating Jesus' ministry in another time and another place.

2. Mark tells the story of a woman who was haemorrhaging (Mk.5:25-34). She touched the hem of Jesus' garment believing it would bring healing. It did. But *"Jesus perceived in himself that power had gone forth from him"* (Mk.5:30). The ministry of Jesus is not one of detachment and disinterest. It is self-giving. So is Christ-like ministry wherever it is found.

To be personally involved, to be self-giving as well as financially giving, is a real challenge to Christians, perhaps even more so in affluent places. The difficulty is compounded when a church is called to respond to global crises or the needs of people of whom we will never have personal knowledge. However, the understandable desire for personal involvement may lessen the benefits which our financial giving might achieve, or be a desire for self-gratification. For example, rather than gifts for general educational or relief programmes in poorer countries, some have opted to support the education in a small impoverished village of an individual child whose name is known by the donor. This can prove most satisfying when the child's progress is monitored and reported. But this has not infrequently led to the gifted - and now educated - child leaving their home village, in theory to "better themselves". As a result the community as a whole is actually further impoverished: as may be the individual who loses something of their natural identity and extended family. Though the motives are without doubt honourable, such giving is not without personal reward. It might therefore be essentially selfish, not self-giving. But the Wisdom of Solomon or the mind of Christ is needed to discern how we might truly be giving of ourselves as well as our wealth in a global economy. Somehow we need to be one with the poor widow who *"put in everything she had, her whole living"*, rather than with those who made *"a contribution out of their abundance"* (Mk.12:41-44). Not giving money when we have it inhibits us from sharing in eternal life, but just giving money is not enough. We must follow the way or example of Jesus more closely, which is the way of self-giving (Mk.10:17-22).

Crucially, Jesus put himself in situations where he could be "touched", where physical contact and emotional demands could be made. The cloistered nature of much church life and mentality does not lend itself to such availability and vulnerability. It is primarily when a church is scattered into the life of the world through the daily lives of its members that a church is capable of a closer following of Jesus' way. Sadly an over-focus on church rituals and "programmes" has often diminished the sense that what "scattered" Christians do in their places of work, their families, and in their neighbourhoods and beyond is ultimately what can be really in keeping with what Jesus would do - be available, with all the risks and opportunities that entails. The priority for the life of a church should be to encourage, and if possible facilitate a Christ-like life in the world for all its members, not to train them for more involvement in their church.

3. Compassionate outgoing ministry can be draining (Mk.5:30). Jesus needed times of respite and refreshment, and so did his disciples. Jesus did his best to take time to rest (Mk.6:30-32), sometimes to pray (Mk.6:36; 14:32), which was not always restful. Sometimes he went to his own house (Mk.2:1; 3:19; 7:17? 10:10?) or to a friend's house (Mk.1:39; 2:15; 14:14). In Mark Jesus is rarely recorded as being alone in the sense of being on his own; though clearly he would have liked some times to be alone for prayer (Mk.1:35; 6:46f. - and even 14:34f.). His ministry is mostly exercised in community and/or in public. There were people who ministered to his needs (Mk.1:31), some of whom were there in the hour of his death and at his entombment (Mk.15:41; 16:47). Christians are rarely called to "go it alone", and a church at its best is a "companionship of people", comrades offering mutual support and hospitality[45]. Unfortunately, rather than the less rarefied words companions, comrades or friends the academic word *fellowship* is generally used in church circles; and used in such a way that someone can belong to a fellowship without actually having anything to do with anyone else in a way that makes demands on them. Jesus did not call people to belong to some "thing", he called his disciples to be with him and each other in a shared living out of God's will; to participate in mutually self-giving community. It is not uncommon for

---

[45] Companion means "sharing bread".

people to go to a particular church because they feel they "get the most out of it"! This, of course, is totally in keeping with the propensity for individualism and self-gratification which marks and mars the present age in Western society, including many churches. But a church true to its founder's genius has always needed to be counter-cultural as well as world affirming. We, like Jesus, are strengthened for service by friends not heroes; co-travellers not role models or leaders; unity not individualism.

4. Underlying all that Jesus said and did was an unimaginable amount of mental as well as spiritually disciplined personal commitment. But the resulting ministry of Jesus was directed toward others. It saddens me that this feature of Jesus' life runs counter to the *modus operandi* of so much church life today. Phillip Blond opined:

> *The great disaster for the church is that at some point it went inside the head and started being about restrictive sexual behaviour. It's almost as if it gave up on the world (but)... I think the church can restore its original mission, which is (to put it in a silly way) to make the world a better place* [46].

To make the world a better place is what Jesus would try to do.

5. There is a fifth consideration in answering the question, "What would Jesus do?" Jesus engaged in a ministry of preaching (Mk.1:14, 39; 2:2) and more commonly teaching (Mk.1:21; 2:13; 4:2; 6:6; 9:31; 11:17f; 12:35, 38; 14:49). Mark tells us of Jesus that "*crowds gathered to him again: and again, as was his custom, he taught them*" (Mk.10:1 my underlining). I think it is reasonable to assume that "*his custom*" was to address the crowd with the spoken word, often in parables (Mk.4:11). But the best teaching is more than words. The teaching of Jesus is also evident in his reactions to certain situations such as his indignation when his disciples discouraged people from bringing their children to him (Mk.10:13ff): or when James and John asked for privileged places in the kingdom (Mk.10:35ff). Everything in Jesus' life has something to teach us. Lessons might be learned from the manner and locations of his continuous teaching ministry, but the main subject matter of Jesus' teaching is possibly even more important; yet in my experience "The Kingdom of God", Jesus' primary subject, is rarely the subject of contemporary preaching or teaching in Jesus' name. If it was the subject and object of the teaching that churches offer, we might be far less self-obsessed. It is to this main subject of Jesus' teaching that we now turn our attention.

---

[46] Phillip Blond interviewed by Nick Spencer *Third Way* March 2012:12

The Kingdom of God

The nearness of the Kingdom of God is the subject of Jesus' very first words in Mark's telling of the story of Jesus' ministry (Mk.1:15). It is clearly an important subject, yet what Jesus meant by the kingdom of God is not at all obvious. Jesus tells his disciples, "*The secret of the kingdom of God has been given to you. But to those on the outside everything is said in parables*" (Mk.4:11). To some extent, we are "*those on the outside*", because we are not privy to the majority of private conversations, teaching and experiences which Jesus shared with his disciples (Mk.4:34) and in particular the twelve (Mk.14:17). As noted earlier one of the lessons from the parables seems to be that the Kingdom of God grows secret should relate with awe. Or as with the meaning of parables, the Kingdom of God is something "secret", to be discovered rather than explained or delivered. In seeking to understand what is meant by the Kingdom of God some light may inevitably be thrown on how Jesus understood himself and his relationship to God.

From reading Mark there are a few things which can be said with some assurance concerning the Kingdom of God. The kingdom can only be received in the way a little child accepts what is offered (Mk.10:14-15). The stern warning against "*causing one of these little ones who trust in me to sin*" (Mk.9:42) might suggest that the childlike quality being commended is that of trust, but we cannot be sure. But we can be sure that it is very difficult to enter the kingdom of heaven if we are rich (Mk.10:23-25). Often what we think we own owns us. We are possessed by our possessions. Kester Brewin makes the point that the enormous internet web we have created to serve us is actually ensnaring us. "*It is not we who are surfing it, it is surfing us*"[47]. Drastic preventative surgery may also be necessary if we are to enter the Kingdom of God and not go, or be thrown into hell (Mk.9:43-48). There is a moral requirement for those who would be part of the Kingdom of God. By "moral" I mean a grasp of what it means to honour God - no less and no more. The only individual to whom Jesus said, "*You are not far from the Kingdom of God*", had shown a sincere moral understanding. The man said to Jesus, "*You are right in saying that God is one and there is no other but him. To love him with all your heart, with all your understanding and with all your strength, and to love your neighbour as yourself is more important than all burnt offerings and sacrifices*". (Mk.12:32-33). A church or a Christian is not called to be judgemental or prudish, but we are called to show our nearness to both Jesus and the Kingdom of God by recognising and living in accordance with that love of God and love of neighbour which Jesus said were the greatest of all commandments (Mk.12:29-31).

---

[47] Kester Brewin reviewing John Brockman's *How is the internet changing the way you think*, Third Way: March 2012 p.42

In several places in Mark there are indications that the Kingdom of God is not here yet. The parables of the kingdom in Mark have a sense of waiting, a reckoning which is yet to come, an approaching time of fulfilment or harvest (e.g. Mk.4:26-32). Joseph of Arimathea is described as someone "*who was himself waiting for the kingdom of God*" (Mk.15:43). Jesus said to his disciples, "*Some here will ....see the kingdom of God come in power*" (Mk.9:1), and he would not "*drink again of the fruit of the vine until that day when I drink it anew in the kingdom of God*" (Mk.14:25). Churches in my experience have often equated the Kingdom of God with the person or presence of Jesus, and have taught that although it is to come in all its fullness, it is already present. That does not seem justified by what is in Mark's Gospel.

With regard to the Kingdom of God we may have unwittingly reduced to a contemporary social construct that which for Jesus had an eternal connotation; and in so doing we may have deprived ourselves and others of the imperative and comfort of a hope which is yet to be realised. This resonates with much that I have experienced in my own and others' lives. A future hope is essential when the kingdoms, the power structures and vested interests of this world dominate, diminish and destroy so much of life. Christians have been accused with some justification of offering "pie in the sky", of focussing on personal salvation in an after-life, rather than giving proper attention to the pressing present demands of social justice. But we have probably allowed that accusation to subvert us from or deprive us of the legitimate future content of our faith - a "kingdom" hope which motivates us in the present and encourages us for the future. We need to regain this perspective, for it is not only a primary element of Jesus' teaching; but is in keeping with the general thrust of his message, so skilfully woven into Mark's method, that here is something which is yet to be fully discovered and fulfilled. Not everything is already revealed - or achieved.

Jesus and Disciples

Mark's Gospel is given a sense of urgency by the repeated use of the words *immediately*, or *at once*, which occur about twenty times in the first nine chapters (Wilhelm counts 41 in total in the Gospel). This verbal cue is indicative of the pace at which the story is told - and perhaps the pace at which Jesus lived. This includes the calling of the first disciples Simon and Andrew. They are said to have *immediately* followed Jesus, who then *immediately* called James and John who followed him (Mk.1:16-20). To read Mark is to feel the urgency of Jesus' mission. Faithfulness in long-term service and witness is not to be decried, but if we follow the example of Jesus as Mark recounts it we shall also be about the work of the kingdom with a sense that tomorrow may be too late for some things or somebody.

There is a saying: "You can tell a great deal about people by the friends they choose". If Mark intends us to explore who Jesus is, looking at Jesus and his disciples may help give insights into Jesus nature. It is often said that Jesus called all different kinds of people to be his disciples. There would seem to be truth in this. The fact that James and John could leave their father *with the hired servants* suggests it was at the least a moderate size family business; and although the description of Simon and Andrew as fishing from the shore may suggest they could not afford a boat, we know from later in Chapter 1 that Simon and Andrew had a house (Mk.1:29). These hard working labourers or entrepreneurs would probably be well respected in their local community. Jesus called those whom we might describe as "ordinary, respectable hard-working people". There can be few churches which do not need such co-workers.

There is little literary, but a sizeable social distance covered when we are told of the calling of the next disciple (Mk.2:14 [48]). He is Levi, a tax collector, an agent of the occupying power, probably not an employee, but an independent agent taking a percentage for himself. Tax collectors were naturally held in low esteem by a population subject to Rome's harsh domination, and they were counted as sinners by the religious authorities, partly because they dealt in money carrying claims of the emperor's divinity. Jesus not only called this tax collector or sinner to follow him, but opened his house and table for many such people (Mk.2:15). Esteemed social status, acceptability and respectability were not prerequisites for being Jesus' disciple. In fact, the normally religiously and socially excluded "outsider" was perhaps especially welcomed by Jesus. Is that so in our churches - or our homes?

The first disciples were called by Jesus to follow him (Mk.1.17). We do not know how many he invited to follow him, but the calling was not confined to the number twelve as the call to the rich man shows (Mk.10:21). The rich man may have declined the offer to follow Jesus, but it would seem that many others were willing to follow him, because it was from a larger number that Jesus eventually appointed *twelve to be with him* (Mk.3:14). Mark having introduced the first four who were called (or five if Levi is equated with Matthew) tells us no more about the other eight (or seven) than their names; with the exception of Judas (Mk.3:14-19). That is the reality in the company of Jesus. There are those whose calling is significant and memorable for others. The story and personality of the majority of Jesus' followers, however, are only known in their own generation and small group, but each has his or her place in the story of Jesus. What does seem to be the case is that it would be difficult to find a common denominator or unifying factor for the twelve other than that they were willing to follow Jesus, and they were chosen by

---

[48] It has been suggested that Levi was Matthew and he became one of the twelve. Because his call so closely parallels the language used in the calling of the four fishermen I am inclined to accept the equation of the two as one person. Whether or not that is the case, Levi was certainly amongst Jesus' followers.

him. Churches which make an attempt in any way to "clone" their membership, or to focus on a particular age or social grouping, should take account of this; and we should all rejoice in, and positively encourage the rich variety of backgrounds, interests, ages and personalities of those who typically make up the membership of many congregations. I once met a minister who said her aim was to have every member of her congregation talking in tongues. One woman in that church, in spite of much pressure, refused to have her own relationship to Jesus manipulated or dominated by a third party, refused to lose her own spiritual identity and direction. I believe she was right to do so. Manipulating people into a common mould would seem quite contrary to the relationships into which Jesus entered.

Mixed in with Mark's account of the calling of the twelve disciples is a very large hint that their life with Jesus, and life as his followers after his death, would be a life with different priorities to those of the religious or political "establishment" and inevitably lead to conflict with them (Mk.13:9). Jesus' disciples were firstly compared unfavourably with the disciples of John the Baptizer (Mk.2:18). John's disciples fasted, Jesus' disciples did not. Being with Jesus was not the same as being with anyone else, even John the Baptizer. Jesus' disciples were then criticised for breaching the Sabbath code of behaviour by plucking ears of corn on a Sabbath; but Jesus held that there were precedents for such behaviour which supported his view that Sabbath observance was not intended to be a punitive law, but a sign of God's grace for humanity. In addition Jesus is *Lord of the Sabbath*, so those who are with him have a higher authority and priority than his opponents recognise (Mk.2:23-28).

Jesus went further when his disciples were criticised for eating with unwashed hands. He went onto the offensive with the accusation that in fact those who accused his disciples of not observing *the tradition of the elders* were guilty of the greater error of abrogating the Law of Moses through their traditions, *"teaching as doctrine the precepts of men"* (Mk.7:1-13. cf.Isa.29:13). Jesus used the specific example of care for one's parents, which the Pharisees said could be neglected if a gift was made "to God" instead. Jesus said this practice meant they were choosing to ignore the *word of God.* This is slightly problematic seeing that Jesus himself appeared to reject his mother (Mk.3:32). Although it is worth noting that Jesus' choice not to see his family follows on from Mark's report that his family (or friends? RSV) wanted to take charge of him because they thought he had gone mad (Mk.3:21). However, Jesus did place following him above staying with parents (Mk.10:29). We may assume this did not mean abandoning the Mosaic injunctions that we "honour" our parents, but was setting all relationships in the context of allegiance to God's will as seen in Jesus. Many Christians have struggled with the need to "honour" and care for their parents whilst giving themselves totally to the work of the Kingdom - and sometimes it does seem to be "either/or". I know of people who have waited for a frail elderly parent to die before responding to their sense of calling to go overseas for missionary service. They have not found this to be an easy decision. Others have made the opposite but no less difficult choice. As so often in Mark, there is no absolute instruction given. What we can say is that following the way of Jesus is likely to mean that we may often do what is not commonly expected of "religiously correct" people, and hard choices will need to be made in faith, not certainty.

We should not be over-critical of those who placed a high value on traditions. To their mind these were interpretations of the Scriptures which made their practical implications clear, so that they could be applied to daily living. Churches have long struggled with the balance between scripture, tradition, and present inspiration. It can be a commendable struggle if it is serious engagement in an attempt to discover and to follow the way of Jesus, to be disciples. Indeed, any church that is not trying to work out how best it can discern God's will, or believes it already knows what it should be doing tomorrow, ignores the complexities of the Gospel. But as a minimum standard, traditions devised by "men" should not take precedence over whatever it is we believe to be "*the word of God*". For Jesus, a Palestinian Jew of his age, this was to be discovered by discerning that Spirit which inspired the Hebrew Scriptures, the Law, the Prophets and the Psalms of David. In seeking to know and do his Father's will Jesus took the scriptures very seriously, even if imaginatively rather than conservatively. For Christians there will be additional writings which may also be regarded as "*the inspired word of God*" and which with due discernment can help give us our priorities. The continuing challenge is to let those priorities be effective in a non-legalistic way in the individual lives of contemporary disciples of Jesus and in the churches' corporate business.

Mark's Gospel repeatedly gives examples of how the disciples did Jesus' bidding. The twelve whom *he called to be with him* were at the same time *called to be sent out* (Mk.3:14). So in the accounts of their calling, their sending, and their reporting back they are called *apostles*, not *disciples* (Mk.6:7-13, 30). In fact they are both, and that is how it has to be. Only being a learner, or exclusively seeing oneself as an agent of mission is not consonant with the gospel. Right from the outset the call of Jesus to his nascent disciples was to *follow* and to be *fishers of men* (Mk.1:17). It was not either/or, but both. For their mission Jesus gave very precise instructions as to the purpose of the mission and how his disciples/apostles were to conduct themselves (Mk.6:7-13). Most of the principles embodied in those instructions could be applied today, although an expectation of cordial, indefinite hospitality might not be realistic. The basic lesson is worth repeating: those who are *called to be with him* (disciples) are also *called to be sent out* (apostles). A church needs its members to be both. To "sloganise" such truth is probably counter-productive; but a motto remembered from church days of my youth did convey a gospel imperative: "*Every member a missionary*". My memory is that, like its predecessor,

"Each one bring one", it did not have any immediate visible effects! A similar effort by a recent General Secretary of the Baptist Union of Great Britain seemed to achieve equally minimal observable results. Nonetheless such reminders of what it means to be a follower of Jesus are important.

Jesus sent his disciples out in twos for their mission (Mk.6:7). The same was true when he needed the donkey for his approach to Jerusalem (Mk.11:1), and when he needed the room prepared for the Passover meal (Mk.14:13). On each occasion two were sent. This could have been because there were genuine dangers for Jesus' disciples on account of their preaching and their association with him. It is hard to imagine that the plots being hatched against Jesus' life would not also put his friends at risk (cf.Mk.14:51). The disciples, like Jesus, were preachers (Mk.6:12). The cause of John the Baptizer's downfall was his preaching. In addition, exorcisms were also not always welcome, especially if the evil spirits appeared to have found a home elsewhere, as in the case of Legion (Mk.5:13, 17). But danger was possibly not the main reason for apostles being sent in twos. Jesus needed others to be with him for his work, to support him, to pray for him. The time to be alone for Jesus and for his disciples was the time for rest and recuperation, not for public ministry. In less dangerous times there may still be a strong case for churches to encourage people to "go out" in twos, or in groups. I suspect this inbuilt mutual support of acting in pairs is partly why Mormons and Jehovah Witnesses are able to persist in their door-to-door visiting in spite of minimal positive response, constant rebuffs and occasional abuse. As a church collecting Christian Aid envelopes door-to-door, we always encouraged this to be done in groups. I remember in the 1960s visiting a Baptist Deaconess who had been sent to live on her own in a new council housing estate in Leeds with the commission to establish a congregation. The aim was commendable, the method was injurious, and remains deplorable. Jesus did not choose to "go it alone"; he was instinctively a co-traveller and encouraged companionship.

The disciples' willingness not only to be with Jesus, but also to do his bidding meant that they were able to share in his ministry. Mark's two accounts of the feeding of a multitude (Mk.6:35-44; 8:1-9) are sometimes referenced as *"Jesus feeds the multitude"*; but it was not accomplished alone. The disciples did the sharing with others of what Jesus had blessed. You may well know Annie J. Flint's meditation which begins; *Christ has no hands but our hands*, and a similar meditation by St. Teresa of Avila. If churches claim to be The Body of Christ it not only behoves us to actually be the hands and feet and eyes and ears and heart through which what is blessed by Christ will be shared with the multitudes, it will also enrich us. The disciples found that after they had shared what Jesus had blessed there was surplus enough for them. Jesus' promise had been fulfilled: *"the measure you give will be the measure you get, and still more will be given you"* (Mk.4:24). Furthermore, when Jesus told his disciples concerning the crowd, *"You give them something to eat"*, they were not really expected to do it without Jesus' guidance and blessing (Mk.6:37ff). The companioned disciples' attentive obedience to Jesus was crucially significant to the needs of the multitudes being met. It remains so today.

The disciples having followed Jesus' instructions and shared the food with the multitude then gathered up the remnants and had sufficient for themselves (Mk.6:43; 8:8). St. Francis of Assisi in his prayer that we should be channels of God's peace included the thought *"it is in giving ... that we receive"*. At the Passover meal Jesus offered bread to his disciples and said that in effect he was giving himself to them. That was surely no less true on other occasions when he took bread, gave thanks, broke it and gave it to them to share. The disciples shared what they had received of Jesus. The disciples received the ministry of Jesus in many ways. The healing of Simon Peter's mother-in law is one of Jesus' earliest recorded healings (Mk.1:3-31). He ministered to their physical needs when their boat was in danger of capsizing (Mk.4:39; 6:51). He ministered to their mental and emotional needs by calling them to be alone with him - even if the attempt to do so was not always successful (Mk.3:7; 6:32). But perhaps his greatest ministry to them was food for their souls given in those times when away from the crowd he would provide them with "explanations" of his parables (Mk.4:34; 7:17-23) and other teaching (Mk.10:10). Jesus said to his disciples including the twelve, *"To you has been given the secret of the Kingdom of God"*. And he went on to say, *"but for those outside everything is in parables"*(Mk.4:10-11). Those who are called to be Jesus' disciples have a wonderful privilege of not only sharing in, but also receiving the ministry of Jesus, and of being privy to a "secret", or some might say a "mystery" which is life giving, but which is not given to everyone. The idea of a "privileged few" might seem at first sight unjust on the many who are apparently not chosen: but the "privilege" is to learn the way of the cross. That offer is actually open to *any man* (Mk.8:34), but it would seem Jesus knew that not everyone had the potential to take up the offer and the cross. If this is so, it might temper some of the unrealistic, and therefore potentially demoralising, expectations of mass conversions championed by some, supposedly in Jesus' name. Jesus was a person of discernment and realism. His disciples should be the same.

Noticeably, Jesus did not even take all of "the twelve" with him on every occasion. There seems to have been an inner core of disciples, Peter, James and John (and sometimes Andrew e.g. Mk.13:3). When the twelve-year-old girl, thought to be dead, was raised by Jesus he took only the three with him (Mk.5:37). Similarly when he was transfigured he took Peter, James and John (Mk.9:2). These were three of the first four disciples he called. Perhaps when people have been in at the beginning of an enterprise it is because their potential has been recognised easily, and staying the course establishes a particular kind of relationship. Mullins quotes R. H. Lightfoot on the transfiguration:

"The whole event, from first to last takes place solely for the sake of the three disciples. He was with them; there appeared unto them Elijah and Moses; there came a cloud overshadowing them; this is my only son hear ye him; and suddenly looking around they saw no one any more, save Jesus only and themselves." (My underlining) [49].

Whilst each one of the twelve had been chosen, and all shared in Jesus' work, some were apparently more capable of trust in special circumstances, or perhaps more susceptible to learning from exceptional moments in Jesus' life (Mk.9:9-13). Similarly there will be those in a church who might be taken into some situations whereas others would rightly be left behind. Jesus' company of disciples were not all the same, no more than is the membership of a church. Not everyone has what is necessary to enter into any or every situation. Wisdom and caution is needed by those who must decide whether one person is or is not suited to serve or learn in particular circumstances; and the decision may best be taken in prayerful dialogue with the person concerned.

If it is the case, as I would suggest, that the whole of Mark's Gospel poses the question, *Who is this?* Then Mark also makes apparent that all twelve disciples had many opportunities to see Jesus in different ways and come to new understandings. They had the same opportunities as the crowds, of course, but so much more. In addition to the privileged insights of Peter, James and John, all the disciples spent many hours with him, accompanying Jesus in his public ministry and sharing time alone with him, but also seeing Jesus calm the storm (Mk.4:39; 6:51) and walk on water (Mk.6:48). They were asked to answer both indirectly and directly who they thought he was (Mk.8:27-30); and on a number of occasions he shared with them how he was destined to be rejected, to suffer, be killed and rise again after three days (Mk.8:31; 9:12; 9:31; 10:34). They shared the intimacy of the Passover meal and were present when he agonised in prayer in Gethsemane and was arrested. Very few had such closeness to Jesus - and it is still a minority who can "walk the walk". The whole church, nonetheless, can still come close to Jesus through his story offered in word, the sacraments celebrated in companionship and sanctuary; and perhaps even more in sharing by faith in his ministry in and for the world. Through all these avenues, as contemporary disciples of Jesus, we also have opportunities to see Jesus in different ways, come to new understandings, and grow closer to him. Others may well make a judgement about Jesus based on the behaviour and attitudes of those who claim to be his followers or friends.

If we are like the first disciples there is a high probability that the opportunities to learn more of Jesus may be there, but understanding will be slow to come. On one

---

[49] TGM cited in TGL p.286

occasion Jesus asked his disciples two related questions: "*Are you also without understanding? Do you not see...?*" (Mk.7:18). Honest answers would have been, "Yes" (we do not understand), and "No" (we do not see). Mark records many instances where the disciples did not fathom the meaning of what they had witnessed. After the first feeding of a multitude Mark says of the disciples, "*They didn't understand about the loaves and their hearts were hardened*" (Mk.6:52// 8:17-18). In the Bible the heart represents the abode of the deepest kind of understanding, probably to some extent both consciously and sub-consciously shaping a person's behaviour. So at the very deepest level the disciples were immune to understanding, and *hearts were hardened* may mean wilfully so. Peter could see that Jesus was The Messiah, but Jesus had to rebuke him because he was not open to seeing, or did not want to see what Messiah-ship would mean for Jesus (Mk.8:33). Being alongside and suffering with, as well as challenging hurting individuals, spiritually and physically hungry crowds, priests, religious purists, politicians and soldiers trapped in inhumane systems, is inevitably a costly business, especially for anyone who gives compassion rather than seeking to control. Genuine full-hearted compassion will involve suffering. The disciples did not grasp how much Jesus gave of himself in his healings and was willing to give (Mk.5:30-31; 10:45), nor the spiritual discipline necessary to respond to severe illness (Mk.9:28), nor the danger of being rich (Mk.10:24-6), nor the value of a child in the Kingdom of Heaven (Mk.10:13). It was all there for them to see, but they saw so little. This fact about the first disciples should serve as a warning to anyone who believes that the meaning of what Jesus said and did was or is immediately obvious, easy to grasp, or solely about what we "know". The work and person of Jesus needs to get "under our skin", into the depths where our attitudes and most influential thoughts are formed - in modern idiom, to the very heart of our being. The story of the disciples is the story of a journey, not just across physical terrain, but a journey of spiritual formation tending toward a wholeness which could only really begin to be realised on the other side of the cross. Jesus understood that new or resurrection life was only possible through death (Mk.8:31). Many churches seem to offer new life without this precondition. They merit the rebuke Peter received for championing the same philosophy (Mk.8:32).

Tuckett suggests the word compassion, and the motive of pity in Jesus is rare in Mark - and in all the Gospels. For Tucket the preferred translation and motivation is "anger". I find that difficult. Mark uses the verb *splanchnizomai* (Σπλαγχνίζομαι) for which I can find no other meaning than *I am filled with tenderness or pity* (Mk.8:2; 9:22). But even if Tuckett is correct, we are surely reading in Mark about Jesus' "righteous anger", which is no less draining, and demands no less an active and often dangerous response of com-passion.

On their journey of faith with Jesus the disciples failed him and themselves, as Jesus knew they would (Mk.14:27). In the earliest days when Jesus sought time and space to be alone to pray "*Simon and those who were with him pursued him*" (Mk.1:35f). This was surely not the kind of following Jesus had in mind for them, and there were harder lessons to be learned. Initially the twelve were "successful". They were sent out in twos with clear instructions as to what they should do; which was to imitate Jesus in his ministry of healing, preaching and exorcism (Mk.6:12f.). They were able to return and report to Jesus on all they had done (Mk.6:30). In a sense they had successfully been in control. But that initial success, as we have noted above was accompanied by the constant failure to understand the nature of the Kingdom Jesus proclaimed and the deeper significance of what Jesus was doing and had to do. Mark in his telling of Jesus' story tells of Peter's acknowledgement of Jesus as the Messiah but also the subsequent and almost immediate rebuke (Mk.8:29-33). Mark follows this with the transfiguration at which the inner three disciples who were present were *very frightened* and *did not know what to say* (Mk.9:6). Next comes the situation where the other disciples had been unable to heal a dumb, spirit-possessed boy (Mk.9:14-29) and Jesus' second foretelling of his passion, death and resurrection (Mk.9:30-31) with the significant comment by Mark, "*But they did not understand the saying and they were afraid to ask him* "(Mk.9:32). This immediately leads to two examples of the disciples "getting it wrong" in a discussion about who is the greatest, or who would have the greatest control (Mk.9:33-37, 42. cp. 10:13-14, 35-44), and a decision about who can or cannot do things in Jesus' name, controlling who is "in" and who is "out" (Mk.9:38-41). The scene is well set for the failures that were to follow when Jesus went into Jerusalem.

The call to be "with" Jesus, both in his self understanding and in terms of the relationship of others to him, is always a call to a deeper humility, never to spiritual arrogance, enlarged ego, visions of empire, control or domination, or a spirit of precious competitiveness. Sadly amongst Jesus' followers today the words *He shall reign,* which might signify an acceptance by those who sing of their own personal call to be obedient followers of Jesus' way, are often misused as a political pronouncement and synonymous with *We shall reign* in the sense that our understandings will one day be dominant. The story of Jesus' disciples should tell us that, yes, he shall reign, though from and through a degrading, humiliating cross, but we will probably fail, and often. The good news is that we are not called to point people to ourselves or our ideas, but to him and his/our heavenly Father.

Mark records the inevitable clash between Jesus and the Jerusalem and temple "authorities" (Mk.Chs.11-12). Conflict has occurred throughout history between those who would do almost anything to maintain the *status quo*, and anyone who proclaims a radical world-changing message. Jesus did not have an agenda for control. But for those who did, Jesus' way of championing those who were dispossessed was an unacceptable threat. The threat was not to Jesus' security alone. There would be a much wider unsettling of the established order. Jesus made predictions about the chaos and mayhem which would come before "*they will see the Son of Man coming in clouds with great power and glory*" (Mk.13:26). These dire prophecies were accompanied by repeated warnings to *take heed,* or *watch* (Mk.13:5, 9, 23, 33, 35, and 37). Sadly, the disciples were unable to *watch* as Jesus wrestled in prayer in Gethsemane (Mk.14:32-43): earning Jesus' sad comment, "*Could you not watch one hour? Watch and pray ...*" (Mk.14:37-8).

Prior to this, one of The Twelve, Judas had set in hand the betrayal of Jesus. This led to Jesus' arrest, at which point the disciples "*all forsook him and fled*" (Mk.14:50-51). Peter did follow at a distance, but when challenged about his allegiance he replied, "*I do not know this man*" (Mk.14:71). Peter was probably speaking the truth at that point in time, even though his words and the crowing of the cock led him to tears. This man, this Jesus, who had now apparently completely lost any control over his own situation, was not the man that Peter had thought he had known. If Mark intends to confront his readers with the question, "*Who is this?*" the twelve disciples were amongst the first to be confronted with the same question, and so often they could not answer it. Wisely did Jesus caution Peter, James and John after the transfiguration to, "*Tell no one what they had seen, until the Son of Man should have risen from the dead*" (Mk.9:9); for until Jesus had died and risen they did not see the crucial clues or accept Jesus' direct teaching as to who he really was and what was integral to his identity. We have noted earlier that a church without a focus on Jesus' death, and which lacks the kind of understanding which places Jesus' death at its centre will proclaim an impoverished message, a worldly Lord, not the kind of Jesus whose kingdom is not of this world and the one whom Peter could not recognise as the Christ in his passion.

Because Mark's Gospel to some extent is preoccupied with "the twelve", in thinking about Jesus' disciples we have been the same. The twelve in Mark are with Jesus at the centre of the story sharing in relationships and journeying together. But there were countless other disciples who also listened to, and followed Jesus – both men and women. Early in Mark Jesus says, "*Whoever does the will of God is my brother, and sister, and mother*" (Mk.3:35). These words strongly suggest that the crowd said to be sitting about him was not all male (Mk.3:32). At his crucifixion three women are named, Mary Magdalene, Mary the mother of James the younger and Joses, and Salome - but there were others unnamed yet important (Mk.15:40). Mark tells us that a group of women were followers of Jesus, and "*when he was in Galilee (they) followed him and ministered to him - and also many other women who came up with him to Jerusalem*" (Mk.15:41). It was possibly one of these women who poured the costly jar of perfumed ointment over his head (Mk.14:3-9). Clearly her action of generous love and spiritual insight stands in utter contrast to Judas Iscariot whose first steps in his betrayal of Jesus immediately follows the anointing. The unnamed woman gives generously: the disciple Judas is out for what he can get (Mk.14:10-11). But we should not be too quick to make saints of the women disciples and sinners of the men. Jesus needed to minister to, and heal both men and women, because all fall short of God's glory as seen by Jesus. Peter followed Jesus after his arrest "from a distance" (Mk.14:54). Exactly the same phrase as used of the women who watched Jesus on the cross "from a distance" (Mk.15:40 ἀπὸ μακρόθεν). At the very end of Mark's original Gospel women are told to give the disciples and Peter a message, but Mark tells us, "*They said nothing to anyone for they were afraid*" (Mk.16:8). Mark leaves us to ponder whether they eventually said something, or whether Jesus himself appeared directly to the disciples.

Mark's Gospel does not allow us to evaluate quality of discipleship according to gender. There may be grounds for saying that the nature of the discipleship was different, because it was twelve "men" who were especially chosen to be with him and to be sent out, but given the itinerant nature of Jesus' ministry and the social norms of the day, such surely had to be the case. However, both men and women were "with him" and "followed him", that is, they were disciples - and it is highly probable that women are often in the text, though unnamed and unspecified. For example, we read, "*And when he was alone, those who were about him with the twelve asked him concerning the parable*" (Mk.4:10). There are more than twelve here. Nothing says they were all men, and this group of probably men and women are almost certainly with him again when the "*great crowd followed him and thronged him*" (Mk.5:24). A woman was able to come unnoticed to touch the hem of his garment (Mk.5:27). That she was unnoticed suggests there were many other women also in the crowd following him. There is a tendency to assume every reference to disciples is a reference to "the twelve" and/or to men, when Mark might just as easily be referring to a wider company of Jesus' followers including men and women. The bottom line is that Mark's Gospel tells us Jesus had women followers (disciples) who ministered to his body. Women ministers! The lesson for any church claiming to be The Body of Christ should not be difficult to learn. Some have put the gospel teaching into practice, but to our shame it is still rejected or overlooked by many.

There is one further thought for which I am indebted to Dawn Wilhelm. Wilhelm makes the point that when the women at the tomb are instructed to let "*the disciples and Peter*" know that Jesus will go ahead of them and meet them in Galilee (Mk.16:7), there is an implicit forgiveness for the disciples' desertion and Peter's denial, a restoration of their role of followers, and a resumption of the call "*to be with him*" [50]. We do well to remember that failure by disciples is more than

---

[50] PGM p.261

matched by the grace of God in Christ. It is the latter which ultimately matters and which helps take us close to the nature of the man called Jesus.

What Does the Lord Require of You?

Jesus then began to teach them that the Son of Man must suffer many things and be rejected by the elders, chief priests and teachers of the law, and that he must be killed and after three days rise again. He spoke plainly about this, and Peter took him aside and began to rebuke him. But when Jesus turned and looked at his disciples, he rebuked Peter. "Get behind me, Satan!" he said. "You do not have in mind the things of God, but the things of men." Then he called the crowd to him along with his disciples and said: "If anyone would come after me, he must deny himself and take up his cross and follow me. For whoever wants to save his life will lose it, but whoever loses his life for me and for the gospel will save it (Mk.8:31-35).

The above words of Jesus immediately follow a conversation between Jesus and his disciples about his identity. The statement by Peter that he thought of Jesus as the Messiah can be regarded as the high point of the Gospel, but what follows in the passage above, is at least equally, and probably more important: for if Jesus is the Christ or Messiah, the way of the cross and self-denial is crucial to his Messiah-ship and is the consequent demand on anyone who would follow or be with such a Messiah. Jesus shared these words with the crowd as well as his disciples. The message was for anyone who would listen.

It is clear that the twelve had "denied themselves". Being with Jesus meant sharing some of the restrictions or privations, and probably the risks which Jesus embraced or encountered. Some of these arose because of Jesus' popularity. On more than one occasion the disciples as well as Jesus were not able to eat because the house they were in became so crowded (Mk.3:20; 6:31). As Peter pointed out, he and the others had left everything to be with Jesus (Mk.1:18; 10.28). Jesus responded that there would be no sacrifice made which would not be rewarded both within the present time and with *"eternal life in the age to come"* (Mk.10:29-31). But such promises had to be received in faith, because their fulfilment was by no means obvious. A disciple, or a church in every age, is called to follow a path which requires sacrifices, and a call to trust in God, which will bring its own reward. However, if the promise of tangible reward becomes the motivating force for ministry, it is not in keeping with the spirit of Jesus. The prayer of Ignatius Loyola which begins, *"Teach us good Lord to serve thee as Thou deservest"*, in its final petition expresses what Jesus asked, that we might be willing, *"to labour and not to ask for any reward, save that of knowing that we do Thy will"*.

"Denying ourselves" may well include giving up or giving away our possessions and security. I am aware of additional interpretations of the story of the poor widow giving her last two coins, but her exemplary action is commended by Jesus for the sacrifice it represents (Mk.12:44). Self-denial can mean even more than this. In earlier days Jesus had hinted at his death: "*The day will come when the bridegroom will be taken away*". (Mk.2:20. See also 3:6 etc.), but in Mark the three clearest predictions of his death which Jesus shared with his disciples come very close together, in this way reinforcing the importance of the message (Mk.8:31; 9:30-32; 10:33-34). Yet immediately following the third prediction Mark tells us that James and John asked for the best seats in the kingdom with consequent discord amongst the disciples. Even if we are generous about the motives of James and John and accept that their request was essentially to be close to Jesus for ever, they still had not understood or accepted what Jesus had been saying. So Jesus' offered them a description of his way of life and death. He told the disciples that he came "*not to be served, but to serve and to give his life as a ransom for many*" (Mk.10:45). Personal ambitions, wanting status, having our needs or wishes met by others, having privileged access or closeness to Jesus, or anything that is a form of self-aggrandisement, is in opposition to the way of the cross. In Jesus' teaching the real sign of being *first* is to willingly be "*last, and the servant of all*" (Mk.9:35; 10:44). Churches need to closely examine how much of their worship and witness and even community work is essentially self-serving and self-satisfying with the perhaps hidden agenda of self-promotion. Sometimes a church's work is even conducted in a spirit of competition with other "disciples" or other churches. The way of the cross, or carrying the cross daily, is not primarily a series of actions, it is the adoption of the spirit or attitude of Jesus, walking in his way. "*He has shown you what is good; and what does the Lord require of you, but to do justly, to love mercy, and to walk humbly with your God?*" (Micah 6:8).

Jesus said he came to serve (Mk.10:45). A life of service is integral to doing God's will. Love of neighbour as well as God is the greatest commandment and of more importance than any religious tradition or ritual (Mk.7:8; 12:30-34). The first healing in Mark (following an exorcism) is of Peter's mother-in-law who as soon as she had been healed took on the role of a servant (Mk.1:31). When Jairus' daughter was healed her parents were invited to serve her need for food themselves (Mk.5:43). The role of the disciples in the feeding stories was to be those who served the needs of others. Jesus said, "*You give them something to eat*" (Mk.6:37), then helped to make that possible.

The manner of Jesus' involvement in the feeding of a multitude is instructive: "*He looked up to heaven, and blessed ...*" (Mk.6:41). On another occasion he gave thanks for the bread and blessed the fish (Mk.8:6f.). The underlying spiritual strength needed for such a ministry was prayer. Jesus said to his disciples, "*All things are possible to him who believes*" (Mk.9:23), but added, "*This cannot be ...*

by anything but prayer.... Whatever you ask in prayer, believe that you have received it and it will be yours" (Mk.9:29; 11:24). Noticeably this trust in prayer was linked by Jesus to a spirit of forgiveness which would make the disciple's trust in God's provision not just a pious feeling, but an active ingredient in their relationships (Mk.9:25). It was not a choice between love of God and love of neighbour: the two are inseparable. Jesus likened the inner spiritual condition which is necessary for right relationships to salt - a purifying and healing agent: *"Have salt in yourselves and be at peace with one another"* (Mk.9:50). The priority Jesus gave to prayer is undeniable and perhaps best exemplified by his obvious distress when the temple had ceased to serve as a place of prayer for all the nations (Mk.11:17). However, if I am honest, the kind of apparently immediate efficacy of prayer which Jesus experienced, even when there is a serious attempt to be at peace with one's neighbours, is not something in which I have found it easy to believe: nor have I witnessed any convincing evidence of it. On the other hand, I have known many people whose faithful prayers seem to have been a blessing for others, and sometimes for themselves. I prefer not to talk about the "power" of prayer, but perhaps more in keeping with Jesus' attitude to maintain an open heart and mind about the possibilities when prayer is offered in humble faithfulness. This, as noted earlier in various ways, is what the Lord requires.[51]

---

[51] Whilst Mark gives minimum details of Jesus' temptation (1:12-13), the whole of Mark's Gospel could be said to provide the outworking of what other evangelists described in greater detail as a singular post-baptismal experience (Matt.4:1-11, Luke 4:1-13). Tuckett sees the story of Jesus' temptation as an *interpretative key for at least part of the narrative to come*, and suggests that the "key" is that *Jesus is victorious in the battle against Satan* (OBC p.889). I prefer a somewhat different and more mundane application. The first temptation was to perform miracles, including turning stones into bread. The first half of Mark's Gospel shows the potential for failure of this way of being the Messiah. People came to Jesus for what he could do for them: understandable, but essentially selfish and therefore the opposite to what Jesus really had to offer, a self-sacrificing way of life. They came for the miracles, not the message or the messenger. The disciples were "successful" in the context of a ministry based on miracles (6:7-13, 30), but once Jesus made clear his path of suffering and death, the way of the cross (8:34-35), their ability to minister seems to have deserted them (9:18b).   The second temptation was to go to Jerusalem and the Temple to demonstrate God's protection for the Messiah. The second half of Mark's Gospel is devoted to what for Mark is Jesus' only visit to Jerusalem, where significantly Mark records no miracles by Jesus (unless one counts the cursing of the fig tree as a miracle - 11:12-14, 20f.), and as his enemies point out he does not receive the protection of God (15:31-2) - a second failure! Finally and noticeably Mark does not end his story of Jesus with Jesus on a mountain top recognised as ruler or lord of the entire world - the third temptation. Sadly churches often choose the way of the temptations rather than the way of the cross, and ignore the lessons from Jesus' life in Mark's Gospel. This perspective would also be beneficial for those who see Matthew 28:18-20 as justification for the building of an empire. Although it should be noted that France effectively rejects the above analysis. He says of the temptations, *It is Jesus' filial trust that is under examination, not his messianic agenda* (RTF p. 131). For me the two are inextricably intertwined.

The Response

> *"In meeting Jesus for the first time most people scarce know what to make of him or what to do with him"*   W. J. Abraham[52].

In Mark's Gospel people who encounter Jesus are regularly described as being frightened, astonished, astounded or amazed - more than twenty times. Some were also offended or angered.

For many present day Christians the notion that people could be afraid of Jesus, or fearful in his presence, would be strange if not unthinkable. Some of us have been raised singing, *"What a friend we have in Jesus"*, but this is no ordinary friend. This is a friend who calms storms and walks on water, and on each occasion we are told his disciples were *afraid* or *terrified* (Mk.4:40; 6:50f.). This is a friend who meets and talks with Moses and Elijah, and his three closest disciples were *"exceedingly afraid"* (Mk.9:6). We might feel that these are exceptional circumstances, but in the normal course of teaching them about his passion, the disciples did not understand, and *"they were afraid to ask him"* (Mk.9:32). Perhaps with good reason as Jesus walked toward Jerusalem we are told, *"Those who followed him were afraid"* (Mk.10:32). They were not the only ones to be afraid. The woman healed of a haemorrhage, when she knew that she would probably have to come face to face with the man through whom she had been healed, *"came in fear and trembling, and fell down before him"* (Mk.5:33). Previous to this in the story of the Gerasene demoniac, the swineherds fled (Mk.5:14), and the local populace, seeing the possessed man now in his right mind *"were afraid"* and *"began to beg Jesus to depart"* (Mk.5:15, 17). The Psalmist said, *"The fear of the Lord is the beginning of Wisdom"* (Ps.111:10). Churches may need to think again about how they present God as seen in Jesus. Jesus was not *meek and mild*, he was, and should always be a force to be reckoned with, a disruptive, often frightening presence.

André Resner Jnr. remarks that in Mark's Gospel whenever there is the combination of *"Jesus + Sabbath the result is conflict or disturbance"*. And Resné asks,

> *"When the church makes its dual confession that a) this is the Lord's Day and b) Christ is truly present where two or three are gathered in his name.... Could the Jesus Mark insists creates Sabbath disturbance (an oxymoron?) wherever he is present be the same Jesus who is present with us? Is anyone threatened by his presence today? Who is awed? Who is prompted to unholy*

---

[52] W. J. Abraham TLC p.164

alliances for destruction? Whose authority is stretched to the breaking point? Whose imagination is stretched and strained beyond the old and safe categories in ways that demand a rethinking of Scripture, tradition, God, everything we thought we were doing for God and everything we thought God was doing for us?"[53]

What the Jesus of Mark's Gospel says and does causes fear, but also astonishment or amazement. When Jesus was approaching Jerusalem he strode on ahead, and those who followed behind were afraid, but also amazed (Mk.10:32). This amazement was there right from the early days of his ministry when he went into Capernaum and the people in the synagogue were *"astonished at his teaching, for he taught them as one who had authority"* (Mk.1:22). This authority included the power to deal with an *unclean spirit* which led to even further amazement (Mk.1:27). Both his teaching (Mk.6:2; 10:24; 11:18) and his healing (Mk.2:12; 5:42; 7:37) caused amazement. Pilate "wondered" (or marvelled) at Jesus' silence. Sometimes this amazement led to his rejection, as with the synagogue congregation in his home town where they were astonished at his teaching (Mk.6:2), but also took offence so that Jesus marvelled at their unbelief (Mk.6:3, 6). The Herodians and Pharisees were amazed at the way he dealt with their questions (Mk.12:17), but their purpose was to *"entrap him in his talk"* (Mk.12:13). These opponents, however, are a minority in Mark. Much more in keeping with the general response is the report that Legion *"began to proclaim ... how much Jesus had done for him; and all men marvelled"* (Mk.5:20). The parents of the little girl restored to life were *"immediately overcome with amazement"* (Mk.5:42). Those who witnessed the healing of a deaf man were *"astonished beyond measure"* (Mk.7:37). Familiarity with the stories, combined perhaps with great difficulty in applying them, may make it hard for a church to share the sense of awe and wonder which Mark so obviously wished to convey. But if Mark's Gospel is to shape a church's life and usher us into the presence of Jesus, the stories must be taken seriously, even if not literally, and proclaimed in such a way that people will still be in awe and wonder when they hear what the Lord has done (and is doing?).

The importance for Mark of these reactions to Jesus comprising fear, amazement, awe and wonder is apparent by the way he chooses to end his telling of the Jesus' story: *"They went out and fled from the tomb, for trembling and astonishment had come upon them; and they said nothing to any one, for they were afraid"* (Mk.16:8). If, as France suggests, Mark's gospel was originally shared by being read in its entirety at one session, this abrupt, surprising and mystifying ending would have had a much greater impact than is possible when the gospel is artificially divided into fragments and never read as a whole. An audience hearing the complete gospel would hear the echoes in the ending, and sense the

---

[53] TLC p.193

culmination of so much in Mark that has gone before. For Mark Jesus is incredibly awe-inspiring. One particular example of this seems most apposite.

> *That day when evening came, he said to his disciples, "Let us go over to the other side." Leaving the crowd behind, they took him along, just as he was, in the boat. There were also other boats with him. A furious squall came up, and the waves broke over the boat, so that it was nearly swamped. Jesus was in the stern, sleeping on a cushion. The disciples woke him and said to him, "Teacher, don't you care if we drown?" He got up, rebuked the wind and said to the waves, "Quiet! Be still!" Then the wind died down and it was completely calm. He said to his disciples, "Why are you so afraid? Do you still have no faith?" They were terrified and asked each other, "Who is this? Even the wind and the waves obey him!"* (Mk.4:35-41)

The experience of Jesus' powerful presence and the consequent awe and wonder are directly linked to, and pertinent to the question Mark has posed throughout his Gospel, *WHO IS THIS?* But in posing the question, *Who is this?* and in answering it with what has been described as *a narrative Christology*, Mark is not inviting his readers to engage in an intellectual exercise, and most definitely not to arrive at simplistic and therefore limiting answers. As George McLeod succinctly put it, *"Christ is a person to be trusted, not a principle to be tested"*[54]. Mark is demanding mental application, but also something deeper, what we might call "spiritual humility" which can take us into the presence of Jesus himself. Mark invites his readers, us, to share the wonder which so often lay behind the question when it was asked by Jesus' contemporaries and to discover for ourselves some of the fascinating, rich, diverse, and life-changing answers.

Mark wants us to be one with the demoniac who *"when he saw Jesus from afar ran to worship him"* (Mk.5:6) and as a result of his encounter with Jesus achieved a right mind, was clothed with a new found dignity, adopted the humble but not humiliating posture of a disciple (Mk.5:15), and could not help but tell others of his experience (Mk.5:20). Mark provides us with an opportunity to be one with the woman who wanted to touch even the fringe of Jesus' cloak and who in her subsequent encounter with Jesus *"came in fear and trembling, fell down before him, and told him the whole truth"* (Mk.5:33). This woman knew what John the Baptizer was talking about when he described Jesus as one *"whose sandals I am not worthy to stoop down and untie"* (Mk.1:7). She therefore adopted an attitude of homage and made a full and humble confession; with the result that Jesus was able to say to her, *"Your faith has made you well; go in peace, and be healed of your disease"* (Mk.5:34). Mark invites us to be one with the Syrophoenician woman who also came and fell at Jesus' feet and humbly yet persistently - and successfully

---

[54] Daily readings with George McLeod 1991 Fount Paperbacks

- pleaded her cause (Mk.7:25-30). Mark wants us to be with the Roman centurion complicit in the crucifixion who was at Jesus' feet and who sensed something really special, some kind of kinship with the divine about this crucified, suffering, dying human being (Mk.15:39) and gave his surprising answer to what for him might even have been the unformed question, *Who is this?*

Mark invited all his readers or listeners, through the recounted experiences of these and so many others, to share their awe, their humble faith, their closeness to Jesus, their questions: but perhaps even more Mark would want us to hear the question posed directly by Jesus himself to his disciples, *"Who do you say that I am?"* (Mk.8:29 my underlining).

To be asked *"Do you know who I am?"* is not always an invitation to immediately define a person by name, title, role or status. It may equally be an invitation to enter into a developing, and let it never be forgotten a productive relationship in which we hear, accept in faith and bear abundant fruit (Mk.4:20). J. D. Kingsbury says that the secrecy motif in Mark serves a catechetical purpose, and Mark guides his readers through a progressive unveiling of Jesus' identity – with the inference that at the end of reading Mark's gospel we will know exactly who Jesus is[55]. Conversely, I regard Mark as drawing his readers or listeners into an ever more engaging mystery within which we might be *lost in wonder, love and praise*. I hope that all who read Mark's gospel will embark on an exciting journey of faith in which there will always remain room for a deeper understanding and the kind of radical answers which demand changes in us.

Furthermore, we might usefully bear in mind that the truth which is to be discovered may be a truth which engages us in a way that is almost beyond human comprehension. Mark's report that at the transfiguration Peter did not know what to say (Mk.9:6) is preceded by the symbol of Jesus' clothes. They were *"white, as no fuller on earth could bleach them"* (Mk.9:3). Theologically, and perhaps literally this testifies to an unearthly experience beyond adequate description, but it gave a glimpse momentarily of the incredible depths of divinity which are always there; treasures waiting to be discovered.

In the side Chapel of All Saints, Northampton, are five stained glass windows adjacent to each other in a horizontal row. Four of the pictures have names. On the extreme left is St. Nicolas with a sceptre and a ship in his hands. To the extreme right is St. Luke holding quill and scroll. Left of centre stands St. George with lance and shield: and right of centre, St. Michael clasps flaming sword and weighing scales. But the central window offers a picture of an un-named figure

---

[55] Jack Dean Kingsbury *The Christology of Mark's Gospel* Fortress Press 1989 pp.14-21

with empty hands. A reasonable assumption is that this represents Jesus. For me the vulnerability yet power of empty hands stands in marked contrast to the others who all hold and potentially wield implements of worldly power. Jesus did not, and does not fit into what many may think of as normal concepts or categories. He has the authority of the humble yet effective servant, and any power he has must be given to him by those whom he would serve in love. In so many ways, though he may share our humanity as the son of man, he offers a unique insight into what it means to be fully human. I have assumed that the central panel is meant to represent Jesus, though his identity is left to the imagination of the beholder. For me, because the figure appears to be Anglo-Saxon, is dressed in royal robes, and has no nail marks in the hands - the figure poses a considerable test for my imagination. It does not accord with my presuppositions, but offers me new possibilities for thinking. This is why it is so "right" as an aid to contemplation of the mystery which is God in Christ.

The Gerasene man with the unclean spirit is perhaps an exemplar in sitting at Jesus' feet properly clothed and in his right mind. But when he asked to follow Jesus he was told instead to go back to his friends and "*tell them how much the Lord has done for you, and how he has had mercy on you*" - and he did (Mk.5:19f). It's the devil in a person who says of Jesus, "*I know who you are*" (Mk.1:24), or thinks that in giving Jesus a title or description they can confine him to their expectations of what can be known, or somehow have control of him (Mk.8:29, 33; 15:26). In contrast, the person who acknowledges their own unworthiness in coming to Jesus and who learns to know him through the questions he poses for us is the one who will find they have gained what really matters (cf.Mk.7:24-30 - The Syrophoenician woman).

MacCulloch, aware of the contributions to spiritual life and theology of Aquinas' *via negativa* and its development in the fourteenth century *Cloud of Unknowing*, nonetheless speaks of "*a constant urge to describe the indescribable*"[56]: whilst Ashton speaks of "*a conceptual system ..... to put the ineffable into words*"[57]. Mark's Gospel invites us to live with the ineffable, to retain the unfathomable mystery, to humbly explore not solve the messianic secret[58]. We are the richer for accepting his invitation not only to live with, but to find life through, the question, *Who am I?* In the journey of getting to know Jesus for ourselves, we might just begin to discover others who are sharing the same excursion[59].

---

[56] D. MacCulloch *A History of Christianity* Penguin 2010 p.421 and p.6
[57] UFG p.228
[58] John Caputo's recent work *The Insistence of God: A Theology of Perhaps* (Indiana Press 2013) postulates: *God asks a question of us, no answers are provided, rather an irresistible urge to find our answers.*
[59] Stoddart's comment is one example: *Theologians (pastoral- practical and others) believe that in some way or other we are invited by God into engagement with the source of life.*

For me, the fact that when one has read Mark's Gospel so many questions remain open is very moving and at times uplifting. Was Jesus the Jewish Messiah, the anointed one, the holy one of God, the gentile's Christos, a Greek, Roman or Hebrew king, a son of God, or The Son of God, the son of man, the man from Nazareth? To different people he was one or more of each of these and so much more; but to say them all is only to have made a selective appraisal. Although twentieth/twenty-first century Westerners seem wired to want to precisely define, or have a proven answer to everything, the depths of any person are not captured by description, nor plumbed by the titles they may be given. Indeed titles may obscure or nullify much of what a person has to offer in a lasting, meaningful, growing relationship. If asked who Jesus is, my answer would have to be something along these lines:-

> *I am sorry, I cannot tell you who or what Jesus is, or might become for you. That's a journey of discovery you must make for yourself. I can tell you a little of what Jesus has meant for others: perhaps even a little of what he has meant and means to me; but that could actually be really unhelpful for you. Please read the story of Jesus in Mark's gospel, learn about Jesus for yourself - and then I would love you to share your discoveries and questions with me* [60].

That such connection is provisional, variegated and far more elusive than perhaps we might wish both analytically and existentially reminds us of the mystery at the heart of the divine-human encounter. Eric Stoddart: *Current Thinking in Pastoral Theology* Expository Times April 2012 p.330.

[60] For those who find a deal of uncertainty as an element of faith an exciting prospect *The Insistence of God: A Theology of Perhaps* by John Caputo (Indiana Press 2013) is commendable.

Chapter Three
LUKE'S GOSPEL – MAGNIFICAT

"At an interfaith consultation for South American religious leaders held in Bolivia Autumn 2011, we invited participants to reflect on the characteristics of God that might inspire us to work for equality. Much of their response was predictable: God's unbounded love moves us to embrace people on the fringes of society, as does God's solidarity with human beings. Much less expected was their understanding of God as a fighter - "lutador" - who in fighting with us and for us brings about transformation." [1]

[46]And Mary said:
"My soul glorifies the Lord
[47]and my spirit rejoices in God my Saviour,
[48]for he has been mindful
of the humble state of his servant.
From now on all generations will call me blessed,
[49]for the Mighty One has done great things for me—
holy is his name.
[50]His mercy extends to those who fear him,
from generation to generation.
[51]He has performed mighty deeds with his arm;
he has scattered those who are proud in their inmost thoughts.
[52]He has brought down rulers from their thrones
but has lifted up the humble.
[53]He has filled the hungry with good things
but has sent the rich away empty.
[54]He has helped his servant Israel,
remembering to be merciful
[55]to Abraham and his descendants forever,
even as he said to our fathers." (Lk.1:46-55 NIV)

There are a number of passages in Luke's Gospel which might be chosen to exemplify or encapsulate the main thrust of Luke's work. For example, the birth, life and death of John the Baptizer is in many ways an abridged, parallel story to that of Jesus. Jesus' reading from Isaiah and brief sermon - sometimes together described as Jesus' manifesto - plus the mixed reactions to him and his message in 4:16-30 might also serve as drawing together into one episode many of the main strands of the larger story Luke has to tell. Chapter 15, with its three stories of "lost and found" set in a context of both dangerous distrust and joyful listening, might again be considered to embody the whole story of redemption which the

---

[1] Loretta Minghella, Director of Christian Aid, (Expository Times April 2012 p.364)

89

gospel Luke shares. No doubt there could be other candidates too: but I suggest no other passage captures the content and the intention of Luke's Gospel as comprehensively and eloquently as Mary's prayer of praise and revolution set close to the beginning of the story and at the very least setting the scene for all that is to follow. So this work on Luke will use what is traditionally known as The Magnificat as the basis for exploring major themes in Luke, which consistently challenge, sometimes portend destruction, but are always potentially redemptive.

The psalm or prayer of Mary will take us through many of Luke's major concerns: worship, praise and joy, the Holy Spirit, salvation, redemption, forgiveness, humility, perseverance, faithfulness, women and gender balance or bias, Jesus as healer and exorcist, listening, obedience, prayer, the heart, reversal, violence, Satan, the kingdom of God, ministry to the lost and marginalised, blessings for the humble poor, the mortal danger of riches and status, table fellowship/friendship, Jesus as teacher, Jerusalem, and the fulfilment and continuity of God's purposes. It is exciting to use the Magnificat as a key to open up so much in Luke's gospel that might otherwise be hidden. Anyone who shares a similar experience will be moved to say with Mary, *"My soul magnifies the Lord"*.

My Soul Magnifies the Lord (1:46)

We will consider Mary as a character in due course, but her prayer begins in her soul! Later in her song Mary will refer to the "inmost thoughts" of others (NIV) or the "imagination of their hearts" (RSV) (Lk.1:51). For Luke the combination of heart, soul and mind constitutes the essence of our inner being. Along with strength they are the essentials which are to be totally dedicated to God (Lk.10:27). Simeon in blessing Mary says, *"A sword will pierce through your own soul also ...the thoughts out of many hearts may be revealed"* (Lk.2:35). When some teachers of the Law and Pharisees inwardly questioned Jesus' right to pronounce forgiveness of sins, his question to them was, *"Why do you question in your hearts?"* (Lk.5:22. see also 8:39f). To some Pharisees Jesus says, *"God knows your hearts"* (Lk.16:15). In marked contrast to those whose hearts are not right, out of Mary's heart and soul comes praise, just as two unnamed disciples on the road to Emmaus had their *"hearts set on fire"* by the presence of Jesus (Lk.24:32). *"The seed in good soil stands for those with a noble and good heart"* (Lk.8:15). *"The good man brings good things out of the good stored up in his heart, and the evil man brings evil things out of the evil stored up in his heart"* (Lk.6:45). Often it seems that churches want to, or feel the need to organise the response people make to God. The results can be quite shallow. Luke's gospel invites us into something deep and profound, and encourages us through Mary's example to be touched within by what God has done and to respond out of the depths of our being.

What comes out of the depths of Mary, her heart and soul, are worship, praise and joy. Mary's soul "*glorifies the Lord*" (Lk.1:46 - magnifies RSV) and "*rejoices in God*" (Lk.1:47).

Not only is worship evident at the beginning and end of Luke's gospel, and consistently featured throughout, but close to both the beginning and the end of the gospel there are templates for worship. The shepherds in chapter 2, "*... hear the word, believe it, set out in search of the child, find and identify the child, bear witness, and give glory and praise to God (Lk.2:15-20)*" [2]. In chapter 24 the two disciples *sharing a journey* to Emmaus heard *the word*, shared *the bread*, recognised they had been in *the presence of Jesus* then hurried and *told others*.

These two disciples were amongst the disciples who later that day experienced the risen Jesus standing amongst them. They were called to spread their witness further afield. They received a blessing, shared "*great joy*" and were "*continually blessing God*" (Lk.24:13-43). Worship as consciousness of the presence of God in Christ might not always lead to a sense of being blessed and exhilaration, but Luke's gospel suggests such outcomes might reasonably be expected.

Zechariah, whose story effectively opens Luke's gospel, is first encountered playing his part as a priest in the corporate worship offered by God's people. Throughout the gospel Jesus is regularly to be found in the synagogue or in the temple, places of worship; and significantly Jesus himself evokes attitudes of worship. Peter is not the only one to be found at Jesus' feet in a posture indicative of worship offered in response to God's holiness or to God's power being recognised in Jesus (Lk.5:8 see also 7:38; 8:28, 35, 41, 47; 10:39; 17:16; 23:47). However, it is worth noting that the worship is of God. The worship is often in response to Jesus "authority" or "holiness", or what Jesus does, but Luke, unencumbered by Trinitarian formulae, does not seem to legitimise substituting Jesus as the object of worship in place of God. Mary's song is inspired by, but not addressed to her son.

As already noted, Luke's gospel, especially but by no means exclusively the opening chapters, is full of worship, praise and joy. Zechariah may have been troubled and fearful (Lk.1:12), but the promise was that he would have "*joy and gladness*" (Lk.1:14) - a joy experienced by Elizabeth and shared by her family and neighbours (Lk.1:58). The child, John, still in Elizabeth's womb "*leaped for joy*" (Lk.1:44) and Zechariah proclaimed, "*blessed be God*" (Lk.1:68). Similarly the fear of the shepherds when surprised by an appearance of the angel of the Lord was met with the assurance that the angel "*brings good news of a great joy*" (Lk.2:10) which led immediately to a heavenly host, and subsequently the shepherds,

---

[2] TGL p.138

"glorifying and praising God" (Lk.2:13f, 20). In Luke 15 this same heavenly host are pictured as being full of joy when the lost are found (Lk.15:7, 10), and the compassionate father can do no other than *"make merry"* when his lost child comes home and can be restored to a former dignity (Lk.15:23).

We've already noted how the gospel closes with Jesus' disciples *"blessing God"* (Lk.24:53), but probably the most telling story with regard to joy inspired by Jesus is that of Jesus approaching Jerusalem on the descent of the Mount of Olives. A great crowd of his disciples spread their garments on the road.

> *"They began to praise God with a loud voice for all the mighty works they had seen ...and some of the Pharisees in the multitude said to him, 'Teacher, rebuke your disciples'. He answered, 'I tell you, if these were silent, the very stones would cry out'"* (Lk.19:36-40).

This is that irrepressible response to God at work in Jesus which Luke identifies and into which the reader is invited time and again[3]. Mary is the archetypal worshipper. Jesus had become an integral, radicalising factor in her life. Her response was to magnify and rejoice in the Lord God. When Jesus becomes part of a church's DNA, when a church knows it has the privilege and responsibility of delivering Jesus into the world, perhaps only then can there be a spontaneous outpouring of the soul in praise, thanksgiving and worship which is the natural response of the hosts of heaven and an invitation to all on earth *"On whom God's favour rests"* (Lk.2:14).

"My Spirit Rejoices"(1:47).

The context in which Mary says these words, would suggest that Mary here refers to the Holy Spirit within her. Zechariah had been told by the angel of the Lord that his son, John (the Baptizer) would be full of the Holy Spirit (Lk.1:15). Mary, similarly, was told by the angel of the Lord that through the medium of the Holy Spirit the power of the Most High would "overshadow her" with the consequence that the child to be born to her would be holy (Lk.1:35). When Mary and Elizabeth met, Elizabeth was filled with the Holy Spirit and was full of praise for Mary and the child within her (Lk.1:41-45). All this led to Mary's description of what it was in her that rejoiced - her spirit - or the Holy Spirit at work in her. The same spirit which was also upon both Zechariah and Simeon and inspired their praise and prophecy would also be upon Jesus in his ministry of preaching (Lk.1:67-79; 2:26-7; 4:18).

---

[3] For other instances of praise and joy as a recurring mood in Luke see 2:38; 5:33-35; 10:17-20; 13:17; 17:15; 18:43; 19:6.

One of the remarkable things about Luke's gospel is that he establishes very clearly in the early chapters that the principle characters in Jesus' pre-natal and infant world were "spirit filled". Then through John's ministry and Jesus' post-baptism prayer, comes the promise that Jesus would baptize with the Holy Spirit with which he himself had been anointed (Lk.3:16; 4:22). However, after these early chapters the Holy Spirit is hardly mentioned again. After the return of the seventy disciples from their mission, Jesus is said to be *"full of joy through the Holy Spirit"* (Lk.10:21). When teaching his disciples about prayer Jesus referred to the Holy Spirit as a gift which a heavenly father is willing to give (Lk.11:13), and which must not be denied (Lk.12:10). Furthermore, reflecting Jesus' own experience (Lk.4:1ff) the Holy Spirit would provide the disciples with any necessary words in times of trial (Lk.12:12). But that is it. Almost all references to "spirit" following on from the beginning of chapter four are to evil spirits.

Why does not the Holy Spirit feature more? It has been suggested that in the synagogue in Nazareth Jesus declared the Spirit of the Lord to be upon him and he made plain how that Spirit would be evidenced: preaching good news to the poor, proclaiming freedom for the prisoners, recovery of sight for the blind, release for the oppressed; proclaiming the acceptable year of the Lord. The rest of Luke does not mention the Spirit by name, but gives an account of the Spirit at work in and through Jesus. My preferred option for the absence of references in most of Luke to the Holy Spirit is that in the early part of his story of Jesus Luke has shown us the kind of people in whom the Holy Spirit can dwell and through whom the Holy Spirit can be channelled - people whose reaction to God at work in Jesus is sincere, properly humble, welcoming and positive. Luke will introduce us to more of these people as the story unfolds, and they too will know the fullness of joy that comes through the Holy Spirit which is God's gift. Luke has given the discerning reader the signs of the Spirit: further explication is redundant.

It could also be noted that if Luke's gospel was written as part one of a two-part story (Luke/Acts), then the Holy Spirit in the Gospel is to some extent synonymous with the person and work of Jesus. Only after his death, resurrection and ascension would the work of the Holy Spirit be separately identified as the major influence in the lives of Jesus' followers. But Luke's gospel makes sufficient reference to the Holy Spirit, the Spirit of inspiration, for the reader to learn that God's Spirit was always at work in people's lives - always life-giving – always literally an inspiration to rejoice.

In God My Saviour (1:47)

The spirit in Mary rejoiced *"in God my saviour"* (Lk.1:47). In fascinating and multiple ways Luke follows through Mary's recognition of God as saviour at work in Jesus. These include messages or stories of salvation, redemption or rescue, mercy and forgiveness. Jesus' entire ministry could be seen as salvific. For example, when later we look at his ministry of healing and exorcism, an element of "being saved" (being *"delivered from evil"*) can always be inferred. But Luke also has explicit references which underlie and develop Mary's thought.

At the annunciation, the angel said to Mary: *"You shall call his name Jesus"* (Lk.1:31), which led after his birth to the temple naming ceremony when *"He was called Jesus, the name given by the angel before he was conceived"* (Lk.2:21). Whilst Luke does not spell out the meaning of the name Jesus (God saves) in the foregoing passages, the information is given to the shepherds, *"To you is born this day in the city of David, a Saviour, who is Christ the Lord"*, and is implicit in Zechariah's words, *"Praise be to the Lord, the God of Israel, because he has come and has redeemed his people, and raised up a horn of salvation for us"* (Lk.2:11;1:68). At the temple, following the naming of Jesus, Anna *"gave thanks to God and spoke about the child to all who were looking forward to the redemption of Jerusalem"* (Lk.2:38): but perhaps Simeon most fully expresses what Luke wanted to transmit from his "eye-witnesses" (Lk.1:2). Simeon spoke of the redemption and salvation he foresaw resulting from the birth of Jesus and said, *"My eyes have seen your salvation"* (Lk.2:30).

It must be acknowledged that how these early characters saw salvation and redemption was not literally fulfilled. For Zechariah salvation was being saved, *"from our enemies and from the hand of all who hate us .... to rescue us from the hand of our enemies, and to enable us to serve him without fear in holiness and righteousness before him all our days."* (Lk.1:71-73) Jesus' disciples struggled to appreciate the true nature of the salvation in which Jesus believed, so that even after his death the two disciples on the road to Emmaus could say, *"but we had hoped that he was the one who was going to redeem Israel"* (Lk.24:21). It is a part of the abiding value of such "saints" that although they could not discern exactly how God would fulfil their dreams, they lived, declared and celebrated their faith in a way that kept hope alive.

Unpalatable as it may have been for some, the salvation evidenced in the ministry of Jesus as portrayed in Luke, in spite of the Magnificat, was not overtly political in nature, even though taken seriously it would have dramatic and radical political and social consequences. Salvation in Luke is salvation from "sinful" conditions which prevent people from trusting in God as love and living a new life rooted in forgiveness. John the Baptizer preached *"a baptism of repentance and the forgiveness of sins,"* (Lk.3:3) and he exhorted the people to *"bear fruits that befit repentance"* (Lk.3:8). Repentance, forgiveness and fruitfulness would be the hallmarks of people who would live life in a new way.

In the ministry of Jesus his attitude to forgiveness was perhaps one of the major causes of unease amongst the religious of his day. Jesus, impressed by the faith of the friends of a man lowered through a roof, said to him, "*Man, your sins are forgiven you.*" This provoked the question, "*Who is this that speaks blasphemies? Who can forgive sins but God only?*" Jesus responded "*The Son of Man has authority on earth to forgive sins*" (Lk.5:20-24). An almost parallel story unfolds at Simon the Pharisee's home where a woman anointed Jesus' feet. He told the woman her sins were forgiven. In response to the critical thoughts and questions he encountered, Jesus gave his justification: "*I tell you, her sins, which are many, are forgiven, for she loved much, but he who is forgiven little, loves little*" (Lk.7:48). On close examination this is confusing - and one could ask, "Which comes first, the love or the forgiveness?" But that is to miss the point. The woman's actions beautifully reflected God's unction - which is not a mechanical process, but the action of a spirit which is truly free. Forgiveness is the appropriation in faith of the freedom which God is always willing to offer. On another occasion to the question put to him by bystanders, "*Who then can be saved?*" Jesus replied, "*What is impossible with men is possible with God*" (Lk.18:26f).

The action and motivation of the woman who anointed his feet was a trigger for Jesus' parable of the two forgiven debtors. Salvation is inseparably linked to forgiveness (Lk.7:41-43, 47 cp. 8:48). Zechariah viewed salvation as "*from our enemies*". That seems to be diametrically opposed to Jesus' teaching and example. Jesus taught "*Love your enemies*" (Lk.6:27, 35), return good for evil, and like God be merciful and non-judgemental (Lk.6:27-38). However, in fairness to Zechariah, loving our enemies may be the best way of being saved from their enmity: and he did believe that his son, John the Baptizer's work would be, "*To give knowledge of salvation to his people in the forgiveness of their sins, through the tender mercies of our God, when the day shall dawn on us from on high*" (Lk.1:77-78). As Mullins says,

> *The ministry of Jesus turned out to be very different from what John the Baptizer and like-minded people expected. Far from destroying sin and sinners Jesus proclaimed the forgiveness of sin and he ate and drank in the company of sinners* (Lk.5:29-32). *Far from promoting self-righteous zeal in the face of wrongdoing he emphasised an attitude of forgiveness and compassion like the forgiveness, generosity and compassion of God* (Lk.6:27-38)[4].

To his disciples Jesus said, "*If your brother sins, rebuke him, and if he repents, forgive him. If he sins against you seven times in a day, and seven times comes back to you and says, 'I repent,' forgive him.*" (Lk.17:3f). Even for those who

---

[4] TGL p.238

crucified him he prayed, "*Father forgive them for they know not what they do*" (Lk.23:24).

Jesus' teaching, given to "*a great crowd of his disciples and a great multitude of people from all Judaea and Jerusalem*" in the "Sermon on the Plain" (Lk.6:17-49) begins with four blessings and four woes (Lk.6:20-26; cp. the six woes in 11:37-52) which taken together echo sentiments in the Magnificat (Lk.1:52-53). The sermon continues: loving enemies is more worthy than loving friends, "*Love your enemies; do good to those who hate you; bless those who curse you and pray for those who persecute you*" (Lk.6:27-28). In an "eye for an eye" culture this potentially breaks cycles of violence. It also reflects God's merciful and generous nature (Lk.6:27-36); although it makes no sense to those Pharisees and Lawyers who rejected John's ministry (Lk.7:30) and now reject that of Jesus, being willing to neither join the fasting of John nor the feasting of Jesus (Lk.7:31-34). Jesus enjoined generosity in regard to others' faults and humble awareness of one's own. He encouraged a non-judgemental and magnanimous forgiving attitude (Lk.6:37-42).

If forgiveness is essential for understanding Jesus' salvation, the concept of "lost-ness" is also important. In his dealings with Zacchaeus Jesus said, "*Today salvation has come to this house .... For the Son of Man came to seek and to save what was lost*" (Lk.19:9-10). The conjunction of three stories of "the lost" in Luke 15 is surely quite deliberate. The lost coin, the lost sheep and the lost son, climax in the words of the father: "*This your brother was dead, and he is alive; he was lost, and is found*" (Lk.15:32).

A question asked over the years by many Christians, and a cause of much pain and division, was put to Jesus by an unnamed interrogator. "*Lord, are only a few people going to be saved?*"(Lk.13:23). It was only indirectly answered on that occasion by Jesus, but may have already been answered by Luke who in considering John the Baptizer's ministry and that of "*the one who is to come*" cites the prophet Isaiah "*All mankind will see your salvation*" (Lk.3:6). Seeing is not necessarily the same thing as receiving; and it should be noted that Jesus believed some might see and yet not see (Lk.8:10). Jesus warned his disciples as the time approached for his death, "*When these things begin to take place, stand up and lift up your heads, because your redemption is drawing near.... watch at all times*" (Lk.21:28, 36). If his lifting up on the cross was a supremely important and highly visible part of Jesus' work of salvation, there were clearly some who did not see it for what it was. "*He saved others; let him save himself if he is the Christ of God, the Chosen One .... If you are the king of the Jews, save yourself*", they taunted (Lk.23:35, 37). They seemed to have no idea that it is in self-giving, not self-serving or self-preservation that the life which Jesus taught, exemplified and promised was to be discovered and experienced. In Mary's open-hearted self-giving lay her capacity to be blessed and to know God as her saviour. As Mother Teresa put it, *"It is in giving that we receive"* - furthermore, only that which is acknowledged as having been lost, including "lost souls", can be legitimately described as having been found, and in that sense "saved".

He Has Been Mindful of the Humble State of his Servant. From Now on all Generations Will Call Me Blessed (1:48)

If Mary was involved in self-giving, for her it was also a time of humbly receiving from God. The majority of us who are steeped in the Christian tradition may take it for granted that we are personally noticed and loved by God. For those who are truly humble it is a surprising and deeply moving insight. That *"the humble poor believe"* and become the recipients of God's blessing is a major strand of Luke's gospel. Need, or poverty, comes in many forms. It may be physical, social, psychological, material, or spiritual, but a key component for redress is that people have the humility to accept that they are in need, that they are unworthy to be blessed, but that they are in the presence of redemptive holiness.

This sense of need and unworthiness was evident in the lives of many who were part of Jesus' story. Zechariah and Elizabeth were probably not poverty stricken in financial terms, because he was a priest, but they knew the stigma-cum-social-poverty of having no children (Lk.1:5-7). It is interesting that inspired at least in part by Elizabeth's conception in old age, Mary's psalm in many ways parallels the psalm of Hannah who also after many years of barrenness became the mother of Samuel (Lk.1:46-55; 1 Sam.2:1-10). Elizabeth was speaking to and about Mary when she said: *"Blessed is she who believed that there would be a fulfilment of what was spoken to her from the Lord"* (Lk.1:45), but the belief is a shared one, as is much of their experience. Mary's words, *"From now on all generations will call me blessed ... His mercy is upon those who fear him"* (Lk.1:48, 50) are confirmation of, as well as inspired by Elizabeth's belief and exemplary encouragement.

According to Luke, Jesus at birth was laid in a manger *"because there was no room for them in the inn"* (Lk.2:7). Jesus begins life literally as an impoverished outsider in humble surroundings. It is shepherds, religiously and socially marginalised people, who are the first non-family members to hear and to respond positively to the news of Jesus' birth (Lk.2:8-20). These "outcasts":-

"........ receive a sign especially for them. They will behold a saviour born as a nomadic shepherd; not inside a settled person's dwelling, but in the 'outside' nomadic dwelling of a shepherd on the move with the flocks, and

strips of cloth which served to keep the child's limbs straight, recall the covering of a shepherd child [5].

It was to the poor and humble that Jesus came. Reading from Isaiah and applying it to himself, Jesus said, "*He has anointed me to preach good news to the poor*" (Lk.4:17). And again, "*Blessed are you poor, for yours is the kingdom of God*" (Lk.6:20).

Alongside poverty goes humility, often associated with the attitude of a child or a servant, those with no legal possessions or social status. So Mary describes herself as "*the handmaid of the Lord*" (Lk.1:38). Simon Peter's mother-in-law, having been healed of a fever, literally became a servant of the Lord (Lk.4:39). When an argument breaks out amongst Jesus' disciples as to which of them was the greatest Jesus talked about receiving children in his name and said, "*He who is least among you all is the one who is great*" (Lk.9:46-48). In the same vein, "*Let the greatest among you become as the youngest, and the leader as one who serves*" (Lk.22:26). On another occasion Luke tells us, "*Jesus rejoiced in the Holy Spirit and said, 'I praise you, Father, Lord of heaven and earth, because you have hidden these things from the wise and learned, and revealed them to little children'*" (Lk.10:21).

The desired attitude was childlike, or that of a servant, which at times resulted in a posture of humility. On his first recorded meeting with Jesus in Luke, "*Peter fell down at Jesus' feet saying, 'Depart from me, for I am a sinful man'*" (Lk.5:8). Others too assumed the posture. "*A man named Jairus, a ruler of the synagogue, came and fell at Jesus' feet, pleading with him to come to his house*" (Lk.8:41). Or the tax collector in the parable "*would not even lift his eyes up to heaven*", but simply and humbly said, "*God be merciful to me a sinner*". Jesus said that "*He went down to his house justified*" (Lk.18:13f). This parable found graphic expression in real life in the positive response tax collectors made to Jesus' teaching (Lk.15:1), and in the encounter between Jesus and Zacchaeus (Lk.19:1-10). Jesus set the principle forth in a story of a father and his two sons. When the younger of the sons came to his senses, he realised what he needed to say to his father: "*Father, I have sinned against heaven and against you. I am no longer worthy to be called your son; make me like one of your hired men*" (Lk.15:18f). The wayward son adopted the attitude, humility, and the ambition, to be a servant. This enabled a father's love to restore his child.

Yet we need to recognise that Luke sets alongside the "sinners", others for whom Jesus had a high regard. These are the genuinely righteous people - "*those who fear God*" (Lk.1:50). They appear throughout the Gospel. Luke says of Zechariah and Elizabeth: "*Both of them were upright in the sight of God, observing all the Lord's*

---

[5] TGL pp.138-9

commandments and regulations blamelessly" (Lk.1:6). Zechariah's vision is, *"that we being delivered ...might serve him without fear in holiness and righteousness before him all the days of our life"* (Lk.1:74f). Mary and Joseph name Jesus and make a thank-offering for him *"according to what is said in the law of the Lord"* (Lk.2:21-24). Of Simeon it is said, *"this man was righteous and devout"* (Lk.2:25), and of Anna, *"She did not depart from the temple, worshiping with prayer and fasting night and day"* (Lk.2:37). These people were of one spirit with Jesus who was recognised as *"a righteous man"* by the centurion at the crucifixion (Lk.23:47). Just as these sincere law abiding people had been present throughout his life, so in his death he is served by Joseph of Arimathea, who is a member of the Council, but is described as *"a good and righteous man"* (Lk.23:50). Though much lauded and showcased in certain church circles, to have been a notorious or outstanding villain, or a reprobate in society's eyes, to have been "wayward" and now obviously changed for the better, is not an essential prerequisite for being part of the company of those who can serve and can be served by Jesus. Faithful, devout, law abiding, yet humble souls have their place too.

Faithfulness, often allied to perseverance, is another motif which appears throughout Luke's Gospel. We tend to focus on the climax of the event, but Jesus was forty days fasting and being tempted in the wilderness. The ultimate test of self-sacrifice on the cross was not embraced without a daily commitment to the way of the cross. Jesus' testimony that God as father is ready to give, was prefaced by the parable of the importunate neighbour who persevered in knocking and asking (Lk.11:5-13. See also Lk.18:1-8). In the service of others and God (Lk.16:11-13), in marriage (Lk.16:18), in times of trial (Lk.18:1-8; 22:28) and in extremis (Lk.21:19), faithfulness, perseverance and endurance are the marks of those who serve in God's kingdom. The true disciple is the one who having heard the word will *"hold it fast"*, and who will bring forth fruit *"with patience"* (Lk.8:15). Faith is not best portrayed by spectacular, five-minute wonders. The outworking of faith is more truly demonstrated by faithfulness, and the intimate connection should not be overlooked.

Mary was a woman. Being a woman in most societies has habitually tended to carry with it various degrees of "poverty". The physical nature of a woman can put her at a distinct disadvantage to men through less immediately available muscular strength, and through what are sometimes called "women's problems"; but also through established discriminatory legal codes and social customs. A number of the women in Luke seem to some extent to have overcome, or perhaps defied some of these and other restraints[6].

---

[6] There are those who consider Luke as deliberately belittling women. D'Angelo's work (1990 cited in Otterman 2007 p.112f) leads Ottermann to conclude that Luke deliberately changed the traditions about early women leaders in order 'to control and cut down the role

The twelve were with him and also some women who had been cured of evil spirits and diseases: Mary (called Magdalene) from whom seven demons had come out; Joanna the wife of Cuza, the manager of Herod's household; Susanna; and many others. These women were helping to support them out of their own means (Lk.8:2-3).

Unfortunately it still needs to be highlighted and emphasised that these women literally ministered to the needs of the body of Christ. They were faithful followers, disciples. They were there at his crucifixion: "*All those who knew him, including the women who had followed him from Galilee, stood at a distance, watching these things*" (Lk.23:49). They were there at his internment. "*The women who had come with Jesus from Galilee followed Joseph and saw the tomb and how his body was laid in it. Then they went home and prepared spices and perfumes*" (Lk.23:55), but because they were law-abiding," *they rested on the Sabbath in obedience to the commandment*" (Lk.23:56). They became the first witnesses to the resurrection. "*It was Mary Magdalene, Joanna, Mary the mother of James, and the others with them who told this to the apostles....* (even if the apostles) *did not believe the women, because their words seemed to them like nonsense*" (Lk.24:10f). It seems reasonable to suggest that Luke in recording the gender-based, prejudiced, negative, incredulous reaction of the male disciples is admonishing them and any who share their mentality.

Most of these women disciples seem to have been law-abiding, respectable women, but Jesus related to less respectable and socially unacceptable women too.

"When a woman who had lived a sinful life in that town learned that Jesus was eating at the Pharisee's house, she brought an alabaster jar of perfume, and as she stood behind him at his feet weeping, she began to wet his feet with her tears. Then she wiped them with her hair, kissed them and poured perfume on them. When the Pharisee who had invited him saw this, he said to himself, 'If this man were a prophet, he would know who is touching him and what kind of woman she is—that she is a sinner'." (Lk.7:37-39)

But the climax of the story is that Jesus said to the woman, "*Your faith has saved you; go in peace.*" (Lk.7:50). Almost the same words are said to the ritually unclean woman who touched the hem of his garment and found healing from her "issue of blood": "*Daughter, your faith has healed you. Go in peace*" (Lk.8:48; cp.17:19; 18:42). Jesus' work was to offer wholeness, restoration, shalom, whatever the starting condition might have been, and whatever the required

---

of women leaders in his time'. Ottermann regards Luke as androcentric, macho and Christocentric to the point of denying the dignity of the people with whom Jesus interacted.

remedy. Jeffrey John offers helpful insights into just how much, and what kind of "faith" this woman needed to approach Jesus. Constant haemorrhaging would have socially excluded this woman because she would have been considered unclean. For her to approach and touch a rabbi such as Jesus would put her in real physical danger of mob violence: but equally for Jesus to commend her for her action was tantamount to him challenging the social and religious mores of the society in which he lived – probably one more nail in his coffin![7]

How Luke perceived women is a contentious issue, but he definitely saw them equally as capable of faith as men. Both Luke and Jesus used them as exemplars. For instance, Jesus seeing a poor woman making her offering remarked, "*She out of her poverty put in all the living she had*" (Lk.21:4): and of the sinful woman with the ointment he said that in marked contrast to Simon the Pharisee, "*She loved much*" (Lk.7:47). Women have the capacity to listen and to contemplate. Luke recounts: "*Mary* (the mother of Jesus) *kept all these things, pondering them in her heart*" (Lk.2:19); and another Mary (sister to Martha) "*sat at Jesus' feet listening to what he said*" (Lk.10:39).

Perhaps most significant is that the immediate context for Mary's Psalm is a meeting between two women who hold centre stage. Mullins reflects on Mary's visit to her relative Elizabeth at the six-month point of Elizabeth's pregnancy (Lk.1:39-56). In this scene both women were accepting of God's role for each of them, and they are totally supportive of each other. Mary stayed nearly three months (i.e. nearly up to Elizabeth's full term). Mullins notes that this is strictly a female encounter in which two representatives of true piety "*theologise and speak with authority about God's newest deeds – and the reader is led to regard them as trustworthy characters and to adopt their theological interpretation of the impending births*"[8]. By suggesting that Mary's Magnificat is the key to appreciating the whole of Luke's gospel, Mullins' view which is limited to an interpretation of Jesus' birth is considerably extended in this work.

It has been pointed out by a number of commentators that in Luke's genealogy (Lk.3:23-38) there is a noticeable absence of women. But Luke points out that the line of male descent is only "supposed" (Lk.1:23). "Supposed" because there were those who were not privy to the union of the (female?) Holy Spirit and the female Mary who was anointed as the medium for Jesus' entry into the world. However,

---

[7] For further on the economic means and status of Jewish women in New Testament times see Sheena Orr *Women and Livelihoods in 1st Century Palestine: Exploring Possibilities* Expository Times Aug.2010 Vol.11 pp539-547. For a much fuller and most valuable exposition of the story of the woman with a haemorrhage see Jeffrey John *The Meaning of Miracles* pp 8-10, 98ff SCM/Canterbury Press 2001.
[8] TGL p.127

the list of male ancestors did provide an alternative male route back to God as a balance to the female origin. This is in keeping with Luke's consistent inclusion of parallel stories involving male and female characters. Some examples of this are Simeon and Anna (Lk.2:25-37), a young man (son) and a young woman (daughter) both raised from death (Lk.7:14f; 8:54f), the daughter of Abraham (Lk.13:16) and the son of Abraham (Lk.19:9), the importunate woman complainant (Lk.18:1-8) and the importunate male neighbour at night (Lk.11:5-13), the shepherds who are told about, and testify to the birth (Lk.2:8-20) and the women who are told about, and testify to the resurrection (Lk.24:5-10); two men in a bed and two women in a field (Lk.17:34f). The three stories told to encourage his followers and to challenge his critics invited his listeners to imagine themselves as a shepherd, a woman, a brother and/or a father (Lk.15). Luke has no bias toward either gender, but in giving significance and parity to women he undoubtedly challenged the chauvinism of his day, and ours, as well as extremist feminism[9]. All humble servants, women or men, as Mary sang, can rightly be described as recipients of God's favour, blessed (Lk.1:48).

He Who is Mighty Has Done Great Things (1:49) ... He Has Shown Strength With His Arm (1:51).

Although these words from Mary's psalm undoubtedly make reference to the past works of God, and to the immediate action of God in the lives of Mary and Elizabeth, in the context of Luke's Gospel they are probably just as much an indication of what God is capable of doing, and would do in Jesus. Of course, the great things will include every aspect of Jesus' life, but for his contemporaries the most common and public demonstrations of the power of God at work in Jesus were undoubtedly healings and exorcisms.

When John the Baptizer sent two of his disciples to ask if Jesus was "*he who is to come*", Luke tells us

> "*At that very time Jesus cured many who had diseases, sicknesses and evil spirits, and gave sight to many who were blind. So he replied to the messengers, 'Go back and report to John what you have seen and heard: The blind receive sight, the lame walk, those who have leprosy are cleansed, the deaf hear, the dead are raised, and the good news is proclaimed to the poor'*" (Lk.7:21-2; cp.Lk.4:18f).

Healing was a significant feature of Jesus' ministry. It was obviously practised prior to the account of the episode in his home town synagogue where he notes that

---

[9] For a succinct and well balanced discussion on whether Luke is a "friend to women", including some feminist critiques of this, see TGL p.55-59

the congregation will be thinking of him as a renowned "physician" (Lk.4:23). Healing was part of Jesus' life right through to the incident in the garden of Gethsemane where he restored the severed ear of the High Priest's servant (Lk.22:50-51). There is a tendency to see every act of healing by Jesus as a "miraculous event". It is possible that his contemporaries did not see it in this way. His reputation was as a "physician", and Jesus described his own work as that of a doctor (Lk.5:31). The physician's work of healing was a deliberate focus for Jesus, entirely in keeping with his teaching that the poor, the crippled, the lame, and the blind should be the prime recipients of godly generosity (Lk.17:13-14). Jesus on a number of occasions asked people not to publicise what he had done for them (e.g. Lk.5:14). Nonetheless he showed a compassionate response to the crowds who looked for his help: "*The crowds ... followed him. He welcomed them and spoke to them about the kingdom of God, and healed those who needed healing*" (Lk.9:11).

Alongside these physical healings were exorcisms. Jesus described this two-fold ministry in response to warnings about Herod's malign intentions toward him. "*He replied, 'Go tell that fox, 'I will keep on driving out demons and healing people today and tomorrow, and on the third day I will reach my goal'* " (Lk.13: 32). Luke tells us that "*demons came out of many people*" (Lk.4:41), that this ministry was shared by the twelve (Lk.9:1-2), then by the seventy-two disciples whom Jesus sent out in his name (Lk.10:17f). We have already remarked that some of his regular female companions had been "*cured of evil spirits and diseases*" (Lk.8:2). There were others who had been healed who would have liked to accompany him (Lk.8:38), and he was willing for a healing ministry to be exercised in his name by those who were not amongst his chosen disciples (Lk.9:49). Though neither healings nor exorcisms need be seen as exceptionally miraculous (both were common place), there is no doubt that for Luke Jesus' two-fold healing/exorcism ministry was a demonstration of God's power, the "*stretched out mighty arm*" [10].

Luke tells us there were "*a great number of people ...... who had come to hear him and to be healed of their diseases. Those troubled by impure spirits were cured, and the people all tried to touch him, because power was coming from him and he was healing them all*" (Lk.6:17-19). Luke also records the exclamation, "*What words these are! With authority and power he gives orders to impure spirits and they come out!*" (Lk.4:36); and, "*they were all amazed at the greatness of God*" (Lk.9:43) [because] "*the power of the Lord was with Jesus to heal the sick*" (Lk.5:17). That Jesus was fully aware of the power at work through him is shown in the story of the woman with the haemorrhage who touched him. She did so in the midst of a crowd pressing him on all sides, yet Luke tells us, "*Jesus said, 'Someone touched me; I know that power has gone out from me'*" (Lk.8:46).

---

[10] It is worth noting that Luke rarely uses the word "miracle". It occurs only twice (Lk.10:13; 19:37).

For many this testifies to a draining experience for Jesus, but it could equally or simultaneously have been a source of strengthening - *It is in giving that we receive!* I would hope it is true for many who minister to others that there have been times at the end of the day when physical and mental exhaustion are experienced, and yet at the same time there is an enrichment of the soul and mentally there is exhilaration. It is akin to climbing a very steep mountain to the summit when every limb aches with satisfaction! Such is the stretched out arm of God in Jesus' ministry.

Just as Mary's sense of the mighty arm of God being stretched out inspired her to express praise and wonder, so Luke tells us of others who were amazed and gave praise to God. When the paralysed man got up and walked off with his bed: *"They were filled with awe and said, 'We have seen remarkable things today'"* (Lk.5:26). When the widow of Nain's son had been restored to life, *"they were all filled with awe and praised God.' A great prophet has appeared among us,' they said, 'God has come to help his people'"* (Lk.7:16). When the spirit of Jairus' daughter returned to her, *"her parents were astonished"* (Lk.8:55); and when a blind beggar received his sight not only did he *"follow Jesus, praising God"*, but, *"When all the people saw it, they also praised God"* (Lk.18:43).

The sense of awe and wonder, however, was on occasions mingled with fear of such power, as in the case of the Gerasenes who begged Jesus to leave their region. *"Then all the people of the region of the Gerasenes asked Jesus to leave them, because they were overcome with fear"* (Lk.8:37). The reasons for their fear have been the subject of much speculation, but there is no doubt the fear was real. When demons are let loose, whatever form they may take, the consequences can be terrifyingly unpredictable (cf. Lk.8:33; 10:18; 11:20, 26).

In addition to fear, wonder and praise, the power and authority which Jesus demonstrated also brought suspicion, scepticism, criticism, argument and hostile opposition. For example, when Jesus was in the same room as a man suffering from abnormal swelling of his body, *"he was being carefully watched"* (Lk.14:1-2). Although the outcome of the situation was that his critics *"had nothing to say"* (Lk.14:6), his prioritising of healing over the accepted norms for Sabbath observance was a running sore (cf. Lk.6:1-5, 6-9; 13:10-17). Similarly his declarations that someone's sins had been forgiven, as in the case of the man let down through the roof, was regarded as blasphemous. *"When Jesus saw their faith, he said, 'Friend, your sins are forgiven.' The Pharisees and the teachers of the law began thinking to themselves, 'Who is this fellow who speaks blasphemy? Who can forgive sins but God alone?'"* (Lk.5:20f).

Criticism regularly came from religious or legal "professionals", but there were others too. Sometimes adverse comment came from members of the crowd: *"Jesus was driving out a demon that was mute. When the demon left, the man who had been mute spoke, and the crowd was amazed. But some of them said, 'By Beelzebul, the prince of demons, he is driving out demons'"* (Lk.11:14f).

This opposition is often juxtaposed with the faith which regularly accompanied healing. The faith of the friends who let the man down through the roof clearly moved Jesus (Lk.5:20), as did that of the centurion whose servant was close to death (Lk.7:9). In two instances Jesus suggested the faith of the person concerned had actually brought about their healing. To the woman healed from a previously incurable haemorrhage Jesus said, *"Daughter, your faith has healed you. Go in peace."* (Lk.8:48), and to the blind beggar on the roadside near Jericho, *"Jesus said to him, 'Receive your sight; your faith has healed you'"* (Lk.18:42).

Jesus said,

> *"Your eye is the lamp of your body. When your eyes are healthy, your whole body also is full of light. But when they are unhealthy, your body also is full of darkness. See to it, then, that the light within you is not darkness. Therefore, if your whole body is full of light, and no part of it dark, it will be just as full of light as when a lamp shines its light on you."* (Lk.11:34-36).

These words perhaps encapsulate the holistic intention which informed the ministry of healing and exorcism in which Jesus engaged. This ministry seems not to have been intended to inspire faith; it was rather a response to faith. But it was more than that, it was an encouragement for faith to work its own miracles, because faith is the means by which the outstretched arm of God can reach the lost-ness of peoples' hearts and bodies - the means by which they, like Mary, can be called "blessed".

Holy is His Name (1:49).

(Note: Whilst most of these reflections on Mary's words have a natural progression and I hope are easy to follow, two of them seem to invite several sub-themes. Where this is the case, as in this section, I have used sub-headings.)

Jesus was asked by his disciples to teach them to pray. He taught them to include in their praying the petition to God, *Hallowed be your name* (Lk.11:2). How can one begin to be a part of the answer to this prayer that God's holiness will be genuinely acknowledged? Luke offers a number of guidelines which include the humility already discussed, but also the need for attentiveness (listening and looking), for obedience, for prayer and for generous, joyful living. It is to these ingredients for honouring God's name as holy that we now give attention.

Chapter 3 - Luke

i. Listening

Luke in his only story of Jesus' boyhood tells us that Jesus was in the temple *"listening and asking questions"* (Lk.2:46). That is, he was listening attentively and responsively. At the commencement of Jesus' ministry he listened well enough to hear the voice from heaven which said, *"Thou art my beloved son; with thee I am well pleased"* (Lk.3:22). We may too easily, and probably erroneously assume that for Jesus a voice from heaven would not require on his part an attitude of being open to hear, the attentiveness which would make it possible to hear, and the trust which could accept what was heard. But Jesus was well aware of these requirements. Following on from the voice from heaven (Lk.3:22), in two of his three conversations with the devil, the devil tries to undermine what heaven had said with the words of doubt, *"IF you are the son of God"* (Lk.4:3, 9). Jesus' life is full of that listening with discrimination which is an essential prerequisite for any pastoral work, relevant preaching, or godly living.

The story of the two sisters Martha and Mary has this description of Mary; *"Mary sat at the Lord's feet listening to what he said"*. Jesus commended Mary for this by saying, *"Mary has chosen what is better, and it will not be taken away from her"* (Lk.10:39-42). And a clear sign that the demon-possessed Legion had been made whole by the ministry of Jesus was that Legion was *"sitting at Jesus feet"* (Lk.8:35), the posture of a disciple who is listening attentively to his or her teacher. Throughout the gospel there are people who earnestly listen. As a result their lives are changed and they become useful in the service of God. In the parable often titled 'The Sower', but perhaps better called 'The Parable of Seed and Soils', Jesus climaxed the parable in this way, *"But the seed on good soil stands for those ..... who hear the word, retain it, and by persevering produce a crop"* - listeners and doers of the word (Lk.8:15).

There were times when many people wanted to listen to Jesus: *"The people pressed upon him to hear the word of God"* (Lk.5:1; see also 6:17), but even his disciples were not always to able to understand the meaning of his words (Lk.9:45; 18:34): this in spite of the voice which came from the cloud, telling them, *"This is my Son, whom I have chosen; listen to him"* (Lk.9:35). Yet Jesus continued to encourage them to listen in such terms as, *"Therefore consider carefully how you listen"* (Lk.8:18) or *"Let these words sink into your ears"* (Lk.9:44). Listening may need to happen for a long time before understanding dawns. Significantly, Mary, the handmaid of the Lord, *"kept all these things and pondered them in her heart"* (Lk.2:19).

ii. Looking

Jesus combined his calls for attentive listening with the need to look, to be watchful. The parabolic words of Jesus, *"Be dressed ready for service and keep your lamps burning, like servants waiting for their master to return from a wedding banquet, so that when he comes and knocks they can immediately open the door for him. You also must be ready, because the Son of Man will come at an hour when you do not expect him"* (Lk.12:35.40), prepares Luke's readers for the later words of Jesus,

> *At that time they will see the Son of Man coming in a cloud with power and great glory. When these things begin to take place, stand up and lift up your heads, because your redemption is drawing near.... When you see these things happening, you know that the kingdom of God is near. Be always on the watch, and pray that you may be able to escape all that is about to happen, and that you may be able to stand before the Son of Man* (Lk.21:27f, 31, 36).

Sadly, even if understandably, the disciples often failed to be watchful, but Luke tells us of others who serve as good examples. Simeon was looking for the consolation of Israel (Lk.2:25). Anna could speak to a number of people who were looking for the redemption of Israel, whilst at the other end of the gospel Joseph, who provided the tomb for Jesus, *was looking for the kingdom of God* (Lk.23:51). At the crucifixion *the women who had followed him from Galilee, stood at a distance, watching these things* (Lk.23:49). Those same women *saw the tomb and how his body was laid in it* (Lk.23:55). It is small wonder that those who faithfully watched and waited for the post-Sabbath dawn were the first to "see" that this was no ordinary dawning.

Listening in the manner of a true disciple and faithful watchfulness are part of that obedience which is a proper response to God's holiness.

iii. Obedience

Zechariah and Elizabeth were both of them *"righteous in the sight of God, observing all the Lord's commands and decrees blamelessly"* (Lk.1:6). Mary says to the angel, *"I am the Lord's handmaid. Let it be to me according to your word"* (Lk.1:38). Luke tells us four times, in respect of Jesus' presentation at the temple and the attendant sacrifice, that Mary and Joseph acted *"according to the law of Moses"* (Lk.2:22, 24, 27, 39). Of the women who watched at the cross and at the tomb Luke says, *"On the Sabbath they rested according to the commandment"* (Lk.23:56b). These are all obedient people, obedient to what they believe to be God's will.

In their obedience to the law these people, some of whom appear at the beginning and others at the end of the gospel, embody the spirit, example and teaching of Jesus. In keeping with the fourth commandment, Jesus was obedient to his parents (Lk.2:51). When tested by the devil Jesus' response is twice, "*It is written*"; and the third time, when the Devil tries to misuse scripture, Jesus replies, "*It is said*" (Lk.4:4, 8, 12). Obedience based on internalised scripture used with discernment is part of Jesus' personal discipline. The way of the cross is for him a way of obedience, of subordination to his Father's will. This is apparent in Jesus' words, "*I have a baptism to be baptized with; and how I am constrained until it is accomplished*" (Lk.12:49). The penultimate expression of obedient surrender is, "*Father, if you are willing, remove this cup from me; nevertheless, not my will, but yours, be done*" (Lk.22:42). And finally, "*Father into your hands I commit my spirit*" (Lk.23:46).

Amazing as it is, this "obedience unto death" is the basis for the "eternal life", or life in the kingdom, which Jesus offers. "*If any man would come after me, let him deny himself and take up his cross daily and follow me*" (Lk.9:23); "*Whoever does not bear his own cross and come after me, cannot be my disciple*" (Lk.14:27). Scott Hoezee on *bearing one's cross* notes how this for many has become a response to unfortunate things that happen *to* a person rather than a lifestyle consciously chosen *by* a person. What Jesus surely intends *is a cross-shaped life: a life with a thoroughgoing kingdom perspective*[11]- a life of obedience.

When Jesus was asked by a lawyer how to inherit fff, Jesus' responded with the question, "*What is written in the law? How do you read?*" The lawyer cited Deuteronomy 6:5 and Leviticus 19:18 which are a call to love God with the entirety of our being, with complete self-surrender, and to love one's neighbour as much as we love ourselves; and Jesus issues a call to obedience, "*Do this, and you will live*" (Lk.10:25-28). The Good Samaritan is one who loves his neighbour at considerable personal risk and cost, and in so doing shows his love of God and his obedience to "*what is written*" (Lk.10:29-37). It is evident from Jesus' words and his own example that he believed the scriptures contained the necessary guidance for a life to be lived in obedience to God's will. The challenge is always to trust in the word and to live responsively.

The way of obedience to what we know of God's will establishes kinship with Jesus, who said, "*My mother and my brothers are those who hear the word of God and do it*" (Lk.8:21). When a woman in the crowd called out, "*Blessed is the mother who gave you birth and nursed you.*" Jesus replied, "*Blessed rather are those who hear the word of God and obey it*" (Lk.11:27f). In keeping with this

---

[11] TLC pp.405-6

principle, and true to the example of Mary and Joseph, Jesus said to a man healed of leprosy, *"Don't tell anyone, but go, show yourself to the priest and offer the sacrifices that Moses commanded for your cleansing, as a testimony to them."* (Lk.5:14). In effect, "Do what you know from the scriptures God requires".

There were many who heard God speak to them through Jesus, and they were obedient to his word. So Peter in what may have been his initial personal encounter with Jesus says to Jesus, *"At your word I will let down the nets"* (Lk.5:5); when Jesus said to the paralysed man, *"I say to you rise, take up your bed and go home"*, he did it (Lk.5:24f). The factor of obedience in many of the healing and exorcism stories is easily overlooked, when in fact it is often crucial and is an essential demonstration of the trustful response which Jesus recognised as conducive to healing.

A centurion is perhaps the supreme example of acknowledging the authority of Jesus' word. He said to Jesus, *"Say the word, and let my servant be healed"* (Lk.7:7f). The disciples seem compelled to acknowledge a divine authority in Jesus' words following the calming of the storm. They asked one another, *"Who is this that he commands even wind and water and they obey him?"* (Lk.8:25). In Luke's gospel obedience to and recognising the authority of Jesus are at times indistinguishable.

It is surely significant that following on from Peter's obedience to Jesus' word and its outcome, Peter fell at Jesus' knees and said, *"Depart from me, for I am a sinful man, O Lord"* (Lk.5:8). The holiness of Jesus is clearly recognised, and as with the holiness of God, humility and active obedience are appropriate responses. James, John and Peter *"left everything and followed Jesus"* (Lk.5:11). This is the kind of sacrificial obedience Jesus expected. As Mother Teresa put it, we will *"serve Thee as Thou deservest, and not ask for any reward, save that of knowing that we do Thy will"*. Jesus said: *"When you have done all that is commanded you, say, 'We are unworthy servants; we have only done what was our duty'"* (Lk.17:10).

Furthermore, Jesus believed that a failure to act obediently is not without cost. Jesus taught this through some of his parables: *"That servant who knew his master's will, but did not make ready to act according to his will, shall receive a severe beating"* (Lk.12:47). Following Jesus' questioning observation, *"Why do you call me Lord, Lord, and not do what I tell you?* Jesus offered the parable of the two house-builders. Non-obedience leads to the collapse of all we build up in our lives, whilst obedience provides a sure foundation to come through the trials and tribulations of life and death (Lk.6:46-49).

Chapter 3 - Luke

iv. Prayer

Luke's gospel leaves little room for doubting that for Jesus the attitudes of listening and obedience were predicated on prayer. It could be argued that Luke interwove a thread of prayer through the entire web of the gospel he wanted to share (e.g. Lk.5:15-16; 6:12; 9:18, 29; 22:32, 41-44; 23:34, 46).

Luke's gospel bursts into life with the story of the then childless parents of John the Baptizer. As John's father-to-be, Zechariah, burnt the incense in the temple the multitude were outside praying (Lk.1:8-11)[12]. An angel of the Lord appeared to Zechariah who told him, "*Your prayer is heard*". His wife would have a child (Lk.1:13). If Zechariah was praying for this, then in spite of his questions (Lk.1:18), his prayers embodied hopes way beyond any normal expectations. However, Luke is leading us to the words of the angel to Mary, "*With God nothing will be impossible*". Mary's answer to what she heard, "*Let it be to me according to your word*" (Lk.1:37) was a prayerful amen, humbly accepting the notion of doing God's will as her duty. The idea of God's right to rule our life is a challenge to anyone's faith, but probably the only proper basis for the prayerful relationship into which Luke's gospel invites us.

These opening prayers in Luke continue with three more prayers: that of Mary often called *The Magnificat* (Lk.1:46-55), the less well known psalm of Zechariah (Lk.1:68-79), and the *Nunc Dimitis,* Simeon's prayer in the temple (Lk.2:29-32). The same occasion in the temple, the infant Jesus' presentation, includes the insightful and disturbing prophecies of Hannah, described as a woman "*worshipping with fasting and prayer night and day*" (Lk.2:37). Later Luke records Jesus' words, "*And will not God vindicate his elect, those who cry to him day and night?*" (Lk.18:7). What Luke tells us of Hannah's prayer life seems to be what Jesus did: he cried, or prayed to God day - and night.

After baptism Jesus was praying when the Holy Spirit came upon him and he received God's benediction (Lk.3:21), and although Luke does not tell us Jesus was engaged in prayer when he was "*tempted by the devil*" (Lk.4:1-13), there are indications elsewhere in Luke that Jesus "*withdrew to the wilderness and prayed*" (Lk.5:16). Following an evening of intensive healing and exorcism Jesus, withdrew to a lonely place - probably to pray (Lk.4:42). As noted elsewhere, prayer for Jesus was seldom a public activity; but it was a regular if not unceasing necessity.

Moments of major significance in Jesus' own life were marked by prayer, as were those in his relationship to his disciples. Jesus withdrew to the hills to spend a night in prayer prior to choosing twelve from amongst his followers (Lk.6:12-16) and to

---

[12] It is interesting to compare and contrast the situation thirty years later (19:46)

delivering what might be called his keynote speech, the sermon on the plain (Lk.6:17-49). Luke tells us that Jesus was praying alone, though "*the disciples were with him*", when Jesus asked his disciples, *"Who do the people say that I am?"* which in this context of prayer led to the second and crucial question, "*But who do you say that I am?"* (Lk.9:18). The background tapestry of prayer for this momentous exchange adds an often missed dimension that it is probably part of Jesus' prayerful exploration of his own identity as much as an education for his disciples. In giving an account of what is sometimes called the transfiguration, contrary to how the story is sometimes interpreted, Luke does not indicate that Jesus went up the mountain to be transfigured, he tells us that Jesus went up a mountain to pray, this time with just three of his disciples. It was "*as he was praying the appearance of his countenance was altered and his raiment became dazzling white*". And from the cloud which overshadowed them a voice came which repeated the affirmation Jesus had received whilst praying after his baptism, "*This is my son*" (Lk.9:28-35). This time through Jesus' prayers the message is heard by his closest followers.

Jesus is a man of prayer, day and night, whose prayers are heard and answered. He is also one who encourages others to pray.

Toward the end of his apocalyptic prophecies Jesus says to his disciple, "*But watch at all times, praying that you will have the strength to escape all these things and to stand before the Son of man*" (Lk.21:36). When Jesus sent out another seventy disciples they were instructed to "*pray for the Lord of the harvest to send out labourers into his harvest*" (Lk.10:1f). When these seventy return after what seemed to be a successful mission, Jesus "*rejoiced in the Holy Spirit*" and offered a prayer of thanksgiving to the "*Father, Lord of heaven and earth*" (Lk.10:21).

Jesus' example of a prayerful life led to his disciples asking him to teach them to pray. He offered them a very simple prayer of five petitions (Lk.11:1-4), but with the important rider of the parable of the persistent needy neighbour. This emphasises that prayer is not a matter of instant gratification (Lk.11:5-8; see also the parable of the importunate widow and the unrighteous judge 18:1f.). Nonetheless it will be the "*Father's pleasure to give* (the disciples) *the kingdom*" (Lk.12:32 cp. Lk.11:2), and prayer is addressed to a heavenly father who will "*give the Holy Spirit to those who ask him*" (Lk.11:13). This last gift of God is not one of the five petitions in what we call the Lord's Prayer. There is more to praying than beginners can appreciate.

It should be noted that Jesus shared a parable with his disciples in which people also knocked persistently on a door, but their lives were such that for them the door was locked and they were told very firmly to go away: "*Depart from me all you workers of iniquity*" (Lk.13:25-27). In similar vein the rich man's prayers to Father

Abraham are refused because his life made him incapable of receiving such blessing (Lk.16:24ff). Jesus' observations regarding the Pharisee's and the tax collector's prayers make a related point (Lk.18:10f); and he very bluntly advised his disciples to beware of "*the pretence of long prayers*" as practised by the scribes whose behaviour belies their apparent devotion (Lk.20:47). Prayer, as with fasting, is of little or no real value when it is divorced from humility and self-giving (Lk.18:12). Indeed, true prayer is the expression of, and inspiration for these.

The prayers in the early chapters of Luke are often a grateful response to what God has done or can do, and the blind man near Jericho is moved to praise God (Lk.18:43). But gratitude as a motive for prayer seems sadly lacking in those who appear in much of the rest of Luke's Gospel. When a Samaritan, realised he had been healed of leprosy, he was the only one of ten who "*praised God with a loud voice* (and who) *fell at Jesus' feet giving him thanks*" (Lk.17:15f). Through the story of the ten lepers Luke records Jesus' awareness of the scarcity of such a grateful response. This should give us cause to reflect on how much we receive for which perhaps we neither feel nor express gratitude.

Throughout Luke's gospel prayer is ever-present, but perhaps even more so when Jesus approaches his death. He knew his death was to be in Jerusalem, the city which in Luke's account of Jesus' life was the scene of many episodes. Luke's gospel begins in Jerusalem when Zechariah is on duty in the temple. It is presumably the setting for the meeting of Mary and Elizabeth in which Mary praised God in her psalm (Lk.1:46-55). Jesus was taken there for his dedication (Lk.2:22ff). We are told that his Bar Mitzvah was one of the annual trips his parents made to Jerusalem (Lk.2:42). He was taken there in his temptation (Lk.4:9ff), and in a way "Jerusalem" sometimes came to him - "*Teachers of the Law and Pharisees came from every village in Galilee and Judaea, and from Jerusalem*" (Lk.5:17-26). Luke gives repeated reminders that Jesus is "*on the way to Jerusalem*" (Lk.9:52, 56, 57; 10:1; 13:22, 31-34; 14:25; 17:11; 18:31, 35; 19:1, 11, 28). It was in Jerusalem that Jesus shared his final meal and conversations with his disciples before his death (Lk.24:36-49). Jesus' believed his destiny lay in Jerusalem, the place which killed the prophets (Lk.9:31-36, 51f; 13:22, 31-33; 18:31-35), but he lamented over it because it was doomed (Lk.13:34f; 19:41-4; 21:20-24). On the temptations, one of which is set in Jerusalem, Charles Campbell says:

The context here is Jesus' engagement with and resistance to the powers of the world, here embodied in the figure of the devil. These powers are the great forces of the world that hold people captive; they are the institutions and systems, along with the driving spirit within them, that promise people life but in fact lead along the way to death[13].

At the heart of the city which Jesus wanted to cherish was the institution of the temple. This should have been "the prayer-filled centre of the nation's life", a symbol of all that God intended for the city and "his people". Instead it embodied the corruption which would inevitably lead to its destruction. Instead of feeding God's people, it fed off them, even squeezing the last penny out of them (Lk.21:4). So Jesus drove out the traders from the temple because, "*It is written, my house shall be a house of prayer, but you have made it into a den of thieves*" (Lk.19:45f). Prayer was not just a personal option for Jesus and his disciples. Jesus did not teach his disciples to pray for *my* bread, but *our daily bread.* Prayer had a corporate dimension; it needed to be at the centre of all life. Sincere and humble engagement in prayer is the basis of a life which is pleasing to God and of a hope which is greater than the present moment or individual history. The plight and prospect of the dying thief who prayed to Jesus on the cross is worthy of contemplation in this regard (Lk.23:42-43). Conversely, where there is an absence, and even more the discouragement, of such prayer it is an indicator that all is not, and will not be well.

If others failed, Jesus remained a man of prayer. When Jesus took the bread and the cup at the Passover meal, even as he contemplated his suffering (Lk.22:15), he *gave thanks* before giving the cup and the bread to his disciples (Lk.22:17, 19). The same action of prayer or blessing over the bread opened the eyes of the two disciples travelling to Emmaus to see that Jesus, who had died, had been journeying with them (Lk.24:30f). At the last supper Jesus told Peter he had prayed for him, prayed that Peter's faith might not fail (Lk.22:31f). On the Mount of Olives, whilst he wrestled with his own perplexity, Jesus told his disciples to pray for themselves that they would not *enter into temptation* (Lk.22:40,46 cp. Lk.11:4). Although strengthened by an angel, the intensity or earnestness of his prayer is graphically portrayed by Luke with the words. "*His sweat became like great drops of blood falling down to the ground*" (Lk.23:44). Jesus knew he had *a baptism to he baptised with* and he was *constrained until it was accomplished* (Lk.12:50), but having endured the baptism of the cross, Jesus' last words before death are a prayer, "*Father into your hands I commit my spirit.*" This moves the centurion to praise God (Lk.23:46). No doubt Luke intended his readers to be similarly inspired.

Jesus' death, of course, is not the ending of the prayerful relationship between him and his disciples. That would continue; and Luke's Gospel concludes with Jesus praying over, or blessing his disciples and their joyful, obedient and prayerful

[13] TLC p.319, 321

response (Lk.24:50-54). As Mary rejoiced in God her Saviour before Jesus was born, so his disciples also rejoiced after he had died and come to new life.

v. Generous, joyful living

Peter Marty speaks of the first disciples after Jesus' resurrection appearances to them:

"The disciples took the word and the blessing of Jesus to heart. Two things distinguished their earliest moments of togetherness: worship and joy. ... great joy! ... joy of the exhilarating and contagious variety (see Lk.2:10). And this joy would lead the church into the work of love and service that never ends"[14].

Not a programme, but a response! Zacchaeus' response, in keeping with the call of John the Baptizer for repentance and a new life in response to the coming of Jesus, was to give an assurance that he would rectify any wrong he had done and respond generously to the needs of the poor. The joy Zacchaeus experienced at being host to Jesus and accepted as of worth by God spilled over into practical deeds to bring joy into the lives of others. This joyful response by Zacchaeus is a proper response to God's kind of holiness (or wholeness) and leads to Raymond Bailey's observation:

Joy is a recurring theme in Luke's Gospel. Zechariah was told that John would bring joy to many (Lk.1:14), and Mary's visit to Elizabeth prompted John to jump for joy in the womb (Lk.1:44). The angels proclaimed great joy for all people when they appeared to the shepherds (Lk.2:10). Luke's sermon on the plain recorded Jesus telling the disciples that even rejection and suffering in God's service should evoke rejoicing (Lk.6:23). Joy is the refrain of those who hear and respond to Christ's good news (Lk.8:13; 10:17; 15:7, 10; 24:41, 52). The African American tradition more than most others has maintained a spirit of celebration of the hope embodied in Jesus even during periods of oppression. Some traditions have presented the gospel as a burden, bad news rather than good news. Preaching from Luke requires an emphasis on joy[15].

---

[14] TLC p.471
[15] Ibid. p.437

He Has Scattered Those Who Are Proud in Their Inmost Thoughts / the Imagination of Their Hearts ((1:51 NIV / RSV).
He Has Brought Down Rulers from Their Thrones (1:52)

These words of Mary invite a consideration of the many kinds of reversal which Jesus championed in word and deed; and the life or kingdom which emerges when the reversals have taken place [16].

Mary had pondered these things "in her heart" (Lk.2:19). Zechariah was told by an angel that his son, John, would "*turn the hearts of the parents to their children and the disobedient to the wisdom of the righteous*" (Lk.1:17). The heart can be the seat of compassion as is the case when Jesus sees the sorrow of the bereaved widow of Nain. Luke says, "*When the Lord saw her, his heart went out to her*" (Lk.7:13), but predominantly in Luke the heart is the seat of our deepest motives which produce so many of our actions. The heart can be the inspiration for all kinds of good or all kinds of evil. Jesus teaches, "*A good man brings good things out of the good stored up in his heart, and an evil man brings evil things out of the evil stored up in his heart. For the mouth speaks what the heart is full of*" (Lk.6:45 - see also 8:12, 15; 10:27; 12:34; 21:34). In Mary's psalm of praise the focus is placed on those "*who are proud in the imagination of their hearts*". Jesus more than once focused on a similar thing: "*You are the ones who justify yourselves in the eyes of others, but God knows your hearts*" (Lk.16:15 - see also 11:43; 20:46).

The dispersal or downfall of those who "*justify themselves in the eyes of others*", who see status in human society as their prerogative, is part of the great reversal which Mary foresaw and Luke elaborated. The Sermon on the Plain (Lk.6:17-49) with its blessings and woes includes these words, "*Woe to you when everyone speaks well of you*" (Lk.6:26). The story Jesus told about those who go to a feast and take the best places further emphasises the folly of this kind of self elevation (Lk.14:7-11), but probably the most forceful "parable" in this regard is that of the tax collector and the Pharisee:-

> "*To some who were confident of their own righteousness and looked down on everyone else, Jesus told this parable: "Two men went up to the temple to pray, one a Pharisee and the other a tax collector. The Pharisee stood by himself and prayed: 'God, I thank you that I am not like other people— robbers, evildoers, adulterers—or even like this tax collector. I fast twice a week and give a tenth of all I get.' "But the tax collector stood at a distance.*

---

[16] C.S. Song is worthy of note: "*God's politics does not consist of attempts to seize power. What it aims at is the transformation of power.. of human politics. It does not seek to dominate or to rule, but rather to effect a repentance/metanoia of power*" (*Third-Eye Theology: Theology in Formation in Asian Settings* Orbis Books1979).

He would not even look up to heaven, but beat his breast and said, 'God, have mercy on me, a sinner.' "I tell you that this man, rather than the other, went home justified before God. For all those who exalt themselves will be humbled, and those who humble themselves will be exalted" (Lk.18:9-14).

Mary's psalm foretold a great reversal which Jesus endorsed; but this reversal cannot be accomplished without cost. A friend, on hearing that I was studying Luke's Gospel said, *"Oh, I love Luke, it is such a gentle Gospel"*. I think not.

The ... great stumbling block in the stride toward freedom is the white moderate who is more devoted to "order" than to justice; who prefers a negative peace which is the absence of tension to a positive peace which is the presence of justice .... Every step toward the goal of justice requires sacrifice, suffering, and struggle; the tireless exertions and passionate concern of dedicated individuals[17].

The downfall of individual pride is followed in Mary's psalm with the downfall of political hierarchies which find their zenith in kingship, *"He has brought down rulers from their thrones"* (Lk.1:52). This will include the "spiritual" ruler of this world, Satan or the Devil. Jesus might on occasions encourage or give the blessing of peace (Lk.10:5; 24:36), but the reversal of world orders cannot be accomplished without violence. The theme of reversal is found throughout Luke's Gospel, and violence is never far away. I believe that sometimes we can be so familiar with the words, and read them so distanced by history, that we miss the nature of the reversal embodied in Jesus and the violence which was both prophesied for the future and a present reality in Jesus' life. There was a widely held belief that:-

"the Messiah would be a glorious and manifestly victorious figure to whom defeat and suffering would be entirely foreign....The messiah would confound the forces of moral, political or social evil experienced by the people....Jesus' understanding of Messiah runs counter to these expectations – moral, political and social forces will seem to overpower him – his fate will be one of ignominy, defeat and suffering"[18].

Jesus said, *"The Kingdom of God is preached, and everyone enters it violently"* (Lk.16:16 RSV). The proclamation and institution of "God's" kingdom involved a message and actions which challenged the power of other kingdoms, rulers and authorities. Inevitably there would be conflict. Simeon's words to Mary, *"A sword will pierce through your own soul"* (Lk.2:35), are an early indication that trouble lies ahead. Jesus' own words indicate he knew this; *"I came to cast fire upon the*

---

[17] Martin Luther King Jnr. (1963)

[18] TGL p.277 cf. the three main passion predictions in Luke 9:21-27; 9:43-45; 18:31-34

earth" (Lk.12:49). There may or may not be a political (Roman?) dimension to the "eagles" in *"Where the body is, there the eagles will be gathered together"* (Lk.17:37), but the saying certainly serves to highlight the gathering tension as Jesus' ministry approached its violent climax, and it parallels the martyrdom of the likes of Bonhoeffer, Romero and countless others. Being or becoming part of God's kingdom is not an easy matter. Tom Wright reflecting on baptism as a symbol of entry into the community of the kingdom says, *"Nobody drifts into the kingdom of God. Sooner or later there must be a dying and rising"*[19].

According to Jesus conflict and potential violence are of the very essence of his way of life: *"If anyone comes to me and does not hate father and mother, wife and children, brothers and sisters—yes, even their own life—such a person cannot be my disciple. And whoever does not carry their cross and follow me cannot be my disciple"* (Lk.14:26f). Most commentators suggest that "hate" for one's family as a condition of discipleship should be considered as a comparative term, that is, a disciple's family must take second place to loyalty to God's will, which is in keeping with Jesus' own example (Lk.8:19-21). But any downgrading of the importance of family for Jesus' contemporaries, and for many in the world today is unlikely to happen without familial conflict and social disapproval or even violent reaction. An over-familiarity with the symbol must not blunt the reality that the cross was an extremely violent and humiliating process of tortured execution involving extreme suffering: not to be embraced lightly.

John the Baptizer preached a message of repentance for forgiveness of sins (allied to Isaiah 40:3-5), and gave a warning of judgement *"Every tree that does not bear fruit is cut down and thrown into the fire …. He who is mightier than I is coming … he will baptize you with the Holy Spirit, and sift the wheat from the chaff "*(Lk.3:2b-19). Separation of wheat from chaff would have been by tedding, vigorously or violently throwing both together up in the air to divorce the heavier grain from the lighter husks which would subsequently be destroyed. This symbol or message of violent action against those who fail to respond to the inauguration of God's reign is present in a number of Jesus' parables. The servant who knows his master's will but does not do it *"shall receive a severe beating"* (Lk.12:46). The news of sacrilegious murders at Pilate's behest and the deaths resulting from the fall of the tower of Siloam leads to Jesus saying, *"Unless you repent you will all perish likewise"* (Lk.13:1-5). A postscript to the parables of the servants trusted with a nobleman's money says: *"But as for these enemies of mine … bring them here and slay them before me"* (Lk.19:27). And perhaps most significantly and prophetically, the parable of the vineyard, or of Israel, includes the beating of servants and the killing of the heir, with the outcome that the tenants themselves are destroyed (Lk.20:9-20). The parable includes Jesus' self-reference as the

---

[19] Tom Wright: *Virtue Reborn* - p.242   SPCK 2010

rejected cornerstone: "*Everyone who falls on that stone will be broken to pieces, but he on whom it falls will be crushed*" (Lk.20:18).

As the parable of the vineyard makes clear, violence is perpetrated not only against those who fail to offer an obedient response to the nobleman or king, but also against the messengers and the heir to the kingdom which Jesus proclaimed. The fullest declaration of this is in Luke 18:31-33; "*Jesus took the Twelve aside and told them, 'We are going up to Jerusalem, and everything that is written by the prophets about the Son of Man will be fulfilled. He will be delivered over to the Gentiles. They will mock him, insult him and spit on him; they will flog him and kill him. On the third day he will rise again*". The four-fold repetition of the prophecy in Luke is indicative of the importance which he attached to it (Lk.9:22, 44; 13:34, 17:25).

Jesus made it clear that his disciples, the servants or messengers of God's kingdom, would experience this violence, "*They will lay their hands on you and persecute you, delivering you up to the synagogues and the prisons*" (Lk.21:12). But violence will have much wider ramifications than simply being an individual matter. Luke certainly includes forecasts by Jesus of violent happenings at a personal level, but also at a national level, "*Then let those who are in Judaea flee to the mountains*" (Lk.21:21), international level, "*Nation will rise against nation* " (Lk.21:10) and cosmic proportions, "*the powers of the heavens will be shaken*" (Lk.21:26), because as Jesus put it "*these are days of vengeance*" (Lk.21:22). Seeds of violence sown in the rejection, persecution and killing of the messengers and the son of God would reap an unimaginable harvest of violent disorder and disaster.

Reports of violence or violent intent appear throughout Luke's gospel. It begins with the fate of John the Baptizer whom Herod shut up in prison and subsequently caused to be beheaded (Lk.3:20; 9:9). Herod probably intended the same fate for Jesus (Lk.13:31), but Jesus' most dangerous opponents were the "religious authorities". "*The Pharisees and the teachers of the law began to oppose him fiercely and to besiege him with questions, waiting to catch him in something he might say*" (Lk.11:53f). This intensified when he came to Jerusalem. When Jesus was questioned about the source of his authority he posed an unanswered question about John the Baptizer (Lk.20:1-8). His interrogators were "*the chief priests, teachers of the law together with some of the elders*" (Lk.20:1) the very people Jesus mentioned in his first passion prediction (Lk.9:22). Mullins sees this as "*the classical challenge between prophecy and institution ... (and)...the classical reaction of the institution*"[20]. As Luke tells us, "*Every day Jesus was teaching at the temple. But the chief priests, the teachers of the law and the leaders among the people were trying to kill him* "(Lk.19:47; 22:2). With the assistance of the Roman

---

[20] TGL p.441

governor, Pontius Pilate, they were successful. While under arrest at the high priest's house Jesus was subjected to verbal and physical abuse. The high priest's soldiers and then Herod and his soldiers "*treated him with contempt and mocked him*" (Lk.22:63-65; 23:11). Finally Jesus and two others were crucified (Lk.23:32f). But even his death, or baptism as he sometimes referred to it, would not bring peace but division in households because he came "*to cast fire upon the earth*" (Lk.12:49) and not to bring peace: "*Do you think I came to bring peace on earth? No, I tell you, but division*" (Lk.12:51)[21].

We can only speculate as to how much resistance Jesus believed his followers should make to violence against themselves. Jesus said to his disciples, "*Let him who has no sword sell his mantle and buy one*" (Lk.22:36): to which they replied, "*Look, Lord, here are two swords*", and he said to them, "*It is enough*" (Lk.22:38). The implication of this is that the disciples were already armed for the purpose of self defence. The arrest of Jesus, itself an act of violence, included the cutting off of an ear with one of the swords (Lk.22:47-54). Nonetheless, ultimately Jesus allowed himself to be crucified. He applied to himself his own words "*Do not fear those who kill the body, and after that have no more they can do*" (Lk.12:4).

The film, *Raiders of the Lost Ark* includes a spectacular scene in which the lid of the Ark of the Covenant is lifted. Upon this desecration an almighty destructive power is released which fills the earthly space and opens up the heavens. Luke pictures the outcome of the desecration of Jesus, the new ark, or embodiment of the new covenant, in a similarly dramatic way. Luke's account of Jesus' crucifixion includes a portent of the violence of national and cosmic proportions which was to come: "*The sun's light failed and the curtain of the temple was torn in two*" (Lk.23:45). Jesus may be the one who according to Zechariah will "*guide our feet into the way of peace*" (Lk.1:79) but this only happens after deliverance "*from the hands of our enemies*" (Lk.1:73-79).

Jesus both teaches and represents a radical reconstruction of society, and reversal of power. The tearing of the old cloth and the bursting of old wine-skins are graphic symbols of the violence involved in introducing the new into the old (Lk.5:36-39). This teaching follows Jesus' reminder that Elijah's miracles were contrary to expectations. They were not for Israel, but for foreigners (Lk.4:24-27). This blunt talking led to an attempt to kill Jesus (Lk.4:29). Jesus prophesied a great reversal "*Some who are last will be first, and some who are first will be last*" (Lk.13:30). Vested interests were threatened by such a message, fearful of it, and tried violently to suppress its promulgation.

---

[21] It should be noted that the angels' forecast of peace associated with Jesus' birth is "*to men on whom his favour rests*" (2:14) - soon to be followed by Anna's prophecy of the piercing sword (2:35)

But, reversal there would be. Crooked paths straightened, valleys filled, mountains brought low, the crooked made straight, rough made smooth, all symbolise the great reversal (Lk.3:4-6); and it is more than rhetoric. Jesus at times seemed bent on creating upheaval. Jesus preached to acclaim in Galilean synagogues for his unique "authority" (Lk.4:14-15), but after this initial approbation he provoked hostility in his home town of Nazareth (Lk.4:16-30). Eric Franklin says that according to Luke's gospel Jesus seems to invite or foment feelings against him[22]. Certainly the company he kept, his behaviour as a "guest", and his direct criticism of scribes, lawyers, Pharisees and priests were not designed to endear him to those powerful people who were the targets of his woes.

Early in his gospel Luke set the life of Jesus in the time of Tiberius Caesar, Pontius Pilate, Herod of Galilee, Philip and Lysanius, plus Annas and Caiaphas (Lk.3:1-2). These taken together constituted the political powers and religious authorities of Jesus' day – the establishment elite, underpinned with military might and social control. But Luke knew, and invited his readers to appreciate that according to Jesus, *"What is exalted among men is an abomination in the sight of God"* (Lk.16:15). However, as noted earlier, the main reversals on which Jesus seems to focus are not political, but religious, and social. Given the nature of his society these latter two were inextricably linked. The parable of the prayers of a Pharisee (socially upper class and religiously acceptable) and the tax collector (social pariah and religious outcast) reversed the normal expectation as to whose prayers would be acceptable to God (Lk.18:9-14). The parable of the rich man (blessed by God according to popular belief) and Lazarus (being punished by God with poverty) ended with the rich man in Hades and Lazarus in the bosom of Abraham (Lk.16:19-23 - see also 14:16-24 the parable of the great feast). These are powerful story pictures reinforcing a number of Jesus' sayings with the message *"Everyone who exalts himself will be humbled, and he who humbles himself will be exalted"* (Lk.14:7-11 see also 9:14; 13:29-30; 19:26; 22:26); and echoing Mary's, *"He has brought down rulers from their thrones but has lifted up the humble. He has filled the hungry with good things but has sent the rich empty away"* (Lk.1:52f).

The words of Jesus presage and then reinforce the greatest reversal of all: *"Whoever tries to keep their life will lose it, and whoever loses their life will preserve it"* (Lk.17:33). This is the ultimate choice which Jesus and everyone must make It has to be acknowledged that so often Christians and Christian institutions have chosen the latter option, setting as priorities self advancement or self preservation. In consequence the essentials of life which Jesus offered are lost. Self preservation and an avoidance of conflict may be regarded as "natural" human

---

[22] OBC p. 922

instincts, but capitulation to these is tantamount to rejecting what was integral to the battle in which Jesus engaged.

Also running throughout Luke's Gospel, although by no means a prominent motif, is another battle in which Jesus is personally engaged but which affects far more than just him. Jesus is in conflict with the devil, demons, or Satan, or Be-el-zebul. The evil, destructive forces with which Jesus and his disciples must contend are given all these different names.

The temptations for Jesus at a personal level as posed by the devil in or of the wilderness resulted in a moment of victory for Jesus (Lk.4:2-13). But the devil is neither defeated nor deterred: "*When the devil had ended every temptation, he departed from him until an opportune time*" (Lk.4:13). The battle would be rejoined, and the work of the devil continued. Although the devil may have failed with Jesus in the wilderness, in Jesus' explanation of the parable of the sower and the seed, the devil is still actively preventing other people from retaining the word in their hearts (Lk.8:12).

The devil is also credited with causing the physical ailments of some people. Luke describes Jesus as casting out a "*demon that was dumb*", with the result that the man dispossessed could then speak. There followed an accusation that he was in league with the prince of demons, Be-el-zebul. Jesus refuted the accusation, but clearly accepted the existence of Be-el-zebul, of other lesser demons, and of Satan (Lk.11:14-18). A woman who spent eighteen years unable to straighten up her body is described by Jesus as "*a daughter of Abraham whom Satan has bound for eighteen years*" (Lk.13:16). And when the seventy two disciples returned from their mission and reported that, "*Even the demons are subject to us in your name*", Jesus offered them the enigmatic picture, "*I saw Satan fall like lightning from heaven*" (Lk.10:17f).

As with Jesus' victory in the wilderness over the devil, the fall of Satan from heaven is not a final victory, for Luke tells us that when the chief priests and scribes in Jerusalem at the time of the Passover were seeking to find a way to put Jesus to death, "*Then Satan entered into Judas called Iscariot*" (Lk.22:3). Judas began the path of betrayal; just as others would follow a path of denial or desertion. Jesus was fully aware of this. At the last supper Jesus said to Simon Peter, "*Simon, Simon, Satan has asked to sift all of you as wheat. But I have prayed for you, Simon, that your faith may not fail. And when you have turned back, strengthen your brothers*" (Lk.22:31-32).

If Jesus was in conflict with, and tempted by the devil, demons, Satan, or Be-el-zebul, it seems reasonable to believe that those who truly follow him will inevitably share the same experience, contend with the same forces: though in the twenty-first century we may use different names for the ungodly or anti-Godly forces which confront or cajole us.

Undoubtedly Luke perceived in the works of God through Jesus the fall of the proud and the mighty and the raising up of poor and marginalised people. But are those who are raised up to assume the power of the mighty which in God's economy needed to be removed? Surely not: for what would be the point of such a reversal? What is needed is a new order or dispensation, which Jesus calls The Kingdom of God.

When Jesus' disciples asked him to teach them to pray, the second petition in the prayer Jesus invited them to say was "*Thy kingdom come*" (Lk.11:2). A possible repetition or expansion of the idea of the kingdom is given in the words, "*Thy will be done on earth as in heaven*", although some see this as a separate petition. There are those for whom the kingdom which is to come, and which will be the will of God, seems to have had a political dimension. We have mentioned earlier how Zechariah prophesied the downfall of "*our enemies*" (Lk.1:71, 73b), and the angel made what is a political forecast about Jesus to Mary, "*The Lord God will give him the throne of his father David*" (Lk.1:32f). When Joseph of Arimathea is described as one who was "*waiting for the kingdom of God*" (Lk.23:51), we cannot know how he perceived this kingdom, but for some it was a kingdom of and in this world. However, to rule over the kingdoms of this world is the second of Jesus' temptations in the wilderness, which is seen by the devil as in his gift, and therefore seen by Jesus as an unacceptable alternative to worshiping and serving God (Lk.4:5ff). As we have noted earlier God is not served best by "ruling over" people. Neither Mary's prayer, nor Luke's gospel as a whole, provides any support for the idea of even a benevolent dictator or monarch.

Commenting on Jesus' first mention of the kingdom of God (Lk.4:43), Mullins says,

It is very difficult to give a clear definition of the kingdom of God (or kingdom of heaven)...which is not a state or system brought about by good, religious, God-fearing people. It is "God's project", a divine plan to which one must respond. The mysteries of the kingdom are a gift of revelation of what is partly seen and partly hidden, partly present and partly future.... (in the, yet beyond) here and now. This calls for a paradoxical outlook on life and the world with its established assessments and values[23].

I would add that the great reversal of which Jesus speaks takes place through, or as a result of living out the values of God's kingdom. The kingdoms of this world

---

[23] TGL p.180

cling to different values. As long as they remain kingdoms of "this world" they will not change.

Whatever forms the kingdom may take in Luke's account of Jesus' teaching, the kingdom is an oft repeated subject. The beginning of the ministry of Jesus in Galilee is described as one of authoritative teaching (Lk.4:15ff, 31f), exorcism (Lk.4:33f, 41) and healing (Lk.4:39f) which leads to his declaration, "*I must preach the good news of the kingdom of God to the other cities also; for I was sent for this purpose*" (Lk.4:43. cp.8:1; 9:11). When Jesus sent out the twelve, and later the seventy, their commission included "*to preach the kingdom of God*" (Lk.9:2; 10:9, 11); and to the would-be disciple who wished to bury his father before following Jesus, "*Jesus said to him, 'Let the dead bury their own dead, but you go and proclaim the kingdom of God'*" (Lk.9:60).

But what exactly is this kingdom? Any commentator worth reading understandably struggles to answer this question because at best we have only hints, and at worst conflicting messages.

In Luke Jesus offers two parables, the mustard seed and the leaven, with the preamble, "*What is the kingdom of God like?*" (Lk.13:18-21), but we are given little information beyond the notion that it starts off as something very small, but full of potential or potency; so that it will grow, expand or work in ways which are beneficial to others. If potency and altruism are indicators of God's kingdom they can be seen in Jesus' own ministry. For example, of his exorcisms Jesus said, "*But if I drive out demons by the finger of God, then the kingdom of God has come upon you*". (Lk.11:20). But this saying raises a further question. Has the kingdom of God already come in or with Jesus? Although quite clearly Jesus was already living out the life of the kingdom, others were not. It seems to me that on balance, the evidence suggests that for Jesus the kingdom was still to come, although the time scale for its coming was by no means clear.

Jesus said, "*Truly I tell you, some who are standing here will not taste death before they see the kingdom of God*". (Lk.9:27). This saying leads directly into Luke's account of the transfiguration of Jesus in the company of three of his disciples (Lk.9:28ff). There are commentators who interpret this sequence as a prophecy followed by its fulfilment; but later as Jesus and his disciples approached Jerusalem, the disciples thought the coming of the kingdom of God had not yet happened, although it was imminent. Jesus responded with a parable of a nobleman who went away to a far country and left his servants to act faithfully and wisely. If, as seems most likely, the nobleman in this parable refers to Jesus, it could be said that the nobleman was already there, but the nobleman's going away and returning were prerequisites for being proclaimed as king (Lk.19:12). Within the Roman Empire this would have been readily understood, being normal practice for many of Rome's subservient territories in which puppet kings only took up their roles after a trip to Rome for permission to be requested and subordinate authority granted.

"Once, on being asked by the Pharisees when the kingdom of God would come, Jesus replied, 'The coming of the kingdom of God is not something that can be observed nor will people say, 'Here it is,' or 'there it is'' because the kingdom of God is in your midst." (Lk.17:20-21).

"The kingdom of God is in your midst" is difficult to interpret. It could mean that Jesus is amongst them and he embodies the kingdom, or as some translators have suggested it might mean the kingdom is within you; that is, in each person's being. Franklin, however, suggests that such a meaning would be *"unique in the New Testament"*[24]. On the other hand there is clearly a future or apocalyptic dimension to the kingdom of God, perhaps captured by a later phrase in Luke, *"sons of the resurrection"* (Lk.20:36).

The plain meaning of Jesus' words sometimes infers that the kingdom was still to come:

"Even so, when you see these things happening, you know that the kingdom of God is near. Truly I tell you, this generation will certainly not pass away until all these things have happened". (Lk.21:31-32),
"For I tell you, I will not eat it again until it finds fulfilment in the kingdom of God...... For I tell you I will not drink again from the fruit of the vine until the kingdom of God comes" (Lk.22:16-18).

Yet there is evidence that the kingdom, or at least its benefits, are for *this age* as well as *the age to come; "Truly I tell you,"* Jesus said to them, *"no one who has left home or wife or brothers or sisters or parents or children for the sake of the kingdom of God will fail to receive many times as much in this age, and in the age to come eternal life"* (Lk.18:28-30).

The expected outcome of these benefits is a different attitude toward the needs of the present moment. Jesus cautioned his disciples against worrying about the basic necessities of life such as food and clothing, and said, *"But seek his kingdom, and these things will be given to you as well. Do not be afraid, little flock, for your Father has been pleased to give you the kingdom"* (Lk.12:30-32). For this reason the poor are blessed, that is, already living the life which has room for the kingdom because it is not full of this world's goods: *"Blessed are you poor, for yours is the kingdom of God"* (Lk.6:20). Of little children who have no property, but who come

---

[24] OBC p.949

for a blessing, Jesus said, "*The kingdom of God belongs to such as these. Truly I tell you, anyone who will not receive the kingdom of God like a little child will never enter it*" (Lk.18:16-17). The property-less, those with no earthly power, the poor are blessed, but "*the rich are sent empty away*".

A rich man asked Jesus what he needed to do to inherit eternal life. The idea that it would be possible to "inherit" eternal life is an indication of a mindset which is probably a hindrance in itself. Unsurprisingly the call to dispose of his riches and to follow Jesus proved too much to ask. So, "*Jesus looked at him and said, 'How hard it is for the rich to enter the kingdom of God! Indeed, it is easier for a camel to go through the eye of a needle than for someone who is rich to enter the kingdom of God'*" (Lk.18:24f). Just how hard it has always been for those who are rich to accept that worldly poverty was Jesus' chosen way is exemplified by an event in Marseilles in the fourteenth century. Four men deemed to be heretics were burnt to death at the stake. Their "crime" or heresy, as identified by Pope John XXII, was to dare to say that Jesus lived in absolute poverty![25] The present Pope (2014), Pope Francis, eschewing opulence seems to stand in sharp contrast to many of his predecessors. When I was a student in Manchester I preached at a Baptist church in the Midlands. In the sermon I suggested Jesus might have been the son of a poor peasant girl. Someone wrote to the college principal to complain.

The humble poor (spiritually and materially) are blessed, but

"*The converse of this is that the rich, the full, the satisfied and the easily accepted are challenged and made to face the consequences of their lot. This leads to a self-satisfaction and self-sufficiency which is not only in danger of shutting them off from the grace of God but which also encourages a manipulation of their fellow human beings. At a number of points in his gospel, Luke will reveal his strong suspicion of riches and the challenge he believes they pose to would-be disciples (Lk.14:33; 16:1-15, 19-31; 18:18-30)*"[26].

Jesus spoke about the misery some would experience when they found themselves outside of the kingdom of God. Life in the kingdom is pictured as a meal at a table in company with "*Abraham, Isaac and Jacob and all the prophets*" and people gathered from all four corners of the earth (Lk.13:22-30). That this picture of the kingdom of God including a meal was current is shown in the comment of one of the guests at the house of the Pharisee, "*Blessed is he who shall eat bread in the*

---

[25] D. MacCulloch *A History of Christianity* Penguin 2010 p.411
[26] Franklin OBC p.935

kingdom of God" (Lk.14:15)[27]. But this led Jesus directly into a parable which foretold the reversal of expectations about who would actually be included in the kingdom (Lk.14:16ff). The disciples themselves may be surprised to be included, but Jesus at the Passover supper tells them: "*You are those who have stood by me in my trials. And I confer on you a kingdom, just as my Father conferred one on me, so that you may eat and drink at my table in my kingdom and sit on thrones, judging the twelve tribes of Israel*" (Lk.22:28-30).

In Jesus' teaching on the kingdom we have the presence of figures from the past, Abraham, Isaac and Jacob. This, combined with the experience in the present of Jesus at the table with his disciples for Passover, his prophetic words that he will never again eat until "*it finds fulfilment in the kingdom of God*" (Lk.22:18), and the indeterminate timing of the gift of a kingdom to his disciples, all lead me to conclude that to place the kingdom of heaven within a particular time-frame based on Luke's Gospel is not possible. What is possible is to say what kind of life and attitudes typify those who could be included in the kingdom Jesus proclaimed, and those who could not. The sermon on the plain (Lk.6:20-38) would serve well as a summary of the Q.E.D. for life in the kingdom of God.

……. But Has Lifted Up the Humble. (1:52)

Although Mary rooted her blessed state not in her own faith but in God's choosing of her (Lk.1:46-49), as a "*lowly servant*" Mary is a perfect example of the poor and humble, who in the new order will be lifted up.   We have noted earlier how the humble poor are blessed. A development or expansion of this feature of Luke's Gospel is to note how Jesus' own ministry is specifically targeted at those who could be described as "lost" or "marginalised", "brought low", and how these humiliated people, as well as those who humble themselves in the presence of Jesus, are lifted up.

Anyone who in any way was considered "unclean" was believed to be a threat to the well being of others. Understandably they would have been marginalised. It is therefore surprising that a man who "*had the spirit of an unclean demon*" should be in a synagogue in Capernaum (Lk.4:33), but this may be an early indication that Jesus throughout his ministry attracted and welcomed "unclean" people. Where this description is a reference to what today would be called mental illness, such a condition still has a marginalising effect for many, whether through self-imposition or the reaction of others. But all societies tend to have people who are labelled in some way as unclean or unacceptable, an underclass who are consequently

---

[27] It is not my intention to consider separately what Jesus' fellow guest might have meant by the phrase, *Kingdom of* God. But for a succinct and helpful treatment of the subject see N.T. Wright's *Jesus and the Victory of God* pp. 202-204 Pub: Augsburg Fortress 1997.

marginalised, even demonised. In England current examples are people labelled as unemployed or immigrant "scroungers"!

Luke's gospel is full of people who are on the margins. The first two characters to be introduced by Luke were Zechariah and Elizabeth. Luke's description is specific, *"Elizabeth was barren, and they were both advanced in years"* (Lk.1:7). But Zechariah's prayer was heard (Lk.1:13). Elizabeth conceived and was able to say, *"The Lord has done this for me ... In these days he has shown his favour and taken away my disgrace among the people"* (Lk.1:25) Someone who being barren would have been regarded as "dis-graced", outside of God's blessing, was lifted up out of that "dis-regard".

The first people, outside of the family to be told of the birth of Jesus were shepherds, who according to most commentators were regarded as ritually and probably physically unclean, living *outside* and with their sheep. Yet these outsiders became a paradigm for faithfully responding to the good news of Jesus. They were properly in awe of the heavens telling out the glory of God (Ps.19:1). They were obedient to what they heard. They sought out Jesus as a matter of urgency. They shared the good news they received, and they returned to their duty of care giving glory and praise to God (Lk.2:8-20).

Luke saw the ministry of John the Baptizer as a preparation for the work of Jesus (Lk.1:17). Among the multitudes who asked John the Baptizer what they should do were soldiers and tax collectors (Lk.3:10-14). The crowds would be fickle in their responses to Jesus, but two soldiers who were Centurions and gentiles, later served as exemplars of faith (Lk.7:1ff ; 23:47): and tax collectors in particular seemed to have been surprisingly positive in their relationship first to John and then to Jesus. *"All the people, even the tax collectors, when they heard Jesus' words, acknowledged that God's way was right, because they had been baptized by John"* (Lk.7:29). Jesus' call of Levi the tax collector to be his follower, and the subsequent saying, *"I have not come to call the righteous, but sinners to repentance"* (Lk.5:27-32) are indicators of the central thrust of Jesus' ministry. The parable of the Pharisee and the tax collector (Lk.18:9-11) and Jesus' encounter with Zacchaeus the tax collector (Lk.19:1ff) further reinforce this interest, as does the accusation which Jesus sarcastically reports, implicitly accepts and overtly recognises when he says, *"The Son of Man came eating and drinking, and you say, 'Here is a glutton and a drunkard, a friend of tax collectors and sinners'"* (Lk.7:34).

It appears to be commonly accepted amongst commentators that along with barrenness and unfit occupations, poverty, sickness or physical impairment were also regarded as indicators of being outside of, or beyond God's blessing – or even under God's curse. I question whether this was so for all those who were sick. My feeling is that the same class and wealth distinction operated which always does. With a few exceptions Jesus' ministry was to people on the streets, or to people brought out of their homes by friends to Jesus. These were almost certainly people who either always had little or no money, or people who had spent all they had on "treatments". They were poor as well as sick, and it was this combination which led to the popular perception of them as un-blessed. In truth, Jesus saw people in these conditions as those who were most open to receiving God's blessing. To John the Baptizer's enquiry whether Jesus is *"he who is to come"* Jesus' replied, *"Go back and report to John what you have seen and heard: The blind receive sight, the lame walk, those who have leprosy are cleansed, the deaf hear, the dead are raised, and the good news is proclaimed to the poor"* (Lk.7:21-22). Even to a thief on the cross Jesus said, *"Today you will be with me in paradise"* (Lk.23:43). This kind of inclusivity still challenges all those, including some who claim to be following Jesus, who put others into groups for approval or disapproval and claim divine sanction for so doing.

The opening statement of Jesus in his home town about his own work paralleled his response to John. It was taken from Isaiah: *"The Spirit of the Lord is on me because he has anointed me to proclaim good news to the poor. He has sent me to proclaim freedom for the prisoners and recovery of sight for the blind, to set the oppressed free, to proclaim the year of the Lord's favour."* (Lk.4:18f; cf. Isa.61:1f; 58:6). Whilst his declaration that this prophecy was being fulfilled was at first welcomed, when Jesus pointed out that no prophet is acceptable in his own country; and illustrated this with reference to the great prophets Elijah and Elisha who performed their miracles for foreigners, the result was hostility toward Jesus (Lk.4:22-27). If barren women, shepherds and the tax collectors were *persona non grata*, foreigners, especially Samaritans, were even more so. The disciples would willingly have destroyed the Samaritan village which refused to accept Jesus because he was going to Jerusalem, but Jesus rebuked them for such a thought (Lk.9:51-56). The story of the ten lepers, in which only one returned to Jesus, honoured him and gives thanks, praises a foreigner. The Samaritan was acting in a way which was more acceptable to God than the other nine who it would seem were Jews. Jesus said to the Samaritan, *"Your faith has made you well"* (Lk.17:11-19). This augmented Jesus' earlier expression regarding the gentile centurion that he *"had not found such faith in all Israel"* (Lk.7:9). Foreigners might have been outside the circle of acceptable Jewish society, but as far as Jesus was concerned they were within the compass of God's love and capable of exemplary faith.

The ministry of Jesus may have been situated predominantly in Jewish territory, but it is quite clear that his ministry was directed to those who were largely rejected within contemporary dominant Jewish norms of social and spiritual inclusion and exclusion. Perhaps significantly, the chapter completely dedicated to three stories of the lost (Lk.15:3-31), is prefaced with *"tax collectors and sinners drawing near to hear him"*, that is Jesus. The Pharisees and scribes, models of religious probity and social acceptance, probably in all senses chose to be at a distance from *"the sinners"*, and muttered their disapproval (Lk.15:1). The Pharisees and scribes may have had difficulty identifying themselves with the central characters of the first two stories, a shepherd and a woman, but related more easily to the wealthy father with sons who will inherit his wealth. However all three of the stories of lost sheep, lost coins and lost people appear to be told to both audiences with the inevitable lifting up of the spirits of those who know they are lost and consternation for those who hold "the lost" in contempt.

The ministry of Jesus is one of lifting people up physically and psychologically. The song of Mary his mother was an expression of her uplifting. Probably the most graphic illustration of the poor being lifted up is the healing of the woman bent over for eighteen years (Lk.13:13). But Peter's mother-in-law (Lk.4:39), Jairus' daughter (Lk.8:55), the widow of Nain's son as well as the widow herself (Lk.7:12ff), are just a few of countless numbers who were put down by the circumstances and mores of their day, but were lifted up, or uplifted, by the overriding compassion of Jesus' ministry.

He Has Filled the Hungry with Good Things (1:53a).

As is the case when sickness and poverty are properly bracketed together, so the descriptions "the hungry" and "the poor" often refer to the same people. The parable of the rich man and hungry Lazarus, who tried to live off crumbs from the rich man's table, is equally a parable of one who is well fed and one who is poor (Lk.16:21f). Jesus' target audience are those who are poor: *"He has anointed me to proclaim good news to the* poor" (Lk.4:18). The blessing of God shown in the compassion of Jesus is toward those who are poor and hungry (Lk.6:20), and on occasions he literally feeds them, as instanced by the feeding of the crowd of five thousand (Lk.9:12-17).

Jesus did not ignore wealthy people *per se*, for when the ruler of the synagogue's daughter was seriously ill Jesus went to her. Following her healing Jesus directed that she should be given something to eat (Lk.8:55); which may well have been part of the healing process which Jesus initiated. Conversely Peter's mother-in-law after being cured of a fever brought food to Jesus (Lk.4:39). It is interesting, but little commented upon, that Jesus himself post-crucifixion and resurrection asked his disciples for something to eat (Lk.24:42). Where the need for food was obvious Jesus knew provision should be made, and it was right to ask God to make such provision, *"Give us each day our daily bread"* (Lk.11:3). The seventy, who went out with scant provisions, sharing the lot of the poor, are told to expect and accept food and drink from willing hosts (Lk.10:5-8). *"Blessed are you that hunger now, for you shall be satisfied"* (Lk.6:21). The most obvious connotation for filling the hungry is food to eat, and we shall look at Jesus' actions and attitudes in this regard in a number of ways. But people may also be hungry for "the word that satisfies". In due course we shall also give this consideration, but there are other considerations related to Jesus sharing food on which it is worth reflecting. We turn to these now.

i. Mealtimes

The sharing of food and sitting at someone's table carried with it the demands of social and religious propriety. The meal at the house of Simon a Pharisee demonstrated how meals were about much more than just eating:

> Then he (Jesus) *turned toward the woman and said to Simon, " Do you see this woman? I came into your house. You did not give me any water for my feet, but she wet my feet with her tears and wiped them with her hair. You did not give me a kiss, but this woman, from the time I entered, has not stopped kissing my feet. You did not put oil on my head, but she has poured perfume on my feet".* (Lk.7:44-46).

Simon had not treated Jesus as an honoured guest might expect. On the other hand Jesus did not always behave as a gracious host might expect. Jesus on one occasion admonished his host with words regarding cleaning the outside whilst the inside is *"full of extortion and wickedness"*, but in the light of his host's understanding of acceptable praxis, what we might call good manners, Jesus was being rightly, though not openly, criticised because he did not wash before a meal at the Pharisee's house (Lk.11:37ff). It may well be that Jesus' omission was a deliberate provocation, dismissing by his words and actions the priorities of the affluent in favour of justice and inclusion for the poor and marginalised. As I know well from my sojourn in rural Jamaica, water can be a scarce commodity: using it for ablutions an unavailable luxury.

On another occasion when dining at a Pharisee's house Jesus healed a man with dropsy on the Sabbath (Lk.14:1-6). He then told two parables: one stressing the need to be humble by taking a lower place at table (Lk.14:7-11), the other about some who reject an invitation to a great banquet at which juncture the outsiders, the poor were invited (Lk.14:15-24). Filling the hungry with good things was not just something Jesus did, but his guidance for others too. Jesus, accused of receiving and eating with sinners, told three parables - the lost coin, lost sheep and lost son - the third of which includes a climactic celebratory feast on the son's (but also the sinner's!) return (Lk.15:1-2,23-24,32). But what we might very aptly call "the punch-line" was that his older self-righteous brother would not, or could not bring himself to be a participant in the meal (Lk.15:28-30).

A significant impediment for the kind of generosity Jesus encouraged was the notion that if you merited God's blessing God would make you rich. On this basis the poor were obviously not blessed by God and were therefore sinners, along with all those whose work was considered less than Godly. The Pharisees would know very well verses such as Ps.1:1-2 *"Blessed is the man who walks not in the counsel of the wicked, nor stands in the way of sinners"*. So when Levi, the tax collector, made a great feast for Jesus and his disciples, the rebuke they received for eating and drinking with "sinners" would seem to be justified by scripture. But Jesus was not walking *in the counsel of the wicked*, nor standing *in the ay of sinners*. Although his ministry was not for *the righteous*, he had come to call sinners to repentance (Lk.5:29f). For this reason his guest list was very different to those of the Pharisees in whose houses he sometimes ate: and the company he chose was just as different. It is especially noteworthy that Jesus' invited himself to Zacchaeus' house (another tax-collector) and thereby chose to become the guest of a sinner (Lk.19:5ff). It can be so much easier to be a benefactor for the poor than it is to be their guest or companion.

Jesus counsels against worrying about food and clothing (Lk.12:22, 26, 29), but concern and provision for those in need is Jesus' command to his followers: "*You give them something to eat*" (Lk.9:13) and *"Be generous to the poor"* (Lk.11:41).Churches have largely chosen to remember Jesus by recalling the feast of the unleavened bread in a room which was prepared (Lk.22:7-13) in which Jesus eats and drinks with his disciples (Lk.22:14-30) and at which he promises them a place at the table in his Father's kingdom. But effectively this has removed from the table of Jesus his requirement to give priority to the poor and to fill them with food and drink. Even worse, it has turned the table into an altar where Jesus is once again sacrificed for the satisfaction of those who are "in".

I would like to examine this a little further.

Mullins says of "the last supper" (Lk.22:14-38) that this is the last of a number of significant meals recorded in Luke as part of Jesus' ministry[28]. Although Mullins omits the hospitality at the house of Simon (Peter) which possibly played a significant part in Peter's response to Jesus' invitation for Peter to follow him (Lk.4:39; 5:2-10), Mullins lists the great banquet at the house of Levi (Lk.5:27-32, cp 15:32), the great dinner at the house of Simon the Pharisee (Lk.7:36-50), the multiplication of the loaves and fish at Bethsaida (Lk.9:10-17), the meal at the home of Martha and Mary (Lk.10:38-42), the midday meal at the home of a Pharisee (Lk.11:37-54), a Sabbath dinner at the home of a leading Pharisee (Lk.14:1-24), hospitality at the home of a chief tax collector, Zacchaeus (Lk.19:1-10), and the" last" supper (Lk.22:7-38) - to which, I suggest, must be added the

---

[28] TGL p.477. See also Hebrews 13:9ff

post resurrection meal shared with two disciples on the road to Emmaus (Lk.24:28-30) and the piece of broiled fish when perhaps only Jesus ate (Lk.24:42). This corresponds with the occasion when Jesus told her parents to give their young daughter something to eat after her life was restored (Lk.8:55). Taken together, the bread of Emmaus and fish in the upper room resonate with the feeding of the five thousand, but they are also a post-resurrection continuation of Jesus' multiple use of meals as symbols of tradition-challenging and inclusive hospitality.

Pazdan says: "*Ritual meals and table fellowship constitute major images for Jesus' community in Luke-Acts. Jesus welcomed everyone at his table*"[29]. Almost everything in this statement is open to question - at least with regard to Luke's gospel. The word "*ritual*", except in its broadest sense and with the one probable exception of the Passover meal, hardly applies as a normal description of most of the meals in which Jesus was involved. Furthermore, in Luke most meals are significantly not in *Jesus' community*, they are part of his involvement in wider society: and in my reading of Luke I cannot find a place where Jesus has 'his' table other than possibly the last supper which being held in an upper room would seem to have been something of a private affair. Furthermore not everyone was welcomed. There is little evidence that women and men were together at the table in most of the meals in which Jesus participated. And from his teaching, especially at some of the meals he attended, it is clear that all kinds of people were not invited to many of the meals in which he shared. Although Jesus' words consistently challenged this, as did the actions of some women, we should not go beyond the evidence.

Rather than inviting all and sundry to "his" table, Jesus accepted the hospitality of all kinds and conditions of people and, as in the case of Zacchaeus, even invited himself (Lk.19:5). Mullins makes a valid point when he says, "*Hospitality is a mark of a God-fearing person and the hospitable household is a sacred congregation in itself*"[30]. But so much of church life is predicated on, "*You come to us*". *We are the ones who have something to give.* Perhaps we need to learn to ask, *Can we come to you?* This would be a welcome acknowledgement that there is so much we need to receive or accept from others if we are ever to be of real service to them and faithful to what we know of Jesus. We are often chary of asking others to give to us (apart perhaps from their money), but Jesus' followers were encouraged to divest themselves of all that made them self-sufficient; then to ask for what they needed, and to accept food and drink from whomever was willing to provide it (Lk.9:1-3; 10:5-8). In the parable Jesus told Lazarus had it absolutely right. He showed the attitude Jesus' encouraged in his disciples, when he was

---

[29] TLC p.353
[30] TGL p. 269

prepared to feast on the left-overs[31], whereas the rich man was totally condemned when he thought of his meals as a private and exclusive matter. It would seem clear that according to our circumstances we may either be right to ask others for what we need, or if we have more than enough we are called as God's people to give others the food allowance they need at the right time (Lk.12:42-44). We are called to be servants. One of the duties of a servant is to provide food (Lk.17:8); but the servant is also worthy of being fed (Lk.10:7).

Roger E. van Harn on Luke 15 says that the three parables given in response to the criticism that Jesus received sinners and ate with them *"disclose that in his table fellowship with sinners, Jesus was already rejoicing in the restoration of the lost"*. Joy dominates and climaxes the first two of these stories with an obvious and telling muting of this at the end of the third. Harn asks what a church would be like if it were shaped by Jesus' table fellowship with sinners? He believes:-

> *"The church would be a party house where celebrations happen. The rejoicing of the angels can be heard and sung in the songs. The church is a fellowship that reaches forward to the new heaven and the new earth and brings its joyful songs into the present. Jesus heard the songs of the angels at his table of fellowship with sinners. The church that is shaped by that table can do no less"[32].*

ii. All are welcome

To a comment made to Jesus, *"Blessed are those who shall eat bread in the Kingdom of God"*, Jesus responded with the parable of invited guests who made excuses with the consequent, seemingly compulsory, inclusion of the urban poor, maimed, blind, and lame – as well as those who lived in the hedges and roadways outside of the city (Lk.14:15-24). Compelling the "poor" to come in is a definitive move against the social stratification which excluded such people from society – positive discrimination! However, rather than in-drag, which has some justification, if a church is to truly follow the example of its Lord, its members need to get out more. There is a need to join in other people's parties, or at least to create the kind of shared meals in times and places where others need them, not those which are convenient to us. The feeding of the five thousand is crucial in understanding how food is best shared in the name of Jesus.

> *"Here in the desert, in Galilee where Jews and Gentiles lived in close proximity to each other and to the surrounding pagan areas of Tyre, Sidon*

---

[31] Lazarus' action might be favourably compared with that of the disciples following the feeding of five-thousand where they also ate the leftovers (9:17)

[32] TLC pp.413-4

and the cities of the Decapolis, there are no special invitations, no boundaries between people on grounds of righteousness or sinfulness, ritual cleanliness or uncleanness, Jewish or Gentile background. All are fed with the food over which Jesus has said the blessing. In a gesture highlighting his prophetic and messianic roles, Jesus gives food to the world at large"[33].

Though Franklin says Luke in his story of feeding the masses does not use verbs which make the connection explicit[34], Mullins says, "*Jesus' words and actions reflect the words and actions by then established in the Eucharistic liturgy. Taking the five loaves (and two fish), looking up to heaven, saying the blessing, breaking the loaves, distributing them, are all words familiar from the liturgy*"[35]. The notion that the feeding must be read through the lens of what was "*by then established in the Eucharistic liturgy*" can only be sustained if Luke has attributed actions to Jesus which do not describe what really happened at the mass feeding. If Jesus did perform these actions at that time, the "last supper" could not be a reference point because it had not yet taken place. No "Eucharist" had become "established". The intrusion of later church praxis into interpreting the narrative which Luke offers invites drawing the wrong lessons, putting ritual before service to one's neighbour, and locating Jesus' action of self-giving primarily in a single, largely private meal in proximity to his death, rather than in his life-giving ministry of feeding the bodies, minds and hearts of any who knew their need and were wiling to participate.

Mullins says, "*The narrative offers a picture of Jesus as compassionate toward the leaderless people and concerned about their physical hunger. A church that invokes the name of Jesus must be concerned about the spiritual and physical hunger of people today*"[36]. Whilst agreeing with the lesson Mullin takes from Jesus' example, its expression has an inherent danger. Namely, it might still put churches in the driving seat and effectively lose the responsive and sacramental nature of the feeding of the multitude. A balance between "power over" and "power for" is not easy to achieve or maintain. In Luke's telling of the story of the feeding of five-thousand, the totally inadequate provisions of the disciples are blessed then set before the people and it seems most likely that they then fed each other (Lk.9:16).

The story of the Road to Emmaus (Lk.24:13-32) has been used to justify the elevation of the Eucharist above all other meals or feeding programmes. The comment is made that in the story we are told Jesus was known in the taking,

---

[33] TGL p.272
[34] TLC p.939
[35] TGL p.272
[36] TGL p.273

blessing, breaking and sharing of bread, which has become known as the fourfold action of the Eucharist. However, we are also told that these two disciples returned to share their experience with "the eleven". This most probably means they were not present in the upper room at the Last Supper[37], yet they still recognised Jesus in the breaking of the bread. Though churches have tried to make it so, the breaking of the bread in the upper room, for all its powerful symbolism, was not a unique or defining action: and in keeping with Luke's Gospel the Passover sacrifice, the crucifixion of Jesus is not the definitive saving act of God, but rather, along with the resurrection and ascension puts the seal on the salvific life-giving work of Jesus. In every age disciples travel with a Lord who is *incognito*. It is when the stranger breaks bread for us we may perhaps glimpse the action and the presence of Jesus with us wherever we are. This is worth repeating, because it runs counter to much which dominates churches' thought and practice. It is when the stranger breaks bread for us we may perhaps glimpse the action and the presence of Jesus with us wherever we are. How rarely do churches experience, or help others recognise this miracle?

Pazdan asks: "*While all may be welcome at the table of the Word, who speaks? Who is addressed? Who is left out? Why? While all may be welcome at the table of the Eucharist, who presides? Who serves? Who is nourished? Who is not fed? Why?*"[38] Honesty compels us first of all to acknowledge that church discipline means that in many churches *all* are not *welcome at the table of the Eucharist* as Pazdan suggests they are. Making the Last Supper a ritual and giving this ritual priority and an institutional pedigree has given large numbers of churches justification for a "closed table" or "altar". Many Protestants as well as Roman Catholics practice discrimination with regard to who can and who cannot participate in the sharing of bread and wine, the Lord's Supper. This is likely to remain so for as long as the emphasis is on The Lord's Table or the altar in a church, in especially reserved sacred spaces, rather than sharing the Lord's ministry of feeding which was "out there", and for those "outside", on the margins, in the world. The most astounding act of feeding by Jesus was in "*a lonely place*" (Lk.9:12), not in a building, not confined in any way[39].

---

[37] Though Luke tells us that the Last Supper was held in a large room (Lk.22:12). Jesus told Peter and John the preparation to be made was for "*us to eat the Passover*" (Lk.22:8) and they are to judge the twelve tribes of Israel: all of which strongly suggests only the Twelve were at the Last Supper.

[38] TLC p.353-4

[39] John's Gospel, by not including a pre-crucifixion "last supper", may deliberately have tried to restore the balance to Luke's account for those not predisposed to see the Eucharistic ritual predating and trumping the feeding of the multitude. The open air mass feeding, along with Jesus' meals with sinners/outsiders, was a challenge by Jesus to those who wanted to keep meals confined to members of their own circle of acceptance. It remains as a challenge to the churches.

Unlike the "*table of the Eucharist*" everyone, at least in public worship, may be *welcome at the table of the Word*, but it is extremely difficult to find a way to share the Word which is genuinely inclusive, which makes everyone feel welcome. For some, like me, too many visual aids will prove an annoying distraction. Others will find a twenty-thirty minute sermon overreaching their attention span or out of keeping with every other way in which they are engaged in learning and communicating in the twenty-first century. At a ministers' conference I was invited to pray with the aid of a spoken prayer said by the person conducting the worship. Simultaneously a series of pictures were each briefly projected on to a screen, and some music was played in the background just loud enough not to be easily ignored. There were those who were full of praise for this multi-media experience. I wanted to scream, then find a quiet room and shut the door. Being inclusive in a post-modern world may mean offering a range of different experiences from which people can make their own selection; but something important about churches as "inclusive communities" may be lost.

John Donne speaking in a bygone age wrote, "*No man is an island, entire of itself. Each is a piece of the continent, a part of the main*". In an age which has seen the introduction and proliferation of the aptly named "I"-pods and "I"-pads there is every encouragement to become disconnected from others. Fortunately modern technology also offers tremendous opportunities for social interaction to increase and new kinds of "communities" to be formed. The internet presents possibilities for new ways of being inclusive: but can churches seize the moment? Will we even want to venture into these often lonely places?

iii. Not by bread alone

Some Christians have been guilty of falsely interpreting Jesus' words, "*Man shall not live by bread alone*" (Lk.4:3), as "*people do not need bread to live*". Jesus' example should rule out any such thinking. The way of Jesus is not to deny people bread, food and drink, but to offer them more than this; to give them food which nourishes body, mind and heart.

As Bell and Maule put it in their hymn:

> *By the Galilean lake*
> *where the people flocked for teaching,*
> *the most precious Word of Life*
> *fed their mouths as well as preaching,*
> *for the good of us all* [40].

---

[40] J. Bell & G. Maule *Baptist Praise & Worship* No.199

One key element in the stories of Jesus' feeding multitudes is that along with the bread he offered himself. In a global society it may not always be possible or appropriate for there to be personal involvement in the entire process feeding mouths as well as preaching. This was explored in more depth when considering Mark's gospel in the section "What would Jesus do?" and will be considered again (e.g. in the introduction to John's Gospel), but suffice it to say here that the example of Jesus suggests the churches' efforts to feed the hungry need in some sensitive and genuinely beneficial way to involve self-giving as well as what can be disinterested donations.

iv. Teaching and Preaching

*"Luke portrays Jesus as a prophet and healer but also as a teacher like the great sages of Israel and the Greco-Roman world. He introduces him as a teacher at the beginning of his ministry on his return to Galilee (Lk.*4:15) *having already cast him in the image of a future great teacher in the scene with the doctors in the Temple* (Lk.2:46-7). *Jesus is spoken of as teacher or described as teaching several times throughout the gospel* (Lk.5:17; 6:6; 13:10, 22; 19:47; 20:1). *He is addressed as teacher even by his adversaries* (Lk.10:25; 11:45; 12:13; 20:28). *Luke's portrayal of Jesus at formal meals also reflects the practice of symposium meals where a renowned teacher is invited as guest of honour to lead discussion and answer questions. The sermon on the plain* (Lk.6:17-49) *... is an epitome or summary of teaching for the Christian community"*[41].

If it is necessary to make a distinction, we might say that on balance Jesus was more of a teacher than a preacher, for although Jesus on one occasion said *"the good news of the Kingdom of heaven is preached"* (Lk.16:16), only once does Luke record that Jesus was actually preaching (Lk.4:44). But Jesus was consistently called "teacher" (Lk.7:40; 8:49; 9:38; 10:25 in addition to Mullins' references above) and Luke repeatedly tells us Jesus was teaching (Lk.4:15, 32; 5:17; 6:6; 13:10, 22; 19:7; 21:37). As Mullins notes, Jesus was addressed by others as *teacher*, and on occasions used this as a self-description: *"A disciple is not above his teacher, but every one when he is fully taught will be like his teacher"* (Lk.6:40; cp. 22:11). A line between teaching and preaching, however, is not always easy to draw, nor perhaps always necessary.

It is commonplace to note that teaching in the time of Jesus of Nazareth was often conducted by progressive question and counter question. In this sense it might be that Jesus as a boy in the temple listening and asking questions was already

---

[41] TGL p.212

involved in the teaching process (Lk.2:46). Luke tells us that as an adult Jesus began his ministry teaching in the synagogues (Lk.4:15). After an initial warm reception (Lk.4:22) he was rejected in his home town of Nazareth (Lk.4:29), but he amazed people in Capernaum both with his teaching and with an exorcism (Lk.4:31f, 35). On more than one occasion Jesus' teaching on the Sabbath in a synagogue involved question and answer and was accompanied by an action of healing or exorcism. For example, when Jesus asked, "*Is it right on the Sabbath to do good or harm, to save life or destroy it?*" his question related to objections to him healing a man with a withered hand on a Sabbath. It invited reflective counter-questioning (Lk.6:6; cf.13:10-17 where a woman is healed in similar circumstances).

Although Jesus' ministry of teaching sometimes took place in the synagogues (Lk.4:44), Jesus taught from a boat (Lk.5:1-3) and elsewhere (Lk.5:15; 6:17; 8:1). In 9:51 Luke tells us that Jesus "*set his face to go to Jerusalem*". That journey was marked by teaching: "*He went on his way through towns and villages, teaching and journeying toward Jerusalem*" (Lk.13:22). When he arrived in Jerusalem the teaching continued. "*He was teaching in the temple daily*" (Lk.19:47f - also 21:37) which provoked a question from the chief priests and the scribes about his authority for doing this (Lk.20:1). The accusation against Jesus given to Pilate serves as a summary of Jesus' teaching ministry "*He stirs up the people teaching throughout all Judaea, from Galilee even to this place*" (Lk.23:5). There is more evidence that the "authorities" were *stirred* up than the people, but that his message was disruptive Jesus himself acknowledged: "*The Law and the Prophets were until John; since then the good news of the kingdom of God is preached and every one enters it violently*" (Lk.16:16).

Some of Jesus' teaching was by direct statements. For example, "*The son of man is Lord of the Sabbath*" (Lk.6:5); or Jesus' words to John the Baptizer's disciples: "*Go and tell John what you have seen .... the poor have good news preached to them*" (Lk.7:22). The commissioning and the work of the twelve included an instruction "*to preach the kingdom*" (Lk.9:1-2, 6), and this mission is a reflection and extension of Jesus' own ministry of teaching about the kingdom of God and healing (Lk.9:9-15). When his disciples asked Jesus to teach them how to pray his response was not a counter question, but instruction, "*When you pray, say ....*" (Lk.11:1f). There are exceptions, for example when Jesus used a child as a teaching aid about true greatness (Lk.9:46ff), or used bread and wine as symbols (Lk.22:17-20); but in Luke, when dealing with his disciples, Jesus' teaching seems mostly to have been by clear statement rather than by parable or question and counter question. Even when crowds are present, Jesus addressed his disciples first, and taught them (Lk.12:1-12): though they were cautioned, "*Take heed then how you hear*" (Lk.8:18).

Again, there are exceptions, notably the sermon on the plain (Lk.6:17ff), but in contrast to his teaching method with his disciples, much of Jesus' teaching for the crowds and at times his response to his critics, was by way of parables. Wilson, helpfully for those using a Greek New Testament, notes a difference in Luke between the word *oxlos*, used negatively for a crowd who are generally hostile to Jesus (Lk.3:7, 10; 11:14; etc.), and *laos* used for a crowd of those who are favourable toward him (Lk.2:18; 3:15; etc.)[42]; but the context is usually a sufficient indicator. Jesus' caution to his disciples about the nature of their listening followed on from the parable of the sower, seed and soil (Lk.8:1-15) addressed to a crowd (Lk.8:4). Similarly the three parables of the lost and found in chapter 15 are addressed to a crowd (Lk.15:1), but also directed specifically at his critics (Lk.15:2) as were a number of other parables such as old and new cloth (Lk.5:36); blind guides leading the blind (Lk.6:39); the rich fool (Lk.12:13ff); the Pharisee and the tax collector (Lk.18:9ff); the guest list (Lk.14:12ff); the great feast (Lk.14:16:ff); the vineyard (Lk.20:9ff) and the talents or pounds (Lk.19:11ff).

The specific nature of the audience for other parables, the Good Samaritan (Lk.10:25ff, 39), the parable of the importunate neighbour (Lk.11:5ff) and the shrewd manager - or dishonest steward (Lk.16:1 - cf. 16:14) are harder to determine. Perhaps this is deliberate on the part of Luke, because whilst a parable might be directed to a certain person or group, the relevance of the teaching could have wider application. For example, the parable of the dishonest steward makes the universally valid point that how we use money now can have future repercussions. However, the tailoring of many parables to a specific target audience should caution against the common assumption - especially when preaching - that all parables are easily given a universal application.

My own delight in Jesus' parables is bound up with the fact that they are all based on perceptive observations of life. Social stratification, the varied world of paid employment, housework, the treatment of material wealth, the experience of poverty, health and sickness, hospitality - sometimes grudgingly given, religion and ritual, human behaviour and the world of nature (Lk.12:22ff; 13:6; 18, 21:29), and so much more. The good teacher and preacher must be equally alert to seeing the rich diversity of life and to discern where a lesson might be learned and perhaps a blessing or a woe given. In my final year of college training for ministry, Greek Street Baptist Church in Stockport gave me Michel Quoist's, *Prayers of Life*. More than forty years on I still turn to it from time to time as a book of 1970's parables, many of which are as relevant today, and all of which mirror the spiritual perceptiveness of Jesus. As George Herbert put it in the seventeenth century:

---

[42] TLC pp.312, 315

Chapter 3 - Luke

"A man that looks on glass,
On it may stay his eye;
Or if he pleaseth, through it pass,
And then the heaven espy."

Two further thoughts about Jesus' teaching need to be mentioned. The first is that at the last supper Jesus told his disciples that the scriptures had to be fulfilled in him (Lk.22:37; Isa.53:12), and on the road to Emmaus *"beginning with Moses and the prophets, he interpreted to them in all the scriptures the things concerning himself"* (Lk.24:27 see also Lk.9:22; 17:25; 24:44f). Given the context of this scriptural self-referencing by Jesus, the use of scripture as a basis for teaching is important. But it seems to have been used by Jesus only with his disciples, and even with them used sparingly. Apart from the opening of Jesus' ministry when the scriptures were handed to him and Jesus said to the synagogue congregation, *"this day is this scripture fulfilled"* (Lk.4:21), Jesus rarely used the scriptures as a basis for teaching or preaching. Churches in contrast use it extensively, and in church circles it can seem that knowledge of the Bible is honoured above knowledge of life. This imbalance means that much of the time churches mentally inhabit a distant place in a bygone age and unsurprisingly preach to or teach themselves not others.

The second and perhaps most important thing to be said about Jesus' teaching is that it was by example as well as words. He welcomed the sinner and the outcast; he stayed calm in the face of danger; he filled the hungry with good things; he stood and spoke against hypocritical and oppressive religion and the abuse of power; he prayed privately and sincerely; he said, *"Father, forgive them, for they know not what they do"* (Lk.23:34); he gave his body and his blood, and in death he entrusted his soul to his father God (Lk.23:46). He was the Good Samaritan, and he still says to those who will listen and learn from his teaching, *"Go and do likewise"* (Lk.10:37).

The Rich He Has Sent Empty Away (1:53b)

i. Riches -an impediment

John the Baptizer invited people to prepare the way for the one *who is to come.* When the crowd asked John, *"What should we do then?"* he answered, *"Anyone who has two shirts should share with the one who has none, and anyone who has food should do the same."* (Lk.3:7-11). Even before Jesus' ministry began Luke set out the basic principles of generosity and social responsibility which Jesus saw as essential for life in all its fullness for everyone. Throughout his teaching Jesus echoed the dictum that if someone has more than enough, and someone else has nothing, it is not acceptable to ignore the need: "*Every one to whom much is given of him much will be required*" (Lk.12:48a).

A rich ruler came to Jesus asking what he had to do to "*inherit eternal life*" (Lk.18:18). Jesus did not pick up on the odd notion that eternal life could be *inherited*. Instead he commended the rich ruler for his faithful observance of the Law of Moses, but went on to challenge the rich man, "*You still lack one thing. Sell everything you have and give to the poor, and you will have treasure in heaven. Then come, follow me*". (But) w*hen he heard this, he became very sad, because he was very wealthy. Jesus looked at him and said, "How hard it is for the rich to enter the kingdom of God!*" (Lk.18:22-24). Luke then contrasts the rich ruler who cannot give up his wealth with Jesus' disciples who have, and records Jesus' promise, "*Truly I tell you,*" Jesus said to them, "*no one who has left home or wife or brothers or sisters or parents or children for the sake of the kingdom of God will fail to receive many times as much in this age, and in the age to come eternal life.*" (Lk.18:29-30). What the rich man wanted, eternal life, was only available when his riches became unimportant to him. The same is true for all.

Jesus' sermon on the plain reversed contemporary thinking which held that the rich were to be seen as blessed and the poor as cursed. Jesus said: "*Blessed are you who are poor, for yours is the kingdom of God. Blessed are you who hunger now, for you will be satisfied.*" But, "*Woe to you who are rich, for you have already received your comfort. Woe to you who are well fed now, for you will go hungry*" (Lk.6:20f, 24f). The word *woe* should probably be read sometimes in the sense that it naturally has when someone says "*Woe is me*". That is, it is not so much condemnatory. It is rather a bewailing, an expression of profound regret for the lost-ness such as that experienced by the rich man above and in the parable of the rich man and Lazarus (Lk.16:19ff). On the other hand the word "Woe" can convey both the desire to see something cease and of damnation. Contemporary examples might be practices of people trafficking, or of imprisonment without trial. In a most obvious rendition in story form of Jesus' blessings and woes, the rich man ignores the poor man at his gate, and Abraham talking to the rich man after both he and the poor man have died, says, "*Son, remember that in your lifetime you received your good things, while Lazarus received bad things, but now he is comforted here and you are in agony*" (Lk.16:25). Young's literal translation of this passage possibly captures the meaning best when it uses the word *distressed* in place of *in agony*. The physical torment is not paramount, but rather the loss of God's favour as shown by the great and unbridgeable chasm separating the rich man from Abraham. Abraham is the archetype of acceptance by God because in common with Jesus, and Jesus' disciples at their best, Abraham was prepared to leave all and give all.

ii. Right priorities

Eternal life is a way of living informed by distinctive priorities. A request for Jesus to arbitrate in an inheritance matter led to the parable of a rich, but foolish, selfish and self-satisfied farmer. Jesus' said, "*So is he who lays up treasure for himself, and is not rich toward God*" (Lk.12:13-21). This parable is followed with Jesus' advice to those who follow him not to be anxious about life, food and drink, clothing, stature, which *all the nations* seek, but rather to seek the Father's kingdom which the Father will be pleased to give them. And Jesus concluded:

> "*Sell your possessions and give to the poor. Provide purses for yourselves that will not wear out, a treasure in heaven that will never fail, where no thief comes near and no moth destroys. For where your treasure is, there your heart will be also*" (Lk.12:22-34).

The parable of the astute, but dishonest steward (Lk.16:1-9) should caution against too readily drawing conclusions about Jesus' thinking with regard to the use of wealth. Jesus said, "*I tell you, use worldly wealth to gain friends for yourselves, so that when it is gone, you will be welcomed into eternal dwellings*" (Lk.16:9); but also says, "*Whoever can be trusted with very little can also be trusted with much, and whoever is dishonest with very little will also be dishonest with much. If then you have not been trustworthy in handling worldly wealth, who will trust you with true riches?*" (Lk.16: 10f). The steward whom Jesus commends for his astuteness has been untrustworthy and dishonest. But the point is surely that he has acted to alleviate the debts or poverty of others. The money is secondary to acts of generosity. When Jesus said, "*No one can serve two masters. Either you will hate the one and love the other, or you will be devoted to the one and despise the other. You cannot serve both God and money*" (Lk.16:13), he probably had in mind the Pharisees described in verse 14 as *lovers of money*, but the words might equally apply to the dishonest steward who put care of his neighbours before his duty to preserve the wealth of a master who apparently allowed his tenants to get into serious levels of debt. No wonder Jesus advised his disciples to consider carefully how they listened (Lk.8:18). Moral codes must be superseded by compassionate action.

A similar prioritisation with regard to received "right behaviour" was evident, "*when a Pharisee invited Jesus to eat with him*". The Pharisee was surprised when he noticed that Jesus did not first wash before the meal. "*Then the Lord said to him, 'Now then, you Pharisees clean the outside of the cup and dish, but inside you are full of greed and wickedness. You foolish people! Did not the one who made the outside make the inside also? But now as for what is inside you—be generous to the poor, and everything will be clean for you'*" (Lk.11:37-41). The Pharisee, like the rich young ruler (Lk.18:18) kept the law, but also kept his money, and failed the test of getting his priorities in the right order.

Jesus' words, "*be generous to the poor, and everything will be clean for you*" merit emphasis. They bring to mind watching a priest's actions at the end a Eucharist in which bread not wafers had been used. He meticulously ensured that every single crumb was gathered up so that, to use his words, "*the Body of Christ is properly respected*". This particular priest is but one of countless examples of attention to correct procedure. I know I am strongly influenced by the teaching I received in my youth against any notion of transubstantiation. Even taking that into account, Jesus is surely not best honoured by such ritual niceties, but by a generous outpouring of costly love for the poor who need his ministry today (Lk.7:36-50).

Perhaps to counterbalance the parable of the dishonest steward, Luke also records Jesus' parable of ten servants who are each given an equal amount of money with which to trade (Lk.19:11-28). Those who increase their master's wealth are rewarded *pro rata* with extra trust. In contrast, the one who failed to even invest the money is roundly condemned. His money is taken from him and given to the one who made the most money. This leads to Jesus' judgement, "*To every one who has will more be given, but from him who has not will be taken away even that which he has*" (Lk.19:26). On the surface this seems to be in direct contradiction to Jesus' teaching that the wealthy in this world will be the ultimate losers. However, it is important to note that all the master's servants received equal sums of money, they were equally wealthy. But one servant failed to use his master's wealth for any good purpose. One rich man kept his wealth in barns; another kept it for himself on his table; another kept it hidden in a napkin; all have missed their opportunities to be generous; and all are lost - sent empty away.[43]

In considering Luke's account of Jesus and those with wealth, it should not go without comment that wealth and power often go hand in hand, as do power and corruption. The consequence of this is danger. Jesus saw it in Herod's treatment of John the Baptizer. Herod had John shut up in prison (Lk.3:19-20) and beheaded (Lk.7:9). Jesus saw it in the behaviour of the scribes who "*devour widows' houses*" (Lk.20:45-47). And he knew it in the activities of the Scribes and Pharisees "*lying in wait for him to catch at something he might say*" (Lk.11:53f). We see it in England today when a strident dissident voice (Brian Haw) in Parliament Square has been literally out-lawed, when illegal imprisonment or detention of migrant

---

[43] C. S. Song offers a persuasive contextual, political and social interpretation of Luke's parable of the pounds. However, given this parable's resonance with other parables told by Jesus I suggest it is reasonable to regard the parable as intended to evoke a more personal evaluation of whether we are generous with what God has entrusted to us. (C. S. Song *Third-Eye Theology* pp.223ff Lutterworth Press)

children or migrants with mental illness has been practised by the British Home Office[44], and Guantanamo Bay Prison operated by an "ally" contrary to most standards of human rights remains largely unchallenged. As I write, the British government are "lending" £2.5 billion to the corrupt regime in Oman so that Oman can buy gun helicopters made by British Aerospace: what the Jubilee campaign call a "dodgy deal". Similar and worse examples of the abuse of power and the corrupting nature of wealth abound across the world.

In Jerusalem there was great wealth as well as abject poverty. In Jerusalem the rich and powerful would conspire to put Jesus to death, not realising that in this total self giving Jesus lived and died in fulfilment of his own teaching. It is therefore perhaps unsurprising that in Jerusalem Jesus drew a lesson from the offerings of *"the rich* who *contributed out of their abundance"* and the widow who gave *"all the living she had"* (Lk.21:1-4). Sacrificial generosity is *sine qua non* for those who would follow Jesus' way. Those who would keep their wealth for themselves Jesus knew to be those who were really lost and empty.

His Mercy is Upon Those Who Fear Him From Generation to Generation.
He Has Helped His Servant Israel, in Remembrance of his Mercy,
As He Spoke to Our Fathers, to Abraham and to his Posterity for Ever.
(1:50,54f)

All of Mary's emotions and words in her prayer of praise and prediction were grounded in her trust in the faithfulness of God. Jesus and his followers were called to be faithful, to persevere and to endure, because that is to reflect the nature of God, to embody the Spirit of God. The bedrock of Jesus' self commitment was his trust in the continuity of God's purposes which had been witnessed, could still be seen, would continue to be revealed, and would be fulfilled.

Whilst the present is always in some sense created by what has gone before, Luke fully appreciated that especially in the work of Jesus there is a drawing together in the present of past and future. This is perhaps evident when Luke's gospel itself is said to be based on the testimony of *"eyewitnesses and ministers of the word"* (Lk.1:2). It is interesting to note that at the end of his Gospel Luke records Jesus words to his disciples; *"You are witnesses of these things"* (Lk.24:48). Perhaps some were the very witnesses used by Luke. In recent times there has been a growing appreciation of the role in ancient societies of *eyewitness* who had a duty to accurately remember events and ensure their transmission. In no sense was this some game of Chinese Whispers. It was a very serious engagement in passing on from generation to generation the stories or events which were part of the genetic

---

[44] for details of specific cases go to http://www.bhattmurphy.co.uk/bhatt-murphy-89.html

construction of a people or nation. Their past gave them their present identity, and strength and guidance to face the future.

Unsurprisingly the eyewitnesses who inform Luke's gospel referred to other writings or characters whose stories had previously been passed on. Zechariah was *of the division of Abijah*. His wife Elizabeth was *of the daughters of Aaron* (Lk.1:5). Joseph was *of the house of David* (Lk.1:27). The work of John the Baptizer was seen as being *in the spirit and power of Elijah* (Lk.1:17ff), and later as fulfilling a prophecy of Isaiah (Lk.3:4-6). Zechariah's prophecy included what might be seen as a summary of Luke's view of the past feeding into the present. Zechariah rejoiced that God *"has raised up for us a horn of salvation in the house of his servant, David"*: and he echoes Mary's words (Lk.1:54f) when he speaks of *"the mercy shown to our fathers ... the oath which he swore to our father Abraham"* (Lk.1:69-73). Luke in fact took his readers way back beyond Abraham. By means of a genealogy going right back to God Luke affirmed that the entirety of human history has been the outworking of God's initiative in the begetting of Adam, and had been leading up to the birth of Jesus (Lk.3:23-28).

The words in Luke's prologue, *"The things that have been fulfilled amongst us"* (Lk.1:4) were an early indication of Luke's conviction that what unfolded in the story of Jesus was "necessary", in the sense that it continued and fulfilled the Old Testament story of God and God's people. Jeffrey John makes the valid point that in considering the gospels, *"the key to unlocking the meaning will often lie in the Old Testament"*[45]. Jesus' story was part of God's will, plan or design (cf. Lk.9:22, 44; 12:50; 13:33; 18:31-34; 24:26-27). Luke wished to emphasise the continuity of God's purposes, but this certainly did not mean a simple repetition of what has been in the past. The naming of Zechariah and Elizabeth's son as John (Lk.1:13, 61) was one example of there being a break with the past as well as assurances for the faithful from it. Hence a break from the past was not a rejection of it. Jesus may already as a twelve year-old have recognised that in his life a heavenly father's rights were paramount. He nonetheless observed the fifth commandment to honour his father and mother (Lk.2:49-51). And in his teaching, three parables - mending old cloth with new material - putting new wine into old wine skins - drinking new wine after old - led to the possibly unexpected and oft overlooked conclusion that *"The old is good"* (Lk.5:39)

There are many ways in which Luke presented deeds and sayings of Jesus as mirroring the lives of the prophets and the words of the scriptures. The most obvious being when Jesus began his ministry, he was given the scroll of the prophet Isaiah and he announced that the prophet's words found their fulfilment in him (Lk.4:17-21). But there are other examples. Luke offered a very brief account

---

[45] Jeffrey John *The Meaning of Miracles* p. 8. SCM/Canterbury Press 2001

of five loaves and two fish, blessed and broken, feeding five-thousand men. Terse details such as the people being divided into companies of fifty, food provided in the desert, and baskets of left-overs (Lk.9:12-17), are all reminiscent of Old Testament stories from Exodus, Numbers and Deuteronomy (see especially Elisha in 2 Kings 4:42 -44). It is surely also legitimate to see the stories of a gentile soldier whose faith exceeds that found in Israel, closely followed by Jesus restoring to life the son of a widow who lived in Nain (Lk.7:1-17), as having parallels in stories of Elijah and Elisha (1 Kgs.17:17-24; 2 Kgs.4:32-37; 5:1ff). It is possible that Luke's readers would have equated Nain with the town of Shunem, where Elisha performed a similar miracle[46]. Jesus' reference to *"the stone which the builders rejected"*(Lk.20:9-18) is a quote from a Psalm (Ps.118:22; cp.20:42 & Ps.110:1). Jesus' death was being actively sought, as Luke reiterates, at the time of the Passover (Lk.22:1f, 7f, 13) and Jesus presaged his death in the Passover ritual of a special meal (Lk.22:7-13). Jesus not only knew the scriptures but he used them to shape his life and thought. However, the story of the transfiguration (Lk.9:28ff) is perhaps the most graphic expression of both the continuity and discontinuity of the great prophets and the Son of man. Jesus told his disciples, *"Many prophets and kings desired to see what you see"* (Lk.10:23f). In Jesus something was happening which had been longed for, but never before realised. Moses and Elijah have importance beyond words as prophets, but, *"This is my Son, whom I have chosen: listen to him"*.

The life of Jesus was neither a simple, natural continuation of the past, nor just something new which arose solely as a result of present circumstances. For Luke, what was happening had always been intended by God. Jesus as God's son (Lk.3:22; 9:25) had to live the life, die the death, and enter into the greater life which God had both planned and foretold through his prophets. Jesus was walking a predestined path. Luke hammers home this point. The Son of man *must* suffer many things (Lk.9:22).

> *"The Son of man is to be delivered into the hands of men* (Lk.9:44).
> *I have a baptism to be baptized with, and how I am constrained until it is accomplished"* (Lk.12:50).
> *"The Son of man must suffer many things and be rejected by this generation - as it was in the days of Noah"* (Lk.17:24-26).

At the tomb the women were reminded of what Jesus told them in Galilee *"that the Son of man must be delivered into the hands of sinful men, and be crucified, and on the third day rise"*(Lk.24:1-11).

---

[46] cf. Craig Evans TLC p.349 or David Holwerda TLC p.345

In his account of Jesus' arrest, Luke uses the words, *"When the hour came"* (Lk.22:14). Given that Jesus himself shortly afterward told those who come to arrest him, *"This is your hour and the power of darkness"*, it is probably not reading too much into this as signifying an hour or time that was predestined. There was not just a broad outline plan in God's purposes for Jesus, but, as the writer of Ecclesiastes says, for everything there was a time. Thinking back to the story of the shepherds, it is important to remember that the praises of the shepherds followed on from the praises of the angels. If as Franklin suggests *"the world is on the move"*, so were the heavens: and, as we have already seen in the angel activity toward Zechariah and Mary, so was God. It can only be said in faith, but God's time had come.

All of these things which *must* happen had been foretold in the scriptures. Jesus told his parents, *"I must (dei) be in my Father's house"* (Lk.2:49)[47]. Jesus told the twelve disciples that they were going up to Jerusalem, *"and everything that is written of the Son of man by the prophets will be accomplished"* (Lk.18:31). To the two disciples on the road to Emmaus Jesus explains, *"Was it not necessary that the Christ should suffer these things and enter into his glory. And beginning with Moses and all the prophets he interpreted to them in all the scriptures the things concerning himself"* (Lk.24:26-27). There are those who are wary of interpreting the Old Testament in the light of the New. Jesus seemed not to share this concern. However, it must be remembered that Jesus read the scriptures both as a Jew and as a guiding influence for his life. The difficulty for most of us of the first point, and the enormous challenge of the second, might caution us in our use of the Jewish scriptures and in any attempt to see Jesus behind every verse - especially as Luke's account of Jesus' use of the scriptures suggests Jesus made a highly selective use and a radical interpretation of them.

Three points can be made in conclusion on the subject of Jesus as part of God's plans.

First, although Jesus' path had been predetermined or predestined by God, this did not mean for Luke that Jesus had no other option than to walk that path. The story of Jesus being tested in the desert (Lk.4:1ff) is an early indication that Jesus had choices. He determined upon the path he believed God had prepared for him. Midway through the Gospel Luke tells us of another crucial choice made by Jesus. Jesus *"set his face to Jerusalem"* (Lk.9:51), fully aware that *"it cannot be that a prophet should perish away from Jerusalem"* (Lk.13:33). Then on the Mount of Olives toward the end of Jesus' life we are told that Jesus consciously and painfully set God's will above his own, *"Not my will, but yours, be done"* (Lk.22:42), which

---

[47] See Marty TLC p.307 for the significance of the word *dei* as *"characterizing Jesus' entire life"*.

enabled the final surrender, *"Father, into your hands I commend my spirit"* (Lk.23:46). If God had a plan for Jesus' life, it was not self-evident, it needed to be lived in faith, and it could have been avoided. The same will be true for each of us.

Second, when Jesus appeared to his disciples after his death he used looking back on the fulfilment of scripture in his death and resurrection as a springboard for the purposes of God which were yet to be fulfilled: *"Repentance and forgiveness of sins should be preached in his name to all nations"* (Lk.24:44-47). As Jesus said, *"No one who puts his hand to the plough and looks back is fit for service in the kingdom of God"* (Lk.9:62 // 1 Kgs.19:20). To draw on the prophetic insights of the past is to follow in Luke and Jesus' footsteps, but even more we should be allowing those scriptures to propel us into a future inspired by the same prophetic faith, and yet more so by the spirit and example of one who was greater than all the prophets.

Third, it seems to me that many commentators are so preoccupied with the demography of the commission (Lk.24:47), that its substance is overlooked. *"Beginning with Jerusalem"* may be of importance in the context of Luke's account of the life of Jesus, and interpreted as "starting where we" may be a principle worth embracing: but the content should surely be of greater import than the context. The singular hope of Jesus' commission in Luke is *"preaching of repentance and forgiveness of sins"*. Is that really the churches' primary and costly message? And of greater importance we should be asking, is it our practice? Are we people who are repenting, living changed lives, and who forgive others as God is ready to forgive us – *Remembering to be merciful*?

Luke's Gospel invites us, the readers, to follow in the steps of John the Baptizer preparing people for *"the one who is to come"* and in a spirit of faith and hope to rejoice with Mary that his coming into our lives will change us and has the potential to transform the entire world into God's kingdom. As Fred Kaan expressed it in his well known hymn:-

Sing we a song of high revolt;
Make great the Lord, his name exalt:
Sing we the song that Mary sang
Of God at war with human wrong.
Sing we of him who deeply cares
And still with us our burden bears;
He, who with strength the proud disowns,
Brings down the mighty from their thrones.

By him the poor are lifted up:
He satisfies with bread and cup

The hungry folk of many lands;
The rich are left with empty hands.
He calls us to revolt and fight
With him for what is just and right
To sing and live Magnificat
In crowded street and council flat.

Fred Kaan 1929-2009

Chapter Four
JOHN'S GOSPEL: JESUS - GIFT AND GIVER

Introduction

For many years I found it helpful to liken John's Gospel to a symphony in which the major motifs are set out at the beginning[1]. These are then developed and augmented as the piece proceeds until there is a glorious resolution. I think there is still much to commend this approach. However, in re-reading John for this study of the gospels it felt more akin to listening to the bagpipes, because although a wide range of melodies are played and often replayed in various keys and with a range of harmonies, underneath it all a consistent and persistent drone gave the whole work its constant harmonious quality and unique character. The constant which I discern within the whole of John's gospel is that Jesus is God's gift who can be received or rejected (Jn.1:10f; 14:17). As the disciples came to know, everything that Jesus had was a gift from his Father, including themselves (Jn.17:6f); but everything Jesus received from his Father he offered back to his Father. The relationship is one of total reciprocity - *"All I have is yours, and all you have is mine"* (Jn.17:10). This mutual indwelling and outpouring of Father and Son is the keynote of the Fourth Gospel and which will sound throughout the following commentary.

The development or elucidation achieved by progressive repetition of key phrases[2] and the variations on this central theme of giving means that the division of John into discrete chapters is not generally helpful. So the chapter numbers which appear in parenthesis in the commentary below are given only as guides to where the main references are to be found for the subject under review, they are not markers of concrete ends or beginnings or divisions. Kiefer, following D.F. Strauss, likened John's Gospel to the seamless undergarment of Jesus, *woven in one piece from the top* (Jn19:23)[3]. Dorothy Lee possibly better than any other has presented the case for reading the fourth gospel as *unified literary and theological utterance*[4]. And Richard Baukham offers a very convincing literary case for seeing John's gospel as a unified work in which the prologue (Jn.1:1-18) and the epilogue (Jn.20:30 – 21:25) are carefully constructed so that the narrative epilogue of 496 words is not some later addition, but is designed by the author to deliberately

---

[1] Burridge likens it to an *overture* TLC p.472

[2] "Progressive repetition" W. Meeks *The Man from Heaven in Johannine Sectarianism* Journal of Biblical Literature Vol. 91, No.1, 1972

[3] OBC p.960 & UFG p.19 n17

[4] Dorothy A. Lee *Flesh and Glory, Symbol, Gender and Theology in the Gospel of John* (New York: Crossroad 2004)

balance the poetic prologue of John 1:1-18 which has 496 syllables[5] In another work Baukham clearly states his view, *"In my view the gospel is an integral whole, including both the prologue and the epilogue, and was designed as such by a single author."*[6]

But there are those who dispute the integral unity of John and espouse alternative views. I have engaged critically with two of these, Ashton and Michaels. Although I may take a different view at times to those espoused by these scholars, their works have nonetheless been extremely helpful as well as challenging[7]. For those readers who may wish to further consider what Ashton and Michaels have to say I have included an extensive footnote at the end of this chapter. This may well not be of value to every reader.

Suffice it to say here that Ashton holds that John's gospel as we have it today was subject to many revisions and additions in its earliest days of existence, on which basis Ashton suggests we can discount large parts of the fourth gospel. Ashton also says that the gospel was produced to encourage a group of Jewish Christians who had been expelled from their synagogue and can only be properly understood with that in mind[8]. Both Ashton and Michaels accept Bultmann's dictum that in John's gospel *Jesus as the revealer of God reveals nothing but that he is the revealer*. This dictum has been tremendously influential in Johannine scholarship, but I find it unhelpful for two reasons. First it means the gospel must be read and understood within a very rigid framework of interpretation, which is quite contrary to the freedom of spirit to which the gospel itself testifies. Second, an overemphasis on revelation has a tendency to prioritise creed over gift, and even to extinguish completely John's testimony to Jesus as gift and giver.

The theme of Jesus as gift and giver finds a variety of expressions in John's gospel. Before working through the gospel in a more systematic way it is worth pondering some features of the fourth gospel which are instructive. For example, John does mention that Jesus had twelve disciples, though not often (Jn.6:67, 70, 71; 20:24). Some of Jesus' twelve disciples are never named, and most get scant personal recognition, or make cameo appearances; Peter being the one exception. The whole

---

[5] R. Baukham – *Jesus and the Eyewitnesses* 2006 Eerdmans p.364f
[6] R. Baukham – *The Testimony of the Beloved Disciple* Grand Rapids 2007
[7] The Gospel of John - J. Ramsey Michaels - Eerdmans NICNT 2010 and John Ashton *Understanding the Fourth Gospel* Oxford (2nd Edition) 2007
[8] Snodgrass would reject any such assertion. *"I find it unlikely that any of the gospels was written for a specific local or serves 'primarily' to address the problems of such a community. They are direct communication written for a broad audience to convey material about the teaching and life if Jesus in order to create followers of Jesus"* (Klyne R. Snodgrass *Stories With Intent* Eerdmans 2008 p.33).

of John's Gospel is predicated upon the testimony of one disciple, the unnamed *"disciple whom Jesus loved"* (Jn.21:20-24). This unnamed disciple testifies that Jesus himself was God's gift (Jn.3:16), was the recipient of God's gifts (Jn.3:35; 5:22-7; 6:37-39; 10:28f; 12:49; 13:3; 17:2, 6-8, 11f, 22- 24), and was the giver of those gifts (Jn.3:34; 4:10; 5:21; etc). Indeed, at one point Jesus himself affords his Father's gifts the greatest priority: *"That which the Father has given me is greater than all things"* (Jn.10:29). God was offering through Jesus more than anything anyone could ever imagine. It seems akin to criminal that commentators should miss out on recognizing the gospel's witness to a mind-blowing offer.

Part of what is astounding in John is the multiple ways in which Jesus offers himself. For example, the statements of Jesus which begin, *"I am"*. These, might superficially seem to be self-promotion, arrogant or revelatory, especially since *I am* can be regarded as a name for God. But at the heart of John's Gospel is the message that in Jesus the generous self-giving, even self-sacrificing spirit or activity of God was presently at work.

Jesus' giving of what his Father has given to him and gives through him is often couched in terms of the obedience of Jesus as a son to God as his father. Jesus acknowledged his dependency on his Father. If Jesus was the vine, his Father was the vine grower (Jn.15:1-5). If Jesus was the bread of life, the Father is the one *"who gives the true bread from heaven"* (Jn.6:48, 58). It was the overflowing life of the Father which was always overflowing through Jesus (see e.g. Jn.4:46-54; 11:25). It was there to be seen in Judaea and Galilee in the one who in John's Gospel is *"The Man from Nazareth"* (Jn.1:45f; 18:5, 7; 19:19 - cp. 7:40ff.). The life-giving word was given to and for the world in flesh and blood.

Jesus is the medium or gateway, or channel for God's gifts. *I am the gate* is the gift of freedom and plenty with security (Jn.10:9; 8:36). *I am the way* is the gift of guidance through example and mutual trust (Jn.14:4, 6 - Fackre suggests *reconciliation*). *I am the truth* is the gift of trustworthiness (Jn.14:1, 6)[9]. Michaels speaks of *doing the truth* and links this with the Hebrew sense of *"acting faithfully as one who gives allegiance to God"*[10]. But he also sees *Jesus' truth* as the same thing as *truth about Jesus*[11]. These two notions, however, are essentially different. Jesus words, *I am the truth,* as with all the *I am* sayings, is not primarily a description or revelation of who Jesus is, but an intimation of what Jesus gives, or offers, and what can be received through him of the life or spirit of God which pulsates in, through and out of Jesus like living water (Jn.4:10, 14; 7:38; 19:34). The grace and truth which Jesus brings, he brings from the Father (Jn.1:14). It is

---

[9] Fackre suggests *revelation*, and for "life" *redemption* TLC p.548
[10] TGJ p.208f
[11] Ibid. p.838

God who is truth-full (Jn.3:3). The *I am* sayings give verbal expression to the nature of God, and in this sense they are prophetic. Once this is acknowledged it is not essential to accept Ashton's suggestion, utilising form criticism, of a repository for the "*I am*" sayings pre-dating and independent of the fourth gospel. Although Ashton's point is well made that what Jesus offers most of all is himself, he overstates his case by asserting that Jesus came to bring "*nothing other than himself*"[12]. Jesus' words are what the Father has given him, and his ultimate gift is the love of his Father and the comfort and guidance of his Father's spirit, not himself - "*For the one whom God has sent speaks the words of God, for God gives the Spirit without limit*" (Jn.3:34; 14:10; 17:8).

John's Gospel has been referred to as *the book of signs,* sometimes restricted to seven in number. In my experience there has sometimes been an unhelpful equating of signs with miracles, with connotations of supernatural powers. Only two signs in John's gospel are given a number: turning water into wine, and the healing of the royal official's son. They are connected not only by location (Jn.2:1; 4:46 - Cana in Galilee) but both are only performed with a recorded measure of unease by Jesus. To his mother he says, "*Woman why do you involve me?*" (Jn.2:4), and to the royal official, "*Unless you see signs and wonders you will never believe*" (Jn.4:48). Following the feeding of about five thousand people, Jesus said to the crowds who came looking for him, "*Very truly, I tell you, you are looking for me, not because you saw signs, but because you ate your fill of the loaves. Do not work for the food that perishes*" (Jn.6:26f). Jesus knew the danger. They saw miracles, short-term satisfiers, not signs, or "in-sights" which could provide spiritual nourishment and challenge.

A few years ago I was at a conference attended by about sixty Baptist ministers. The speaker, Pat Took, asked us how we might use the story of the raising of Lazarus (Jn.11:1ff) in our preaching or in a pastoral way. For a while no one answered, so I made the point that as a miracle the story has no practical use. Our people die, and to proclaim that they can be called out from their grave (or more commonly the crematorium's flames) after four days would be a cruel hoax - just as it would be to send five loaves and two fish to the starving thousands in the horn of Africa. But to share the stories in John's gospel as signs of love-inspired generosity, of death-defying hope, and of a spirit which generates peace through trust: to share these things which God offered and signified in and through Jesus gives a genuine and valuable gospel basis for pastoral work in every circumstance. Put bluntly, looking for miracles is a quest for the naïve, superstitious and shallow. Signs, on the other hand, are for the one who does not follow the crowd (Jn.6:66-68), the genuine seeker after truth (Jn.14:6), the one who abides in the word and in whom the word abides (Jn.15:6f). Michaels is right to say, "*The signs*" ... *are not*

---

[12] UFG pp.125, 128

necessarily miraculous, but full of revelatory significance". Jeffrey Johns adds further food for thought. Miracles are "*literary creations with a theological purpose*" and "*with different levels of meaning*". Among the levels he discerns are Christological, typological, eschatological, symbolic and sacramental[13]. Jesus' actions as signs offer all of this and much more.

It is perhaps helpful to think of the signs in John's Gospel as related to the contribution the word 'sign' makes to the word significant. John was aware that a number of moments and sayings in the story of Jesus were of particular significance; not only signifiers of what he had to give, but also at times sign-posts indicating Jesus' direction of travel and where he was on his journey. For example, he was heading toward his "hour" (Jn.13:1, 17:1), but since it had not yet arrived the wedding feast and rejoicing must go on (Jn.2:4). He was going to, and showing the way to his Father from whence he had come (Jn.14:6, 20:17). Using the word "significance" as a key to understanding John's Gospel provides a literary and theological rationale for those parts of John's Gospel in which an event or saying is accompanied by debate or teaching. As with Jesus himself, the "signs" are not ends in themselves; they are an invitation to contemplate and as much as we are able to accept what God has to offer.

(Chapter 1)

Often in the fourth gospel an action is followed by narrative. In chapter one the teaching or proclamation is given first, by the author of the Gospel and in the ministry of John the Baptizer.

> "*In the beginning was the Word, and the Word was with God, and the Word was God. He was in the beginning with God. All things came into being through him, and without him not one thing came into being. In Him was life*" (Jn.1:1-4a).

Crucial here is that "*the Word was God*", and since this so clearly echoes the opening chapter of Genesis, this is the Word which God uttered, God "expressing" Godself, God's very essence being "fleshed out" - earthed as well as universalised. God's word makes things *egeneto* - happen, come to pass. In all creation from the very beginning Godself was God-giving - or indeed, God's self-giving was and always is the beginning. John tells us that in all creation, in history, and now in Jesus, God's own life or spirit or word was active in self-giving, making things happen, being poured out -. "*What has come into being in him was life - and the life was the light of all people*" (Jn.1: 3b-4a). "*He gave power to become the*

---

[13] TGJ p.173. See also Jeffrey John *The Meaning of Miracles* pp 5-7 SCM/Canterbury Press 2001

Chapter 4 - John

children of God"(Jn.1:12): and, perhaps the crucial text for all that follows, "*from his fullness we have all received grace upon grace*" (Jn.1:16).

The *fullness* of Jesus is partly expressed in the various titles he is given. Here, in Jesus, was someone who had everything to offer that had been promised to God's people. He was *Messiah/Christ* (Jn.1:41), *someone of whom Moses wrote, and of whom the prophets wrote* (Jn.1:45), *Son of God ... king of Israel* (Jn.1:49). Jesus was also what was needed, *Lamb of God* (Jn.1:36), *Rabbi* (Jn.1:38). Jesus was that for which people hoped, *Son of Man* (Jn.1:51). Additional evidences of Jesus as God's gift are given by John the Baptizer when he is questioned about Jesus' successful ministry. Consider the gifts and how they are given which is evident in these words of Jesus:

"*No one can receive anything except what has been given from heaven*"(Jn.3:27). "*He whom God has sent speaks the words of God, for he gives the spirit without measure. The Father loves the Son and has placed all things in his hands. Whoever believes in the Son has eternal life; whoever disobeys the Son will not see life, but must endure God's wrath*" (Jn.3:34-35).

The gift and the giver may be accepted or refused, but there can be no doubt that John wants his readers to know what is on offer, and that God the Father in heaven is the ultimate source and arbiter of all that can be received or rejected.

The action in chapter one includes comment that this incarnation of the Word, and the offer of life through Jesus, evoked a response of scepticism in those who had been sent by the Pharisees (Jn.1:24-5). Conversely a welcoming response came in the nascent discipleship of Andrew and his un-named co-disciple: then Andrew's brother Simon Peter, Philip and Nathanael[14]. These first disciples are the first recipients of an insight into the relationship of Jesus and his Father: "*No one has ever seen God. It is God the only Son, who is close to the Father's heart, who has made him known*" (Jn.1:18). This is a relationship which they will see in action, into which they will enter in due time, and which is offered to them as a gift. As Jesus put it pictorially to Nathanael, "*Very truly I tell you, you will see the heaven opened and the angels of God ascending and descending upon the Son of Man*" (Jn.1:51). The modern idiom is apt: when the heavens open they pour out their contents.

(Chapter 2)

Chapter two actually offers two "signs", though only one is thus described. First, John recounts an incident at a marriage feast. At Jesus' behest six stone jars filled

---

[14] cf. Jn.3:19-21; 5:43; 7:12, 30ff; 8:24 for further evidence of this contrast in reactions to "the light" which had come into the world.

156

to the brim with 20-30 gallons of water became the best wine (Jn.2:6-9). Intriguingly, John offers no additional comment on this sign other than to tell us that this was *"the first of his signs in Cana of Galilee"* (Jn.2:11 see 4:54; 20:30). Self evidently it was a gift to meet the need of a friend and/or the concern of his mother, but within John's account of this sign Jesus said to his mother, *"My hour has not yet come"* (Jn.2:4). Then his mother *said to the servants,* *"Do whatever he tells you"* (Jn.2:5); and John follows this up by informing his readers that the Steward did not know from where the wine had come, *"though the servants who had drawn the water knew"* (Jn.2:9). Commentaries often focus on the "miracle" of turning water into wine, and/or the superabundance of the wine provided. Bauckham holds that *the extravagance of Jesus' gift is integral to the story's significance*[15], and is prescient of Jesus' words, *"I am come that they might have life, and have it abundantly"* (Jn.10:10). The overwhelming, joy-producing giving is of importance. But the *hour* and the *servants who knew,* and who are *obedient* are also aspects of this sign which will feature throughout this gospel. They are applied not only to his followers, but to Jesus himself, and are linked to *his glory* in ways which a focus on the miraculous can easily obscure (Jn.2:11 & see below on 17:7ff).

It may also be worth noting that the "best" wine is rarely if ever wine which has just been produced, or which is produced with a lack of tradition and experience behind it - it lacks vintage! If the new wine represents Jesus, or what Jesus was offering, it is not new in the sense of being a novelty. Jesus had taken time to mature, and his work was drawing on the lived and recorded faith of countless generations as well as the fathomless resources of the supreme viticulturist, his Father in heaven.

Another sign in Galilee was to follow later (Jn.4:54). Only these two Galilean signs are numbered, but there were many others. For example, John describes the feeding of five-thousand as *"what he had done as a sign"* (Jn.6:14). There were many signs in Judaea and Jerusalem (Jn.2:23; 3:2, 6:2, 14; 12:18, 37; 20:30). The ubiquity of signs in John undermines James Matthew Thompson's view, shared by Ashton, that John used a *Book of Signs* the contents of which only last to the end of chapter 12. To justify his conclusion the reference to signs at 20:30 has to be relocated to the end of chapter 12[16]. In fact, in John's gospel, although all the named disciples who were chosen by Jesus were found in Galilee (discipleship is also a gift!), the majority of Jesus' recorded ministry was located not in Galilee, but in Jerusalem. Contrary to Thompson and Ashton, John tells us that in Jerusalem

---

[15] TLC p.491
[16] UFG p.50

many believed in Jesus "*because of the signs he was doing, but Jesus on his part would not entrust (give) himself to them, because he knew all people*" (Jn.2:23f; see also 5:42; 16:30; 21:17). In John's Gospel Jesus may be the man from Galilee (Jn.7:42), but it is most evident in Jerusalem that he comes to his own and his own will not receive him (Jn.1:11).

If there is a division in John's Gospel it is more between a receptive Galilee and a hostile Jerusalem or Judaea than a ministry of signs and a postscript of passion. It is a generalisation, but has truth in it to say that Judaeans "looked down" on people from Galilee or Nazareth. France emphasises the considerable divide between Judaea/Jerusalem and Galilee as geographic, political, cultural, linguistic and religious; to which one could add historical. The late twentieth/early twenty-first century North-South divides of countries such as Chad, Sudan or even to some extent England provide parallels to first century Palestine[17].

The second, but unnumbered, "sign" in chapter two took place in Jerusalem: the clearing or cleansing of the temple. Taking the temple back for God and giving it, or opening it up to those who should have been able to worship God in freedom (Jn.2:14-16). Although John does not designate this as a sign, it may be regarded as a sign since it led to the question and answer session in which Jesus told the Jews about the impending destruction and raising up again of the temple, with John's editorial comment that Jesus was referring to his body (Jn.2:19-21). The Jews who incongruously asked Jesus for a sign or miracle to justify his action are typical of all those who are not able or willing see the significance of Jesus' words and actions played out in front of them.

(Chapter 3)

It would seem that Jesus did not recruit any disciples for his inner circle in Jerusalem, but it was because of Jesus' signs that Nicodemus came to Jesus by night - secretly (Jn.3:2). Later John tells us of Joseph of Arimathea who was also a secret disciple, "*for fear of the Jews*" (Jn.19:38). It was in this Jerusalem context of fear, political control, repression and danger that Jesus said to Nicodemus, "*For God so loved the world that he gave his only Son, so that everyone who believes in him may not perish but may have eternal life*" (Jn.3:16). In the midst of angst the offer of hope and salvation is given. This text (Jn.3:16), which Martin Luther called *The Gospel in brief*, has naturally and rightly achieved prominence. Jesus is the gift and the giver. John 3:16 expresses this concisely and supremely. Perhaps most of all because, *to love / agapan* is not so much a feeling as a choice; and "*the striking even shocking thing about God's love for the world in relation to God's*

---

[17] For a fuller treatment of the Judaea/Galilee divide see Wayne Meeks *Galilee and Judaea in the Fourth Gospel* Journal of Biblical Literature Vol. 85, No. 2, Jun., 1966

love for his one and only Son, is that the former takes priority"[18]. God gives his beloved Son for love of the world. God not only sends his Son, but gives him, and gives him up to die that the world through believing or trusting in him might find eternal life. Michaels with good reason says:

> *"If the Father gave up the Son whom he loved above all to death on a cross, how great must be His love for us and for our world. Just as the Spirit was God's immeasurable gift to his Son, so the Son is God's immeasurable gift to the world".*[19]

Whilst a precise "definition" of *eternal life* is reserved for later in the gospel (Jn.17:3), even in this address to Nicodemus the term is followed by Jesus speaking of belief and unbelief. This coupled with obedience/non-obedience is at the heart of the eternal life which is in Jesus and which is offered through him (Jn.12:50; 17:2). However, eternal life in the final analysis is received by being *"born from above"* (Jn.3:3) - *"the spirit gives birth to the spirit"* (Jn.3:6), which is not something we can do for ourselves, not something to be accomplished by us. It is a gift: the gift of a relationship with the world, with other people and with God - it is *communional*[20]. As John the Baptizer said, *"A person can only receive what is given them from heaven"* (Jn.3:27). If I am honest I must admit how seldom I sense this humble spirit of absolute dependency on God's generosity in myself or in others.

The testimony of John the Baptizer to Jesus had been that he had seen, and others would see, that the one on whom the Spirit would *"come down and remain is the one who will baptize with the Holy Spirit"* (Jn.1:32f). Jesus himself can give this Spirit, *"without measure"* (Jn.3:34). The conversation with Nicodemus serves to progress the teaching about God as spirit, or the Holy Spirit, and the need for the new birth which first found expression in chapter one: *"To all who received him, who believed in his name, he gave power to become children of God, who were born not of blood or of the will of the flesh or of the will of man, but of God"* (Jn.1:12f). So now Jesus says to Nicodemus, *"What is born of the flesh is flesh, and what is born of the Spirit is Spirit ... You must be born from above"* (Jn.3:6-7 NRSV footnote: *anew)*. Sadly John 3:7 has often been interpreted without reference to John 1:13 as though being born *anew*, or *from above* is a decision to be made rather than a gift to be received. The frequent translation of the Greek *anothen* (ἄνωθεν) as *again* (e.g. NIV) is probably neither the best nor the most helpful rendering since it loses the connotations of "upward" which the Greek most

---

[18] TGJ p.202
[19] Ibid. p.227
[20] See Bogdan Lubardić *Orthodox Theology of Personhood: A Critical Overview Part 1* Expository Times Aug. 2011 pp.527, 530

naturally embraces. It is often overlooked in regard to these words of Jesus that physically speaking we cannot choose to be born, or choose our parents: our life is their gift, and we are a gift for them. Whilst to push the analogy of physical and spirit birth too far would not be in order, the same underlying principle might legitimately be applied to both.

I was raised in a Christian culture which saw "making a decision" as the beginning of one's spiritual journey. Indeed, I was one of thousands who went forward at a Billy Graham crusade in which we were invited to make a decision. The subsequent nurturing in my own church meant this became an important moment in my life. But I am quite convinced that it was not "my" singular decision which meant I became accepted as a child of God - or was born again - any more than Jesus' baptism did. Jesus' life was full of decisions. It was even more full of God's graciousness. Jesus told his disciples, "*Ask and you will receive*" (Jn.16:24), but it remains God's prerogative as to what is given and when (Jn.14:26). That is not a decision which I can make.

The importance of this teaching for Nicodemus about the working of God's Spirit is perhaps shown when some of its main themes are repeated almost immediately in the story of Jesus' encounter with a Samaritan woman at Jacob's well. So, for example, Jesus said to the Samaritan woman, "*The true worshippers will worship the Father in spirit and truth, for the Father seeks such to worship him. God is spirit, and those who worship him must worship in spirit and in truth*" (Jn.4:23f). The notion explored with Nicodemus of the Spirit being like the wind so that trying to locate or confine it is futile (Jn.3:8) is paralleled by Jesus telling the Samaritan woman that talking about worshipping on this or that mountain shows a lack of understanding of God as Spirit (Jn.4:21). It may be legitimate to recognise when God's Spirit is at work, but all decisions related to where, when, and how the Spirit moves belong solely to God.

Michaels offers an important commentary on the encounter between Nicodemus and Jesus. Nicodemus came in the dark, at night, the symbol of the working of evil (cf. esp. Jn.13:30). Nicodemus came in the darkness to Jesus who was the Light which was coming into the world (Jn.1:9). In spite of his fear, something moved Nicodemus to seek out Jesus, and Michaels notes the Johannine principle; *no one "comes to the Light", or to Jesus, without being "given" and "drawn" to him by the Father* [21] (cf. Jn.3:27; 6:37, 39, 44, 65; 10:29; 17:2, 6, 24). Nicodemus does not decide, he responds.

Nicodemus is typical of many in John's gospel who were drawn to Jesus, but who did not understand (Jn.3:10). "The Jews" and Jewish opponents (Jn.8:27; 10:37ff;

---

[21] TGJ pp.210, 217

12:40), the Pharisees (Jn.10:6); and even his disciples (Jn.12:16; 13:7, 12; 16:18; 20:9) consistently did not understand. Although a few are said to have "believed", belief would be better thought of as trust than as understanding. It would seem that only after Jesus' death could real understanding become possible, though trust or faith would still be paramount. In this sense all the encounters between Jesus and others in the gospel stories are preliminary, provisional, precursors of *the hour* when his true glory would be revealed.

(Chapter 4)

Jesus' conversation with a Samaritan woman is the story of someone who came to draw water, but through an exchange of words, was drawn to Jesus. The process began with Jesus asking, "*Will you give me a drink?*" (Jn.4:7). The woman's surprised riposte to Jesus' demonstration of disregard for prevailing cultural prejudices led to Jesus saying to the woman:

> "*If you knew the gift of God, and who is saying to you give me a drink, you would have asked him, and he would have given you living water* (Jn.4:10) ... *The water that I give will become in them a spring of water gushing up to eternal life*" (Jn.4:14).

Jesus himself is a gift of God. To "receive" him is to receive through him "*living water ... gushing up to eternal life*".

As is true of John's entire gospel, there is a lot of giving evident in this story. Jesus, in response to the woman's mention of a Messiah who was to come, said, "*I am (he,) the one who is speaking to you*" (Jn.4:26). Jesus is constantly referred to as the Messiah throughout the fourth gospel from Jn.1:41 to Jn.20:31 (cf. esp. Martha's confession Jn.11:27), which suggests this was important for the writer of the fourth gospel. Probably more important is Jesus as "The Word" - one who speaks and whose followers listen (Jn.10:3, 16, 27). Michaels notes that Jesus as light appears through to chapter 12; but the description of Jesus as "The Word" never appears in John's gospel after chapter 1 (Jn.1:1, 14) - where it is an obvious inference not an explicit statement.. Michaels, however, make this astute comment; "*The text begins with audible revelation ("Word"), moving on to visible revelation ("light") and thence back and forth between the two (embodied in Jesus' signs and discourses) as the story unfolds*"[22]. For John Jesus is the Word, and speaking, uttering or offering words is a form of gift, of self-exposure - as a conversation with a Samaritan (!) woman (!) amply illustrates. For Brueggemann, "*The new reality is not really available until it is uttered*"[23].

---

[22] TGJ p.46
[23] Cited by C. L. Campbell TLC p.483

This God-self-giving as literally uttered word is surely part of the theological rationale for the long conversations and extended monologues of Jesus which are included in the fourth gospel. So even in chapters where it may be less easy to identify specific gifts the word made flesh is still being offered, and accepted or refused. Rejecting Jesus' words is tantamount to self-condemnation (Jn.12:47f), whereas abiding in Jesus' words, allowing his words to dwell in us, enables Jesus to give whatever is asked in his name (Jn.15:7). So it is with the Samaritan woman's neighbours. Having first believed because of the woman's testimony, they came to believe *"in him because of his word"* (Jn.4:39). Similarly with the royal official at the end of chapter four whose son was cured; *"Jesus said to him, 'Go, your son will live'. The man believed the word that Jesus spoke to him"* (Jn.4:50. see also 6:63, 68; 14:10; 17:8). It is made apparent throughout John's gospel that Jesus is the incarnation of the Word of God, the Word which gives life.

(Chapter 5)

The healing of a royal official's son is closely followed by the healing on a Sabbath of a man by a pool at the Sheep Gate in Jerusalem (Jn.5:1-9). The man was obedient to the word or command of Jesus and received the healing for which he had longed for thirty-eight years. This gift of restored health leads in chapter five to a short confrontation initially provoked because Jesus' command to the man to pick up his mat and walk was considered by those whom John describes as *"the Jews"* to constitute a breach of Sabbath observance (Jn.5:10). Following their criticism of his encouragement for Sabbath indiscipline, Jesus spoke to his persecutors of his calling to follow *"My Father's"* example of being about his work. Jesus' call by God to work is not a new theme in John's gospel. In chapter four Jesus had answered his disciples' request that he ate something by saying to them, *"My food is to do the will of him who sent me and to complete his work"* (Jn.4:34). But the reference to *"my Father"* caused further offence because it was seen by his opponents as *"making himself equal to God"* (Jn.5:17-18). There follows a substantial, dense monologue by Jesus (Jn.5:19-46). Ashton rightly observes, *"the relationship between God and Jesus is nowhere more fully articulated than in the dialogue and discourse in John 5:19-30"*[24]. We can register again the notable element in Jesus' description of the relationship he had with his Father, his claim to have the authority for giving the life they shared to others.

> *"Just as the Father raises the dead and gives life to whomever he wishes, so also the Son gives life to whomever he wishes. The Father judges no one, but has given all judgement to the Son. For just as the Father has life in himself, so he has granted the Son also to have life in himself"* (Jn.5:21, 26).

---

[24] UFG p.227

Jesus pointed out to his critics that both John the Baptizer (Jn.5:32f) and the scriptures (Jn.5:39) testified to him, "*Yet*", he says, "*you refuse to come to me to have life*" (Jn.5:40). "*I have come in my Father's name and you do not accept me*" (Jn.5:43). Both the gift and giver are refused. Ultimately the giver is God because Jesus could do nothing on his own (Jn.5:19, 30). Rejection of Jesus by the Jews was in effect a rejection of what they claimed as their own identity, namely to be "the children of God" (Jn.8:42-4).

(Chapter 6)

But there were many people who seemed willing to receive something of what Jesus had to offer: and his offer of life runs as a powerful undercurrent, occasionally surfacing, particularly in this part of John's gospel. John tells us, "*A large crowd followed him because they saw the signs he was doing for the sick*" (Jn.6:2). Hardly any of these signs are described in any detail, but the gift of restored health was clearly an important, and for many an attractive feature of Jesus' ministry. This particular phase of Jesus' ministry would in time find its climax in the restoration to life of his friend, Lazarus (John 11:1ff. and see on Jn.5:21 above).

The terse reference to why crowds followed him is followed in John's gospel by Jesus' withdrawal to "*the other side of Galilee*" to a mountain with his disciples. The crowds followed - about five thousand (Jn.6:10) - and with the help of his disciples, and the resources of a child, Jesus fed them all (Jn.6:4-13). That this *sign* (Jn.6:14) happened near the time of the Passover Festival (Jn.6:4), that the grass was green (Jn.6:10), that Jesus gave thanks before distributing the bread and then the fish (Jn.6:11), that the result of all this was acknowledgement of him as "*the prophet who is to come into the world*" (Jn.6:14) and that Jesus withdrew when he realised the crowd intended to force him to be their king (Jn.6:15), are all elements in the story which have legitimately been given attention by commentators and preachers. The fish is not without its significance (see on Jn.21:9 below), but for Jesus in John's gospel the major talking point which results from the feeding of the multitude is the *bread*. The bread represents Jesus himself, offered, gratefully and prayerfully received, and abundantly shared, even to the extent of there being twelve baskets of bread left over. It is of note that John tells us that Jesus performed this feeding as a sign, but then makes it clear that the significance of what was being done was not appreciated by those who were fed. Their immediate reaction was to politicise the event, wanting to make Jesus a king. Later Jesus tells them that they come to him not because they saw the signs, but because they *ate the loaves and were satisfied* (Jn.6:26). This is confirmed when the people ask Jesus for a sign to substantiate his claim that God wanted them to believe in him as the one God had sent (Jn.6:30). As stated earlier, they saw miracles, short term satisfiers, not signs, or "in-sights" which could provide spiritual nourishment and challenge.

The story of Jesus walking on rough water (Jn.6:16-21) sits oddly in a chapter otherwise largely devoted to Jesus as the bread of life. Michaels suggests the miracle which should command our attention here is not walking on water, but the fact that Jesus could cross the lake, and therefore, by inference, was like the wind or the spirit, able to go wherever he wished in a way that was beyond his disciples', let alone the crowd's comprehension[25]. But the most obvious focus of the story is surely Jesus walking on the water. The sharing of bread produced short-lived amazement for the crowds: but Jesus walking on the water in the midst of a storm seems to have produced more lasting awe in the disciples. Both stories serve as preparation for the climax and aftermath of Jesus' teaching about bread when many of his disciples left him (Jn.6:66), but the twelve through Simon Peter said, "*Lord, to whom should we go? You have the words of eternal life. We have come to believe and know that you are the Holy One of God*" (Jn.6:68f)[26].

Jesus said to the crowd who after the feeding of five thousand came looking for him, "*Do not work for the food that perishes, but for the food that endures for eternal life, which the Son of Man will give you*" (Jn.6:26). This leads to the succinct declaration, "*I am the bread of life. Whoever comes to me will never be hungry*" (Jn.6:35), plus an extended exposition of what this meant. At the heart of Jesus' words are these, "*I am the living bread that came down from heaven. Whoever eats of this bread will live forever; and the bread that I give for the life of the world is my flesh*" (Jn.6:51). The bread of a child, blessed, broken and shared was a sign of Jesus' own self-giving, which was also life-giving, because to receive what Jesus offered of himself was to receive the life which Jesus shared with his Father: "*Just as the living Father sent me, and I live because of the Father, so whoever eats me will live because of me*" (Jn.6:57; cp.5:26). This does not mean that those who receive Jesus will not physically die, but "*all who see the Son and believe in him may have eternal life; and I will raise them up on the last day*" (Jn.6:40; cf. 6:44). Noticeably, all of this is said within the context of Jesus as the recipient and steward of the gifts of his Father, "*This is the will of him who sent me; that I should lose nothing of all that he has given me*" (Jn.6:39f).

---

[25] TGJ p.358

[26] Since there are those who believe John's Gospel was written in a way that elevates Peter above other disciples, it is interesting to note that this declaration by Peter is followed in John by Jesus noting the devil at work in Judas (6:70f), whereas in the Synoptics it is Peter who follows his declaration of faith with words which Jesus attributes to the devil's inspiration (Matt.16:23; Mark 8:33).

The offer or gift of his flesh to eat was probably amongst the most difficult offers Jesus made to his contemporaries, and even more so his blood to drink (Jn.6:53). Not only would these cannibalistic notions have been anathema to the Jews whom Jesus addressed, they are still a challenge to those who "hear" the words. Some have gotten round the difficulty by suggesting Jesus is here referring to the Eucharist, which makes his talk of flesh and blood symbolic, or a matter of transubstantiation. But as Michael's points out, when this offer of his flesh and blood was made the Last Supper had not yet been held[27], and in John's gospel there is no wine mentioned at Jesus' last pre-crucifixion meal. It has also been suggested that the best way of understanding Jesus' offer of his flesh and blood is by reference to the feeding of five thousand following which Jesus does say, "*The bread is my flesh*" (Jn.6:51). But this is not a reference to the loaves of bread shared with the crowd, but to "*the bread that comes down from heaven and gives life to the world*" (Jn.6:33); the bread which is Jesus himself (Jn.6:35, 48). As with John's account of Jesus' last pre-crucifixion meal with his disciples, there is no wine mentioned in the feeding of five-thousand. This passage with its offer of eating the flesh and drinking the blood of Jesus must be considered in its own right and context.

The people had wanted to seize Jesus and make him a King. However, Jesus came not to yield to human coercion, nor to command obedience, but to inspire obedience by feeding on him as the bread of heaven, and drinking in his life. The extent of his own obedience would be shown by his death in which his flesh would be "offered up" and his blood would flow. Jesus said many things which only made sense later. This meant that his word had to be taken on trust. Only some had it in them to be so trusting; perhaps those whom the Father was drawing to him (Jn.6:44, 65 - and see 3:27). One of the most likely interpretations of Jesus' invitation to eat his flesh and drink his blood is that Jesus was inviting his "followers" to be willing to share in his manner of death[28]. This would certainly be more challenging than asking them to ignore dietary regulations. It is also more challenging than being invited to share in a Eucharistic meal. More is being offered and asked than that.

(Chapter 7)

John chapter seven is set at the time of the Festival of Booths. Jesus' brothers had possibly been present at the first sign in Cana and stayed in Capernaum with Jesus and their mother (Jn.2:12), but John tells us they did not believe in him (Jn.7:5). For motives which can only be a matter of speculation they tried to persuade Jesus

---

[27] TGJ p.396
[28] Ibid. p.397

to go to Judaea for the festival, where his life would be under threat (Jn.7:1-9) [29]. At first Jesus opted to remain in Galilee on the basis that "*my time has not yet fully come*" (Jn.7:8). However, Jesus subsequently went to Jerusalem for the festival, secretly at first (Jn.7:10), but then teaching openly in the temple (Jn.7:10ff); teaching which provoked a number of questions and a mix of favour and hostility.

The source, and therefore the legitimacy or authority of his teaching was questioned. Jesus answered by saying that the originator or author of his teaching was not himself, but "*the one who sent me*" (Jn.7:16f). His Father gave him the words he spoke and commanded him to speak them (Jn.13:49). His supposed breach of Sabbath regulations (cf. Jn.5:1-18) obviously still rankled with his critics. He told them that Moses gave the law to them, but they did not keep it (Jn.7:19). They were willing to perform the minor surgery of circumcision on the Sabbath to avoid breaking the Law of Moses, yet contrarily are angry with Jesus because he heals a man's whole body on the Sabbath (Jn.7:23f). It would appear that they could not, or would not see the illogicality, let alone the heartlessness of their stance.

Jesus responded to questions about where the Messiah would come from implicitly in his use of the words "*him who sent me*" (Jn.7:18) or "*the one who sent me*" (Jn.7:16, 28f), but then shifted the emphasis on to where he was going: that is, "*to him who sent me*" (Jn.7:33). Burridge notes "*the image of God sending Jesus is one of the most common in John's gospel, occurring over fifty times*"[30]. But it is not a one-way trip. Jesus is also returning to the one who sent him.

John tells us that when Jesus was in Jerusalem for the Festival of Booths "*there was a division in the crowd because of him*" (Jn.7:43), a fact which is evident throughout the chapter. The crowd complained at his initial absence, but "*some were saying, 'He is a good man'*" (Jn.7:12; cf. 7:30f; 7:40-42). Some people asked, "*Can it be that the authorities really know that this is the Messiah?*" (Jn.7:25ff), but others, including the chief priests and Pharisees, held that the Messiah could not, like Jesus, come from Galilee (Jn.7:41, 52). John also records unsuccessful (Jn.7:44) and controversial (Jn.7:51) attempts to arrest Jesus whose "*hour had not come*" (Jn.7:30, 32). In the midst of all this controversy and the threatening Jerusalem environment, on the last day of the festival of Booths, Jesus cried out,

---

[29] For the relationship between Jesus and his brothers see Matt. 12:46-50; 13:55; 19:29; Mark 3:31-35 (6:3?); Luke 8:19-21; 14:12; (16:28?); John 2:12; 7:3-10; (20:17? which in the light of 20:18 is usually taken to refer to the disciples, although Jesus said *Brothers*). Verses such as Matthew 10:21//Mark 13:12 "*Brother shall deliver brother to death*", plus the many references to the need for brothers to forgive one another may all have an autobiographical connotation, even if a much wider application. See also the story of the Prodigal Son in Luke 15.

[30] TLC p.500

"Let anyone who is thirsty come to me, and let the one who believes in me drink. As the scripture has said, 'Out of the believer's heart shall flow rivers of living water" (Jn.7:37f). Jesus was still offering himself as gift and giver. According to John the gift is in some sense in the future, *"Now Jesus said this about the Spirit, which believers in him were to receive; for as yet there was no spirit, because Jesus was not yet glorified"* (Jn.7:39), but the import of Jesus' words is of a gift for believers which was there in Jesus waiting to be received and shared, even, or especially, in Jerusalem. Put simply, it is when the going gets really hot, when the temperature rises, that refreshing water becomes most necessary and welcome. Jesus can give what believers need when times are hard.

Michaels suggests that in spite of a similar proclamation to the Samaritan woman (Jn.4:14) the statement by Jesus that *living water* would *flow out of the believer's heart* (Jn.7:38) should be understood as a self-referencing quote from scripture by Jesus. Jesus was declaring that he would always be a source of living water for those who came to him; according to Michaels Jesus was not saying that his disciples would themselves become such sources: *"The point is not, as is often thought, that the believer will necessarily become a channel of living water to others, but that the believer's own well will never run dry"*[31]. I beg to differ. John offers an aside/commentary on Jesus' words, *"By this he (Jesus) meant the Spirit, whom those who believed in him were later to receive"* (Jn.7:39). Jesus believed that after he had gone away and the Spirit had been given to his disciples they would do greater things than he (Jn.14:12). For me the most plain meaning is the preferred option. Living water will flow out of believers' hearts because they will be filled to overflowing by the abundant life-giving spirit of Jesus. Indeed, if the gift was just for personal enrichment, that would not be in keeping with the self-giving nature of God manifested in Jesus: it could not be "God's" spirit which had been received.

(Chapter 8)

Its omission in some ancient manuscripts of the story of *the woman caught in adultery* (Jn.8:1-11) has led many commentators to suggest that it does not belong at this point in John's original telling of Jesus' story. Indeed, Kiefer says it was not in the original gospel at all[32]. However, the fact that the woman was obviously being used to trap Jesus in some way makes it not altogether out of place and possibly reinforces the hostile environment described in chapter seven. The story is a perfect tool for contrasting the basis of Jesus' judgement with that of his opponents (Jn.8:15f). There is also a kind of ironic envelope formed by the

---

[31] TGJ pp.464ff
[32] OBC pp.974, 999

abandonment of the "legal" stoning of the woman at the beginning of the chapter, whilst the chapter ends with an "illegal" attempt to stone Jesus himself.

Nonetheless, it might be conceded that there does not seem an obvious relationship between this story (Jn.8:1-11) and the discourse which immediately follows it. This discourse which begins with Jesus self-description as the Light of the World (Jn.8:12ff), would fit somewhat better and more naturally with the healing of the blind man in chapter nine (Jn.9:1ff) when Jesus' claim to be the Light of the World is repeated (Jn.9:5). But a case can be made for the story of the woman taken in adultery being included where it is, not only for the reasons given above. The story is in some ways a living parable echoing the fourth gospel's proclamation: "*For God did not send his Son into the world to condemn the world, but to save the world through him*" (Jn.3:17). Undoubtedly this woman was "saved", was not condemned, and was given the call or opportunity to find a new life – no longer "lost". In that sense Jesus did bring "light" into her life - "*In him was life; and that life was the light of men*" (Jn.1:4).

Whilst some have pointed out that chapter six is possibly a later addition to the original gospel[33], an unsubstantiated proposition that I find unnecessary, it has to be acknowledged that chapters five to nine taken as a whole seem not to have an obvious logical progression. This, of course, actually undermines the contention that our current script is a revised or more polished version of "an original". Many of the criticisms of John's Gospel as we now have it are only necessary when a strictly logical progression is deemed essential to support some preconceived, superimposed straight-line structure for the fourth gospel in its entirety. In chapter eight Jesus says, "*I am the light of the world. Whoever follows me will never walk in darkness, but will have the light of life*" (Jn.8:12); but there is no development of this thought in chapter eight. Instead John returns, with some variations and development, but also considerable repetition, to the dispute which filled chapter seven. Jesus talks again about the validation of his teaching or judgement through his relationship with his Father (e.g. 7:16 //8:16); about going where he cannot be found or followed (Jn.7:34 // 8:21); and words about the ignorance of his opponents concerning his Father. "*You do not know him*" (Jn.7:28) parallel, "*You know neither me nor my Father*" (Jn.8:19). Those who "*have the light of life*" stand in marked contrast to the Pharisees in Jerusalem to whom Jesus said, "*I told you that you would die in your sins, for you will die in your sins unless you believe that I am he*" (Jn.8:24). In other words, typical of the fourth gospel, themes are echoed rather than grouped conveniently for scholarly analysis[34].

---

[33] See Kiefer OBC p.971

[34] Burridge makes a related point about chapters 14-17, saying, *There is no clear structure to these chapters.* He helpfully goes on to suggest they are *better understood through prayerful meditation than by analysis* (TLC p.545). Wise advice to follow at times for much,

Earlier John recorded Jesus' prophecy that just as Moses lifted up the snake in the wilderness, "*so the Son of Man must be lifted up*" (Jn.3:14). This prophecy is now repeated, but with a specified outcome: "*When you have lifted up the Son of Man, then you will realise that I am (he)*" (Jn.8:28). The immediate impact of his words was that some believed him. However, in keeping with John's previous indication that Jesus did not trust Jerusalem converts (Jn.2:23), Jesus did not seem to welcome these "believers". Instead he issued the challenge, "*If you continue in my word, you are truly my disciples; and you will know the truth, and the truth will make you free*" (Jn.8:31f), plus the accusation, "*Yet you are ready to kill me*" (Jn.8:37, 40 cf. 7:19). This leads on to thoughts about freedom as freedom from sin (Jn.8:33-49), and Jesus as coming from his Father, God (Jn.8:42). This is in marked contrast to the Jews who claim Abraham, or God, as their father (Jn.8:39, 41), but who according to Jesus are slaves and are the children of the devil (Jn.8:34, 44).

As is often the case in John, all this controversy provides a context for promises or gifts from God through Jesus. The first gift is freedom (Jn.8:31f). A. J. Cocksworth reflecting on freedom says, *It is not something of human possession, it is gifted to*

---

if not all, of scripture. For an example of the kind of analysis which is certainly of great academic and theological interest to Johannine scholars, but in my opinion adds nothing to the value of John's Gospel as a text intended to draw its readers closer to God in Jesus, see volume 2 of *The Gospel and Letters of John*, by Urban C, von Wahlde; pub. Eerdmans 2010. Taking almost a thousand pages, Wahlde proposes three successive editions of the gospel, each increasing in size, and sees theological development accompanying the addition of new material. Hence, if we accept Wahlde's proposals, we have an original Johannine gospel and associated theology, plus two developments of both the text and the theology. Bultmann's approach of *a patchwork pieced together by an intelligent compiler* (UFG p.149) still creates the need to divide the text as we have it into discreet portions for separate and different consideration. However worthy these analyses might be it only adds to the complexity which Burridge acknowledges can detract from allowing the text as we have it to be a word of God for us. Michaels actually makes a very clear choice, giving *priority to understanding the text in its present form, just as it has come down to us, rather than tracing the history of how it came to be - - The task of interpreting the gospel is formidable enough without undertaking to re-write it* (TGJ pp.764, 996, 1006). Michaels describes my own approach precisely when he says, *the approach taken here is synchronic, not diachronic* (TGJ p.xii; 996 n.41). In contrast Ashton sees *rigorous diachronic analysis* as a necessary supplement to the synchronic exegetical approach (UFG p.302. See also UFG p.12 for reference to the roots of diachronic v synchronic approaches in Ferdinand Saussure's *Cours de Linguistique Générale*). Unsurprisingly Ashton adopts a three-editions stance and on that basis elects to restrict his commentary to what he considers to be the first edition (UFG p.136). Lindars, however, sees no reason for extensive redaction because *the evangelist's style permeates every sentence of the gospel*" (Barnabas Lindars *Behind the Fourth Gospel* SPCK 1971) *us in Jesus Christ ... it is that which we are drawn towards by a prior movement of grace*[35]*.* The second gift is deathless life. *"Very truly I tell you, whoever continues in my word will never see death ... Whoever keeps my word will never taste death"* (Jn.8:51,52). *"Continue in my word"* and *"keep my word"* should be taken as caution against short-term enthusiasm, and a commendation of faithfulness or perseverance. Contrary to the wishes of those who like to have everything in neat sequences, John typically chooses not to develop the idea of deathless life at this point. It will be referenced again in both story and conversational form in the story of Lazarus and his sisters (cf. John 11; esp. 11:26).

(Chapter 9)[36]

What John does in chapter nine is to return to the words of Jesus, *"I am the light of the world. Whoever follows me will never walk in darkness, but will have the light of life"* (Jn.8:12) with an associated "sign". Chapter nine records the healing of a man born blind (Jn.9:1-12). A question from his disciples as to who sinned occasions Jesus' response that the blindness is not the result of sin, but so that *"God's works might be revealed in him"* (Jn.9:3). To which Jesus' added, *"As long as I am in the world, I am the light of the world"* (Jn.9:5). Not only is the man's blindness not the result of his sinfulness, but he was someone in whose life God could be at work, and who through Jesus might learn to "see". In sharp distinction from those in whom Jesus could do nothing, for example, some of the Pharisees mentioned later (Jn.9:16, 40), this man hears Jesus' words and without "seeing" physically is obedient to Jesus' word. Furthermore he becomes a witness, a believer and a worshiper (Jn.9:33, 38). As with the man by the pool at the Sheep Gate (Jn.5:9), the healing of the blind man happened on a Sabbath (Jn.9:14) and again produced controversy, dividing opinion amongst the Pharisees. They questioned the blind man, then his parents, and then the blind man again, who not only defended Jesus, but criticized the Jews for not knowing where Jesus came from. As a result he was driven out (Jn.9:30-34). Jesus found him and asked, *"'Do you believe in the Son of Man?' He said, 'Lord, I believe and he worshiped him'. Jesus said, 'I came into this world for judgement so that those who do not see may see, and those who do see become blind"* (Jn.9:35b; 38f). Jesus offers the interrelated gifts of light in place of darkness (Jn.8:12), sight for blindness (Jn.9:39) and day rather than night (Jn.9:4. cf.13:30). Some, sadly, will be blinded

---

[35] Expository Times Aug 2011 p.570

[36] In considering chapter nine I have chosen not to focus on 9:22. For diachronic readers of the gospel this verse merits major attention, and draws attention away from themes consistently found in John's gospel other than that of gathering hostility toward Jesus and his followers in his own lifetime: hostility which resulted in his death. This point seems to be overlooked by those like Ashton who see the whole controversy as related not to Jesus of Nazareth but to the notional Johannine community. UFG p.74.

by the light (Jn.9:39), prefer the darkness (Jn.3:19), and behaving like Judas go out into the night (Jn.13:30).

(Chapter 10)

Within the context that believers are his sheep, the gift of his Father to him (Jn.10:29), Jesus pronounced three "I am" sayings. Unlike the thief who takes away and destroys, each of these "I am" sayings of Jesus is indicative of a gift of Jesus which provides safe-keeping. "*I am the gate for the sheep*", says Jesus (Jn.10:7). Jesus is the way in and out for the sheep and in this way creates a safe haven. "*I am the gate. Whoever enters by me will be saved, and will come in and go out and find pasture*" (Jn.10:9). Jesus provides protection and personal pastoral oversight for the sheep - "*They shall never perish; no one will snatch them out of my hand* (Jn.10:28b). "*I am the good shepherd. The good shepherd lays down his life for the sheep*" (Jn.10:11, 14f). Jesus gives his life for his sheep: but he gives them more. He gives them a relationship in which they know his voice, and he knows them individually by name in a way which parallels the relationship he has with his Father, "*I know my own and my own know me, just as the Father knows me and I know the Father*" (Jn.10:14f, 30, 38). Indeed, his Father, the watchman, has the primary role in Jesus' teaching in John 10. His presence is not always recognised or appreciated, but it is the watchman (not Jesus) who opens the gate (John 10:3). That is, Jesus is the agent of the Father whose will is being done and who enables it to be done (Jn.14:31).

Through this relationship with his Father Jesus gives eternal life to the followers whom God has given to him (Jn.10:28). John makes the point that even though it was in obedience to his Father's command, which itself is a gift, Jesus' laying down of his life for his sheep as the good shepherd was an entirely voluntary act, an act of love, in some ways a priestly act of sacrifice, of self-sacrifice. His life was not "taken", but "given": "*I lay down my life ... of my own accord. I have power to lay it down, and I have power to take it up again. I have received this command from my Father*" (Jn.10:17f). Jesus is a donor but also the recipient of a direct command given within a supremely precious relationship which overrides all other considerations; "*What my Father has given me is greater than all else*" (Jn.10:29). The result of his words was further division amongst *the Jews* (Jn.10:19-21). Jesus recognised that there were unbelievers who were not of his sheep (Jn.10:26). Nonetheless Jesus proffered or prophesied inclusivity and unity for his sheep, present and future: "*I have other sheep that do not belong to this fold. I must bring them also, and they will listen to my voice. So there will be one flock, one shepherd*" (Jn.10:16). Again, typical of the fourth gospel, the themes of inclusivity and unity are introduced or touched upon here but not immediately developed. They are left to be worked out in greater detail later in the gospel (e.g. 17:22f). This is John's way of sharing the gospel. Not to accept this is to be pushed into ever more convoluted theories in order to reduce the fourth gospel to pedantic prose offering a straight-line history rather than a work of art displaying great depth and variety.

(Chapter 11)

The death and calling back to life of Lazarus (Jn.11:1ff) might be regarded as tangible evidence for Jesus' earlier claim, "*Very truly I tell you, whoever keeps my word will never see death*" (Jn.8:51). But Lazarus does *taste death*, and his story is more in keeping with the somewhat different and perhaps developed declaration of Jesus to Martha, "*I am the resurrection and the life. Those who believe in me, even though they die, will live, and everyone who believes in me will never die*" (Jn.11:25f). The gift of Jesus to those who believe is, as Sidney Carter put it in *Lord of the Dance*, "*The life that'll never, ever die*" - a life which is neither defeated nor nullified by death. To believe in Jesus is to receive him and with him all that he offers, which includes eternal life and resurrection out of death. It should be noted that almost always eternal life is seen as something which precedes resurrection. "*For my Father's will is that everyone who looks to the Son and believes in him shall have eternal life, and I will raise them up at the last day*" (Jn.6:40). "*Whoever eats my flesh and drinks my blood has eternal life, and I will raise them up at the last day*" (Jn.6:54). The common notion that believers will be resurrected to eternal life has no basis in John's gospel. Eternal life is the gift of God through Jesus in this life, and it is this eternal life which leads to resurrection, not the other way around. Jesus said, "*I give them eternal life, and they shall never perish; no one will snatch them out of my hand*" (Jn.10:28).

There are many elements of the story of the raising of Lazarus in which Jesus can be seen as giving of himself. But he was also receiving - not least in his friendship with Lazarus and his family in Bethany; in the love which was shared. John tells us that Lazarus' sister Mary "*was the one who anointed the Lord with perfume and wiped his feet with her hair. Her brother Lazarus was ill*" (Jn.11:2f See 12:1-8). The snippet of information about Mary precedes the actual account of her action, but is indicative of the relationship of mutual love and devotion which is possibly the most important ingredient in the story. John tells us that Jesus saw Mary weeping, and the Jews who came with her (Jn.11:33), at which "*he was greatly disturbed in spirit and deeply moved*" (Jn.11:33). Jesus began to weep, and the Jews commented, "*See how he loved him*" (Jn.11:36). It may be that the Jews, as was so often the case, were "in the dark", not realising that Jesus' tears were less likely to have been caused by his love for Lazarus, whose death would lead to God being glorified, than a response to the tears of Mary whom, with Martha and Lazarus, we are specifically told Jesus loved (Jn.11:5). There is surely an echo of this to be found in John 20 when another Mary, Mary Magdalene, stood outside a tomb weeping, heard Jesus say her name, and wanted to hold him (Jn.20:11ff)[37]. It is highly significant that the author of the fourth gospel is consistently described, not as the one who believed (even though he did - 20:8), but as the one who was loved - a relationship rooted not in revelation, but in reciprocal giving and receiving.

It has been suggested that Jesus' tears of anger were his response to the death of his friend and the pain it had caused. Given Jesus' delayed response to the invitation to come to Bethany, and his expressed views on death, this seems unlikely. Michaels offers an alternative explanation for Jesus' tears. He suggests that Jesus' tears were caused by the anger he felt because he found the presence of the Jews intrusive and wished to be alone with Lazarus' family[38]. In placing the emphasis on Jesus being angry, Michaels presents a convincing case, but my preference in explaining the tears of Jesus is to place the emphasis on Jesus' love and compassion, which does not exclude anger, but which, for me, provides a more likely motive for his tears. Jesus' anger was more likely to produce actions and words which directly addressed the cause of his anger (e.g. 2:14ff).

As well as being a vehicle to show Jesus' love, John uses the story of Lazarus to tell his readers that death followed by resurrection is "*for God's glory so that the Son of God may be glorified through it*" (Jn.11:4). In other words, Lazarus' story is also Jesus' story. Kiefer suggests: "*In the fourth Gospel Jesus' crucifixion, his hour of death and departure, coincides with the hour of Jesus' glorification* (Jn.3:14; 8:28; 12:32f). *By his death Jesus will be glorified with his Father*" (Jn.13:31f; 17:1-5)[39]. The glory of God is seen by those who believe. To Martha, who had declared her belief in Jesus as "*the Messiah, Son of God, the one coming into the world* "(Jn.11:27), Jesus said, "*Did I not tell you that if you believed you would see the glory of God?*"(Jn.11:40). Just one example of parallels of the stories of Lazarus' and Jesus' deaths and rising to life is that when Lazarus came out of the tomb in his grave cloths, Jesus said, "*Unbind him and let him go*" (Jn.11:44). Resurrection includes leaving the clothes of the grave behind - being set free from them. In the story of the first Easter Sunday morning, Peter and the other disciple saw the linen wrappings of Jesus internment laying there in the tomb (Jn.20:4-7), perhaps unbound by the two angels whom Mary saw (Jn.20:12). Kiefer makes a very important point, that in the story of the raising of Lazarus, "*The passage from death to life corresponds to the transition from unbelief to faith*"[40].

---

[37] As Paul put it, faith is an abiding spiritual treasure, as is hope, but the greatest gift is love (1. Cor.13:13; cf. John 17:23)

[38] TGJ pp.636-40. The Greek text here need not imply anger at al, but simply passion.

[39] Kiefer OBC pp.992

[40] OBC p.981

In so many ways the raising of Lazarus prefigures Jesus' own path through death to new life - for example, it is on the third day that Jesus responds to the message of Lazarus' illness (Jn.11:2) although exact parallels are clearly not intended since Lazarus is in the tomb four days (Jn.11:17). In fact Jesus' tears could have been for himself, not in a selfish way, but because of the betrayal, fear, ignorance and hatred which would combine to crucify him. It is not uncommon for the death of friends to evoke strong intimations of one's own mortality.

The immediate aftermath of the raising of Lazarus in John is that the event is reported to the Pharisees. They met with the chief priests, and John tells us the Sanhedrin was worried that the popularity of Jesus would lead to the Romans taking away "*both our temple and our nation*" (Jn.11:48). Caiaphas said to them, "*It is better for you to have one man die for the people than to have the whole nation destroyed*" (Jn.11:50) Although this led to a successful determination to take Jesus' life, in Caiaphas' words John sees an unwitting prophecy: "*He (Caiaphas) prophesied that Jesus was about to die for the nation*"; with the additional words, "*and not for the nation only, but to gather into one the dispersed children of God*" (Jn.11:51f). This is perhaps a reference to Jesus' mission and concern for "*other sheep, not of this fold*" – though it could relate as easily to the Jewish Diaspora (Jn.10:16). Caiaphas' words also resonate with Jesus' own teaching that a single grain of wheat "*if it dies, it bears a great crop*" (Jn.12:24). One death, Jesus' death, would lead to many lives, perhaps better expressed as "life for many".

Caiaphas is a representative of those who did not walk in the light. Jesus said, "*Are there not twelve hours of daylight? Those who walk during the day do not stumble, because they see the light of the world. But those who walk at night stumble, because the light is not in them*" (Jn.11: 9f). The light was not in those who plotted Jesus' destruction. Predictably they arranged his arrest to be at night and held his mock trials during the hours of darkness. Such plots led to Jesus withdrawing with the disciples to Ephraim "*near the wilderness*" (Jn.11:53f), which perhaps forms an envelope with 1:23 in which John was "*a voice crying in the wilderness*" and certainly seems to be a literary break point in John's Gospel, before the beginning of the climaxing story which begins, "*Now the Passover of the Jews was near*" (Jn.11:55). "The Jews" were going to sacrifice the lamb (cf.1:29; 19:14)!

(Chapter 12)

John chapter twelve begins, "*Six days before the Passover Jesus came to Bethany*" (Jn.12:1). Jesus once again was on his way to Jerusalem. John's Gospel can be read as a ministry punctuated by Jerusalem festivals: a Passover provides the backdrop for the commencement of his public ministry (Jn.2:13, 23). An unnamed festival at which John records the first act of healing as part of Jesus' ministry (Jn.5:1) is followed by a second Passover when five thousand were fed (Jn.6:4) although not in Jerusalem on this occasion. Jesus then made two more festival appearances in Jerusalem. At the first, the Feast of Tabernacles or Booths, Jesus was acclaimed as a remarkable teacher (Jn.7:2, 15). At the second, the Feast of Dedication, his Messiah-ship was seriously questioned and attempts to dispose of Jesus intensified (Jn.10:22). Then less than two-thirds of the way through his gospel John takes us into the last six days of Jesus' life. John offers a little reminder that we are for a third time in Jerusalem for the Passover (Jn.13:1) and will later recount that Jesus died on the *Day of Preparation*, the day before the great solemn Sabbath (Jn.19:31). This final Passover for Jesus would be the hour of his passage through death to resurrection life.

Very much in keeping with the proposition that Jesus was God's gift, is the suggestion made by a number of commentators that Jesus himself can be seen as a new form of provision replacing or fulfilling the purposes and values of the Jews' festivals, rituals and venerated ancestors. Baukham says the festivals "*find their true, eschatological meaning and fulfilment in Jesus and the salvation he brings*"[41]. Jesus' proclaimed at the festival of booths that in him and through him came both water and light. That these elements featured in this particular festival's rituals can be seen as a support for such thinking[42]. At the Feast of Dedication, Jesus claimed to be the one sanctified (or dedicated) by God (Jn.10:36) as earlier he had spoken of his body being the real temple (Jn.2:19-21). John indicates that Jesus had more to offer than Abraham (Jn.8:58), or Jacob (Jn.4:12ff; 1:51?) or Moses: "*The Law indeed was given through Moses; grace and truth came through Jesus Christ*" (Jn.1:17). A new covenant was replacing the old - or *grace upon grace* was fulfilling the old covenant (Jn.1:16). When Jesus' body was taken down from the cross with bones "unbroken" this might be seen as Jesus becoming the new paschal lamb (cf. Exodus 12:46). Burridge reflected on the traditional seven *I am* sayings in John: bread of life; light of the world; door of the sheepfold; the good shepherd; the resurrection and the life; the way, truth and life; and the vine. He says, "*These descriptions are all central images of the Jewish faith and Law now fulfilled in Jesus*". Taken together these are a powerful indicator that Jesus was new wine replacing or transforming the old ritual water (Jn.2:6-9).

John's account of Jesus' last six days before his death begins with a meal (Jn.12:2)[43]. This "supper" is the first of three meals which help shape the rest of John's gospel. The second was also a supper, but with his disciples, preparing them for his death (Jn.13:2-17:26). The third meal was a post-resurrection "breakfast" on the sea shore with a smaller group of disciples (Jn.21:4. 9f). It is fascinating to note

---

[41] Bauckham TLC p.530

[42] Kiefer OBC p.975

[43] 12:2 NRSV *dinner,* Greek δεῖπνον - the same word used in 13:2, NRSV *supper*

the times of day/night which punctuate and dramatise the story-line: *evening* (Jn.13:2; 20:19)... *night* (Jn.13:30; 21:3)... *still dark* (Jn.20:1)... *early in the morning* (Jn.21:4) - time to break the fast!

The first of the three meals was with friends in company with Lazarus, who had recently been called out from the tomb, and his two sisters. Martha and Mary together and individually gave something to Jesus. They gave a meal at which *"Martha served"* (Jn.12:2), whereas *"Mary took a pound of costly perfume made of pure nard, anointed Jesus' feet, and wiped them with her hair "* (Jn.12:3; cf. 11:2). Judas questioned the misuse of such an expensive commodity, but Jesus explained Mary's action as related to his burial. In publicly anticipating his entombment, her act showed deep insight and an acceptance of his death, or going away, which no one else seems to have shared (Jn.12:7 - cf.19:40). Was this the act which inspired Jesus to wash his disciples' feet (Jn.13:54ff)? There is much in this account of a meal six days before Jesus' death which prepares a reader of John's gospel for the intimate time Jesus would share with his disciples over a meal, and which portends his suffering and death. The account of his anointing by Mary ends with words of Jesus laden with pathos: *"You always have the poor with you, but you do not always have me"* (Jn.12:8). The threat to Jesus which would result in his death is emphasised and widened by John to include Lazarus, because what Jesus had done for Lazarus resulted in many of the Jews believing in Jesus rather than listening to the chief priests. They were bound as a result to take action against Jesus - and Lazarus (Jn.12:10f. see also 12:18). As Jesus would make very clear to his disciples, to be his friend, to respond to his call, to follow his way, is to risk his fate (Jn.15:18-21).

The next day (five days before the Passover) Jesus, approached Jerusalem. He was greeted by great crowds of pilgrims waving branches and offering praises. Jesus found a young donkey on which to ride into the city (Jn.12:12ff). The crowd was attracted at least in part because of the witness of those who had been present when Lazarus was called back from death (Jn.12:17f), with the result that the Pharisees confessed their helplessness because, *"the world has gone after him"* (Jn.12:19). John had said earlier that Jesus was given because of God's great love for *the world* (Jn.3:16 - cf. 12:47). The world, or at least a representative sample of it, was in Jerusalem for the Passover. So John tells us that some Greeks, representatives of the world beyond Judaism, told Philip they would like to see Jesus. To Philip and Andrew's relay of the request Jesus responds: *"The hour has come for the Son of Man to be glorified. Very truly I tell you, unless a grain of wheat falls into the earth and dies, it remains just a single grain; but if it dies, it bears much fruit"* (Jn.12:23f). John does not record that those particular Greeks saw Jesus. The time, or *hour* had come when Jesus' ministry to individuals would be surpassed by his being lifted up (Jn.3:14; 8:28) - *"And I, when I am lifted up from the earth, will draw all people to myself"* (Jn.12:32).

176

It is worth noting that John, who records the request of Greeks to see Jesus, later tells us that the inscription Pilate ordered to be put on the cross, "*Jesus of Nazareth, the King of the Jews*" was written in Aramaic, Latin - and Greek (Jn.19:20). The man from Nazareth would be seen no more, but the crucified, glorified, raised up and ascending Christ could be seen through the eyes of faith by everyone and acknowledged as the king he was (See on Jn.17:1-3 below). In John's Gospel the man from Nazareth was always the man for everyone (Jn.3:16), but also the "man from heaven" (Jn.1:9, 51; 3:13, 31; 6:33, 41f, 51) who would return, or be received back into heaven (Jn.8:21; 13:1; 14:3; 16:7; 20:17). The scope of his mission was truly comprehensive.

Chapter twelve is an account of Jesus' last public ministry prior to his death. In chapter thirteen John shifts the locus from the public arena to the private intercourse of Jesus with his disciples. It is therefore no surprise that in chapter twelve some of the earlier major themes are reiterated and sometimes expanded or deepened.

There is the familiar contrast of light and darkness. "*Jesus said to them, 'The light is with you for a little longer. Walk while you have the light, so that the darkness may not overtake you. If you walk in the darkness, you do not know where you are going. While you have the light, believe in the light, so that you may become children of light'*" (Jn.12:35f). Or more succinctly, "*I have come as light into the world, so that everyone who believes in me should not remain in the darkness*" (Jn.12:46).

John also reflects again on the relationship between Jesus and his Father which has been the oft stated justification for the authenticity of his public teaching. "*I have not spoken on my own, but the Father who sent me has himself given me a commandment about what to say and what to speak. And I know that his commandment is eternal life*" (Jn.12:49f). Furthermore, the believer participates in this Father-Son relationship: "*Whoever serves me the Father will honour*" (Jn.12:26): "*Whoever believes in me believes not in me, but in him who sent me. And whoever sees me sees him who sent me*" (Jn.12:44f). In various forms the words of Jesus which relate to *believing* in him occur throughout the gospel (Jn.1:50; 3:18; 6:69; 9:35ff; 11:26-40; 12:36, 44; 14:1, 11, 29; 20:27) - but this belief is never an end in itself.

For John, Jesus is Saviour rather than judge. But people are judged by their response to Jesus and his words. "*I do not judge anyone who hears my words and does not keep them, for I came not to judge the world, but to save the world. The one who rejects me and does not receive my word has a judge; on the last day the word that I have spoken will serve as judge*" (Jn.12:47f).

John has already indicated that Jesus is the good shepherd who lays down his life for his sheep (Jn.10:15), but he lays it down in order to take it up again (Jn.10:17); and to those who put their trust in him, he gives them eternal life (Jn.10:28). Indeed, he is the resurrection and the life (Jn.11:25). Just as God was glorified through Lazarus' passing through death (Jn.11:4, 40), so it will be with Jesus; "*And what should I say "Father, save me from this hour"? No it is for this reason that I have come to this hour. Father, glorify your name. Then a voice came from heaven, 'I have glorified it, and I will glorify it again'*" (Jn.12:27f). Jesus' willingness to lay down his life and to take the way through death to new life is the example for all who believe: "*Those who love their life lose it, and those who hate their life in this world will keep it for eternal life. Whoever serves me must follow me, and where I am there will my servant be also*" (Jn.12:25f). The approach of Jesus' suffering and death did not leave Jesus unaffected. This would not be easy for Jesus, who confessed, "*Now my soul is troubled*" (Jn.12:27 cf. Jn.11:33). Nor would it be easy for his disciples. So John now gives us an extensive account of how Jesus tried to prepare his disciples for his self-giving in death, and for their own costly discipleship.

(Chapter 13)

John begins his account of Jesus' time with his disciples by telling us "*Jesus knew that his hour had come to depart from this world and go to the Father. Having loved his own who were in the world, he loved them to the end*"(Jn.13:1). Although one particular disciple is called "*the one whom Jesus loved*" (Jn.13:23; 20:2; 21:7, 20), it is quite clear that Jesus loved all his disciples in a way that was not possible in relation to those who were not committed to him; those who "*loved human glory more than the glory that comes from God*" (Jn.12:43). Though Michaels prefers a temporal emphasis for Jesus' words *to the end*, seeing it as related to *his hour had come*[44], Kiefer points out that the Greek words used here for *to the end*, could equally mean *perfect*[45]. Whether or not in a temporal framework, Jesus' love for his disciples was to be perfected, made complete by his laying down of his life for them (Jn.10:11; 15:13).

It is noteworthy that the word *love* (or *loved*) appears in a positive way just ten times in the first twelve chapters of John, but more that forty times in the remaining nine chapters, reaching its conclusion in Jesus' persistent questioning of Peter about his love for him (Jn.21:13-17), and Jesus' enigmatic prophecy about the disciple whom he loved and who, significantly, was still following Jesus – and

---

[44] TGJ p.722
[45] OBC p.985

Peter (Jn.21:20-23). This particular three-way relationship (Jesus – Peter - the disciple whom Jesus loved) is also evident at the supper table when the question of who would betray Jesus is under consideration (Jn.13:23f), and in essence at the tomb (Jn.20:2-10); but here (13:1) Jesus makes explicit for the first time the love he gives to all his true disciples. This abiding, self-giving love is the subtext for all that follows. This includes what is often referred to as the "farewell discourse", but is seldom specifically said to be an extended expression of Jesus' deep desire that his disciples should literally "fare well". Through his actions, shared thoughts and prayers at the meal table Jesus showed how much of himself, of his own emotional energy, spiritual capital and personal mission, he had invested in and was entrusting to his disciples (cf. Jn.4:34f; 5:24; 6:38f, 44; 17:18, 23; 20:21).

The setting for Jesus' interaction with his disciples is a last supper (Jn.13:2, 12, 23-27) the details of which we are not given over and above the fact that there was bread which was dipped into a dish (Jn.13:26). As noted earlier, the supper setting for Jesus' last pre-crucifixion teaching of his disciples provides an interesting literary link to the breakfast setting for the final resurrection appearance of Jesus as recorded by John (Jn.21:12). But it was during supper, as a demonstration of the true nature of his love for them, that Jesus washed his disciples' feet (Jn.13:4-11). Peter objected strongly to Jesus wanting to wash his feet (Jn.13:8); but Jesus said to Peter, "*Unless I wash you, you have no share in me*". Even if Jesus was also rightly understood to be their *Teacher and Lord* (Jn.13:13), Jesus offered himself to his disciples as a low ranking servant and wanted to be received and imitated as such (Jn.13:14). Peter would know that foot-washing was a duty confined to the lowliest servants in a household. It was considered so demeaning that it could not be required of a male Jewish servant. It was a task for foreign slaves. It is also possible that Peter would have in mind the action of Mary anointing Jesus' feet. In this action Jesus follows the example of a woman (Jn.12:1-3) and fulfils the common duty of a foreign slave. It is difficult for us to imagine how shocking and unacceptable such abasement would be in an honour-based world. Such a world, including *his own people* (Jn.1:11), could not receive him, but nor was it easy for his disciples to accept the ways in which Jesus offered himself to them - ways which in the eyes of many would be regarded as humiliating. It is easy for us to overlook the fact that crucifixion was designed to be humiliating. But for Jesus proper humility was the hallmark of that genuine love and obedience which made him, and could make them, channels for God's blessing: "*If you know these things you are blessed if you do them*" (Jn.13:17)[46].

---

[46] To my mind it is highly regrettable that along with John's account of Jesus' death, this story is not included as a Sunday lesson in the Revised Common Lectionary. It means that the majority of Christians will never be invited to reflect on these crucial stories.

Chapter 4 - John

A number of commentators have read references to baptism in Jesus' words to Peter, "*One who has bathed does not need to wash, except for the feet, but is entirely clean*" (Jn.13:10). But baptism plays little part in John's gospel, and the subject is not developed here or elsewhere. Some commentators are convinced that both Jesus and his disciples baptized people[47]. The reference in Jesus' conversation with Nicodemus to being born of "*water and the Spirit*" (Jn.3:5) is generally not regarded as a reference to a double baptism. However, on the basis of 3:22; 3:26 and 4:1, two of which texts are hearsay accounts of Jesus baptizing people, and choosing to discount the very clear declaration in 4:2 that Jesus himself did not baptize people, it has been claimed that "*the purpose of the baptisms performed by Jesus*" was to make people Jesus' disciples[48]. None of the disciples whose calling is recorded are said to have been baptized by Jesus - other than as promised with the Holy Spirit after his death and resurrection (Jn.20:22). Indeed John's gospel makes a point of contrasting John the Baptizer who baptizes with water, with Jesus who in John is not baptized with water, but with the spirit coming down on him like a dove from heaven (Jn.1:32), and who will therefore baptize not with water, like John, but with the Holy Spirit (Jn.1:3[49]). The fact is that John's gospel shows no interest in what have become central, often dominating sacraments in the life of many churches. Numerous commentators have tried very hard to read Christian rituals of Baptism and Eucharist into John's gospel narrative but it is *eisegesis* not *exegesis*. Jesus' remark about being "*entirely clean, though not all of you*" (Jn.13:10) is not a reference to the churches' future practice of baptism, but a reference to Jesus' washing of his disciples feet, and a preparation of the reader for the hard fact that betrayal by one of Jesus' own inner circle, one of the twelve, Judas, was imminent. If we hold in mind that receiving and believing are almost synonymous in John[50] and that Jesus had called himself *the bread of Life* and declared that to eat of him was to have life, there is deep pathos and irony in what follows. In John's account of a last supper Judas alone is recorded as having been given the bread which had been dipped in the dish by Jesus (Jn.13:25f). John tells us, "*After receiving the piece of bread, he* (Judas) *immediately went out. And it was night*" (Jn.13:30).

Intriguingly this passing of Judas into the night evoked in Jesus a repetition or confirmation of his sense that God was being glorified in what was happening to him, that it was an essential part of his individual journey back to his Father, and that the appropriate response of his disciples to these things was to obey the new commandment he was giving them to love one another as Jesus had loved them. This in turn prompted Peter's claim that he would lay down his life for Jesus, but

---

[47] See e.g. TGJ p.183
[48] Ibid. pp.214, 233
[49] Ibid. p.268
[50] Ibid. p.68

180

Jesus' prediction that Peter would very shortly deny him three times (Jn.13:37f). The frailties and shortcomings of Jesus' disciples at this time are set alongside the purposeful intensity of Jesus' devotion to the path laid out for him by his Father. John perhaps indicates the commitment of Jesus to his Father's will and the extent of Jesus' love for his disciples by the length of Jesus' teaching and prayer at this point. With only minor interventions (just 7 verses), the words of Jesus at the last supper total 110 verses (Chs.14-17), one eighth of the entire gospel.

Jesus, close to his own time of suffering, offered his disciples comfort, guidance and hope undergirded with promises and prayer. Prayer itself is a gift of God, a way of communicating with God: but equally it is a gift to God by the person who prays. In fact, prayer expresses in a practical form the mutuality of Jesus and his Father, and between a believer and God which was expounded by Jesus especially in his own prayer (chapter 17). Prayer as gift and giving is inextricably linked to a number of promises given by Jesus.

(Chapter 14)

The first promise is of the gift of a place which Jesus would go to prepare and which his disciples would receive after passing through death: *"I go to prepare a place for you"* (Jn.14:2f). But this promise is predicated on the invitation to trust in God and also in Jesus (Jn.14:1). The generous spirit of God has already been seen at work through Jesus. It is evident in the abundance of wine at the wedding in Cana (Jn.2:6), in multiple healings (Jn.6:2, 7:31), in the surplus gathered even after feeding five thousand (Jn.6:12f), in his willingness to give his life (Jn.10:15). This same generosity will manifest itself in the *"house with many dwelling places"* or as the King James Version so grandly puts it, *"many Mansions"* (Jn.14:2). Death will not make of naught, nor bring to an end, the action of God's generous spirit as seen in Jesus. Indeed, Jesus' death will result in the release of even more of his Father's generosity (e.g. Jn.14:26 *"The Advocate, the Holy Spirit, whom the Father will send in my name, will teach you all things and will remind you of everything I have said to you"*).

Jesus further promises that having gone to prepare a place for his disciples he would come again and take them to be with him in his Father's house (Jn.14:4). In this sense at least Jesus is "the way" to the Father (Jn.14:6); although Jesus makes it plain, as he has done on many occasions, that intimacy with the Father is already possible because *"If you really know me you will know my Father also. From now on you do know him and have seen him ... Whoever has seen me has seen the Father "* (Jn.14:7, 9; cp. 1:14, 18). Jesus also further promised his disciples, *"Anyone who loves me will obey my teaching. My Father will love them and we will come to them and make our home with them"* (Jn.14:23). Jesus is always with, or one with the Father. He is giving an insight into his Father by his very presence in the world and the relationship they share in life and through death (Jn.12:44f, 14:9). His close disciples would share in this relationship, but he would be drawing all people toward himself, and therefore into the presence of his Father, through his being lifted up - on the cross and in resurrection-ascension.

A crucial element of what Jesus gives is a unique way to God as the Father. This promise, as with all Jesus' promises or pronouncements, would be validated by Jesus acting in accordance with and completing his Father's will. "The way" is not a physical pathway to a geographical place, but a spiritual journey within and into an ever expanding, death-defeating relationship. So Jesus can say, "*You know the way*" ... and the way is to "*come to the Father through me* (Jesus)" (Jn.14:4, 6). "The way" is neither a simple, nor an isolated concept understandable without reference to other aspects of Jesus' teaching and example. For instance, although here Jesus talks about the disciples being taken to God's house or dwelling place, as noted above Jesus also talks about the Father with Jesus coming to make a dwelling place right beside or in the disciples (Jn.14:23).

John also associates Jesus as the way with Jesus as truth and life (Jn.14:6). In this context truth is surely better associated with trustworthiness which liberates, rather than the all too common association, or even infatuation, with factual correctness which so easily acts as a ring-fence against honest, open enquiry. There is no need to go with Dodd and see truth as Platonic, nor with Bultmann's truth as quasi-Gnostic. Ashton says that De La Potterie [1977] "*has shown conclusively that Dodd is wrong ... and ... Bultmann is wrong*"[51]. But one does not have to accept Ashton's own quasi-Gnostic proposition that truth is a riddle and has "*an esoteric meaning reserved for those 'in the* know' "[52]. Truth is not separate from the active, self-giving word or spirit of God with which the gospel began. Truth is closely linked to grace (Jn.1:14, 17), and with the spirit (Jn.4:23f) which has the freedom of the wind (Jn.3:8) and which God is free to give. This is truth with freedom to express itself in myriad ways with potential to set people free. The "signs" in John's gospel all testify to the liberating power of the truth Jesus lived. I remember reading about two ways in which we might read the Bible. It can be read as though we are in a long narrow space with a low ceiling, and it can take us undeviating along the restrictive corridor. Or it can be read as though we are on a trampoline, propelling us to new heights, and evoking in us a sense of release from earth's downward pull (Jn.14:17). John's Gospel invites us to be on the trampoline. Because Pontius Pilate did not comprehend what Jesus meant by truth he was unable to set Jesus free or himself (Jn.18:37ff).

---

[51] UFG p.346
[52] Ibid. p346

Of course, truth is associated with truth telling, with words, because when a person is liberated through faith in God's trustworthiness, is sanctified by truth (Jn.17:17), there is no place for lies or deceit (Jn.3:21). Truth as offered in John has to do with life rooted in loving honesty and faithful commitment to the One who not only speaks, but embodies truth. This is a far cry from self-justifying certainties or dogmatic correctness; what Bogdan Lubardič describes as "*intellectual idols...* *psychological strongholds of egocentric security and emotional self-protection furnished by rationalist propositions*"[53]. Such things are the stock in trade of Jesus' enemies, not his friends (Jn.5:39f).[54]

Just as Jesus' kind of truth cannot be comprehended by worldly definition, so the life of which Jesus spoke is not about physically breathing or having consciousness. Life in John's gospel is a gift to be received. It is the outworking of having faith in Jesus (Jn.3:15f; 5:24; 6:47; 11:25; 17:3; 20:31), drinking the water (Jn.4:14), eating the bread or food of life which Jesus offers (Jn.6:27, 33); eating and drinking Jesus flesh and blood (Jn.6:51, 54); receiving the words of Jesus which are full of the *spirit of life* (Jn.6:63, 68; cp. 1:1-4); following Jesus, ("*Whoever follows me will never walk in darkness, but will have the light of life*" 8:12); and being willing, like Jesus, to lose one's life (Jn.12:25), even if, as in the case of Peter, the willingness is not always matched by the ability (see 13:37f). In keeping with all of John's gospel, to acknowledge Jesus as the way, the truth and the life is not to make a creedal statement, nor even to be invited to marvel at what is being revealed, but to accept the gift of Jesus himself, and all that is offered by his Father through him; "*I am in the Father and the Father is in me*" (Jn.14:11). Knowing Jesus and trusting in him and the Father who sent him is to have "eternal" life (Jn.3:15f, 36; 5:24; 6:40, 47; 17:3) – life not measured by years but by participation in God's ever-creative purposes.

Kiefer describes eternal life as *the goal of believers*[55], but it is not a goal, it is a gift. Mary Pazdan on John 11:25f says, "*The assurance of everlasting life beyond the grave is emphasised*"[56]. In spite of such commentators and some translations, eternal life is not *everlasting* life, not best understood as time-related[57]. Michaels cites John's inclusion of festivals as evidence that "*it* (John's Gospel) *wants to be*

---

[53] Expository Times Sept. 2011 576 *Orthodox Theology of Personhood: A Critical Overview - Part 2*

[54] For an interesting short but enlightening discussion on just one approach to the matter of "truth", see Oliver Crisp *Analytic Theology* Expository Times July 2011 pp. 475-6.

[55] OBC p.985

[56] TLC p.536

[57] Note: France speaks of the false modern assumption that 'eternal' is a synonym for 'everlasting' RTF p.966

taken seriously as history"[58]; but it seems to me the purpose of using the festivals is theological not historical. A new covenant or relationship is being established with God through Jesus which is not dependent on a religious, or any other kind of calendar. Michaels is convinced that *historical truth* in John should not be distinguished from *theological truth* [59], yet reflecting on Jesus' words that those who keep his word will *never see death* (Jn.8:51) Michaels himself acknowledges that "*Jesus is not using this kind of language in the normal, that is, literal, way*"[60]. Pazdan is probably much nearer the mark with her commentary on John 20:17: "*The theological rather than the chronological and spatial intention of verse 17 also indicates a new relationship which the disciples will enjoy with the risen Jesus and the Father*"[61].

So, to *live for ever* (Jn.6:51, 58) is not a promise of life as we know it for an infinity of years. It is rather a promise that to partake of Jesus' life is not to be lost now or ever in spiritual, or through physical death (Jn.6:39). Eternal life is a life of mutual indwelling, mutual blessing: participating in that action of giving and receiving which was always the nature of God, and which by comparison makes time lines irrelevant. Jesus, and the life he shares with his Father and with his disciples, transcends both time and the negative human perception of life as confined to a specific period of time ending with death as complete annihilation. Jesus' words stand in direct contradiction to the notion that death has the last word for obedient believers:

> *Very truly I tell you, whoever hears my word and believes Him who sent me has eternal life and will not be judged, but has passed over from death to life. Very truly I tell you a time is coming and has now come ..... (Jn.5:24f).*

Michaels interprets these words as indicating a *two-stage affair*, a chronological sequence "still to come": somehow related to the resurrection of Jesus, and subsequently of others, and yet already present in Jesus at the time the words were spoken[62]. The chronological reference is unhelpful and unnecessary. C. H. Dodd's "realised eschatology" may have enjoyed only passing and minority popularity, and Michaels might arguably restrict its scope to judgement and not salvation (which he regards as *a divine intention for the future*)[63], but the insights of realised eschatology are still worthy of consideration and serve as a challenge or corrective

---

[58] TGJ p.28
[59] Ibid. p.26
[60] Ibid. p.526
[61] TLC p.590
[62] TGJ p.532
[63] Ibid. 204 footnote p.119

to time-bound expositions of John's gospel. Eternal life is "*the life of the age*", the age of living within God's will in contrast to living with the concerns of this world as the be-all-and-end-all of our existence. Michaels suggests that salvation seen as a promise for the "future" needs to be balanced by both the fact that this "future" is connected with "*the last day*" – (an impossible/unintelligible chronological concept) – and, to use Michaels' own words, "*is more than a future hope. It is a present possession... something a person "has" here and now*"[64]. This has sometimes been expressed as *already-but-not-yet*[65]. In my reading of, and reflection on John, I have not felt it necessary to look as some do for an *apocalyptic key* [66]. I consider [realised] eschatology a more helpful and appropriate tool. Ashton criticises Dodd for failing to take the eschatological element into account when thinking of God's judgement. For Ashton judgement "*of its very nature is God's last act, his ultimate verdict upon the human race*", therefore for Ashton Dodd's term *realised eschatology* is actually de-eschatology, and a contradiction in terms. But why should one choose Ashton's impossible to relate to life "end-of-history-scenario" in preference to Dodd's understanding of a present and continuous relationship with God who is without history? A relationship which includes ultimate - not final – judgement.

John the Baptizer said, "*The One coming after me has come ahead of me, because he was before me*" (Jn.1:15), Jesus said to the Samaritan woman, "*The time is coming and now is*" *(Jn.4:23; 5:25)* and to the Jews in Jerusalem, "*Before Abram was, I am*" (Jn.8:58). None of this makes chronological sense. What Jesus has to offer is not time-bound; and Jesus' pre-existence (Jn.1:1-5) is a-historical, only comprehensible as theology, that which takes "God-beyond-history" into account. My granddaughter's question at the age of eight, "*When was God made?*" perhaps like the parallel question, "*When was I conceived?*" can only be satisfied with a theological answer. The "journey" Jesus made from the Father and to the Father, is not limited to a specific period of time nor trajectory through space, but is the ever-present pattern of Jesus' life in God, from God and to God (Jn.1:1-3), of continuous ascending and descending, as seen with the eyes of faith (Jn.1:51). Eternal life is not defined by, or confined to, any particular place or space - or time - in which it is experienced. John emphasises that Jesus, living the resurrected life, could come into a room with locked or closed doors (Jn.20:19, 26); but living eternal life pre-resurrection he had been able to walk on water (Jn.6:19). The life of the spirit, as we have noted elsewhere is not physically constrained, but has the freedom, the eternal life, which is in God and which is offered in and through Jesus. To contemplate these things is not only to experience great excitement

---

[64] Ibid. p.398
[65] Ibid. p.696 Michaels on 12:31
[66] UFG p.viii

mingled with awe and wonder, but also to be challenged to accept eternal life, life rooted in trust in God which expresses itself in perfect freedom.

The consideration of how times and places fit into understanding God is not merely an academic subject. It has pastoral implications and ramifications. I recently talked with a "religious, but non-church" person whose brother, in his early twenties, had committed suicide two years earlier. Amongst the many difficulties her brother had were gender problems and addiction to drugs. In addition he suffered from mental sickness including devastating depression. But in her eyes he was most of all a much loved and sorely missed brother. We talked until I felt we had covered, though certainly not answered all her questions and I suggested we might agree to rest the business there, but I would be available for further conversation if she felt it might be helpful. And then she asked, *"Right. So where is he?"* And we began to talk about what was at the root of her angst. So I talked with her about John 14 and how some people find contentment through trusting in Jesus' words to his friends that God has a place prepared for them. But we also thought about how the things that really matter, spiritual things like faith, hope, love, cannot really be, and are better not confined to a time or place. So her love for her brother and her brother's "spirit" did not last for the time span of 20+ years and then cease to exist. And just as their relationship of love was maintained in whatever (often different) places they might have been during his life-time, the fact that he was now out of sight did not devalue that loving relationship. She could, and quite obviously still did love him: and if, as I believe, God is best known where love is, then she might have trust that something of God was holding her brother through her love which her brother's death would not diminish – and had conceivably deepened.

This relationship of trust, based upon Jesus' giving of himself in the love and life which death cannot destroy, is the foundation of the work of Jesus which will continue through his disciples and especially through their prayerful petitions offered in his name to him (Jn.14:12-14). Eternal life is not a life yet to be discovered in some other post-death place, nor in realms beyond time. Eternal life is life as lived by Jesus of Nazareth, life in all its fullness for each and every age. So the comfort beyond death which Jesus offered for disciples is complemented by the promise of comfort in the here and now; as Jesus expressed it: *"I will not leave you orphaned"* (Jn.14:18). By over-analysis it is so easy to miss the encouragement offered by Jesus to his friends that they would do greater things than he: and all the other ways in which in Jesus' pre-crucifixion words to his disciples a kind of nurturing was taking place which Jesus' followers would do well to emulate. Jesus invited his disciples to trust or believe in him, but equally, if not more so, he was putting his trust in them. Believing in people is of equal importance to believing in Jesus.

Jesus' promised comfort, or companioned-strengthening, for his disciples is expressed in three ways.

The first, paradoxically, relates to the fact that Jesus is going away. Whether this going away refers to Jesus' crucifixion or to his ascension, or to both, is not said. In any case, in John's gospel the dividing line or difference between these two is not altogether clear. But whatever is meant by "going away", the world would no longer see Jesus, but the disciples faithful adherence to his commandments will mean that he will love them and will, amongst other things, reveal himself to them. So they will see him again (Jn.14:19f). I think it is fair to say that Jesus' love for his disciples was not conditional upon their obedience, but their obedience allowed him to love them - or even made them loveable. Jesus' and his Father's spirit of love could dwell in them as they abided in his words.[67]

The second and related medium of comfort for disciples is the Father's gift to them of the Holy Spirit as their counsellor who will live in them (Jn.14:16f). The Spirit will replace Jesus as their teacher enabling them to remember what Jesus had said to them (Jn.14:26 - and see 20:22), and guide them *into all the truth* (Jn.16:3).

Third, Jesus promises a parting gift of his peace, which is the basis for his repetition of "*Do not let you hearts be troubled, and do not let them be afraid*" (Jn.14:1, 27), even though, "*in this world you will have distress*" (Jn.16:33 - and see 20:19, 21, 26). Perhaps to reassure his disciples Jesus then offered them a reminder that what was going to happen to him should not cause them undue angst, because *the ruler of this world* might be coming, but Jesus' willing obedience to his Father's will is still the controlling factor. They should see his death as the clearest possible demonstration of Jesus' love for his Father (Jn.14:30), and of the intimate relationship of Father and Son - into which Jesus invited his disciples, using the symbols of the vine, branches, and fruit, and explicitly in his prayer – "*Father, just as you are in me and I am in you. May they also be in us*" (Jn.17:21). The Holy Spirit will be their comforter, with them and providing strength to live as Jesus had shown the way to live.

The ending of chapter fourteen "*Rise, let us be on our way*" (Jn.14:31b) sits oddly in what is apparently a monologue which continues to the end of chapter seventeen. Some see this as one of many evidences of the revisions of editors or redactors; but it could just as easily be taken as one of those natural occurrences when there is an intention expressed to move on, but in fact it doesn't happen at that point. In fact, if redactors were at work, it would seem reasonable to suggest that these words would have been excised. (See also my comments on 18:1 below.)

---

[67] cp. 5:38 where some do not dwell in his words and effectively refuse eternal life.

(Chapter 15)

Jesus' words, *I am the true vine* (Jn.15:1), begin a treatise on the disciples being joined to Jesus comparable to fruitful branches being joined to the vine (Jn.15:2-8). His Father is the viticulturist: "*My Father is the vine-grower*" (Jn.15:1). John does not enlarge upon the meaning of *bearing fruit* or being *fruitful*, other than that the fruit will last (Jn.15:16), but Jesus had prophesied earlier that after his death his followers would do greater works than he had (Jn.14:12). This seems the most likely association with the fruit-bearing which Jesus has in mind here - that is, that his ministry of self giving symbolising the true nature of his Father would be continued not just through his present disciples, but through all who came to belief through them and their successors (Jn.17:20). The conversation about being clean which accompanied the foot washing (Jn.13:8ff) is also picked up in the parable of the vine in which unfruitful branches are destroyed and fruitful branches are cleaned or pruned – made fit for purpose. But the central motif of the parable or imagery is the necessity for the disciples to remain joined to Jesus as branches must be joined to a vine if they are to live, be healthy and be fruitful.

The union of Jesus and his disciples is made effective by prayer and obedient, faithful love, with resultant joy. Jesus said to his disciples:

> *If you abide in me and my words abide in you, ask for whatever you wish, and it will be done for you* (Jn.15:7//15:16c//16:24). *This is my commandment, that you love one another as I have loved you* (Jn.15:12, 17). *I have said these things to you that my joy may be in you, and your joy may be complete* (Jn.15:11).

Jesus lays down his life for those who live in obedient love for him and loving service of one another. They are his friends (Jn.15:13) and their love for one another would demonstrate to others the loving obedience of Jesus which united them; it would be a witness (Jn.13:35). This has parallels with Lazarus, whom Jesus described as *our friend* (Jn.11:11), and whose relationship to Jesus, which overcame death, was a potent witness (Jn.11:45). I live in a town where the proliferation of new churches gives an impression of an ever more divided church. To tell the truth, from their earliest days churches have never managed to give real priority to the command to love one another in such a way as to come together in order to be an eloquent witness to those who are in need of seeing the love of Christ evident in relationships between his "followers". Michaels commenting on John 17:21 puts it very well:

> *The point is that it must be a visible unity, a "sign" to the world, testifying not only to their relationships to each other but to their relationship to Jesus and to the Father. Implicit in the notion of unity - in itself a very abstract concept*

- is the concrete imperative of loving one another (as in Jn.13:34-5; 15:12, 17) and obeying Jesus' commands (as in Jn.14:15; 15:10). These are things even "the world" can see, and those things, he implies, are the heart and soul of the disciples' mission to the world - consequently the world's only hope[68].

Having spoken about the love which unites Jesus with his disciples and should unite them with one another, Jesus turned his thoughts to the reality of hate. Jesus had experienced the hatred of some people toward him, and their hatred would bring him suffering and death. The disciples should expect to be treated by "the world" in the same way as Jesus (Jn.15:18ff), including being killed (Jn.16:2). But they should not be deterred from being faithful witnesses to what they had experienced as companions of Jesus *from the beginning* (Jn.15:27) because they will receive the gifts they need, not just to endure, but to be victorious (Jn.16:33). The gifts to a large extent are a repetition of the gifts already promised in chapter 14, (e.g. Holy Spirit and peace), but their value is seen in different ways. This is typical of the fourth gospel in offering echoes which being heard in a different setting are capable of being appreciated with new subtleties.

(Chapter 16)

The first gift, the companionship of the Holy Spirit, would guarantee they would not be witnessing alone. They would be sharing in the work of the Holy Spirit who was promised (Jn.14:16, 26). The companionship they knew with Jesus would be replaced or replicated in their companionship with the Holy Spirit. The Spirit would be bearing testimony (Jn.15:26). It would be an advocate to convince the world of the truth which Jesus came to share (Jn.16:7-11). The Holy Spirit would bring back to the minds of the disciples things Jesus had shared with them, and would guide them and show them the way ahead (Jn.14:26, 16:13). In effect the fourth gospel is the product and a foretaste of the Holy Spirit's work. It is a manifestation of one of God's gifts. Indeed, the gospel enables those who never heard Jesus of Nazareth speak to bring his words to mind.

The second gift was a promise that the weeping, mourning, pain and suffering which the disciples would undoubtedly endure, including the distress of a time when Jesus would have to leave them, would not last for ever. Just as after painful labour and childbirth the wonder of a new life can outweigh, overshadow, even make forgettable the pain. Jesus said to his disciples, *"So you have pain now; but I will see you again, and your hearts will rejoice, and no one will take your joy from you"* (Jn.16:20ff). It is not obvious how this promise to Jesus' first disciples has relevance to their successors. But the death of Jesus is not the only death which has brought fear and sorrow. Many need to believe that they will see their loved ones

---

[68] TGJ p.876

again and find the kind of joy which cannot be taken away. All Jesus' promises can only be received by faith. It seems to me that some may require more trust than others.

Other promises or gifts, such as peace, are briefly touched upon in this particular chapter. The Father loves the disciples and will give to them whatever Jesus asks (Jn.16:26f). Jesus forecast that they would all be scattered and desert him (Jn.16:32). In fact at least one disciple did not abandon Jesus and was there at the cross (Jn.19:26), but the promise remained true that Jesus would never be alone primarily because the Father was always with him - and that should give them peace in Jesus (Jn.16:33; cf.20:21).

Finally, Jesus says they should *take courage;* (because) "*I have conquered the world*" (Jn.16:33) - that is, he offers the example of his own victorious life and death for their encouragement and inspiration. The Greek word (νενικηκα) translated by NRSV as "conquered" has also been translated as "overcome" (e.g. NIV, Youngs) or "defeated" (GNB). All of these can put the emphasis on the destruction or humiliation of the enemy, "the world". But John tells us God loved the world (Jn.3:16), so defeat and humiliation can hardly be what is meant here. The use of the same Greek word in the legend of the Greek runner, Pheidippides, may be helpful. He was sent from the town of Marathon to Athens to announce that against all expectations the Athenian forces had defeated the Persians in the battle of Marathon. It is said that he ran the entire distance without stopping, but moments after proclaiming his message " νενικηκαμεν " (nenikekamen, "We have won!"), he collapsed from exhaustion. It was not the defeat and humiliation of an enemy which made the event so memorable - these are countless. Rather it was because the victory had been won against all the odds as far as the world was concerned. It was the kind of victory which was truly inspirational - as was the way the message was delivered (cf. Jn.19:30). Even if Jesus can foresee the destruction of his enemies resulting from their rejection of all that he stands for, he does not pray for it, nor exult in it, but rejoices only in the way God is glorified by those who are faithful, even unto death - "*I glorified you on earth by finishing the work that you gave me to do*" (Jn.17:4). It is not triumphalism, but truly victorious loving, living and dying which is the glory of God (see Jn.12:27f).

(Chapter 17)

So, as he looked to heaven, Jesus began his prayer: "*Father, the hour has come; glorify your Son so that the Son may glorify you*" (Jn.17:1). Looking up, in common with being "*born from above*", is not indicative of a spatially oriented perception of spiritual realities, of where God is to be found (Jn.3:7f). Looking "up" to heaven in prayer not only parallels Jesus' symbolic action at the tomb of Lazarus (Jn.11:41), it is in keeping with John the Baptizer's testimony that he saw the spirit coming "down from heaven" and remaining on Jesus (Jn.1:32). It also reflects Jesus' own conviction that he had come down from heaven (Jn.6:38), and especially the vision Jesus offered to Nathaniel at the beginning of his ministry. Nathanael would "*see heaven opened and the angels of God ascending and descending upon the Son of Man*" (Jn.1:51). Nathaniel would "see" evidence of the journey Jesus himself was making from and back to the Father (Jn.1:14; 6:62; 8:14, 21f; 13:1; 14:5, 12, 28; 16:17, 28; 17:5, 24; 20:17). This would not be in a space ship - or even using a physical ladder, but by way of glorification, what we might call spiritual elevation. The constant nature of the ascent and descent of the angels "*upon the Son of Man*" may well be a symbol of the intercourse between Jesus and his Father in heaven, including the delivery of the gifts from the Father which Jesus was offering in his Father's name. Traditionally many Christians bow their heads and close their eyes to pray, probably as a sign of respect. The body posture for such praying easily becomes inward focussed. It was at one time dangerously disrespectful to look at a king. But Jesus' gave an example of "looking up" as an accompaniment to prayer. I have tried it. It evokes a quite distinctive sense of relationship to God - sometimes a different, expansive kind of prayer.

Jesus now knew *the hour* had come for his return (Jn.17:1; 13:1), *the hour* Jesus believed could not be pre-empted (Jn.2:4; 7:30; 8:20) and which had been previously heralded (Jn.12:23, 27). *The hour* is probably not best understood as referencing a specific or predetermined time or date, so that all the inestimable millions of actions which impinged on Jesus' life had to be dovetailed together in some predestined pattern. *The hour* is that moment when what was to be accomplished had reached its obvious dénouement (Jn.17:4). As Brutus says in Shakespeare's Julius Caesar, "*There is a tide in the affairs of men, which taken at the flood leads on to victory*". *Carpe diem.*

It is highly significant that Jesus' prayer to his Father at this literally crucial moment in his life is petition rather than intercession. A. J. Cocksworth's comment is profoundly thought provoking, insightful and relevant:

> *Prayer is, after all, the stuff of human freedom and human flourishing; it is precisely in prayer that the ethical agent inhabits the freedom of God into which she is drawn, and actualises her responsibility to the world as a grateful creature of God* [69].

Cocksworth is not actually talking about Jesus, but this rationale for prayer applies as much to Jesus in relation to his Father in heaven as to anyone else. For Jesus to actualise his particular responsibility for the world meant he was to willingly give his life, to die for it. Through prayer he accomplished significant deeds (Jn.6:11,

---

[69] Expository Times Aug. 2011 p.570

15, 23; 11:41), and inhabited the freedom of God, which impelled him toward his destiny. Prayer is the channel through which the gifts of God can be received (Jn.14:13f; 15:7, 16; 16:24). Jesus lived as well as taught this. *"Jesus in this Gospel rarely prays in the conventional sense of the word because his whole life on earth is a prayer, by virtue of his union with the Father"*[70]. This understanding of prayer may be why, as far as I can tell, Jesus never called people to a prayer meeting!

The beginning of Jesus' prayer is different to what follows. It is offered in the third person:

> *"Father, the time has come. Glorify your son, that your son may glorify you. You have given him authority over all people, to give eternal life to all whom you have given him. And this is eternal life, that they may know you, the only true God, and Jesus Christ whom you have sent"* (Jn.17:1-3).

Is Jesus talking as much to his disciples as he is to his Father? Prayer can have a social function as well as a spiritual purpose. It is interesting to note that in his conversation with the Samaritan woman at one point Jesus adopted the third person to speak about himself (Jn.4:10), and in so doing challenged the woman to see more in Jesus than she had hitherto. In other places where Jesus refers to himself not as "I", but as "The Son of Man" it might be for a similar purpose (Jn.6:27, 53; 9:35; 12:34).

The use of the third person in Jesus' prayer may be due to other reasons. It may be John's literary way of taking the "author-ity", the "giving" initiatives embodied in the person of Jesus of Nazareth into a dimension which (to use a Johannine image) is more like the wind which blows when and where it will, down through the ages, all across the face of the earth. The authority is not divorced from Jesus, but it will no longer be related primarily to Jesus as Jesus of Nazareth, nor as son of Joseph (Jn.1:45; 6:42), nor as Son of Man (Jn.1:51; 3:14; etc), but to Jesus as God's son (Jn.1:49; 5:25; 11:27; 20:31). Jesus as the Son of Man is worshipped (Jn.9:35-38), crucified, lifted up (Jn.3:14; 12:23), and in this way glorifies God (Jn.9:28): but who the Son of Man is remains an enigma: *"Who is this Son of man ... who is he?"* (Jn.12:34; 9:36). It is to believe in, put one's trust in Jesus as *God's son* which is to receive eternal life (Jn.3:15f, 36; 4:14, 36; 5:24, 39; 6:27, 40, 47, 54, 68; 11:25; 17:2f). Jesus' prayer begins by affirming his son-ship and the benefits which derive from recognising his son-ship.

Way back in the first *sign* the obedient, knowing servants had been instrumental in helping to reveal the glory of Jesus (Jn.2:7-11). Now as Jesus drew near to his *hour* (Jn.2:4) Jesus prayed to his Father for those who had *"kept your word"*, and who

---

[70] TGJ p.644

"know that everything you have given me is from you ... I have given .... they have received ... and know .... and I have been glorified in them" (Jn.17:7ff). The disciples were obedient, knowing servants of Jesus and his Father. Easily overlooked, but quite crucial in the prayer is the repeated intimation that Jesus *"Gave them the words you gave me"* (Jn.17:8) or had *"given them your word"* (Jn.17:14). It is by abiding in this word, making this gift a permanent "possession", being obedient to it, that Jesus' disciples will be sanctified, or consecrated (Jn.17:17). As Jesus has glorified and been glorified by his Father in completing his work of mission and witness (Jn.17:1, 4f), so they can glorify Jesus (Jn.17:10) by completing their mission (Jn.17:18) and witnessing to the world (Jn.17:23).

The prayer of Jesus for his disciples has both a preamble (17:6-10) and a postscript (Jn.17:25-26). The prayer itself is comparatively short, yet a very powerful set of petitions (Jn.17: 11-24). The prayer that Jesus offered for them includes many themes, most of which are not unpacked within the prayer. In keeping with the character of this gospel as a whole they are expounded in other places.

The first petition of Jesus is for the gift of continuing protection for the disciples, but the nature of this protection is *"by the power of your name"*, and the purpose is *"so that they may be one"* (Jn.17:11f). This is not physical protection, but protection from divisiveness which is the work of the *evil one* and the nature of *the world* to which his disciples do not belong any more than did Jesus. The world will hate them as it hated Jesus (Jn.17:14-16). Rightly the most commonly highlighted theme in Jesus' prayer is that of unity (Jn.17:11ff). Jesus prayed for "oneness" amongst his present and future disciples (Jn.17:20) as a witness to the world (Jn.17:21, 23) - a oneness with each other and with Jesus, embracing the oneness of Jesus with his Father *"so that the love with which you have loved me may be in them, and I in them"* (Jn.17:26). Sadly, as mentioned above, the church as a whole has yet to take to heart and give practical expression to Jesus' conviction that the glory of God is seen supremely in the unity of his disciples - and is marred by any divisiveness[71]. One of the most the most bizarre and saddest illustration of this is that the keys to the Chapel of the Resurrection in Jerusalem are held by a Moslem because the different Christian groups who share responsibility for it cannot come to an amicable arrangement amongst themselves. Conversely, though "uniting" often seems a step too far, there are plenty of examples of Christians from different traditions coming closer together and demonstrating their love for one another. Such experience has been one of the joys in my own long-term involvement in ecumenical endeavour.

Other important themes are touched upon in Jesus' prayer, such as joy (Jn.17:13 - cf.8:56; 15:11; 16:20ff), and sanctification in the truth - *"For their sakes I sanctify*

---

[71] See above on Chapter 15 paragraph 1

myself, so that they also may be sanctified in truth" (Jn.17:19). Truth in this instance for Jesus, is his Father's trustworthy word (Jn.17:17) which Jesus had given to his disciples (Jn.17:14 - and see on 14:6 above). Sanctification is obedience to God's will, which is expressed by being sent into the world. Jesus' disciples do not belong to the world, but they are sent into it (Jn.17:18). When Christians hear the words, *"Go in peace to love and serve the Lord"*, the command *"Go"* should be understood as going into the world, and *"to love"* as love for the world (cf. Jn.3:16; 12:47), for in this dual obedience God the Father of Jesus is served and we are in this way the saints, the sanctified ones – commissioned and committed to share in God's love for the world. A personal relationship with Jesus which does not have an inter-personal dimension is nonsense. The Father of Jesus is not honoured, served or glorified by self-absorbed piety. To follow Jesus means to be sent and to go into the world to love it - perhaps even to die for it.

The prayer in John 17 also picks up Jesus' earlier comforting promise to his disciples that *"where I am, there you may be also"* (Jn.14:3). Jesus prayed, *"I desire that those also whom you have given me may be with me where I am, to see my glory"* (Jn.17:24), the glory his Father had given Jesus because the Father loved Jesus *before the foundation of the world* (Jn.17:24; 1:1ff, 10; 17:5). Although Jesus would be glorified on the cross, other aspects of his glorification had been there throughout his ministry (Jn.1:14; 2:11; 11:4): indeed it existed *before the world was* (Jn.17:5). When the writer of John's gospel says, *"We beheld his glory"* it is an indication that Jesus' prayer had been answered.

The prayer of Jesus for his disciples brought to an end Jesus' pre-Passover teaching in the context of foot-washing and a supper (chapters 13-17). What is really an extended monologue by Jesus began with Judas, *"the one destined to be lost"* (Jn.17:12), and his devilish intention to betray Jesus (Jn.13:2), to bring about his death. The prayer in John 17 is Jesus' final preparation of himself and his disciples - and John's readers - for that death.

(Chapter 18)

Almost as though he is carrying straight on from 14:31, John moves us very quickly from the prayer of Jesus for himself and his disciples into the beginning of the end and its aftermath. Perhaps we should read chapters 15-17 with the sense of urgency which John may have intended by intruding them between 14:31 and 18:1. In fact, 14:31 usually translated as, *"Come now. Let us leave"* might be better understood, as *"Come, on. We need to get on with this"*. Jesus now knows his hour has come. He is going to die. There was much to be said and little time to say it.

"After he had spoken these words, he went out with his disciples across the Kidron Valley to a place where there was a garden" (Jn.18:1). Jesus *"knowing all that was*

going to happen to him" identified himself twice to the soldiers and police who came with Judas to arrest him (Jn.18:2-5). He was voluntarily giving himself into the hands of sinful men - and even more into the hands of his Father. Jesus had said:

> *"No one can take my life from me. I sacrifice it voluntarily. For I have the authority to lay it down when I want to and also to take it up again. For this is what my Father has commanded"* (Jn.10:18).

So when Peter cut off the ear of Malchus, the high priest's slave, Jesus told Peter to sheath his sword, asking Peter the rhetorical yet heartfelt question, *"Am I not to drink the cup that the Father has given me?"* (Jn.18:10f). Jesus was still receiving from his Father, even if it was the cup of suffering, and in obedience to his Father he was still giving, giving of himself, laying down and giving up his life out of love for his friends (cf.Jn.15:13f) whose safety he managed to secure in the garden (Jn.18:8f) and about whom he refused to give details to Annas (Jn.18:19ff).

Michaels pictures the scene of Jesus' arrest as one in which a cohort of six hundred Roman soldiers, plus Judas and officers from the High Priest and Pharisees were in the garden. Whilst the Greek word *speiran* (σπεῖραν - a cohort) is used by John, most translators and commentators have quite reasonably taken it to be a detachment rather than literally a cohort - which would surely have been most unlikely - and as Michaels acknowledges might rather undermine Jesus' claim that he lays down his life and no one takes it from him (Jn.10:17f.[72]). It also throws into question the notion that Jesus could negotiate the safety of his companions (Jn.18:9). In fact, I see no compelling reason to believe that Roman soldiers were involved at all in the arrest of Jesus. If they were, why did he initially face a Jewish trial rather than a Roman one? The more likely reading is that this was a detachment of the chief priests' own guard who had on a previous occasion been sent to arrest Jesus (Jn.7:33, 45f)[73]. This time, to ensure the job is done, they are accompanied by some of the Pharisees and chief priest's officials. As is clear later in the account of Peter's denials, it was one of them whose ear was cut off. It is unreasonable to suggest that six hundred Roman soldiers stood by while this happened and did nothing.

---

[72] TGJ p.891

[73] France cites Blinzler, *Trial* 61-70, who argues the case that all the troops in John's account of Jesus' arrest are Jewish - RTF p.1012 n14. Perhaps most telling against Michaels conjectures of Roman involvement is Matthew's unambiguous statement concerning those who accompanied Judas Iscariot to the garden, *"... a large crowd armed with swords and clubs, sent from the chief priests and the elders of the people"* (Matt.26:47).

John tells us that having been arrested Jesus was bound and taken to Annas, the father-in-law of Caiaphas, who was the high priest that year (Jn.18:12-14). The identity of the High Priest is somewhat confused seeming to be either Annas (Jn.18:15, 19, 22), or Caiaphas (Jn.11:49; 18:24), or both[74]. If, as John tells us (Jn.18:24), Caiaphas was the high priest, and Annas his father-in-law (Jn.18:13) then John gives no good reason for the involvement of Annas, but intriguingly tells us that one of Jesus' disciples was known to the high priest and therefore had access to the house of Annas. This disciple also had enough influence to arrange through "*the woman who guarded the gate*" for Peter to have access to the courtyard. It was this woman's quite logical question about whether Peter was a disciple of Jesus which brought the first of Peter's three denials (Jn.18:17, 25-27). The prophecy of Jesus that before the cock crowed Peter would deny him three times (Jn.13:38) had begun to be fulfilled. There is perhaps an intentional parallel, yet subtle distinction, between John's account of Judas leaving to betray Jesus when "*it was night*" (Jn.13:30) and Peter's denials of Jesus when "*it was cold*" (Jn.18:17). Jesus was sent to Caiaphas, but no account is given of any interaction between Caiaphas and Jesus. We are simply told that Annas sent Jesus bound to Caiaphas (Jn.18:24), and Jesus was taken from Caiaphas to Pilate's headquarters early in the morning (Jn.18:28).

The account which John gives of Jesus in the hands of his Jewish interrogators is sparse and yielded neither specific accusations, nor substantive answers. Furthermore, when Jesus was taken to Pilate he was accused of being a criminal, but with no stated crime (Jn.18:29f). In Pilate's first conversation with Jesus, Pilate said, "*Your own nation and chief priests have handed you over to me*" - a further indication that Roman soldiers had not been involved in arresting Jesus.. Pilate asked Jesus, "*What have you done?*" (Jn.18:35). The reader is left in no doubt that there was no genuine case against Jesus; not even a specific charge. He had done no wrong. John told his readers earlier that Jesus had been condemned without a hearing (Jn.7:45-52) and the members of the Sanhedrin were determined to kill him (Jn.11:53). Michaels suggests: "*In John's gospel the whole public ministry of Jesus (at least from chapter 5 on) is his trial at the hands of the Jewish religious authorities, one in which he is both the accused and the accuser*"[75]. As noted above, Jesus would also have been subject to the negative stereotypes of, or prejudices against Galileans which were common amongst the Pharisees and ruling authorities in Jerusalem[76]. In chapter 18 the false accusations of wrongdoing stand in marked contrast to Jesus' testimony to Pilate, "*For this I was born, and for this I came into the world, to testify to the truth*" (Jn.18:37). Against the background of clandestine, night-time plots and lies Jesus shines out as innocence and truth: and

---

[74] TGJ p.908

[75] Ibid.p.34

[76] Ibid.p.475

Pilate, having found "*no case against him*", moved to try to secure his release - but to no avail (Jn.18:38b-40; 19:6). Barabbas the bandit is preferred to Jesus: "*And this is the judgement, light has come into the world, and people loved darkness rather than light because their deeds were evil*" (Jn.3:19).

(Chapter 19)

Pilate had Jesus flogged, perhaps in the hope that this would placate Jesus' enemies (Jn.19:1-6). As well as flagellation, Jesus was physically and verbally abused, mocked as "King of the Jews". Pilate's first question to Jesus had been, "*Are you the king of the Jews?*" (Jn.18:33). This question, which amounted to a political accusation, did not go away. Pilate made further attempts to persuade Jesus' accusers to carry out their own punishment, but his accusers finally came up with the charge that Jesus claimed to be the "*Son of God*" (Jn.19:7 cf. 5:18; 10:33,36), and threatened Pilate that he might be portrayed as "*no friend of the emperor*" (Jn.19:12). Although three times he had found Jesus not guilty of any crime (Jn.18:38; 19:4, 6), Pilate succumbed to their pressure. The title or claim to be "*Son of God*" would probably have had more of a political than a religious connotation for Pilate, and Jesus' accusers overtly played the political card when they said to Pilate, "*Everyone who claims to be a king sets himself against the emperor*"; inferring that this was the case with Jesus. In spite of his conversation with Jesus, his failure to find any fault in Jesus, and his evident desire to release Jesus, Pilate nonetheless handed Jesus over to "them" to be crucified (Jn.19:16). It is so often true that when institutional powers or vested interests collaborate for self-protection, the fate of an individual casualty (or sometimes of hundreds or thousands of individuals) is deemed to be of no account. The Bhopal Gas disaster of 1984 is a most graphic and tragic examples of this; and others might add Hiroshima and Nagasaki, the killing fields of Cambodia, *ad infinitum*.

Although John tells us that Pilate handed Jesus over to his accusers for crucifixion, it is clear that the crucifixion was carried out by Roman soldiers with Pilate's authority since the Jews had to ask Pilate for the prisoners legs to be broken (Jn.19:31f). There have been suggestions that the Jewish authorities could have carried out the death sentence themselves, though not by crucifixion[77]. Jesus was given back to them to be crucified (Jn.19:16), but as with all John's gospel, the point being made is primarily theological rather than factual. Herein lies the kernel of the fourth gospel. Jesus, who belongs to God, is "given", and gives himself in all his self-accepted vulnerability. "We" must choose what we do with him.

Whoever carried out the death penalty, in worldly terms the chief priests and their allies who demanded Jesus' death were primarily responsible. However, Jesus had

---

[77] TGJ p.931 n80 on Schnackenburg, and Michaels' own view TGJ p.931

197

said to his disciples, "*the ruler of this world has no power over me*" (Jn.14:30), and, although by this he meant Satan, he also said to Pilate, "*You could have no power over me unless it had been given to you from above*" (Jn.19:11; 16:11, 33; see above on 14:30). His aggressive accusers were culpable, as to some extent was Pilate, but all the acts of malicious, fearful and weak individuals which reflect the "power" of Satan and the ways of the world are subordinate to the ongoing will of the Father, and the self-giving obedience of the Son. Jesus was crucified with the inscription, "*Jesus of Nazareth, the King of the Jews*" (Jn.19:19). Significantly the protests, cynicism and wilful ignorance of those who brought about his death were not enough to take away the title - though as Jesus said, "*My kingdom is not from this world ... is not from here*" (Jn.18:36). Jesus did not come to dominate or rule the world, nor to condemn it, but to love it - even unto death (Jn.3:16). In that sense and only in that sense Jesus was a "king". The only acceptable biblical king for God's people is one who will be their shepherd, one who will lay down his life for the sheep. John's gospel makes this quite clear if the gospel is read as all of a piece.

John specifically tells us of Jesus that he carried his own cross "*by himself*" to Golgotha (Jn.19:17)[78] where he was crucified between two others. John's gospel is full of signs, though the majority are not designated as such. Jesus carrying his own cross to "*the Place of the Skull*" is surely amongst the most powerful signs, if not THE most significant moment in the whole of his story (Jn.19:17). Specific mention of the cross is not a feature of Jesus' teaching in John: the significance of his death is (Jn.12:32f; 18:32. cp. 21:19 concerning Peter). Jesus, like the solitary grain of wheat that falls into the ground and dies, (Jn.12:24) gave his individual life so that many might receive life (cf. Jn.11:50; 18:14).

Those who see the raising of Lazarus as "*the seventh and ultimate sign*"[79], are surely wrong, not just in the number seven (cp. Jn.2:23; 3:2), but in using the word *ultimate* for anything other than Jesus' own death, resurrection life and projected ascension. One possible reason for the apparent failure of Kiefer and others to see the foot washing of the disciples, the reported issue of blood and water from Jesus on the cross (Jn.19:34.[80]), Jesus' death and resurrection, and so much more as *signs*, is the division they make of John's gospel into a "book of signs" (Jn.1:19-12:50) and a "book of glory" (Jn.13:1-20:29), enveloped by a prologue (Jn.1:1-18) and an afterword (Jn.21)[81]. This is an artificial and unhelpful division carrying with it the unfortunate likelihood that it will take away the overall unity of John's work. It

---

[78] In all three Synoptic gospels Simon from Cyrene is pressed into service to carry Jesus' cross (Luke 23:26//Mark 15:21//Matthew 27:32).
[79] OBC p.981
[80] See TGJ p.969 for the deep significance of this report
[81] e.g. Gabriel Fackre TLC p.548

seems to overlook the fact that John tells us that it was in his "*becoming flesh and living amongst us*" that "we" were able to see "*his glory*" (Jn.1:14). To emphasise this incarnated glory John tells us that at the wedding in Cana Jesus "*revealed his glory*" (Jn.2:11). Those who do not see the whole of John's story as "glorious" are ignoring what John clearly sets out to convey at the beginning of his gospel; and worst of all it takes away the significance of the cross as connected to, and the climax of everything that had been given before, including ubiquitous signs.

I prefer not to follow those who would divide the content of John's gospel into discreet sections, or even well defined groups of sayings. The traditional selection of seven *I am* sayings serves as a useful example of why this is so. Before returning to chapter 19 we shall take a few moments to consider the artificiality of proposing seven *I am* sayings.

"*I am the vine*" (Jn.15:5) is often cited as the seventh of "the seven *I am* sayings"; but the choice of verse five in chapter fifteen arbitrarily ignores verse one in which Jesus says, "*I am the true vine*"(Jn.15:1). Furthermore, this so-called final *I am* saying is in chapter 15, so do we need a demarcation of the gospel there? [82] A pre- and post- *I am sayings* division would be particularly attractive if revelation is accepted as a key determinant for understanding the gospel. But there are not just seven *I am* sayings in John. They are manifold: starting, some would suggest, with "*the water I give*", which is repeated, and in which Jesus uses *ego,* the strong "I" (Jn.4:14). Certainly Jesus' words, "*I am he*" (ἐγώ εἰμι 4:26) is a definite use of "*I am*" by Jesus. These words "*I am he*", which probably carry the most obvious divine connotation of all the "*I am*" sayings, are used on seven occasions in the fourth gospel (Jn.4:26; 6:20; 8:24, 28, 58; 13:19; and 18:5ff). Jesus as the bread of life (Jn.6:34, 48) is only one expression of an *I am* saying associated with bread. Jesus is also the bread that came down from heaven (Jn.6:41), and the living bread (Jn.6:51). The *I am* sayings, "*I am from above*" (Jn.8:23)... "*I am not of this world*" (Jn.17:16) and the defiant and definitive, "*Before Abram was born, I am*" (Jn.8:58) must all be overlooked in order to preserve the number seven.

"*I am the gate*" (Jn.10:9) inexplicably takes precedence over "*I am the gate for the sheep*" (Jn.10:7): whilst incredibly "*I am the good shepherd*" (Jn.10:11, 14) is preferred to "*I am God's Son*" (Jn.10:36). "*I am the resurrection and the life*" (Jn.11:25) is clearly a pivotal saying in John's gospel, but to be considered as number five of seven is hardly helpful. Again, when Jesus said to his disciples, "*You call me 'Master' and 'Lord', and rightly so, for that is what I am*", this is not regarded as an *I am* saying because it does not fit the accepted formula of the

---

[82] Michaels, though using different descriptions for the two major sections, to a great extent follows the division of the fourth gospel at 12:50. But he acknowledges, *Structure in John's Gospel, as in most great literature, is largely in the eye of the beholder.* TGJ p.37

seven: subject (I) + verb (am) + predicate (bread, etc.)., Had John expressed this as *I am master and Lord*, it might have found its place in some commentators' *I am* tick list.

Perhaps the most glaring omission from the traditional seven *I am* sayings are the words of Jesus predicting that the time will come when the disciples will know that "*I am who I am*" (Jn.13:19 cp. Exodus 3:14)[83]. The point I am making is not quibbling over the number seven, but emphasising the artificiality of any kind of "mechanical" or "forensic" approach to a text throughout which the spirit of *I am* is intended to flow freely.

The words of Jesus "*I am the way, and the truth and the life*" (Jn.14:6) can serve as a statement which encapsulates some of the other *I am* sayings which follow. So Jesus as the way leads to several statements of "*I am going to the Father*" (Jn.14:12, 28; 16:5, 10 etc.) - or "*I am ascending to my Father and your Father, to my God and your God*" (Jn.20:17). Truth would be the subject of discussion with Pilate, but is not extensively treated. Life is probably understood in the context of the three-way relationship of Jesus, the Father and Jesus' disciples. "*I am in the Father and the Father is in me*" (Jn.14:10); "*I am in my Father, and you are in me, and I am in you*" (Jn.14:20); "*Just as I am in you and you are in me ... so ... I in them and you in me*" (Jn.17:20f). This is slightly different to another omitted *I am* saying, "*I am not alone for my Father is with me*" (Jn.16:32), which should be held in association with "*I am ascending to my Father*" (Jn.20:17) and "*I am going to the Father, for the Father is greater than I*" (Jn.14:28). By effectively ignoring all of these *I am* sayings, much of what is central to John's gospel is relegated in importance. And there are two more which ought to be considered as significant. First, Jesus said to Pilate, *You say I am a king* (Jn.18:37). Jesus does not refute this, although he does challenge Pilate's understanding of what kingship means (Jn.18:36). Second, if we take Michael's dictum that the task of the commentator is to interpret the text *as it has come down to us* to its logical conclusion[84], then most of "us" have received the text in its English translation, which would make the final and perhaps the most important *I am* saying of them all, "*I am sending you*" (Jn.20:21). This would rightly turn "*I am*" sayings of Jesus from a narrow, cosy, descriptive tick-list to a missionary enterprise, from control and creed to trust and commission[85].

---

[83] Michaels offers helpful insights into the way in which texts from deuteron-Isaiah may well inform the *I am* sayings in John where *I am* is suggestive of *I am the Lord* TGJ p.534
[84] TGJ p.xii
[85] Michaels suggests that in Jesus "conversations" as given in John, the use of the emphatic first-person singular by Jesus is a literary device often used to mark a change in what the gospel intends to convey (e.g. in chapter 5:19-47 where Michaels notes just such a change at v.30) TGJ p.323

Chapter 4 - John

Jesus was always giving. However, in contrast to when he laid his garments down in order to wash his disciples' feet (Jn.13:4), at Golgotha Jesus did not give up his clothes. They were taken and divided as perks for the four soldiers on crucifixion duty, with lots cast for Jesus' seamless tunic or undergarment (Jn.19:23-25a). John tells us that the division of Jesus' clothes was a fulfilment of Scripture. He cites verse 18 from Palm 22; a Psalm which has often been regarded as prophetic or descriptive of the experience of crucifixion[86]. The division of the sufferer's clothes is not the most obvious choice to show scripture's fulfilment in the death of Jesus; but perhaps, as is so often the case, the sign offered is an invitation to considerably more reflection. Psalm 22 though three-quarters full of agony concludes with "*all the ends of the earth*" turning to the Lord and the affirmation that the sufferer will live for the Lord (Ps.22:27, 29). Furthermore the Psalm ends with a note of resounding triumph, "*Future generations will be told about the Lord, and proclaim his deliverance to a people yet unborn, saying that he has done it*" (Ps.22:30f) - "*It is finished*" (cf. Jn.12:32; 19:30).

Even, or perhaps especially on the cross, Jesus' love of his friends is not diminished; nor necessarily theirs for him. John tells us of four women at the cross, and the disciple whom Jesus loved. At least some of his disciples were not far away from Jesus in his trials and in his hour of death (Jn.18:15; 19:26). From the cross Jesus invited a new relationship of care, symbolised by the gift of a Mother for "*the disciple whom he loved*", and the adoption and protection of a "son" for a mother whose own son was dying on a cross (Jn.19:25-27). This last act of kindness - we might say setting his affairs in order - is the precursor to Jesus being confident that "*all was now finished*" (Jn.19:28). Not everyone has the opportunity, but I have seen on many occasions when a person has approached their death with a kind of satisfaction because they have made sure the affairs of their loved ones were in order and they were going to be looked after. It is not always easy to see Jesus' common humanity in the commanding figure of Jesus who seems to stride so purposefully and masterfully through John's gospel, but here as in other places his humanity shines through (cf.Jn.11:35; 12:7, 27).

John tells us that there was one last fulfilling of scripture when Jesus said "*I thirst*", which prompted the gift to him of bitter wine lifted on a stalk of hyssop[87]. Again, there is much pathos and irony in this situation in which the one who in response to the needs of others turned water into the best wine, in his own hour of need

---

[86] See also Ps.69 cited in Jn.2:17 in connection with the cleansing of the Temple. Psalm 69 also has passages which can be related to the experience of crucifixion.
[87] Though John does not make this scriptural connection explicit, Hyssop was used for smearing the blood on the houses of the Israelites prior to their exodus from Egypt (Ex.12:22) or for ritual cleansing of a house (Lev.4:14ff.).

201

received the poorest (see on Jn.13:25 above). He who gave the promise of rivers of living water (Jn.7:38) was himself thirsty. Yet still the real food and drink for Jesus was "*to do the will of Him who sent me and to complete his work* (Jn.4:34): and out of him flowed living water, water and blood (Jn.19:34 cp. 4:10; 7:38). The work was now complete or accomplished. As Jesus said, "*It is finished .... .Then he bowed his head and gave up his spirit*" (Jn.19:30). In appreciating Jesus as gift and giver, giving up or laying down his life, surrendering his spirit to his Father is perhaps Jesus' ultimate gift to his Father God, to his disciples, and to the world.

Allusions to, rather than quotations from the Jewish scriptures are said by some commentators to abound in the earlier chapters of John. For example, Burgess on the feeding of the five thousand sees at least a dozen possible Old Testament parallels[88]. Jesus often refers to scripture in his debates with opponents (Jn.2:17; 6:31; 7:38; 8:54; 10:33f); and the author of the fourth gospel indicates that scripture is being fulfilled in Jesus' life (Jn.12:38-41). But not till 13:18 is there a specific indication by Jesus that scripture would be fulfilled[89]. It is intriguing just how much John overtly relates the death of Jesus to the scriptures in comparison with his scant specific scriptural reference prior to this. So when the legs of the others who were crucified were broken and Jesus' were not John sees the fulfilling of a prophecy in Psalm 34 regarding a righteous man (Jn.19:34-36. Ps.34:21). Others have drawn parallels with the treatment of the Passover lamb whose bones were not to be broken (Exodus 12:46; Numbers 9:12). Because Jesus was already dead, he was pierced with a spear and we are informed "*at once blood and water came out*" - a direct quote from the prophet Zechariah (Zech.12:10). Actually the scripture quoted is of little help in appreciating the symbolism of the issue of blood and water from Jesus' side, and the call to faith in Jesus which it represents (Jn.19:35). One must look elsewhere in John's gospel for this; but these and other references serve to emphasise John's conviction that even if he limits specific scriptural references, everything about Jesus, especially his death, was in keeping with, and a fulfilment of the scriptures. For John "*These are the scriptures that testify about*" Jesus (Jn.5:39), and as Ashton puts it, "*The evangelist and his readers are the rightful inheritors of the whole biblical tradition*"[90]. This is paged up very early in the fourth gospel: "*After he was raised from the dead his disciples remembered .... And they believed the scripture and the word that Jesus had spoken*" (Jn.2:22). The clause, "*... and the word that Jesus had spoken*" is also important. It was not just the fulfilment of scriptures that the disciples remembered, but through the agency of the Holy Spirit (Jn.14:26) also the fulfilment of all that Jesus had said and prophesied (e.g. Jn.18:32). For John Jesus' words carried the same authority as scripture: "*For John a single saying of Jesus can have the status*

---

[88] TLC pp.506f
[89] cf. TGJ p.739 n91
[90] UFG p.145

of a verse of scripture" (Jn.18:9) *Even more startlingly, Jesus himself can become the object of a Midrash"* (Jn.5:39)[91]. We take it for granted that Jesus' words have the status of scripture since they are given in our (Christian) Bible. For Jesus' contemporaries it was a major departure from their received religion and its associated canon of scriptures.

A word of caution is in order. Allusions to Scripture, as opposed to direct quotations, should not be too easily assumed or used[92]. Early in John's gospel we are told through Philip that Jesus is *"someone of whom Moses wrote in the Law, and of whom the prophets wrote"* (Jn.1:45). It is apparent that the author of John's gospel is well acquainted with scripture and saw it being fulfilled in Jesus, especially perhaps what was contained in the "Books of Moses" (Jn.5:39, 46), but systematically to try to relate everything in this gospel to specific passages of scripture seems neither justifiable, nor a priority for Jesus. The scriptures testify to Jesus, not the other way round: *"You search the scriptures ... (but) ... you are unwilling to come to me that you might have life"* (Jn.5:39f).

John's account of Jesus' death is completed when Joseph of Arimathea asks permission to remove Jesus' body. He and Nicodemus, both secret disciples, took charge of Jesus' body. Whether or not they removed it from the cross we are not told, but Nicodemus at least was an older man (Jn.3:4), so if they did it was literally a labour of love. The cross was not empty because Jesus was raised from the dead. That emptied the tomb. The cross was empty because of the love of two (probably elderly) men for Jesus. Putting themselves at risk they gave Jesus the respect any human being merits in death. Mirroring in many ways the generous actions of Mary who anointed Jesus' feet with an extravagant quantity of perfume (Jn.12:1-8), Nicodemus and Joseph embalmed Jesus' body using the significantly generous amount of myrrh and aloes they provided. They wrapped his body in spiced cloth. Then because of the lateness of the hour, and the approach of the Passover Sabbath, they laid it, possibly temporarily, in an unused tomb which was in a nearby garden (Jn.19:38-42). A garden - where seeds die so that new life is made possible, especially when *"My Father is the gardener"* (Jn.15:1) and there are people in it who are willing to fill it with love.

---

[91] Ibid. p.340

[92] E.g. in contrast to Odeberg (*The Fourth Gospel* 33) and others, Michaels, commenting on, *the angels ascending and descending on the Son of Man* (1:51) says *The allusion in Jesus' pronouncement to Jacob's dream at Bethel (Gen 28:12) is neither as direct nor as unmistakable as is commonly assumed* (TGJ p.136). Unlike Jacob, for Nathanael there is no ladder, there is no dream, there is no covenant promise, and equating Jacob with the Son of Man would be to unreasonably stretch the imagination. On the other hand Michaels also asserts, *Sometimes Jesus' own words are so closely entwined with Scripture that it is difficult to tell which is which (7:38; 19:28)* (TGJ p.170).

(Chapter 20)

John does not tell us in advance about a stone placed at the entrance to the tomb, but early on Sunday morning Mary Magdalene found "the stone" had been removed from the tomb (Jn.20:1-2). Mary assumed "they", presumably Joseph of Arimathea and Nicodemus after the sunset which ended the Sabbath, had moved his body. Mary reported this to Peter and the other disciple whom Jesus loved, adding, "*We do not know where they have laid him*". It is, of course, a reasonable conjecture that enemies of Jesus might have removed his body. The secret burial for Sadam Hussein and sea burial for Osama bin Laden to avoid their post-death veneration is hardly a new phenomenon: but there is no suggestion of this in John's account of proceedings.

John gives no reason, but perhaps to verify for themselves Mary's report, Peter and his co-disciple visited the "empty" tomb and both in turn saw the linen wrappings for Jesus' body and the head-cloth lying separately. To some extent their reactions are the same. They both as yet did not understand the scripture, and they both returned to their homes; but the disciple whom Jesus loved "*saw and believed*" (Jn.20:8). The combination of "*did not understand*" and "*saw and believed*" might seem paradoxical. But perhaps this belief, or faith, is that deep trust which surpasses knowledge, and with minimal evidence, wells up in one who having been the recipient of the love of Christ always lives in hope. I think "believing without understanding" would be a fair description of many Christians, and possibly should be true of us all when we are faced with life's deepest mysteries.

John provides ample evidence that Jesus, even in his death, engendered a great deal of love for himself (See above on Jn.11:2f; 12:1-8). Mary Magdalene makes her first appearance in the fourth gospel standing near the cross (Jn.19:25), but she obviously knew the disciples (Jn.20:2), and was known to Jesus. Mary wept outside the tomb before looking into it (Jn.20:11). In the "empty" tomb Mary now saw two angels in white seated as though the body of Jesus was still between them, one at his head and one at his feet. Michaels makes the point "*Angels play only a minor role in this gospel*".[93] Nathaniel is told he will see angels (Jn.1:51), and some members of a crowd thought they might have heard an angel speaking to Jesus (Jn.12:29); but in fact this appearance at the tomb is their solitary actual appearance in the fourth gospel[94]. Maybe John is telling us that Jesus had guardian angels who had been at work in the tomb. But perhaps only one who loved and who mourned could see it.

---

[93] TGJ p.291 n20

[94] On ten occasions in the other gospels angels are associated with the Son of man, and often in a protective role. See TGJ p.137

And then Mary saw Jesus.

The encounter of Mary Magdalene and Jesus has to be one of the most moving, mysterious and faith-demanding episodes in all of human literature. How many people have cried for their "disappeared" loved ones? How few have ever expected to see them again, yet lived in hope even as they wept? Almost all would at least have found some consolation in knowing where their loved ones were buried; and even more if they could at least hold them for one last time. If Mary's story is to be entered into, then it cannot be her story alone. Yet her story is unique, for her loved one was dead, but now he stands before her and identifies himself by speaking her name. Of course, Mary wanted to hold him. But Jesus said to Mary Magdalene,

> *"Do not hold on to me, because I have not yet ascended to the Father. But go to my brothers and say to them, I am ascending to my Father and your Father, to my God and your God"* (Jn.20:17)[95].

Several times in his teaching Jesus had told his disciples that he had come from his Father and would return to his Father. The resurrection appearances in John are not an end in themselves; they are a way-marker between the cross and the ascension. There is no account in John of ascension, but it is forecast (Jn.6:62; 20:17); and there is a word about Jesus coming again, which would seem to presuppose an ascension without giving details (Jn.21:23 and see 14:3). Jesus' return to his Father from whence he came has been a continuing theme throughout the gospel. Kiefer says *"in the fourth gospel the resurrection and the ascension seem to coincide"*[96], but this is difficult to square with Jesus' words to Mary that he had not yet ascended (Jn.20:17). Just as there is no account of the ascension in John, similarly there are no specific details of the resurrection, but as the story of Thomas highlights, physical evidence should be quite secondary to reception by faith (Jn.20:29).

It was post-resurrection that for the first time, Jesus referred to his disciples as *brothers*. Jesus asked Mary to give a message to his "brothers". Mary probably quite rightly relayed the message to Jesus' disciples, because the message included the words: *"My Father and your Father"*. Jesus' Father is their Father and his God is their God. (Jn.20:17). His death and resurrection cement a familial relationship with his followers.

---

[95] Whilst many translations render Jesus' words μή μου ἅπτου as "Do not touch me", they may be less harsh and could equally be translated, *"Do not keep holding on"*. Why would Jesus treat Mary differently to Thomas? (cf.Jn.20:27)

[96] OBC p.997

Having seen the empty tomb on the Sunday morning, Peter and the other disciple returned to their homes, but by the evening, having received Mary's message, most of the disciples had come together, though behind locked doors out of fear of "the Jews". That evening Jesus appeared to the disciples, greeted them with a blessing, a greeting, and the gift of *Peace/Shalom*. He showed them his hands and side. "*He breathed on them and said to them, Receive the Holy Spirit. If you forgive the sins of any they are forgiven; if you retain the sins of any, they are retained*" (Jn.20:19-23). Jesus was still the gift and the giver: giving as promised at the last supper, peace, the Holy Spirit, and a commission to exercise a discerning ministry of forgiveness - three different but related gifts. Ashton's suggests that these verses (Jn.20:21-23) might have been an "original" ending of the fourth gospel[97]. Whilst I do not accept his proposition, such a climax would fit well with my contention that John's Gospel has as its major underlying theme Jesus as gift and giver.

It is remarkable that in John's telling of the story of Jesus this is the only direct reference to forgiveness, and it is not Jesus who forgives, but his disciples who are called to be agents of forgiveness. However, in the encounter of Peter and Jesus in the final chapter of the gospel, the forgiving, redeeming and commissioning nature of Jesus himself is made plain. The presence of the word "give" within the word "for-give-ness" is easily overlooked. But forgiveness does usually require a great deal of give, ideally, but certainly not always as part of give-and-take. The best in Jesus is saved till last! Those who would see chapter 21 as an unnecessary or even unlikely addition perhaps miss this important point. It is supremely through his followers receiving and then exhaling his own grace-full spirit of forgiveness and love that Jesus can still give new life to the world.

A week after his first resurrection appearance to his disciples Jesus appeared again to the disciples, and Jesus' ongoing compassionate, forgiving nature is evident[98]. Jesus invited Thomas to touch the wounds which he had shown to the other disciples a week earlier, with the implication that Jesus knew that when the others had told him of their experience Thomas had said: "*Unless I see the mark of the nails in his hands, and put my finger in the mark of the nails and my hand in his side, I will not believe*" (Jn.20:25). Thomas' reply to Jesus' invitation to do just that was, "*My Lord and my God*" (Jn.20:28), to which Jesus replied, "*Have you believed because you have seen me? Blessed are those who have not seen and yet have come to believe*" (Jn.20:29). Whether or not, as many people have suggested, 20:31 is the original ending of John's Gospel, Thomas is the archetype of all those who receive the humanly speaking incredible message from others that Jesus who

---

[97] UFG p.485

[98] It may be easily overlooked that Thomas questioned the truth of the other disciples' testimony. Yet they still included him in their company. Perhaps their ministry of forgiveness had already begun – and certainly doubts were no barrier to companionship.

was crucified is alive. Unlike Thomas, without physically seeing for themselves those who hear are invited to believe. So to Thomas' story John adds that much more could have been written, but the aim is to invite belief in *"Jesus as the Messiah, the Son of God, and that through believing you may have life in his name"* (Jn.20:31; and see 3:16; 6:47) ... Jesus is the gift and the giver!

<u>(Chapter 21)</u>

Although Ashton is totally committed to the view that chapter 21 is an appendix or epilogue and uses the "promotion of Peter" as a supporting argument[99], Michaels makes the important point, *"There is no evidence in any existing manuscript of the gospel of John that it ever circulated without chapter 21"*[100]. In spite of the grand and apt conclusion of 20:31, also perhaps because of familiarity, John's gospel does not seem quite complete to me without chapter twenty-one which effectively rehabilitates Peter, who has been the most named disciple in John - over thirty times. Although often mentioned in company with one or more other disciples, and in spite of being the three-time denier, Peter is in a unique way part of the story of Jesus' arrest, trial and resurrection. There are those who say chapter twenty-one was added to promote Peter above the disciple whom Jesus loved[101]. This is on the basis that Peter had previously deferred to the disciple whom Jesus loved. John 13:24 might support this contention. It would seem the disciple whom Jesus loved was sitting closer to Jesus than Peter, and Peter motions to him to ask Jesus a question (Jn.13:23f). But Peter throughout most of the fourth gospel plays a far more prominent and forceful role. For example, Peter is clearly the spokesperson for the disciples (Jn.6:68). The disciple whom Jesus loved waits at the entrance to the tomb, but Peter goes straight in (Jn.21:6). Even in chapter thirteen, when he is close enough, Peter addresses Jesus directly (Jn.13:38). The story of the third resurrection appearance includes the names of three disciples, Simon Peter, Thomas, Nathanael, and lists a further four, the sons of Zebedee and two others. *The disciple whom Jesus loved* plays a significant supporting role, (Jn.21:7, 20, 24), but the focus is manifestly on Peter, to whom Jesus' last *"Verily, verily"* pronouncement was made (Jn.21:18). Ashton notes there are 25 of these "amen" sayings in all, the vast majority related to major Christological affirmations. At the end of the fourth gospel the focus has in some ways now shifted from the work of Jesus to what will be required of his followers. Rather than Peter's *"promotion above others"*, which would have been anathema to Jesus, Jesus' words to him are better understood as his rehabilitation with an integral commission to feed or serve others - teaching he found so hard to accept when Jesus wanted to wash his feet (Jn.13:8).

---

[99] UFG p.14

[100] TGJ p.1006

[101] e.g. UFG pp.30-31

Having appeared to his disciples twice in a house, Jesus made a third appearance to them by the side of a lake where they were fishing. Although this is Jesus' third appearance, John tells us that the disciples still did not recognise Jesus on the shore, and we are left to ponder why this should be so. A simple, yet obvious answer is that distance made recognition difficult. Alternative suggestions, for example that the disciples still did not fully accept that Jesus could come to them, have merit. But when Jesus words were heard, obedience to those words produced "fruit" (actually fish) in abundance. Then one disciple at least knew that the man standing on the shore was Jesus. When the disciple whom Jesus loved recognised Jesus (like Mary before him) he told Peter, who rushed to Jesus whilst the other disciples persevered to land the great haul of fish. Perhaps by his actions Peter was already answering the imminent questions about his love of Jesus.

There was bread. Jesus was already cooking fish, and he invited the disciples to add some of the fish they had caught (Jn.21:9f.). Then John tells us, "*Jesus came and took the bread and gave it to them, and did the same with the fish*" (Jn.20:13). It is surely no coincidence, but rather a memory-jog for his disciples, that the food here corresponded to the food used in the feeding of five-thousand (Jn.6:11). Providing one hundred and fifty three fish (Jn.21:11), more than enough to share, and bread for a breakfast meal in which Jesus shares the task of making provision with the disciples (Jn.21:10), these are reminders that Jesus' work is that of the great provider, the channel of his Father's abundant gifts. This leads naturally into Jesus' command to Peter, the representative disciple, to be a giver, to feed his lambs or sheep (Jn.21:15-17). Jesus is the Good Shepherd (Jn.10:11, 14) who ensures his flock are fed (Jn.10:9; cf. also 6:51 etc). All his followers are invited to do the same, to share in this ministry of giving, and to do so out of love and obedience. Peter will be under the command of Jesus, as will all the other disciples (cf. Jn.13:34; 14:15, 21; 15:10, 12, 14. 17), in the same way that Jesus has been under the command of his Father (Jn.10:18; 12:49; 14:31). But the commands are a gift, because to be obedient to them is to share in the eternal, abundant, overflowing life of the Father and the son[102]. Jesus himself is under the command of his Father, but "*His commandment is eternal life*" (Jn.12:49f); and the intended outcome of the disciples obedience to Jesus' commandments is that they might have joy (Jn.15:11)[103].

---

[102] The concept of God's commandments as gifts is hardly new. E.g. "*When the Lord had finished speaking to Moses on Mount Sinai, he gave him the two tablets of the testimony, the tablets of stone inscribed by the finger of God*" (Exodus 31:18). Of course John 21 reflects this, but also reflects the new covenant prophesied by Jeremiah: "*I will put my law in their minds and write it on their hearts*" (Jeremiah 31:33).

[103] By a rather tenuous connection of this passage to Deuteronomy Ashton following Pancaro and others manages to turn Jesus' commandment to love one another into "divine revelation"(UFG p.434 & p.434 n33): but this is unnecessary and detracts from the

Peter may have denied Jesus (Jn.18:17, 25, 27), but in John's gospel he had been there from the beginning of Jesus' public ministry (Jn.1:41f), had expressed his willingness to die for Jesus (Jn.13:37f); had defended Jesus with his sword in the garden (Jn.18:10); and with another unnamed disciple had followed Jesus to the high priest's house (Jn.18:15). Sometimes Peter failed, but he was committed, and there is good evidence that he was still regarded as a leader amongst the disciples (Jn.20:6; 21:3). Jesus questioned Peter, not about his commitment to him, but about his love for him; noticeably not calling Peter by the name which means *rock* (Jn.1:42), but *"Simon, son of John"* (Jn.21:15ff). Simon comes from the Hebrew meaning "he has heard" (cf. Jn.3:29; 5:24f; 8:47; 12:49); John or Jonah was the prophet who at first ran away from what God said, but whose repentance led to the salvation of a nation. Peter's positive responses to what he hears Jesus asking him led to Jesus' instruction for Peter to behave like a shepherd of Jesus' flock. The good shepherd of the flock will lay down his life for his sheep (Jn.10:11), so Jesus predicted how Peter, as an older man, and a shepherd of his sheep, would die. As Jesus had given his life, so he invited Peter, *"Follow me"* (Jn.21:18f) - an invitation which should be held in tandem with this gospel's repeated invitation by Jesus for his disciples to *abide* (or remain) *in me* (Jn.6:56; 15:4ff, 10). Peter's question to Jesus about the future of *the disciple whom Jesus loved* resulted in the last words of Jesus recorded in John's gospel. They are spoken to Peter (Jn.21:22), and in John's gospel are addressed to Peter for the first time: *"Follow me"*. Jesus had said,

> *"My sheep recognize my voice. I know them, and they follow me"*
> (Jn.10:25)
> *"If any of you wants to serve me, then follow me"* (Jn.12:26).

Perhaps only some of Jesus' sheep are called to be shepherds too, but all are called to follow where he has led.

"The disciple whom Jesus loved" is said to be the witness of *"these things"*, and author of the Gospel (Jn.21:24). Ashton, in keeping with his multi-edition theory, is certain that someone other than the original author of the fourth Gospel added this ascription. Even if this were correct, it would still leave open the question as to who this beloved disciple might be. For convenience, and given the title of the Gospel, I have referred in this commentary to the author of the fourth gospel as "John". One complicating factor is the difficulty of even deciding upon twelve names for Jesus' inner circle of followers. John's Gospel never lists them. Therefore the beloved disciple could well be unnamed and unnameable: but this has not inhibited many in their attempts to justify the choice of a particular individual.

---

relationship of commandment and response which underlies the whole of Jesus' ministry and of true discipleship.

There are those who support the claim that John, one of the sons of Zebedee, was the beloved disciple[104]. I find it intriguing that in fact a disciple called John is never mentioned by name in John's Gospel. Baukham suggests on the basis of *the best second-century evidence, which can be traced to Papias of Hierapolis,* the author of the fourth gospel is another disciple of Jesus called John who was not one of the twelve[105]. Pazdan, perhaps with a mischievous glint in her eye, suggests Mary Magdalene as a candidate for the beloved disciple[106]. Some have suggested, although others disagree, that Leonardo de Vinci's depiction of the Last Supper shows him in agreement with Pazdan; but Mary would also have needed to have been out fishing as one of the disciples (Jn.21:3-7). Although I find the proposition very attractive, I think the case for Mary Magdalene as the beloved disciple cannot be sustained.

Support for Lazarus as the beloved disciple has the benefit of the author of John's gospel not only telling us that Jesus loved Lazarus, but emphasising it three times (Jn.11:3, 5, 36), and the beloved disciple only makes a formal appearance in the Gospel after the raising of Lazarus, though not immediately. *The disciple whom Jesus loved* is first referred to in this way at 13:33. Stibbe goes so far as to say of the beloved disciple, "*He has to be Lazarus of Bethany*"; and he cites a number of earlier scholars who support this view.[107] But there are good reasons to discount Lazarus. The disciple whom Jesus loved was in the upper room sitting close to Jesus. He was, with Peter when Mary reported the disappearance of Jesus' body. He was fishing with Peter, James and John. All these, especially the events in the upper room with Peter strongly suggest that he was one of the twelve (cf.Jn.20:24; 6:67). It is hard, however, to see Lazarus as one of the twelve disciples. Jesus invited his disciples to go to where Lazarus had died, describing Lazarus as *our friend* (Jn.11:11). Nowhere in the story of Lazarus' restoration to life does John suggest he was one of the twelve or even a disciple; and only some time later did Jesus apply that term of endearment to his disciples (Jn.15:14f. *You are my friends if you do what I command. I no longer call you servants, because a servant does not know his master's business. Instead, I have called you friends.*).

---

[104] See Kiefer OBC pp.961, 998, 999. See also G. Beasley-Murray. Beasley-Murray cites a number of second century writings which support the contention that John the son of Zebedee, one of the Twelve was the beloved disciple. But he acknowledges that the "evidence" is open to serious questioning, "*marred by unwarranted elaborations and confusions*". (*Gospel of John* Word Biblical Commentary 1987 pp.lxvif – Beasley Murray's extensive treatment of the subject is covered in pages lxvi - lxxv)

[105] R. Baukham *Testimony of the Beloved Disciple* p.15

[106] TLC p.591

[107] Mark W. G. Stibbe *John as Storyteller* CUP 1992 p.78

Notwithstanding Michael's somewhat arbitrary ruling that the disciple whom Jesus loved "*would not have been sometimes named and sometimes anonymous*"[108], and his tenuous suggestion that it might have been one of Jesus' brothers[109], my own preference for the identity of the disciple whom Jesus loved and *the witness to these things* is Nathanael. We might reasonably assume Nathanael is quietly there in the background from chapter 1 when Jesus demonstrated an immediate affection for him and said Nathanael would be a witness (Jn.1:45ff), but not making another named appearance until chapter 21 (Jn.21:3). Although arriving at a different conclusion, Baukham's argument that the beloved disciple was "*not one of the itinerant disciples who travelled around with Jesus, but a disciple resident in Jerusalem who hosted the last supper*" could in fact be used to support the candidacy of Nathanael[110]

The clearly enunciated purpose of the gospel is that "*you may come to believe that Jesus is the Messiah, the Son of God*" (Jn.20:31). Apart from Martha (Jn.11:27), who it would be very difficult to identify with the disciple whom Jesus loved, and the Jewish leaders, who did not believe it (Jn.19:7), Nathanael is the only one who refers to Jesus in this way (Jn.1:49). His name is also mentioned individually in contrast to John who is referred to only once, in tandem with his brother and not by name (Jn.21:2). Jesus, when he first saw Nathanael, described him as "*truly an Israelite in whom there is no deceit*" (Jn.1:47). Israel, meaning one who wrestles with God, or God strives, was the gift of a new name for Jacob - which means cheat. Light and truth were given to replace darkness and deceit. Jesus, who "knew" all people (Jn.2:24), saw something of the innate honesty or truthfulness which was in Nathaniel. Some of the Gospel's closing words fit so well with Nathaniel as a man with no guile:" *This is the disciple who testifies to theses things and who wrote them down. We know that his testimony is true*" (Jn.21:24) And, of course, the name Nathaniel means *God gives*, which I maintain is the overriding message of the fourth gospel [111].

228

Jesus had said to Andrew and another unnamed disciples of John the Baptizer, "*Come and see*" (Jn.1:39). Though a different Greek verb is used initially, Philip gave the same invitation to Nathaniel, "*Come and see*"; and he did see (same verb -

---

[108] TGJ p.20

[109] Ibid p.958

[110] R. Baukham *Testimony of the Beloved Disciple* p.15 & 27. There is actually a tradition that Nathanael in TFG is the name given to Bartholomew in the Synoptics, which would make Nathanael one of the Twelve. But this theory is by means universally accepted.

[111] It will be apparent to readers that I do not accept the arguments of Stibbe and others that "*the beloved disciple himself is not the actual author of the Fourth Gospel*" (Mark W. G. Stibbe *Op cit.* p.77).

1:46f). On the basis of the slender evidence of what he physically saw at that time Nathanael saw with eyes of faith who Jesus really was, "*the Son of God* " and "*the king of Israel*": and he was promised by Jesus that he would "*see greater things than these. You will see the heavens opened and the angels of God ascending and descending upon the Son of Man*". It is true that Nathanael is not mentioned again by name until Jesus' third resurrection appearance which heralds the end of the Gospel, but he was there at the beginning seeing with eyes of faith, and he was there at the end seeing and recognising the risen Jesus; and if he is the disciple whom Jesus loved, at the end he was still following (Jn.21:20). Through his writing he was still a witness to what he had seen, inviting his readers through eyes of faith to also see and believe[112].

Scholars with innumerable points of view will no doubt debate for many years to come the identity of this disciple[113]. But interesting as the search might be, it could well divert attention from a more important question. Perhaps we should be asking not who the beloved disciple *was*, but who he or she *is*. And the answer is there in John's gospel. It is the follower of Jesus who is there at the beginning - who stays with Jesus on the way, who is close to Jesus when the bread is offered to be shared, who is still close when death does its worst, and who recognises Jesus alive again in the command to fish or shepherd in a different way - whether that command comes at the beginning or the end of our journeying with Jesus. So, by the grace of God, "*the disciple whom Jesus loved" can* be you or me![114] The greatest gift is *the love of Jesus,* in every sense of these words. He is the gift and the giver.

---

[112] For scholarly attempts to identify *the beloved disciple*, J.H. Charlesworth 1995 work *The Beloved Disciple* is commended (Trinity Press International p.127-224). A briefer but helpful and more recent survey can be found in Andrew T. Lincoln *The Gospel According to St. John* (Black's New Testament Commentary 2005 p.17-26), or in Michaels *The Gospel of John* (TGJ p.5-24)

[113] Linders, for example, says that whoever the beloved disciple might be, it is no use looking for her or him in the New Testament (Barnabas Linders *John* JSOT/Sheffield Press 1990 p.23). In marked contrast Moloney suggests that the beloved disciple-cum- author of the Fourth Gospel could well be, as tradition has oft asserted, John the son of Zebedee and one of the twelve disciples (F.J. Moloney *The Gospel of John* Liturgical Press 1998 p.8)

[114] Linders (Ibid p.23) makes a closely related observation, *"The beloved disciple embodies the faith of the evangelist ...but he is one with whom the reader should identify. For the whole purpose of the gospel is to convey the same understanding to every reader"*

Special footnote on Ashton and Michaels.

Since Ashton and Michael's works have contributed so much to my commentary on John's gospel, it seems right to give those readers who wish an opportunity to know the bases of my criticisms of these two commentators. I have found much to commend in both, but also grounds for considerable reservation.

Ashton is perhaps a typical example of those who do not see John's Gospel as holistic. His opinion is that John 21 is *an appendix or epilogue* added later to an original work. This is a major component of his criticism of John as an integrated work; but a view which I do not find compelling (see my comments above on forgiveness in chapters 20-21).

In fact Ashton believes that the Gospel as we have it is the subject of many revisions. This leads him to propose and use a *first edition* as the basis for his work and to ignore any sections he considers to be later additions. For example and to my mind incredibly, Ashton rejects most of what many consider a crucial chapter, chapter 11. It is unnecessary to accept Ashton's assertion about the acrimonious controversies of chapters 5 - 10 and the contents of chapters 14 - 17. Ashton says they are "*projected back into the life of Jesus* ... (and) ... *prove* (my underlining) *that their author was writing for readers whose circumstances were radically different from those of the few followers Jesus had gathered in his own lifetime.*" All this, Ashton says, goes to prove "*this is not a homogeneous text*". Ashton unhelpfully colours his entire work by his total commitment to the notion that "*the Gospel itself ... surely must be (*read*), in relation not to the time of Jesus, but to that of the* (much later) *Jesus group within the synagogue*". (UFG p.62). "*The gospel as we know it was largely inspired by the traumatic experience of the community's expulsion from the synagogue*" (UFG p.65). Ashton sees the acceptance of a Johannine community and an appreciation of its experiences as a prerequisite for commenting on the fourth gospel - and especially on chapters 13-17 - to the extent that the gospel is written as much to preserve the thoughts of a Johannine prophet as to transmit those of Jesus (UFG pp.451-3). So the "*We*" in *We beheld his glory* (1:14) is no longer associated with *became flesh and dwelt among us* and thus an expression rooted in the experience of those who actually walked and talked with Jesus in Galilee and Judaea, but for Ashton becomes a statement of faith by a later notional Christian community (UFG p.505). However, in spite of extensive scholarly acceptance of the existence of a Johannine community and their expulsion from a synagogue, both - especially the latter - are highly speculative, as is this major contention of Ashton. Ashton himself acknowledges that the community cannot be pieced together *without conjecture* or *speculation* (UFG p.239) and without a *shaping hypothesis* which *transforms facts into evidence* (Francis J. Moloney notes the need to differentiate between a Johannine School and the Johannine community. Expository Times Vol. 123 April 2012 p.317).
Baukham is one who challenges Ashton and others of like mind: "*Reconstructions of the Johannine community from the gospel are largely fantasy*" (*The Testimony of the Beloved Disciple* p.13)
Other points made by Ashton to support his multiple editions theory of John's gospel will be considered later (e.g. dislocations in the text, or aporias), but on balance I find the seamless garment of Kiefer and Strauss more persuasive. In order to maintain his insistence on the gospel's primary inspiration as much later than Jesus' own day, Ashton seems completely unaware of the compelling evidence which contradicts his thesis. There was real conflict in Jesus' own day, and, for example, chapters 5-10 fit very well with such a scenario. How can

it be seriously claimed that conflict has to be *projected back into the life of Jesus*, when Jesus patently died as a result of the animosity of his "opponents"?

Bultmann features large in many commentaries on John's Gospel. Michaels work has merited and received considerable attention in the above chapter on John's gospel. Michaels cites a number of times Bultmann's dictum, that *"in John's Gospel, Jesus as the Revealer of God reveals nothing but that he is the revealer"* (e.g. TGJ pp.434, 518. See also UFG p.493 where Ashton cites Bultmann's *Theology* p.66). Michaels follows Bultmann to the extent that he sees the whole of John's Gospel as concerned primarily with revelation - "*revelation is to be the Gospel's theme*" (TGJ p.89). Rowland identifies this use of Bultmann as *the climax of John Ashton's book* (UFG p.vii); and Ashton himself acknowledges "*my debt to Rudolph Bultmann will be obvious to any reader - its Grundkonzeption* (UFG p.xii; pp 6, 305). Or again, *the shadow of Bultmann looms throughout this book* (p.493). In support of his total commitment to Bultmann's focus on revelation Ashton even suggests that the words, λογος (word), δοξα (glory) and αληθεια (truth) could all be "*translated 'revelation' without serious distortion*" (UFG p.492). This is only true if one is already committed to a uniform meaning for the text rather than appreciating a coat of many colours. I would go as far as to say that this Bultmann-induced infatuation with 'revelation' as the sole interpretative key drains the rich colour and sometimes evident spontaneity (Ashton's aporias!) out of the fourth gospel. Ashton's Bultmann-inspired *Grundkonzeption* is not the drone which distinctively enriches the harmony, but the blanket which smothers the fire. The gospel itself reflects the freedom and the rich and multi-faceted generosity of the Man from Nazareth who would, I believe, have hated being constrained and diminished by a scholastic need for everything to be organised within a rigid framework of interpretation. It is a great pity that his work as a whole seems to ignore Ashton's own critique of Bultmann which comes at the end of his book: "*Bultmann's conception of the Johannine theology of revelation, for all its brilliance, has a fundamental flaw. He is too anxious to discard the narrative husk of the gospel in order to get at the kernel of revelation inside. The evangelist's own insight into the meaning of the gospel message is not borrowed from an alien religion, nor is it detachable from the story. He knows the meaning is a mystery*" (UFG p.528).

Turning now to Michaels: he structures the entire gospel on Bultmann's presupposition of revelation as the key to reading and understanding the fourth gospel. So the fourth gospel can be divided into the following sections: *Preamble* (Jn.1:1-5), *The Testimony of John* (Jn.1:6-3:30), *Jesus' Self-Revelation to the World* (Jn.4:1 - 12:43) - 12:44-50 is transitional - *Jesus' Self-Revelation to the Disciples* (Jn.13:1 - 16:33) - John 17 is a transitional prayer - *Verification of Jesus' Self-Revelation in his Arrest, Crucifixion and Resurrection* (Jn.18:1 - 21:25). This includes a very common, but to my mind unhelpful division of John at 12:43/50, which can destroy the gospel's seamless character (TGJ p.36. And see my reflections above on chapter 19 on the division of John into a book of signs and a book of glory). The division at 12:43 ignores the much more obvious transition point at 12:1 "*Six days before the Passover*".

An overemphasis on revelation is unhelpful in its tendency to prioritise creed over gift. Those who adopt this stance rarely pursue the notion that revelation is itself a gift - but one of many., Michaels leads up to this claim that "revelation" is the gospel's theme by saying, "*The one from whose fullness we have all received is after all the 'Word' and the 'Light'*" (TGJ p.89). But then Michaels chooses to put the emphasis on the nouns (word and light) and presses into service as adjectival rather than as adverbial, action-descriptors, within the *fullness* of what *we have all received*. As Gregory of Nyssa put it, "*Concepts create idols*.

Only wonder understands" (Cited in *More Ready Than You Think* Brian D. McLaren Pub. Zondervan 2006).

In keeping with his chosen emphasis Michaels chooses to say of John the Baptizer that his "sole" mission was to testify about Jesus and make him known to Israel (Jn.1:31) (TGJ p.101), but, in the same short speech from which Michaels quotes, John the Baptizer says of Jesus that he "*will baptize with the Holy Spirit*" (Jn.1:33). That is, he will be a giver. Michaels is not wrong to assert that revelation is a major theme in John's gospel, but I believe he is wrong, as are others, in following Bultmann who sees this as the crucial and all-determining factor for reading and understanding the gospel.

The work of Brevard Childs (*Old Testament Theology in a Canonical Context* 1985 & *The New Testament as Canon: An Introduction* 1985) could serve as a useful critique of the historical-critical approach of Bultmann and others which has also been criticised by many commentators such as R. Alan Culpepper's *The Anatomy of the Fourth Gospel. A Study in Literary Design* (pub. Fortress Press 1983). For further on this see F.J. Maloney *Recent Johannine Studies* (Expository Times Vol.123 Apl.2012 p.313ff). Braaten criticises "*the dominant role that revelation plays in modern theology.* He says *Revelation is not the supreme category of Christian dogmatics; salvation is!*" (Carl E. Braaten *That they may believe - A theology of the Gospel and the mission of the church* Eerdmans - Grand Rapids 2008 p 12.) Daniel L. Migliore is well worth reading on the subject of revelation. He offers a less static creedal meaning for revelation as "*a breakthrough in human consciousness that expresses itself in creative imagination and ethical action ... revelation generates self and world transformation*" (Daniel L. Migliore *Faith Seeks Understanding* Eerdmans 2nd Ed. 2004 pp.20-43 esp.p.33f.). Revelation is not an end in itself, just as Jesus is not an end in himself (Jn.14:9, 28). As the story of Lazarus and its aftermath so dramatically demonstrate, Jesus is the means by which the Holy Spirit and life in all its fullness is offered and received or rejected.

Chapter Five
REFLECTIONS

For the main body of this work I set out to allow each of the four gospels to speak to me with the voice of an individual and independent author. I have attempted to demonstrate that each of the four New Testament gospels makes a distinctive contribution to appreciating the life of Jesus. Whilst I would not be at all surprised to find that many people do not agree with the four quite different major emphases I have discerned, I would be disappointed if anyone could still think that when you have read one gospel you have read them all - or that to read one of the Synoptics largely covers what all three have to offer. Matthew, Mark, Luke and John are neither clones themselves nor in the business of creating facsimiles. Each deserves separate consideration and appreciation. Nonetheless, having read and written about all four New Testament gospels it is impossible not to reflect on some of the similarities or parallels and some of the differences. This last section is my attempt to note a selection of those things which can be found in all four gospels; some of which show common ground, whilst others indicate important, insightful, thought-provoking, and often helpful differences. I also hope to show by way of an example - a short sermon - that identifying differences can provide a valuable resource for those whose privilege is to share an exposition of the gospels as part of worship.

I shall look at some of the differences to be discerned in a moment and then move on to some things on which all four gospels agree. But it might be helpful to look first at one particular feature of the gospels which perhaps more than any other shows not only that they are different, but provides evidence that they are intentionally so.

Endings

If you were writing the story of Jesus, how would you end it? I suggest that would depend on what you wanted to be the most significant thought to leave in peoples' minds. Or perhaps the ending might be the most apt conclusion to what you had already written, choices already made, perspectives previously gained. The four New Testament evangelists chose four very different ways to end their gospel.

Matthew's gospel seems to me to be primarily about what it means to be a disciple of Jesus and by involvement with a company of disciples (the *ekklesia*) to work for the coming of the Kingdom of Heaven. He ends his telling of the story with Jesus' command to his disciples to go and make everyone a disciple, with the promise, *"and surely I am with you always to the end of the age"* (Matt.28:20). Mark, I have suggested, intended to raise question, "Who is he?" about an awesome Jesus. Appropriate answers to this question must be found by the reader rather than given

217

by the writer. It is therefore totally in keeping with Mark's aim that his gospel should end with three women who were instructed to tell Jesus' disciples that he was going ahead of them into Galilee; but gripped with fear they said nothing (Mk.16:8). This, I would contend, is why the added endings to Mark (Mk.16:9-20) are most unlikely to be the original work of the author. Luke's gospel, in spite of its underbelly of violent intent, is from start to finish about people who are blessed by God, filled with God's Spirit, and who respond with joyful praise. I have suggested the Magnificat is the finest example of this. Naturally Luke concludes his gospel with an account of how having promised them *"power from on high"* Jesus left his disciples in the act of blessing them, and they, filled with joy, praised God (Lk.24:49-53). John, typically, for he uses echoes throughout the gospel, offered two endings. The first is in keeping with his emphasis that Jesus is the gift and giver. He is the Christ, the son of God, God's gift to the world, and this gift is given so that the further gift of *"life in his name"* might be received (Jn.20:31). But in addition John offers reminders of the life the disciples had already shared with Jesus (symbolised by the great catch of fish and a meal John 21:1-14). Then through Jesus' conversation with Peter, John reiterates Jesus' call for his disciples to love him and one another (Jn.21:13-17): and finally John tells of the cost of discipleship for some (21:18f.) plus the caution not to think about what is required of others: *"You must follow me"* (Jn.21:22). John's two endings taken together make a single point. Jesus is the gift and giver, but that is not a theory to be accepted, it is a truth to be lived as it was incarnate in Jesus (Jn.1:14).

That there are four quite different endings should be enough to convince that they are not about "what really happened". They are not verbatim reports of historical events. The resurrection life of Christ, and the freedom inherent in the way the Holy Spirit works, should take us beyond such confined thinking (see e.g. the symbolism of locked doors which cannot keep out the risen Jesus. Jn.20:19). Each ending in its peculiar way is a final invitation to allow the story of Jesus to fill our lives, and in this way for Jesus to be with us to the end of the age, to fill us with appropriate mystery-filled fear, to know God's blessing as an impetus to praise, and by following him as the way to receive all that God offers in Christ of forgiving love, the refreshing honesty of truth, and an inextinguishable quality of life. These gospel messages are not in competition. No one evangelist's message invalidates any other. They are all part of the riches in Christ which could not be contained by all the books in the world (Jn.21:25). What follows should be read with this always in mind.

Other differences

The endings are by no means the only major differences between the four gospels. From many possibilities I have chosen five which are of special interest to me for relatively brief treatment.

1. Jesus' "Birth".

The two birth narratives in the gospels, the events surrounding Jesus' conception and delivery, "speak" to me in a very personal way. The war-time circumstances surrounding my own birth meant that the Canadian airman whose genes I inherited was never known by me, nor legally recognised as my father. As a result of her "unacceptable" pregnancy, my mother was dismissed from both her Brethren Meeting and from her work by one of the elders who was her employer. We are talking about Strict Brethren in the early 1940's, and people acting in accordance with their "principles". I hold no grudges against those involved - though I cannot help seeing parallels with those "religious" of Jesus' day who put principles before compassion. My subsequent not altogether successful adoption by relatives also contributes to how I read the accounts of Jesus' birth. Did Joseph in effect adopt him? Was Jesus a war-baby? Was the 1940's Canadian airman an agent of the Holy Spirit? Can and should the story of Jesus' birth in occupied territory inform my thinking about the lives of Palestinians in the present-day "occupied territories", and their counterparts in so many other places. Like all Bible stories, the birth stories are capable of multi-layered readings or interpretations and applications.

Mark, has no story of Jesus' birth - perhaps being more interested in the prospect of Jesus' second birth or second coming than his first (Mk.13:8) - and content to use a symbol and a voice from heaven to affirm Jesus' heavenly and spirit-anointed parentage (Mk.1:10f.). In some ways this accords with John's Gospel which also has no specific birth narrative, but in keeping with the prologue (Jn.1:1-5, 10-14) testifies that Jesus' birth or entry into the world is "from above" (Jn.3:31; 8:23). The birth that really matters in respect of Jesus, and John would suggest for anyone, is not that which comes via physical parentage, but that new life or re-birth which comes when Jesus is received as God's gift:

> *"Yet to all who did receive him, to those who believed in his name, he gave the right to become children of God — children born not of natural descent, nor of human decision or a husband's will, but born of God"* (Jn.1:12f; see also Jn.3:5f)

There are ways of reading the stories which discern a marked contrast between Matthew's birth narratives, full of threats and tension, and Luke's, which are full of joy. Yet as we have seen in the chapter on Luke in this work, Luke's gospel is full of threats and tension. Mary's song of praise is also a song of revolution (Lk.1:46-55), and Zechariah's Psalm is not without subversive political content (Lk.1:69-71, 74). Sometimes apparent differences are not sustainable when the gospels are considered in their entirety; but differences there are.

Chapter 5 - Reflections

It comes as a surprise to many people to learn how marginal Mary the mother of Jesus is in Matthew's story of Jesus' birth and its aftermath. The focus is overwhelmingly on Joseph. It is to Joseph that three times *"the angel of the Lord appeared ... in a dream"* (Matt.1:20; 2:13, 19). In John's gospel Jesus is described as *"the son of Joseph"* (Jn.1:45; 6:42), but without Matthew Joseph would be little more than a name; and I believe many very important messages would be lost. I may not have known my "natural" father, but there were those who did their best to stand by my mother. Over the years many have done their best to stand by me; and I hope in turn I have been a "Joseph" for others who have found themselves in strange, and for some "unacceptable" circumstances.

With regard to Joseph Luke is very different. Luke makes a point of saying of Joseph's parentage of Jesus, *"So it was thought"* (Lk.3:23). Although in Matthew Joseph is a man who *"is faithful to the law"* (Matt.1:19) and who *"did what the angel of the Lord had commanded him"* (Matt.1:24), Luke is either unaware of, or chooses to ignore this. Instead Luke concentrates on Mary and others as models of true piety, the *annouim*, the humble, devout poor[1]. By offering his alternative focus, it is as if Luke took an enormous, mostly empty canvass (*tabula rasa*) on which he placed a few distinctive characters; the most prominent being Mary - at this point in the story even eclipsing Jesus. Simeon's *Nunc Dimitis* is immediately followed by words addressed directly to Mary (Lk.2:29-35). It is Mary (not Joseph) who speaks to the teenage Jesus in the Temple, and Mary who *"treasured all these things in her heart"* (Lk.2:31).

After the birth stories, Mary the mother of Jesus is mentioned by name only once in Matthew (Matt. 13:55 - though cf.12:46ff). Mary does not feature at all by name in Mark (cf. 3:33ff), and only makes a couple of cameo appearances in John (Jn.2:2-4; 19:25-27). Even in Luke, after initially highlighting the role of Mary in Jesus' birth and nurture, Luke barely mentions Mary again. Yet it is impossible, so I will not attempt to estimate how much influence Luke's particular focus on Mary has had in the history of Christianity. Suffice it to say the ubiquitous portrayals of the *Madonna and Child* or of the extra-Biblical *Pietà* are indicative of the devotion which Mary has inspired as a long-suffering mother, an obedient servant, a model of humility, and for many a beatified virgin. By comparison Mary's song of revolt, the Magnificat has probably had minimal, though not insignificant impact. There are churches where depictions or statues of Mary are more in evidence than those of Jesus. Perhaps for some Mary is human and therefore "like us", whereas in spite of the "official" line that Jesus is both human and divine, it is difficult to worship Jesus if he is human "like us". Mary is therefore more approachable, and for some a necessary compassionate intermediary. There is also doubtless a not necessarily helpful gender factor at work in which a mother is seen to be "approachable",

---

[1] TGL p.108

whereas a Father or a son is expected to be "stern" even if "loving". Furthermore, the traditional conceptualisation of God as Father, Son and Holy Spirit does not obviously include a feminine "person". Whatever the underlying reasons for Marian devotions, Luke by emphasising the role of Mary offers something which the other three New Testament gospels do not.

Much, much more could be said, but my main contention is that by separately considering each gospel writer's approach to the subject of Jesus' birth or genesis real differences become apparent. This is not a weakness in their testimony. Each offers a distinctive contribution to the life of Christians, their churches and their neighbours. It is a bonus to be welcomed.

2. Genealogies and Parentage

Although Mark centres on questions about Jesus' identity, and John includes speculation as to Jesus' parentage or where Jesus comes from, Mark and John do not include genealogies. They do, however, offer important perspectives which might be said to offer something similar to the genealogies of Matthew and Luke.

Mark does not mention Jesus' father, Joseph, at all. Mark records Jesus' commendation of his disciples for leaving their brothers, sisters, mothers and fathers *"for me and the gospel"* (Mk.10:29); but in Mark the sole reference to Jesus' own parentage is to his mother (and brothers) in the story, also told by Matthew and Luke, of their apparent rejection by Jesus in favour of a different understanding of what constituted his "family": *"Whoever does God's will is my brother and sister and mother"* (Mk.3:31-35 //s Matth.12:46-50; Lk.8:19-21). Matthew uses the word "Father" instead of "God" in recording Jesus' words on this occasion. In fact, Mark speaks very little of God as Father - just four times. First, Jesus will come in his Father's glory (Mk.8:38). Second, only the Father knows *"that day and hour"* (Mk.13:32). Third, the disciples will have their heavenly Father's forgiveness if they forgive others (Mk.11:25). These are the briefest possibly hints that God is Jesus' Father and also the father for the disciples. Yet, typical Mark, it is this Gospel which gives us that most intimate, succinct and possibly uniquely challenging expression of the Jesus/God relationship as Father/Son. Jesus, praying in Gethsemane, addressed God as, *"Abba, Father"* (Mk.14:36).

Perhaps, in spite of all its words about the intimate connectedness of Jesus and God as his Father, John's gospel never quite matches Mark's *"Abba, Father"*. But it certainly reinforces it. As mentioned in the chapter above on John, Jesus has his genesis as the word which was not just in or with God, but was God (Jn.1:1). As throughout the Bible God's word "goes forth", Jesus as God's word or gift is sent or given (Jn.1:14; 2:16, etc.) and will not return void, but will return to God having accomplished what God intends (Isaiah 55:11). So Jesus will return to his Father (Jn.14:12; 16:17, 28). Yet in a sense Jesus has never left his Father, or at least his Father has never left him (8:29; 16:31).

There is one brief reference in John to Jesus as the "*Son of Joseph*", but it is no more than a passing comment in the context of Jesus' words that he is "*the bread that came down from heaven*" (6:41f). His opponents clearly understood the claim Jesus was making:

> "*For this reason they tried all the more to kill him; not only was he breaking the Sabbath, but he was even calling God his own Father, making himself equal with God*" (Jn.5:18)
> "*I and my father are one*" (Jn.10:30; 14:10f).

This is not a relationship which is ring-fenced. Jesus' Father is also the disciples' Father (Jn.20:17). The parable of the vine (Jn.15:1-8) and Jesus' prayer (Jn.17:11, 21-23) are evidence of Jesus' belief that his disciples could be part of, or included in the mutually committed, deeply satisfying relationship Jesus shared with his and their Father. Jesus instruction to Mary to "*Go and tell my brothers*" (Jn.20:17), which clearly refers to his disciples shows how in John Jesus' "family" are his disciples as they are also identified in Matthew (Matt.12:49).

Luke's genealogy (Lk.3:23-38) could be said to make a related, but more universal point. Jesus is the son of God, but so is Adam, and by extension not only all the others whose names are recorded, but all humanity can acknowledge God as their "Father". This is not the same as that special relationship with God as Father which is based on sacrificial obedience, a relationship grounded in following the way of Jesus, but neither is it a relationship to be ignored. I conduct many funerals of people, or for people in funeral congregations, who have never made any obvious commitment to honouring God as their Father. They may actually have disavowed themselves of any such belief. It is never my intention to impose my beliefs on them, but I believe it is legitimate, and I will on occasions share this with families, that the ministry I offer is based on my personal belief that every person, even an unrepentant prodigal, is a child of God and therefore worthy of appropriate respect and love. I sometimes use a reading from the "Wisdom of Solomon" which begins with the thought, "*I also am mortal, like every other human being, a descendent of the first-formed child of the earth*" (Wisdom of Solomon 7:1). I know that very occasionally someone picks up on the theological and Lucan implications of this verse.

Luke, having established the ultimate fatherhood of God for Jesus in his genealogy, makes little further comment on God as Father. The angel's message to Mary pages up the genealogy of Jesus. He will be given "*the throne of his father David*" and "*reign over the house of Jacob*", but he is "*the Son of the Most High*" (Lk.1:32). As we have seen in the chapter on Luke above, Luke's gospel sets out fundamental beliefs in its early chapters through the words of angels and people of true humility and piety. These are then expanded in story form rather than discrete statements. So, for example, when Luke gives his version of the beatitudes with associated "woes" it is to a crowd of disciples "*and a great number of people from all over Judaea, from Jerusalem, and from the coast of Tyre and Sidon*" (Lk.6:17). This is followed by teaching about how to treat enemies, who predominantly would be "unbelievers", but whose treatment should be based on an understanding of God as a merciful "Father". The nature of the audience is important as context for the teaching. Quite naturally, therefore, prayer will be addressed to God who is in heaven as "Father" by Jesus (Lk.22:42; 23:46) and by his disciples (Lk.11:2, 13; 12:30ff).

There are major differences between the genealogies of Matthew, Luke and the Old Testament [2]. Indeed, apart from the "fourteen generations" from Abraham to David and the inclusion of Shealtiel and Zerubbabel, there is little else in common between Matthew and Luke. There is even disagreement as to the name of Jesus' grandfather. Was it Jacob (Matt.1:16) or Heli (Lk.3:23)? But as Meier wisely says in his commentary on Matthew; "*The genealogies of Matthew and Luke are to be understood as theological statements not biological reports*"[3].

Matthew's genealogy, with its neat division of Jesus' ancestry into three sections of fourteen generations delineated by what might be considered the most significant people or events in the history of the Jews, is probably intended to convey that through the history of the Jewish people, though sometimes in spite of them, God's purposes have always been served. In Jesus, as the Messiah, they find their fulfilment (Matt. 1:1-17). Yet Matthew is fully aware that this is not the whole story. The visit of the Magi shows Matthew understands that Jesus was not a Messiah just for Jews (Matt. 2:1-12). Matthew begins his genealogy of Jesus not with God and Adam the progenitor of all humanity, as per Luke, but with Abraham, the recognised founding patriarch specifically of the Jews. Yet as early as the ministry of John the Baptizer Matthew records John saying, "*Do not think you can say to yourselves, 'We have Abraham as our father.' I tell you that out of these stones God can raise up children for Abraham*" (Matt.3:9). It is not the relationship to Abraham as a biological father that matters, but being part of God's ongoing purposes; which now means being part of the work of Jesus and in this way knowing God as "*our Father*" (Matt.6:9. cp. Jn.8:33-42). Jesus put the matter very strongly in saying to his disciples, "*Do not call anyone on earth 'father,' for*

---

[2] For fuller details see TGL pp. 159-162

[3] J. P. Meier *Matthew: New Testament Message 3* p.3 Pub. Michael Glazer 1980. Cited in Mullins p.161

you have one Father, and he is in heaven" (Matt.23:9). It may not be intentional, but it is noteworthy that in the earlier chapters of Matthew references to God as Father are most commonly to *your Father*, that is, the disciples' *Father*; but following Jesus outburst of prayer to God as his Father (Matt.11:25) the balance shifts so that Jesus' talks much more about *my Father*. This is not an absolute divide by any means, but possibly reflects the shift from a teaching ministry toward Jesus' passion and death. Whichever specific relationship is being referred to, in Matthew's gospel the fatherhood of God trumps any other relationship.

All four gospels would agree on the need to prioritise a relationship with God; yet each shares this truth in a very different way. The genealogy or aetiology of Jesus is not set out in similar fashion. For this reason different insights can be gained. A massive, but possibly helpful, over-simplification is to note that in Mark Jesus' origins remain as a question to be asked. In Matthew Jesus has his roots in the ongoing story of God's people. In Luke Jesus' story begins with God. For John, Jesus' life has always been and will always remain in God.

3. Names or Titles for Jesus

The gospel writers record many different names and titles which are used to address or to describe Jesus. Each is worthy of consideration if we are to begin to appreciate what the gospel writers believed about the one who was their subject, but also the inspiration for their lives.

i. Jesus

It may seem to be stating the obvious to say that the most commonly used name for the person who is the main focus of the four New Testament gospels is "Jesus". Both Matthew and Luke tell us the name was divinely ordained (Matt.1:21; Lk.1:31). Matthew even gives an explanation of the name: *"for he will save his people from their sins"*. The name Jesus is used by each gospel an average of 240 times. Yet there is an intriguing anomaly.

Matthew and John report that the name 'Jesus' was part of the wording on the notice Pilate ordered to be fastened to the cross (Matt.27:37; Jn.19:19), whereas Mark and Luke do not include the name. In Matthew and in John, as far as I can tell, no one ever addresses Jesus by his name - though the crowds accompanying Jesus into Jerusalem speak of him by name to others in the crowd (Matt.21:11). Mark and Luke have three parallel occurrences of Jesus being directly addressed by his name: a man with an unclean spirit in a synagogue (Mk.1:24; Lk.4:34), legion, the demoniac (Mk.5:7; Lk.8:28), and a blind man (Mk.10:47; Lk.18:38). Luke adds two further instances. One is in the story of the ten lepers (Lk.17:13); the other is when the dying crucified thief addresses Jesus on the cross, *"Jesus, remember me ..."* (Lk.23:42). So the sparse use of Jesus' name as a direct address is limited to a few people who were in need of saving; but many others who also needed saving did not use Jesus' name. Only second-hand do we learn in John's Gospel that at least some people called Jesus by his name or referred to him as such. The man born blind and healed by Jesus responded to questions about the identity of the man who had healed him with the words; *"The man they call Jesus"* (Jn.9:11).

It was obviously normal practice to address people by their given names, and the name "Jesus" was commonplace: but the fact is that there are only five recorded instances of the name "Jesus" being used by the people who spoke to him. The other nearly one-thousand uses of the name are all by the writers of the gospels in their narration of his story. They use Jesus' name almost exclusively when referring to him. Could it be that only after his death was the full significance or appropriateness of his name, Jesus (God saves), realised and accordingly became the dominant mode of reference? If so, perhaps the gospel writers are to be commended on the faithfulness of their accounts of how Jesus was addressed by those who met him in the flesh, rather than how he was referred to in retrospect. It may be that when people met Jesus "in the flesh" there was something about him which usually led to him being addressed with a title of respect. If so, then the gospel writers have done their best to convey this reality in their records of the encounters between Jesus and his contemporaries.

It has been interesting to note over the years of being a minister how some people find it very easy to address their prayers to Jesus by name. Others feel more comfortable using a title, such as "Lord". Whilst I have known some who felt that they could only pray to God as "Father" or "Heavenly Father", perhaps unconsciously feeling that the role of Jesus was to point people to his Father, God, not to encourage worship of himself, or prayers to himself. There is a difference between praying "in Jesus name", and praying "to Jesus". The former seems more in keeping with the overall testimony of the gospels: but there can be no hard and fast ruling derived from their witness.

ii. Jesus of Nazareth/Galilee

Both Matthew and Luke record that Jesus was born in Bethlehem, yet in common with Mark and John who have no birth narratives, Jesus as an adult is never referred to as a Bethlehemite or a Judaean. He is *Jesus of Galilee; Jesus of Nazareth; a Nazarene; a Galilean*. Similar descriptions appear in all four gospels. Matthew alone offers prophetic justification: *"He will be called a Nazarene"* (Matt.2:23). In keeping with this prediction, Matthew later records the words of the crowds who accompanied him into Jerusalem, *"This is Jesus, the prophet from Nazareth in Galilee"* (Matt.21:11). In Mark the young man in the white robe at the tomb speaks about Jesus to the women as *"Jesus the Nazarene"* (Mk.16:6). The two disciples on the road to Emmaus also refer to *Jesus of Nazareth* (Lk.24:19). John tantalizingly has some unnamed people ask, *"Does not the scripture say that the Christ will come from Bethlehem, the town where David lived?"* (Jn.7:42). But this question remains unanswered, and the thought is not further developed in John.

Peter was accused of being associated with Jesus on the basis of his Galilean accent, so it would seem that Jesus' accent was the same. A common sense view is that if Jesus was raised from a young child in Nazareth, his accent might well have been that of a Nazarene/Galilean. However, sometimes the accents of parents are more influential than that of one's peers. The facts in this regard are complicated somewhat by the implications in Matthew that Joseph was a Judaean and only moved to Nazareth after Jesus' birth and their flight to Egypt (see Matt.2:19-23), whereas Luke suggests Joseph already lived in Nazareth prior to Jesus' birth (Lk.2:4) and both he and Mary were from Nazareth (Lk.1:26; 2:39). The gospels do not unanimously declare Jesus' birth place as Bethlehem, but they are in agreement as to the town from which Jesus was generally believed to have come, which was Nazareth. But they do not speak with one voice on the justification for this belief.

What is most important, as we have noted earlier, but what is hardly recognised by most Christians today, is that the descriptors *"of Nazareth"* or *"of Galilee"* would have been a divisive proclamation, at times used in a derogatory fashion, especially in Jerusalem (see above on John chapter 2). Even Nathanael initially shared the belief about Nazareth that nothing good could *"come from there"* – and no one suggested he had misidentified Jesus' place of origin (Jn.1:46. cp. Jn.7:41, 52). Not all names or titles used of Jesus were complimentary.

iii. Jesus the Christ/Messiah

Jesus is never directly addressed as *"Jesus Christ"* or just *"Christ"*; and depending on the translation this simplified title is used only two or three times by the Gospel writers (Matt.1:1; Mk.1:1; Jn.1:15). But the gospel writers leave no doubt they believed Jesus was "the Christ" or "the Messiah". The terms seem interchangeable as far as translations are concerned. KJV never used the word Messiah in the New Testament, whereas NIV (UK) consistently prefers Messiah to Christ.

Matthew (1:1) and Mark (1:1) both include *"Jesus Christ"* in their opening editorial sentence. Luke's dual birth stories means readers must wait to be told of Jesus that *"He is the Christ"*, but the source of this revelation is an angel (Lk.2:11). John's gospel not only tells us early on that *"grace and truth came through Jesus Christ"* (Jn.1:15), following this up with Andrew telling Peter, *"We have found the Christ"*

(Jn.1:41), but later affirms that his entire gospel has been written with the explicit purpose that "*you may believe that Jesus is the Christ*" (Jn.20:31).

For some the most dramatic or direct expression of this belief is by Peter at Caesarea Philippi in Matthew (16:16), Mark (8:29) and Luke (9:20). However, in John's gospel it is Martha, the sister of Mary and Lazarus, who unequivocally says, "*I believe you are the Christ*" (11:27).

In a few rare instances Jesus seems to refer to himself as the Christ or Messiah (e.g.Matt.23:8, 26:63; Mark 9:41; Luke 24:26; John 4:35; 17:3); but according to Matthew and Luke Jesus also gave orders not to tell anyone that he was the Messiah (Matt.16:20; Lk.4:41). For the gospel writers it was obviously tremendously important that Jesus should be recognised by their readers as the Christ or Messiah. Just how important it was for Jesus himself remains an open question.

Even more worthy of consideration might be the question: "How relevant to the majority of twenty-first-century people is this link to the history and expectation of ancient Jewish (Messianic) or Greco-Roman (*Christos*) thought?" I believe for most Christians in Britain today when the word Messiah is used it carries limited Jewish connotations and does not adequately express their understanding of Jesus as having universal significance. In my experience mention of Jesus as "The Messiah" or "The Christ" has a place in a church's selected scriptures for Advent and possibly Christmas, but perhaps with good reason is seldom otherwise the subject of study by any other than fringe groups such as *Jews for Jesus*. Both in and beyond church circles Jesus may be often referred to as "Jesus Christ", but rarely if ever as Jesus "the" Christ/Messiah. The absence of the use of the definite article probably supports my suspicion that neither element of the name is used as a useful, significant, contemporary description. It generally identifies a particular individual, but says nothing more.

iv. Son of God

At the beginning of the appraisal of Mark's Gospel in this study the question was raised as to how much the ascription *Son of God* carried implications of divinity for the *Son*. It is not my intention to repeat that discussion. Here we are considering the differences between the four gospels. In respect of the attention given to Jesus as *Son of God* these are considerable.

As we have noted earlier, whether Mark's gospel originally included *Son of God* at the beginning (Mk.1:1) and in the testimony of the centurion at the cross (Mk.15:39) is on the balance of the evidence unlikely. However, in his account of Jesus' baptism (Mk.1:11) and transfiguration (Mk.9:7) Mark tells of a voice from heaven or a cloud which unambiguously declares Jesus to be God's son. In Mark such recognition does not form part of Peter's expression of faith at Caesarea Philippi, but evil spirits are said to have regularly called Jesus *Son of God* (Mk.3:11; 5:7). There is just one direct comment by Jesus on a father-son relationship in Mark which most naturally is taken as a word about himself and God (Mk.13:32), and there is an implicit reference in a parable which includes a father and his son (Mk.12:6); but the exchange between Caiaphas who asks, "*Are you the Son of the Blessed One?*" and Jesus who responds directly, "*I am*" is a rather isolated testimony in Mark to Jesus' own belief in this regard (Mk.14:61f). As we have noted in other places, any description of Jesus as *Son of God* is far outweighed by Mark's emphasis on Jesus as *Son of Man* - and there is little if any justification on the basis of Mark's gospel for equating Jesus' son-ship with Jesus' divinity.

Matthew, in common with Mark and Luke records the voice from heaven at Jesus' baptism (Matt.3:17) and Transfiguration (Matt.17:5), but precedes this with a prophetic reference to Jesus as an infant, "*Out of Egypt I called my son*" (Matt.2:15 / Hosea 11:1). In Matthew (Matt.8:29) there is a close parallel to the story of Legion in Mark (Mk.5:7) with demon-possessed men who call Jesus, "*Son of God*". Matthew also includes the parable of the father who sends his son as his envoy (Matt.21:33-41) and the implied subordination of the son to the father who alone knows the ordained "hour" (Matt.24:36), Additionally Matthew includes one instance of Jesus praying, "*I praise you father*" (Matt.11:27; cf. Lk.10:21f). Jesus' response to Caiaphas is more nuanced than in Mark. Caiaphas says, "*Tell us if you are the Christ, the Son of the Living God*", which evokes Jesus' response, "*You have said so*" (Matt.26:63f), rather than Mark's "*I am*" (Mk.14:62). Though later at his crucifixion the chief priests claim Jesus had said he was the Son of God (Matt.27:43) which probably is not unconnected with the subsequent exclamations of the centurion and others, "*Surely this man was the son of God*" (Matt.27:54 - or *a* son of God NIV footnote). Both Matthew (Matt.4:3, 6) and Luke (Lk.4:3, 9) include the probing words of Satan "*If you are the son of God*" - taunting words hauntingly repeated in Matthew by Jesus' enemies when he hung on the cross (Matt.27:40).

In many ways Matthew's references to Jesus as God's son are very close to those of Mark, but there are three significant differences. Matthew tells us that the disciples, having seen Jesus walk on water and the storm calmed, "*Worshipped him, saying, ' Truly you are the Son of God.*'" (Matt.14:33). To Mark's account of Peter's confession of faith at Caesarea, "*You are the Christ*" Matthew adds, "*the son of the living* God" (Matt.16:16). Possibly the most influential contribution of Matthew to the way in which people have thought about Jesus comes in the gospel's penultimate verse with a formula which is unique not only in the gospels, but in the whole of the New Testament, "*In the name of the Father and of the Son and of the Holy Spirit*" (Matt.28:19. cp. 2 Cor.13:14 for a possible parallel). A close relationship between the Father, the son and the Holy Spirit are certainly abundantly evidenced in John and implicit in Luke, but only in Matthew is there this precise expression or formula which has been seen by many as placing Jesus, the Son, on a par with other divine manifestations, equally God. However, it should be noted that there is nothing else in Matthew to support such an exposition.

As noted above, Luke in common with Mathew and Mark records the voice from heaven at Jesus' baptism (Lk.3:32) and Transfiguration (Lk.9:35); and the probing questions of Satan in the desert closely following Jesus' baptism (Lk.4:3, 9 // Matt. 4:3, 6). Luke also offers three close parallels to Mark: in the story of Jesus' dealings with a demon-possessed man called Legion who said to Jesus: "*What do you want with me, Jesus, Son of the most high God*" (Lk.8:28 // Mk.5:7); in his record that many demons who were expelled declared, "*You are the Son of God*" (Lk.4:41 // Mk.5:7); and by including the parable of the son who is killed (Lk.20:13; Mk.12:6; Matt.21:33ff. see above). Luke's account of Jesus' trials is not the same as Matthew, Mark or John, though in a close parallel to Mark. Jesus is asked quite directly by the Council of the Elders, "*Are you then the Son of God?*" To which Jesus replies, "*You are right in saying I am*" (Lk.22:70).

So it is evident that although at times there are subtle differences, Luke incorporates much of the same material as Mark and Matthew in relation to Jesus as God's son. But Luke also has a unique contribution to make. Even if the angel's words to Mary recorded in many translations as, "*So the holy one to be born will be called the Son of God*" should be read as, "*So the child to be born will be called holy*" (Lk.1:35), Luke has already established through the angel that Jesus will be called *the Son of the Most High*" (Lk.1:32). Luke's story of Jesus' conception is itself a testimony to the fatherhood of God in respect of Jesus. Luke perhaps reinforces this twice in his distinctive genealogy: firstly, with the little comment about Jesus that he was the son, "*so it was thought*" of Joseph (Lk.3:23); secondly, by the tracing of Jesus familial ancestry directly back to God (Lk.3:38).

God's fatherhood of Jesus, and by implication Jesus' as Son of God, finds further confirmation in Luke with four occasions when Jesus refers to '*My Father*', a phrase which occurs much more often in Matthew, who has seventeen instances. Mark never uses the phrase '*My Father*', but in Mark, as in Matthew and Luke, Jesus speaks of God as "*The Father*" (Mk.8:38; 13:32). As noted above, Mark alone has that most intimate of addresses by Jesus in prayer, "*Abba*" (Mk.14:36). In Luke Jesus as a boy speaks of *My Father's House* (Lk.2:49), but then the notion seems largely in abeyance until Jesus final passion and its aftermath. In the upper room Jesus says to his disciples, "*And I confer on you a kingdom, just as my Father conferred one on me*" (Lk.22:29). Although Jesus had taught his disciples to address God as "*Father*" (Lk.11:4), only on the Mount of Olives, does

Jesus himself for the first time in Luke pray to God as "*Father*" (Lk.22:42). Jesus uses this form of address twice more - "*Father forgive*" (Lk.23:34); and finally "*Father into your hands*" (Lk.23:46). Though for all three synoptic gospel writers God is clearly the Father of all humanity, the words from heaven or a cloud at Jesus' baptism and transfiguration, along with other instances mentioned above, strongly support the contention that Jesus was son of God in a unique way.

It is, however, when we come to John's Gospel that Jesus as the Son of God, God as the father of Jesus, and Jesus as intimately related to God's Spirit can be seen as dominant motifs - "truths" which are constantly repeated. Not at his trial - although in John Jesus always seems to be on trial - but as part of his ongoing conversation with "the Jews", Jesus says, "*.... I said, I am God's Son*" (Jn.10:36). This has already been stated by the gospel writer (Jn.1:14), John the Baptizer (Jn.1:34) and Nathanael (Jn.1:49). It will be confirmed by Martha (Jn.11:27) and the author of the fourth gospel (Jn.20:31). For John, Jesus as "God's Son" is not just a title, a way of describing or appreciating Jesus, it is at the heart of the faith the gospel seeks to inspire. Believing in Jesus as God's Son is the key to eternal life (Jn.3:36; 6:40). This may be true for the other three gospel writers, but they do not spell it out.

In Matthew (Matt.3:17; 17:5), Mark (Mk.1:11; 9:7) and Luke (Lk.3:22) a voice from heaven says, "*This is my son whom I love*"; but in John it is Jesus himself who declares, "*The Father loves the Son*" (Jn.3:35; 5:20; 10:17; 15:9). The writer of the fourth gospel affirms that Jesus is "*the one and only Son, who is himself God and is in the closest relationship with the Father*" (Jn.1:18). In addition Jesus provides the confirmation, "*I and my Father are one*" (Jn.10:30). Only in John is it made explicit that the son exists and works so that the Father may be glorified through him (Jn.11:4; 13:32) - "*It is the Father, living in me, who is doing his work .... I am in the Father and the Father is in me*" (Jn.4:10f). This emphasis on the relationship of Father/Son between Jesus and God is underpinned or expanded in John's Gospel with numerous references by Jesus to *My Father* (Jn.5:17f; 8:49; 10:18, 25, 29; 12:26; 15:15, 23f; 16:23, 25) or *The Father* (Jn.1:16; 5:36f; 13:1, 3; 14:16, 26; 15:16, 26; 16:10, 17, 28; 20:17). And in John there are more occasions than in the Synoptics on which Jesus directly addresses God in prayer as *Father* (Jn.11:41; 12:27f; 17:1, 5, 24) or *Holy Father* (Jn.17:11, 25).

All four Gospel writers agree that Jesus is rightly called "*Son of God*". But the importance or significance of this seems to vary from gospel to gospel - as no doubt it always will from believer to believer. Each of us must consider what practical difference it makes by saying and believing "*Jesus is God's son*". Perhaps one helpful answer is given in the story of the transfiguration, "*Listen to him*"!

v. Son of Mary

As well as being called "*Son of God*" Jesus is also described in the gospels either directly or indirectly as "*the son of Mary*". Here again the gospels are not united in the attention they give to this.

Mark mentions Jesus' mother Mary by name only once: in a question asked about Jesus, "*Isn't this Mary's son?*" (Mk.6:3//Matt.13:55). Jesus' mother is mentioned only on one other occasion by Mark, an occasion when Jesus posed the question recorded in all three Synoptics, "*Who is my mother and who are my brothers?* (Mk.3:33//s Matt.12:48 // Lk.8:21); with Jesus' own answer that his family consists of those who do God's will. In Mark, Jesus' rejection of his birth family, including his mother, would seem to be final. Yet, on the other hand, Mark records Jesus' chastisement of the scribes and Pharisees because they found a way to avoid their duty to honour their father and mother (Mk.7:9-13). Typical of Mark, readers are left to make their own decisions.

Luke, who in the early chapters of his gospel paints such a positive picture of Mary (Lk.1:26-38, 2:1-7; 2:51), not only includes the story of Jesus prioritising a different kind of family (Lk.8:21), but adds two further bases for acknowledging the rejection by Jesus of special status for his birth-mother. Some women said to Jesus: "*Blessed is the mother who gave you birth*". To which Jesus replied, "*Blessed rather are those who hear the word of God and obey it* (Lk.11:27f). Then in Jesus' teaching he said, "*If anyone comes to me and does not hate father and mother, wife and children, brothers and sisters – yes, even their own life – such a person cannot be my disciple*" (Lk.14:26). It is interesting to note that Luke makes a passing reference to Mary in the Book of Acts (Acts 1:14), but never mentions Mary again. Nor is Mary mentioned by any other New Testament writer outside of the gospels.

Matthew gives an account of Jesus' conception and birth with references to "*his mother Mary*" (Matt.1:18; 2:11) - and precedes his genealogy with the statement, "*Mary was the mother of Jesus*" (Matt.1:16). It seems strange given this beginning that in common with Mark and Luke Matthew tells us nothing more about Jesus and his mother save her abortive effort to take him home (Matt.12:48) - though some might see a reference to Jesus' mother in the description "*Mary the mother of James and Joseph*" (Matt.27:56)[4].

John, as in so many things, provides a different picture. Jesus' mother, Mary, is never mentioned by name in John; but at the beginning of Jesus' public ministry, John tells us "*His mother was there*" (2:1); and she played an active role in the events at the wedding at Cana. John follows this by telling us that Jesus "*went*

---

[4] cf. Matt.13:55; Jn.19:25

down to Capernaum with his mother and brothers and his disciples. There they stayed for a few days" (2:12). Were Jesus' mother and brothers living in Capernaum by that time? If so, it is not unreasonable to suppose that occasionally he went "home" to his mother. In John's account of Jesus' life Jesus visited or stayed in Capernaum a number of times during his early ministry (cf. Jn.6:24, 42). He was certainly enough in touch with his brothers for them to try on one occasion to persuade him to go to Jerusalem (Jn.7:3). Although Mary is not mentioned and seems to have been absent during most of Jesus' ministry in Jerusalem, John tells us *"his mother"* was one of the women at the cross and Jesus ensured continuing care for her courtesy of *"the disciple whom Jesus loved"* (Jn.19:25-7). To unveil John's view of Jesus' mother and her relationship to her son we need to discern the signs.

Though Luke may have used words of Mary to graphically shape his telling of the story of Jesus, on balance, Matthew, Mark and Luke all suggest Jesus had other priorities and turned away from his mother. Because I regularly worship in ecumenical contexts, I have become familiar with "The Stations of the Cross". Recently in a service using the Stations of the Cross, the Roman Catholic priest conducting the worship observed that the only extra-Biblical element in the stations is the intrusion of Veronica. But Jesus meeting his mother, Mary, as he carried his cross; and the sometimes included Pietà also have no firm Biblical foundation. Jesus was undoubtedly the *Son of Mary*, and the fourth gospel strongly suggests that Jesus retained a deep love for his mother throughout his life; but scant evidence is offered in the New Testament gospels to warrant the kind of devotional attention and veneration many Christians have afforded her.

vi. Son of Joseph

According to John, Jesus was also called *"the son of Joseph"* (Jn.1:45; 6:42); though John is alone in using this title and makes no other mention of Joseph. As we know, Luke in his genealogy says of the notion that Joseph was Jesus' father, *"So it was thought"* (Lk.3:23). Luke confirms that indeed *it was thought* by recording the question asked in the Nazareth synagogue, *"Isn't this Joseph's son?"* (4:22). In Luke's birth narratives Joseph is a minor player and receives only one other passing mention (4:22). Joseph is never mentioned in Mark. But what I find strange is that in Matthew's birth narratives Joseph is possibly the most significant character; yet after the return from Egypt to Nazareth Joseph receives just one oblique mention through the question, *"Isn't this the carpenter's son?"* (Matt.13:55). All kinds of explanations have been offered for Joseph's "disappearance", including his early death: but the question in Matthew, which seems most naturally to refer to Joseph as a father who is still alive, and Luke's account of Jesus' visit to Jerusalem as a teenager (Lk.2:41-52) would caution against too readily accepting this or any other theory. Jesus' reply as a boy concerning, "*My Father's house*" to his mother's words, "*Your father and I have been anxiously searching for you*" (Lk.2:48f) would suggest that Jesus gave no greater allegiance to his "earthly" father than he did to his mother - though as a child Luke tells us Jesus was "*obedient to them*" (Lk.2:51). Was Joseph like the father of the prodigal son, waiting at home for his son's return? (Lk.15:20.) If so, Joseph's son would "return" in quite a different way.

vii. Son of Abraham/David

Matthew at the outset of his gospel describes Jesus as the "*Son of Abraham*" (Matt.1:1) - as does Luke in his genealogy, though less directly (3:34). This is not a title used by Mark or John. Matthew and Luke put the matter into perspective in Jesus words, "*Do not begin to say to yourselves, 'We have Abraham as our father.' For I tell you out of these stones God can raise up children for Abraham*"(Matt.3:9). John offers a different basis for according Abraham only relative importance. Jesus says: "*Before Abraham was born, I am*" (Jn.8:58).

I suspect the gospel writers had a similar view of the relationship between Jesus and Abraham to that which they held with regard to Jesus and David. Indeed, Matthew brackets together the two descriptions *Son of Abraham* and *Son of David* (Matt.1:1). In Luke, in spite of the angels words to Mary that God would give Jesus "*the throne of his father David*" (Lk.1:32), Jesus says of the Messiah, that is, of himself, "*David calls him 'Lord.' How then can he be his son?'*" (Lk.20:43). Nonetheless, in the Synoptics "*Son of* David" seems to have been a title that was used either by people in need calling out to Jesus (Matt.9:27; 15:22; 20:30f; Mk.10:47; Lk.18:37, 39) or in praise (Matt.21:9, 15). In John some unnamed people comment on the expectation that the Messiah would be of the house and lineage of David (Jn.7:42); but the idea that Jesus was in some way the son of Abraham or David seems to be foreign to the fourth gospel whose repeated testimony is that Jesus is the Son of God (Jn.1:49; 5:25; 11:27; 20:31).

Son of Mary? Son of Joseph? Son of Abraham? Son of David? Yes, for some people Jesus is one or all of these. But when all four gospels are taken into consideration, Jesus is primarily *Son of God* and *Son of Man*.

viii. Jesus is "Lord".

In Mark's Gospel the Syro-Phoenician woman is unique as someone who calls Jesus, "*Lord*" (Mk.7:28; cp.Matt.15:21-28). Additionally in Mark there are three probable self-references by Jesus to the legitimate use of this title (Mk.2:28; 5:19; 11:3//Lk.19:31ff); and if the later endings of Mark are taken into account there are two editorial references to "*the Lord Jesus*" (Mk.16:20f; cp. Matt.24:3); but as a regular way of speaking about or to Jesus, "Lord" is noticeably absent in Mark.

Very early in Luke's gospel Jesus is recognised as "Lord" when Elizabeth speaks to the pregnant Mary as "*the mother of my Lord*" (Lk.1:43). A variety of people speak to Jesus as *"Lord"* - a leper (Lk.5:12; Matt.8:2), a centurion through his friends (Lk.7:6; Matt.8:6ff), Martha (Lk.10:40), an unnamed person (Lk.13:23), Zacchaeus (Lk.19:8), would-be disciples (Lk.9:59,61), and committed disciples (Lk.9:54;10:17; 11:1; 17:5; 22:38; 24:34; Matt.8:25;) - including Peter (Lk.5:8; 12:41; 22:33; Matt.14:28ff; 17:4; 18:21; 26:22). As well as the parallels already noted in parentheses, Matthew also adds a blind man (Matt.9:28) or men (Matt.20:30-33), and a father pleading for help for his son (Matt.17:15). In many ways Luke and Matthew are one in recognising that Jesus was addressed on many occasions as "*Lord*"; and that the use of this appellation is often part of a cry or plea for help.

But Luke and Matthew also share a caution about the use of the word "Lord". As part of his sermon on the plain Jesus asks, "*Why do you call me 'Lord, Lord,' and not do what I say?*" (Lk.6:46). The words are not enough. But Matthew goes further. Not only does Jesus in Matthew explicitly say, "*Not everyone who says to me, 'Lord' Lord' will enter the kingdom of heaven*" (7:21); but he follows this up with a parable in which five foolish virgins stand at a closed door shouting, "*Lord, Lord*", only to receive the reply, "*I tell you the truth. I don't know you*". Peter also calls Jesus, "*Lord*", but in a way which earns him a solid rebuke (Matt.22:16f). In spite of all these words of caution, Luke and Matthew seem to have little if any reservation themselves as authors in referring to Jesus as "Lord" or "the Lord". Perhaps Mark took to heart the caution against too easily using the word "*Lord*", and this is reflected in a gospel which encourages a more in-depth exploration of how Jesus might be addressed and understood.

If some of the translations of John's gospel are to be taken as a fair translation of the available Greek in context, then John provides a quite different slant on the use of the word, "Lord", or at least the translators have done so. With a few exceptions the word "Lord" is not used by those who speak to Jesus until nearly half way through the gospel (9:38). Jesus is regularly addressed as "*Sir*". This is very often by people in need, not by committed disciples (Jn.4:11, 15, 49; 5:7; 6:34; 8:11; 9:36). But when the gospel (from 9:38 onward) turns its attention much more to Jesus' speaking for the benefit of his disciples, or to conversations with them in mind, the word "*Sir*" as a way of talking to Jesus almost drops out of sight, and "*Lord*" takes its place. Only Mary in the garden is deemed to have used the word "*Sir*" in her ignorance (Jn.20:15). Since it is the same Greek word, Κύριε, which is being translated as both "Sir" and "Lord", it is difficult to draw too hard and fast a lesson from the translations. However, it would seem to be in keeping with the cautionary words in Matthew and Luke that use of the word "Lord" is confined in John to those who are known by Jesus to be his true followers - the man born blind who believed and worshipped (Jn.9:38), Peter (Jn.6:68; 13:6, 9, 36f; 21:15ff, 21), Martha and Mary (Jn.11:21, 32, 39), Mary Magdalene (Jn.20:2, 13 18), Judas not Iscariot (!Jn.14:22), the disciple whom Jesus loved (13:25; 21:7) - and by no means last or least, Thomas (14:5; 20:28 "*My Lord, and my God*").

Calling Jesus, "Lord", amounts to a commitment to follow Jesus' teaching. Although each gospel puts it in a different way, John surely captures the import of all the gospels in the words of Jesus he records:

> "*You call me Teacher and Lord, and rightly so, for that is what I am. (But) Now that I, your Lord and Teacher, have washed your feet, you should also wash one another's feet. I have set you an example that you should do as I have done for you*" (Jn.13:13f).

Jesus is Lord, but this is a Lord who lives as a humble servant and dies as a scapegoat, laying down his life for his people. Jesus expects those who claim him as their "*Lord*" to be willing to do the same.

ix. The Shepherd

John conveys this same truth about the sacrificial nature of the lordship of Jesus using a different title. John reports Jesus as saying, "*I am the Good Shepherd. The Good Shepherd lays down his life for his sheep*" (Jn.10:11). The emphasis has often and rightly fallen on the sacrificial character of the Good Shepherd, yet within the passage on the Good Shepherd there is possibly the equally important task of the shepherd to gather in sheep which "*are not of this sheep pen ... and there will be one flock and one shepherd*" (Jn.10:16).

In Matthew's parable of the sheep and the goats it is interesting to note how the Son of Man (Matt.25:31) mutates into the shepherd (25:32) and then into a king (25:34). This ties in well with Matthew's early quote from Micah of the "*ruler who will be the shepherd of my people Israel*"(Matt.2:6 // Micah .5:2).

Without doubt Jesus as a shepherd has been a most powerful image in Christian history, yet it finds minimal expression in the gospels. It is found in John chapter 10 (Jn.10:1-16), but nowhere else in the fourth gospel. In Mark there is a single reference to "*the shepherd*" when Jesus quotes the prophet Zechariah, "*I will strike the shepherd, and the sheep will be scattered*" (Mk.14:27; Zech.13:7) - a verse also quoted by Matthew (26:31). In addition in Matthew, Herod is told that out of Bethlehem will "*come a ruler who will be the shepherd of my people Israel*" (Matt.2:6 // Micah .5:2). Matthew does use the shepherd image twice more: once in an editorial comment which is more about the crowds than Jesus, "*like sheep without a shepherd*" (Matt.9:36): and as already noted in the parable of the sheep and goats the Son of Man is likened to a shepherd (Matt.25:32). Nowhere in Luke is there a direct reference to Jesus as a shepherd; but some may see the context of the parable of the lost sheep as justifying the concept of Jesus himself as the shepherd who seeks out "the lost" (Lk.15:1-7). Indeed John's gospel climaxes in a conversation in which Jesus encourages Peter to "*Feed my lambs - Take care of my sheep - Feed my sheep*" (Jn.21:15-17).

It might also be noted that the place of the 23rd Psalm in most churches' hymnody, and its frequent use both spoken and sung in high ceremony as well as popular folk religion probably plays no small part in giving prominence to the shepherd image for "*The Lord*". I suggest that many people when they say, "*The Lord is my Shepherd*" may think the word "*Lord*" is being applied to Jesus, since God as a shepherd is not an idea which is broadcast widely. Other hymns based on Psalm 23 aid the identification of the shepherd in the Psalm with Jesus. For example, in "*The King of Love my Shepherd is*" H. W. Baker makes explicit a connection between Jesus and the shepherd in Psalm 23 with the words, "*Your cross before to guide me*". In similar vein Anna Waring in "*In heavenly love abiding*" has the words "*My God is round about me*", but also "*My Saviour has my treasure*" – which many would naturally think of as Jesus.

Although in the gospels Jesus is never spoken to as "*Shepherd*", and overt references to Jesus as shepherd are few, the image has such a capacity to encapsulate the life, ministry and passion of Jesus there is small wonder that its influence has been so outstanding.

x. King of the Jews/Israel

All four gospels include the encounter of Pilate and Jesus. Although there are differences in the overall conversation, all four include Pilate's very direct question, "*Are you the king of the Jews?*" (Matt.27:11; Mk.15:2; Lk.23:3; Jn.18:33). The Synoptics all quote Jesus as answering, "*Yes. It is as you say*". But in John Jesus responds to Pilate with a question, "*Is that your own idea, or did others talk to you about me?*" and a statement, "*My kingdom is not of this world*" (Jn.18:34, 36). The outcome, however, is the same in all four gospels. Pilate had a notice pinned to the cross, which was the official "crime" or charge against Jesus, and probably had the same intention as the mockery of Jesus by his soldiers and others (Matt.27:29; Mk.15:18; Lk.23:37; Jn.19:3). But for the gospel writers and for their Christian readers "*Jesus of Nazareth: the King of the Jews*" may be considered a fitting description (Matt.23:37; Mk. 15:26; Lk.23:38; Jn.19:19ff)[5]. It

---

[5] I cannot remember ever reading or hearing it said that the words Pilate had affixed to the cross were meant as mockery; and as a warning to anyone else with pretensions to kingship. But that seems to me to be the most obvious motive. Any suggestion that Pilate meant these

is within the passion narratives in the gospels that the title *"King of the Jews"* finds its most frequent expression; possibly because in his death Jesus posed the most serious and obvious challenge to the accepted notions of what it meant to be a king. Mocking disbelief confirms that challenge.

Mark uses the title "King of the Jews" only in his account of Jesus' trial and death, whereas in Matthew Jesus is of royal lineage and is *"born to be king of the Jews"* (Matt.2:2). When the crowds welcomed Jesus into Jerusalem Mark says the crowd shouted for the coming *"Kingdom"* (Mk.11:10) not the king; whereas Matthew cites Zechariah *"Say to Daughter Zion, 'See, your king comes to you'"*(Matt.21:5//Zech.9:9). And for Matthew *"the kingdom of heaven is like a king....."* (Matt.18:23; 22:22; 25:34). Even though Matthew records Jesus rejection of the devil's offer to let him rule the world (Matt.4:8-10), he tells us the Magi asked where they might find *"the one born to be king of the* Jews" (Matt.2:2). I am not convinced that Matthew accepted that Jesus' kingdom was not *"of this world"* (cp.Jn.18:36)[6].

Luke seems to have envisaged an earthly kingdom. The angel said to Mary, *"The Lord God will give him the throne of his father David, and he will reign over Jacob's descendants for ever.'* (Lk.1:32f). Simeon declares that Jesus would be *"the glory of your people Israel"* (Lk.2:32), But it is difficult to see how these prophecies have been fulfilled. In Luke when Jesus enters Jerusalem a large crowd of disciples shout, *"'Blessed is the king who comes in the name of the Lord!' 'Peace in heaven and glory in the highest!'"* (Lk.19:38); echoing the message of the angel to Mary (Lk.1:32) and of the angels to the shepherds (Lk.2:13f). But Jesus' entry into Jerusalem being proclaimed as king by his disciples closely follows a parable (Lk.19:11-27). In the parable a man enters a country to be proclaimed as king, but the subjects hated him and did not want him as their king. *"He was made king, however, and then returned home"* (Lk.19:15). The divine intention may have been for Jesus to be the King of the Jews, but in Luke that intention is thwarted.

For me, given that Jesus seems only to have been formally recognised as a "King" on the cross (which therefore was his throne), the verse in Luke, *"He was made king, however, and then returned home"* (Lk.19:15), has a Johannine feel to it.

---

words to be taken literally is unthinkable. Of course, the gospel writers intended their readers to see the truth in what was written by Pilate, but there is no basis for attributing the evangelists' motives to Pilate.

[6] For an interesting, though not altogether convincing perspective on this, see *The Difference Heaven Makes: Rehearing the Gospel as News* in which Christopher Morse suggests that it is this world in which Jesus is king, but it is this world in the radically new order replacing the present order which is passing away - Pub. Continuum International 2010.

Chapter 5 - Reflections

Before Jesus had begun his work Nathanael called Jesus, "*the King of Israel*" (Jn.1:49). But when, following the feeding of five thousand, "*they intended to make him King by* force", Jesus made himself scarce (Jn.6:15). In John's account of Jesus' final entry into Jerusalem the shouts of the crowds include, "*Blessed is the King of Israel*" (Jn.12:13) but noticeably in John it is Jesus himself who finds a donkey so that he can enter Jerusalem in keeping with Zechariah's prophecy (Matt.12:13, 15// Zech.9:9). John chooses not to include the words in Zechariah "*Your king comes to you righteous and victorious, lowly and riding on a donkey*". Given the subsequent washing of his disciples' feet and the gospel emphasis on service as a virtue, rather than *lording it over* others [7], the reader might legitimately and helpfully recognise the kingly humility which Zechariah prophesied as being enacted in John rather than quoted. Any praise of Jesus as "king" in modern worship should be nuanced. Raw adulation of what is in essence an earthly kind of power demanding subservience is unworthy of one who was both humbly born and humiliated in death.

xi. The one who was to come

John the Baptizer, in both Matthew and Luke, sends two of his disciples to ask Jesus, "*Are you the one who was to come, or should we expect someone else?*" (Matt.11:3; Lk.7:19f). Why John sent to ask this we cannot tell. Perhaps Jesus did not live up to what John expected. After all, John's father, Zechariah, confidently expected that "*the horn of salvation*" would bring "*salvation, or rescue, from the hands of our enemies*" (Lk.1:69, 71, 74). All four gospels record John himself forecasting that the one who would come, and for whom he was preparing the way, would be "*more powerful than I*" (Matt.3:11; Mk.1:7; Lk.3:16), or "*has surpassed me*" (Jn.1:15). Mark and John inform us that John the Baptizer expected the one who was to come to baptize "*with the Holy Spirit*" (Mk.1:8; Jn.1:33), to which Matthew and Luke add "*and fire*" (Matt.3:11; Lk.3:16). At the time of John's imprisonment and death the fulfilment of these prophecies was not evident. Jesus offered to John in prison a quite different basis for accepting that he was "*the one who was to come*" - healing, raising of the dead, and good news for the poor (Matt.11:4f;Lk.7:21). We cannot tell whether or not this satisfied John that Jesus was indeed "the one". The continuing existence of "disciples of John" (see Acts 19:1ff) at least raises the seldom recognised possibility that John was not convinced.

In Matthew Jesus is certainly the one who comes and who fulfils the Law and the Prophets. "*Do not think I have come to abolish the Law or the Prophets: I have not*

---

[7] Chloe Lynch on *In 1Peter 5:1-5* notes how in both 1 Peter 5 and in Mark 10:42-45 the same word κατακυριευουσιν, *Lording it over*, is used to emphasise what followers of Jesus should not do - Expository Times Aug.2012 p.537

238

come to abolish them, but to fulfil them", says Jesus (Matt.5:17. cp.); and demonstrates what he means by "fulfilment" in a series of pronouncement which begin, "*You have heard it said, but I say....*"(Matt.5:22, 28, 32, 34, 39, 44). In addition to this, throughout Matthew's gospel Jesus is represented as fulfilling what the prophets foretold (Matt.1:22; 2:15, 17, 23; 3:15; 4:14; 8:17; 12:17; 13:14, 35; 21:4; 26:54; 27:9).

The first fulfilment in Luke's "*account of the things that have been fulfilled among us*" (1:1) is through Mary (1:38, 45). Elsewhere in Luke "*the times of the Gentiles*" will be fulfilled (Lk.21:24), and the Passover meal (the Last Supper) will find its fulfilment "*in the Kingdom of God*" (Lk.22:16). The references may be few in number in Luke, but there is little doubt that for Luke the main fulfilment of God's formerly declared intentions is through Jesus.

In Matthew many of the references to Jesus' fulfilment of the scriptures are editorial. In Luke there are only four statements that in Jesus the scriptures are being fulfilled, but they are all by Jesus himself; three leading up to his death (18:31; 21:22; 22:37) and one after his death on the road to Emmaus, "*Beginning with Moses and all the Prophets, he explained to them what was said in all the scriptures concerning himself*" (Lk.24:27). Mark has only one reference to the fulfilling of scripture. There was a question by the disciples which seemed to make the assumption that fulfilment of what Jesus predicted was inevitable (Mk.13:4), but the words of Jesus himself, "*The scriptures must be fulfilled*" (Mk.14:49) refer to his arrest, and by extension his death. Unlike Matthew, Mark in common with Luke, does not relate specific incidents in the rest of Jesus' life to the fulfilment of scripture.

John has a high view of Scripture: "*Scripture cannot be set aside*" (Jn.10:35). In John, Philip says to Nathanael, "*We have found the one Moses wrote about in the Law and about whom the prophets also wrote*" (Jn.1:45). This is confirmed by Jesus in his words to the Jews in Jerusalem, "*If you believed Moses, you would believe me, for he wrote about me*" (5:46). The fourth gospel has a relatively small, but fairly even mix of both editorial comment (12:38ff; 18:9, 32; 19:24, 36) and words spoken by Jesus himself (13:18; 15:25; 17:12) to support the contention that Jesus was the one about whom the Law and the Prophets wrote. But John has what I consider to be a unique understanding of Jesus in as much as Jesus himself deliberately acted in order to fulfil what was prophesied about him. For example, "*So that the Scripture would be fulfilled, Jesus said, 'I am thirsty'*" (Jn.19:28). Furthermore, any indicators in John of Jesus as the fulfilment of Scripture should be held alongside Jesus' self-knowledge that he is the agent of, and fulfilling God's purposes. Jesus knows that he is "*the one who comes from above .... the one whom God has sent*" (Jn.3:31, 34 - see also 5:38; 6:29, 46; 7:33; 8:29; 10:36; 12:44f; 13:16, 20). So he tells the crowd that he is "*the bread of God ... who comes down from heaven*" (Jn.6:33); and even more plainly tells his disciples, "*I came from the Father and entered the world*" (Jn.16:28, 30).

Perhaps all these indicators that Jesus, as John the Baptizer hoped, is "*the one who was to come*", are given their most dramatic expression by all four gospel writers in their account of Jesus' final approach to Jerusalem. Those who welcome him shout, "*Blessed is he who comes in the name of the Lord*" (Matt.21:9; Mk.11:9; Lk.19:38; Jn.12:13). Words which Matthew and Luke tell us Jesus believed would herald his reappearance (Matt.23:29; Lk.13:35). If the testimony of all the gospels is taken into account, Jesus is "*the one who was to come*" - but also the one who as the Son of Man will come again.

xii. The Son of Man

Having looked specifically in the chapter devoted to Mark at the way in which Mark used the title *Son of Man*, it is not my intention here to repeat those thoughts, but rather to note the similarities and differences displayed in the gospels in their use of this descriptor. The first thing to say is that all four gospels include a number of references to the "*Son of Man*"; but it is always a way in which Jesus refers to himself rather than an ascription used by others in their interaction with him - unless the gospel writers are taken into account. Anyone familiar with the Synoptics will know that Matthew, Mark and Luke have a great deal of material which is common to two of the three, or sometimes all three of these gospels. John expresses possibly the same beliefs but mostly through very different narrative.

The most obvious parallels in the Synoptics in their use of the "*Son of Man*" are found when Jesus talks about or forecasts his passion (Matt. 17:12, 22; 20:18, 26:2, 24. Mk.9: 31; 10:33; 14:21. Lk.9:44; 17:25; 18:31-33; 22:22). Instead of saying, "*I will ...*" Jesus invariably says, "*The Son of Man will ...*" Or in Mark and Luke on some occasions *"The Son of Man must ..."* (Mk.8:31; 9:12; Lk.9:22; 24:7 cp. Jn.3:14; 12:34). These passion predictions find their fulfilment when Jesus' says, "*The Son of Man is betrayed into the hands of sinners*" (Matt.26:54; Mk.14:41. cf. Lk.24:7, 26).

In speaking of what is sometimes referred to in The Lord's Supper as *"his coming again"*, Jesus consistently uses "Son of Man". Mark has three occasions when Jesus speaks of this (Mk.8:38; 13:26; 14:62). Matthew does not have many more (Matt.10:23; 16:28; 19:28; 25:31 - cp.Lk.21:36); but in contrast to Mark's little apocalypse which has only one mention of the *Son of Man* (Mk.13), Matthew's apocalyptic discourse (Matt.24:3-44) is clearly focussed on the Son of Man (Matt.27, 30, 39, 44). It is Luke, however, who records most instances of Jesus speaking about the future coming of the Son of Man in glory and for judgement (Lk.9:26; 10:40; 17:22, 24, 26, 30; 18:8; 21:27, 36; 17:22, 24, 26, 30; 18:8), culminating in Jesus' words to the Sanhedrin, "*From now on you will see the son of man seated at the right hand of the mighty God*" (Lk.22:69//Matt.26:64). Perhaps this more frequent use of the figure of judgement is inevitable given Luke's focus on the ultimate reversal of all earthly orders foretold in Mary's song of praise and revolution.

We are left to wonder why Jesus himself used what amounts to an alter-ego. One plausible explanation is that Jesus needed to convey that what was happening to him, and what he was doing and would do, was not the product of an ego-trip, nor ultimately in his hands. He was acting in accordance with God's purposes which, in virtue of being "God's" purposes, had a dimension which far exceeded the present moment and any individual life; even that of Jesus of Nazareth. Using *Son of Man* gave this breadth of reference. Of course, at a more mundane level, it might have been less emotional, and therefore easier, for Jesus to speak about his suffering and death in the third person, rather than the first.

All three Synoptics report that the Son of Man has authority to forgive sins (Matt.9:6 // Mk.2:10//Lk.5:24) and is "*Lord of the Sabbath*" (Matt.12:8//Mk.2:28//Lk.6:5). Matthew and Luke also tell us the Son of Man had "*nowhere to lay his head*" (Matt.8:20 // Lk.9:58), was said to be a glutton *and a drunkard* (Matt.11:19//Lk.7:34), could be likened to Jonah (Matt.2:40; Lk.11:30), and that to speak against the Son of Man was of less gravity than blaspheming against the Holy Spirit (Matt.12:32; Lk.12:8-10). There seems little doubt that all these are referring to Jesus

In Mark alone Jesus' uses the title "The Son of Man" at Caesarea Philippi (Mk.6:13), and we find the prophecy, "*until the Son of Man has risen from the dead*" (Mk.9:9). Only in Luke does Jesus say people will be blessed if they are hated because of the Son of Man (Lk.6:22); that the Son of Man, "*came to seek and save the lost*" (Lk.19:10); and to Judas, "*Are you betraying the Son of Man with a kiss?*" (Lk.22:48). In Matthew the Son of Man is the farmer who sows good seeds (Matt.13:37) and who will reap the final harvest (Matt.13:41); and the one who comes, "*not to be served, but to serve and to give his life as a ransom for many*" (Matt.10:28). Any attempt at a fuller appreciation of the Synoptic gospels' use of "*Son of Man*" will take all these into account

Use of "the Son of Man" in the fourth gospel is confined to the first thirteen chapters. As with the Synoptics only Jesus uses this title, and it is a self-description. One example of this is Jesus to Nathanael when Jesus' says there will be, "*angels ascending and descending on the Son of Man*" (1:52). But I do not sense in John's use of this title the same connotations of an alter-ego which may be present in the Synoptics. Indeed, when the fourth gospel takes us into Jesus' preparation of himself and his disciples for his death, the use of "a third person" as opposed to the direct "I" would destroy the intimacy between Jesus and his disciples which John so clearly wished to convey. So, for example, Jesus says, "*I am going away and I am coming back to you. If you loved me you would be glad ...*" (14:28); or, "*I am going to Him who sent me ... Because I have said these things you are filled with grief*" (16:5). This is not going to happen to some obscure heavenly being. It will happen to the man they know and love.

We have recognised that the fourth gospel also record Jesus saying, "*The Son of Man*". This is not only to Nathanael, but to others such as Nicodemus (Jn.3:13-14). To the crowds who had been fed, "*food that endures to eternal life*" will be given by the Son of Man who has the Father's *seal of approval*" (Jn.6:27). To bickering Jews, Jesus said they needed to eat the flesh and drink the blood of the Son of Man - or "*You have no life in you*" (Jn.6:53); and to dithering disciples a question: "*What if you see the Son of Man ascend to where he was before?*" (Jn.6:62). On just one occasion in John there is a hint of Jesus using "Son of Man" when referring to his death. He said to the Jews, "*When you have lifted up the Son of Man, then you will know that I am the one I claim to be*" (Jn.8:28). The Jews may have been left still pondering, "*Who is this Son of Man*" (Jn.12:34) But the proximity of "*Son of Man*" and "*I*" in chapter eight leaves the reader in no doubt as to who the Son of Man is. This is reinforced in the story of Jesus and the man blind from birth. Jesus asked him, "*Do you believe in the Son of Man?*" and Jesus went on to say, "*You have seen him; in fact he is the one speaking to you*" (Jn.9:35-37). Furthermore, the one hint of Jesus using "Son of Man" in reference to his death must be held alongside John's conviction that Jesus' death was the hour of his glorification. In John, Jesus says, "*The hour has come for the Son of Man to be glorified*" (Jn.12:23): then, having spoken of his death (12:33) and acknowledged his betrayal as a *fait accompli* (13:18-30), Jesus says, "*Now is the Son of Man glorified*" (Jn.13:31) - and the title "Son of Man" is not used again!

Possibly the closest John gets to the Synoptics' use of "The Son of Man" is when Jesus says, "*He has given him authority to judge, because he is the Son of Man*" (Jn.5:27). But unlike those instances in the Synoptics where the Son of Man is Lord of the Sabbath, or has authority to forgive sins, John's reference here to the Son of Man is in the same "conversation" directly and closely linked to obvious references to Jesus as "*the Son*" (Jn.5:26), and "*the Son of God*" (Jn.5:25). In John, the "Son of Man" is part of, though not a major part of Jesus' public persona. It is not the way in which his closest disciples are encouraged to think about Jesus or to relate to him. In John at least Jesus wants to be able to call his disciples "*friends*" (Jn.15:15), and indeed does so in his last Johannine post-resurrection appearance (Jn.21:5). By implication Jesus is their friend in a two-way, deeply personal relationship. In contrast, from my reading of all four New Testament gospels the title *Son of Man* almost always seems impersonal, even a way of Jesus distancing himself as an individual from the inevitable personal cost involved in his

242

commitment to fulfil the will of God. Perhaps this is why the title as a probable description of Jesus appears only three times in the rest of the New Testament (Acts.7:56; Rev.1:13; 14:14), and in my experience is rarely used as a way of talking about Jesus in the twenty-first century. As a result we probably lose that sense of God's universal and extra-historical action which is necessary to balance, and probably outweigh the idea of Jesus as my personal friend and saviour.

xiii. A Prophet

"Jesus the prophet" was considered particularly in surveying Mark's gospel, but all four gospels include the fact that Jesus was called a prophet. The Samaritan woman in John says to Jesus, "*I can see you are a prophet*" (Jn.4:19). Later in the same chapter John makes an editorial comment that Jesus had said, "*a prophet has no honour in his own country*" (Jn.4:44), whereas in the other three gospels these words are said by Jesus *in situ* (Matt.13:57 Mk.6:4. Lk.4:24). The advice given to Nicodemus, "*Look into it and you will find that a prophet does not come out of Galilee*" might have been "the official line" of the religious authorities (Jn.7:52), but it does not seem to have been the popular conception. Mathew hints that Jesus was welcomed as a prophet when he entered Jerusalem for the last time. The crowds said, "*This is Jesus, the prophet from Nazareth*"(Matt.21:11). The reported view of Herod is that he thought Jesus could be a prophet (Mk.6:14f. Lk.9:8). According to the disciples at Caesarea Philippi, the same is true of people in general (Matt.16:14. Mk.8:27f. Lk.9:19). Others who considered Jesus to be a prophet include the people of Nain (Lk.7:16), the five-thousand who had been miraculously fed (Jn.6:14 "*Surely this is the prophet who is to come into the world*"), the Jerusalem crowd at the Feast of Tabernacles (Jn.7:40) and the man born blind (Jn.9:17).

There were those who directly questioned whether Jesus was a prophet; not only on the grounds of his regional origin, but because of the company he kept (Lk.7:39) and his fate (Lk.22:64). In fact, for Jesus, his death in Jerusalem would serve to confirm his status as a prophet, because Jerusalem was, as he put it, "*You who kill the prophets*" (Lk.13:34). Most telling for me in deciding whether or not to refer to Jesus as a prophet is the story of the two disciples on the road to Emmaus. Not knowing to whom they are speaking they describe Jesus: "*He was a prophet, powerful in word and deed before God and all the people*" (Lk.24:19). It is true that Jesus went on to speak about himself as the Messiah (Lk.24:26), but nowhere does Jesus deny that he is also a prophet, or "*the prophet who was to come into the world*" (Jn.6:14).

Mentioned earlier, but well worth repeating, is the fact that speaking about Jesus as a prophet can be very helpful in interfaith conversations. This is especially so in talks between those who belong to the Abrahamic faith traditions (Judaism, Islam and Christianity). The Qur'an recognises Jesus as a great prophet, and for many Jews the notion of Jesus as a prophet is not a problem. However, it is also worth repeating that to genuinely accept Jesus as a prophet is to take full notice of his role as a spokesperson for God for justice and truth; and his call to follow him.

xiv. Rabbi or teacher

From Matthew's gospel it would appear that Jesus was happy for his disciples to call him *"teacher"* (Matt.23:10 - *"You have only one teacher, the Christ"*), but he disliked *"Rabbi"* and counselled his disciples against using it of themselves (Matt.23:7f). It is noticeable that in Matthew the only person to call Jesus *Rabbi* is Judas Iscariot in the process of betraying Jesus (Matt.26:25, 49 // Mk.14:45). In Mark, Peter also calls Jesus "Rabbi", but without any apparent negative connotations (Mk.9:5; 11:21); as does a blind man (Mk.10:51). Luke does not use the term at all, but in the first half of John's gospel "Rabbi" is used to address Jesus on a number of occasions. Since the first occurrence is by Nathanael who seems to meet with considerable approval by Jesus we might assume that as far as John is concerned Jesus did not brook at being addressed in this way (Jn.1:49; 7:25). In Luke, John the Baptizer is called *teacher* (Lk.3:12), whereas in John's gospel John the Baptizer is addressed as *Rabbi* (Jn.3:26), supporting the impression that in the fourth gospel the title Rabbi is used in a general way with neither negative nor positive inferences.

It would seem that being addressed as "Teacher" met with Jesus' approval. When he despatched his disciples to prepare the upper room for the Passover meal *"the teacher"* was Jesus' suggested way of identifying him to the owner of the house (Matt.26:18. Mk.14:14. Lk.22:11). However, in Matthew, although others do (Matt.19:16; 22:16, 24, 36), Jesus' disciples never address Jesus in this way. Not so in Mark. In their distress in the storm on the lake the disciples cried out, *"Teacher, don't you care if we drown"* (Mk.4:38). The sons of Zebedee approach Jesus calling him *"Teacher"* (Mk.10:35), as had John earlier (Mk.9:38). And as they were leaving the temple, impressed by its grandeur, the disciples addressed Jesus in the same way (Mk.13:1). In Luke the disciples call Jesus "Teacher", just once (Lk.21:7); but, as in Matthew, in Mark and Luke there are a number of other people who also call Jesus "teacher" (e.g. Mk.8:17 // Lk.9:38; 10:25 // Lk.18:18).

To some extent the Fourth gospel confuses the issue as to whether Jesus approved of the title "rabbi" and/or "teacher" by telling us in the story of the calling of Jesus' first disciples that "rabbi" *"means teacher"* (Jn.1:38); which is compounded when Nicodemus says to Jesus, *"Rabbi, we know that you are a teacher"* (Jn.3:2). Actually, John records no instances of the disciples calling Jesus, "Teacher"; but Jesus acknowledges that they do: *"You call me 'Teacher' and 'Lord', and rightly so, for that is what I am .... I, your Lord and Teacher, have washed your feet"*

(Jn.13:13f). On the other hand, Mary, Martha's sister, refers to Jesus as "*The teacher*" (Jn.11:28); and Mary Magdalene is said to have used the Aramaic word, "*Rabboni*" which, echoing his earlier comment on the meaning of "Rabbi", John tells us also "*means teacher*" (Jn.1:38; 21:16). In John's gospel there is only one instance of Jesus directly being addressed as "*Teacher*". It is in the story of the woman taken in adultery (Jn.8:4): a story which some would consider as not originally part of the gospel. Whether or not John 8:1-11 formed part of an "original" fourth gospel, the fact that the writer places words which he deems equivalent to "teacher" in the mouths of the first disciples, the sister of Lazarus who was released from death, and the first witness to Jesus' resurrection may be more indicative of its importance than the infrequency of its use in comparison to the Synoptics.

All four gospels give examples of Jesus being a teacher, but for Luke and John this is a role which after Jesus death will belong to the Holy Spirit (Lk.12:12. Jn.14:26). However, precisely because of the gospels' written record of Jesus' teaching, the envisaged role of the Holy Spirit as teacher or *aide memoire* might not be so vital - though the best teachers are inspirational: viz. *Take my yoke upon you and learn from me, for I am gentle and humble in heart, and you will find rest for your souls* (Matt.11:29).

xv. Less frequent names or titles.

There is no doubt that, as in many other things, in the matter of titles Jesus was given, the Synoptics, Matthew Mark and Luke, have more in common with each other than any one of them has with John; the Synoptics occasionally being exact parallels of each other.

So all three include one or more requests for someone, or the disciples as a group, not to disclose to others what they had learned about Jesus (Matt.12:16; Mk.3:12; Lk.5:14). This includes the warning given after Peter's declaration of faith in Jesus as the Messiah (Matt.16:20. Mk.8:30. Lk.9:21); and at the transfiguration (Matt.17:9. Mk.9:9) - though in Luke the disciples' secrecy seems to be their own initiative (Lk.9:36). In all three, through either an extended or a min-parable, Jesus likens himself to *the bridegroom* (Matt.25:1. Mk.2:19. Lk.5:34). All three record the accusation levelled at Jesus that he was "*a friend of tax collectors and sinners*" (Matt.11:19. Mk.2:16. Lk.7:34; 5:30 & cp.Lk.15:1), but also report Jesus' belief that he had fallen, or would fall into the hands of (the real?) "sinners" when he was arrested (Matt.26:45; Mk.14:41; Lk.24.7).

Chapter 5 - Reflections

a. Master

Another title used for Jesus is "*Master*". Embedded in my memory is a sermon I heard in my teens based on the words, "*The Master needs it*". Jesus told his disciples to say this if anyone questioned them about requisitioning a donkey (Matt.21:3). Yet looking at this verse more than fifty years later I can find this translation only in Weymouth. All other translations choose to translate the Greek κυριος as "Lord". So in the overwhelming majority of versions of the New Testament the title "master" is not applied directly to Jesus in Matthew: though some may see a reference to Jesus in some of his parables (Matt.18:23-35; 24:45-51; 25:14-30), and in the reply of the Syro-Phoenician woman, "*Even the dogs eat the crumbs from their master's table*" (Matt.15:27). It is somewhat similar in John - that is, the title is only applicable by inference. In John Jesus' attitude to use of the title for himself is ambiguous. On the one hand he tells his disciples, "*I no longer call you servants, because a servant does not know his master's business. Instead I have called you friends*" (Jn.15:15); but on the other hand says to them, "*No servant is greater than his master. If they persecuted me, they will persecute you also*" (Jn.15:20). These are the only references to Jesus as master in John, and no one ever addresses Jesus as master. The word "Master" does not appear at all in Mark.

So Luke stands in contrast to the other three gospels by using "Master" (Greek επιστατα) as the title by which Jesus was directly addressed on six occasions: three times by Peter (Lk.5:5; 8:45; 9:33); once by John (Lk.9:49); on one occasion by all the disciples, "*Master, Master, we're going to drown.*" (Lk.8:24); and once by the ten men with leprosy: "*Jesus, Master, have pity on us*" (Lk.17:13). Peter's first use of the title (Lk.5:5) is in a situation where obedience is required, but it should be noted that with this one possible exception, in none of the other instances in Luke does the word "Master" carry connotations of a master-servant relationship. In this sense those commentators who see the term as simply a title of respect, comparable to "Lord", would seem to be right. It is much more by way of some of Jesus' parables that the concept of "Master" as "one who must be obeyed" is evident: and in this regard further decisions need be made about each parable as to whether the Master is meant to be understood as Jesus or as the Father in Heaven. I would contend that "The Master" in the parables is rarely intended to be seen as Jesus, and in some instances the real master or ruler is made obvious: "*This is how my heavenly Father will treat you*"(Matt.18:35).

b. The Holy One

This description or title is not found in Matthew, but in Luke it appears twice. The angel spoke to Mary about "*The holy one to be born*" (Lk.1:35); and near the beginning of his ministry in Capernaum there is a strange confirmation of this when a man with an evil spirit shouts at Jesus, "*I know who you are - the Holy One of God*" (Lk.4:34). Mark has this same story with the same words, but no other use of the title. The Fourth Gospel also uses the title only once, but on a very different occasion. Peter, possibly speaking on behalf of all the disciples, says to Jesus, "*We believe and know that you are the Holy One of God*". This confession is probably the Johannine equivalent to the Synoptics record of Peter's confession of Jesus as the Messiah at Caesarea Philippi. It is intriguing therefore to observe that whereas in the Synoptic tradition Peter's confession is followed by a reprimand for Peter as "Satan" (Mk.8:33), in John Peter's confession is followed by Jesus declaration, "*One of you is a devil*", but with an author's note that Jesus "*meant Judas, the son of Simon Iscariot, who though one of the Twelve, was later to betray him*" (Jn.6:70f). Whoever it was that merited Jesus' reprimand, it would seem to be true that acknowledging Jesus as "*the Holy one*" is no guarantee of ensuing peace. Holiness throughout the Bible is a matter for awe-inspired respect akin to fear. Jesus as "the Holy one" warrants careful regard.

c. Saviour

It may come as something of a surprise to discover that Jesus is referred to as "Saviour" only twice in the gospels. In Luke the angels say to the shepherds, "*Today in the town of David a Saviour has been born to you*" (Lk.2:11): and in John some Samaritan villagers express their faith, "*This man really is the Saviour of the world*" (Jn.4:42). John precedes this declaration with an editorial comment, "*God did not send his Son into the world to condemn the world, but to save the world through him*" (Jn.3:17); and confirms it later when Jesus says, "*I did not come to judge the world, but to save it*" (Jn.12:47). Luke also has other words which convey the sense of Jesus as a saviour. Zechariah's psalm anticipating the birth of his son John, and possibly that of Jesus, declared in faith, "*He has come and he has redeemed his people*" (Lk.1:68). When Simeon saw the infant Jesus he was moved to praise God and said, "*My eyes have seen your salvation*" (Lk.2:30); whilst Anna on the same occasion, "*spoke about the child to all who were looking forward to the redemption of Jerusalem*". Jesus himself says his work is salvific, "*The son of man came to seek and to save the lost*" (Lk.19:10), and for the disciples on the road to Emmaus he provided confirmation of their hope that Jesus would have been "*the one to redeem Israel*" (Lk.24:21).

In some ways the learning experience on the road to Emmaus is also a riposte to those who shouted abusively at Jesus when he was being crucified: "*He saved others ... but he cannot save himself*" (Lk.23:25). These taunts that Jesus "*saved others*" also appear in Matthew and Mark (Matt.27:42//Mk.15:31), but neither refers to Jesus as "Saviour". Possibly the closest Mark comes is in the words of Jesus to his critics, "*It is not the healthy who need a doctor, but those who are ill. I have not come to call the righteous, but sinners*" (Mk.2:17), but the only direct references to Jesus as one who saved were uttered by his tormentors at the cross. In Matthew, of course, *the angel of the Lord* appeared not to Mary, but to Joseph. He is told that Mary would give birth to a son who was to be given the name Jesus, "*because he will save his people from their sins*" (Matt.1:21). There are numerous inferences that Jesus is a saviour, but few outright declarations of it. However, since his name, Jesus, means God saves, the Synoptic gospel writers may well have deemed it tautologous to also refer to Jesus as Saviour.

All the gospels convey a picture, or pictures of Jesus as one who saves others from their ailments. But the belief that his death was a work of salvation is by no means clear in all four gospels. Nor is it transparent that Jesus' saving work was for the whole world rather than just for "*his people*" - which many of the above references seem to imply. As noted earlier in this work, some of the parables in the Synoptics strongly hint that the "Jews" would invalidate their potential benefits from the coming of the Messiah, and others would reap those benefits. Luke has an isolated indicator that Jesus would be "*A light for revelation to the gentiles*" (Lk.2:32); but it is left to John to state clearly that God's purposes in Jesus' death are universal - "*And I, if I be lifted up, will draw all men to myself*" (Jn.12:32 - see also Jn.3:16 - cp. Matt.28:19). The relationship between being drawn to Jesus and "being saved", however, is unclear.

xvi. Titles for Jesus given in only one of the gospels

Some titles appear in only one of the gospels; though a very similar title, or other ways of conveying a comparable message may be apparent to a careful reader elsewhere. For example, Matthew alone, through a quotation from Isaiah, speaks of Jesus as "*my servant*" (Matt.12:18. Isa.42:1). But in Luke Jesus says, "*I am among you as one who serves*" (Lk.22:27). And all four gospels include the notion of Jesus adopting or commending a servant's role, or approving of good servants (Matt.23:11; 25:21, 23. Mk.9:35; 10:43. Lk.17:9; 19:17). In John servants may become friends (Jn.15:15), but, as demonstrated by Jesus washing his disciples' feet, friends serve one another as their servants (Jn.13:14f); and in serving others they serve God (Matt.25:31ff).

In the titles that follow similar parallels might be made, but if all the possible links were followed this work would never end. So a somewhat briefer summation must suffice.

John's gospel has many titles for Jesus which do not appear as titles in the Synoptics. Jesus is the *Word* (Jn.1:1, 14): *Light* 1:4, 9; 8:12//9:5; 12:35, 46): *Life* (Jn.1:4; 14:6; 11:25): *the Lamb of God* (Jn.1:29, 36): *the gate* (Jn.10:9) *the gate for the sheep* (Jn.10:7): *the (true) vine* (Jn.15:1, 5): *Way Truth & Life* (Jn.14:6). There are fourteen references to Jesus as *Bread*, all occurring in John chapter 6. At this point it would be enjoyable to offer a long excursus into the possible links between the feeding of five thousand and subsequent words about "bread" in John chapter six and the accounts of mass feedings and the last supper in the Synoptics. This is not the place.

In John Jesus is *The Only Begotten* (Jn.3:16) who carries "*the glory of the only begotten*" (Jn.1:14). Constant references are made to the nature and implications of Jesus as *God's Son*, and to the Father-Son relationship which later in the fourth gospel indicates the incorporation of Jesus' disciples into the relationship (1:1f, 14; 3:35; 5:19-26; 6:27, 40, 44-46, 57; 8:16-19, 28, 42, 54; 10:15, 30, 38; 12:44, 49f; 13:20; 14:6-14, 20-24, 28, 31; 15:1, 23; 16:15, 26-28, 32; 17:10). Through this relationship Jesus is *the resurrection and the Life* (Jn.11:25).

Some would see a claim to divine status in Jesus' words, "Before *Abraham was born, I am*" (Jn.8:58). This is already implicit in the opening verse of the fourth gospel, "*The Word was with God and the Word was God*" (Jn.1:1); and possibly in the description of Jesus as " *The one and only who is at the Father's side*" (Jn.1:18 NIV); but it is made quite explicit in Thomas' words of worship, "*My Lord and my God*" (Jn.20:28). Matthew may have intended to convey the same message in his unique reference to Jesus as, "*Immanuel - which means, 'God with us'*" (Matt.1:23), but such an intention is not apparent elsewhere in Matthew's gospel.

All of John's titles for Jesus repay serious contemplation, yet in my own pilgrimage of faith there are three further titles, each of which appear in only one of the gospels and only once, but all of which feed my soul and challenge my life.

A. The Carpenter

Only in Mark is Jesus "*The carpenter*". Mark tells us that in his home town the people in the synagogue expressed their surprise and indignation, "*Isn't this the carpenter? Isn't this Mary's son and the brother of James, Joseph, Judas and Simon? Aren't his sisters here with us?' And they took offence at him*" (Mk.6:3). On other occasions it was Jesus' place of origin that people used as an excuse to belittle or dismiss him. Here in Mark it is his occupation, and possibly the relatively low social and religious status which is therefore ascribed to his family - they are "Working class"! Finding reasons to dismiss the claims of Jesus - or of other people upon us - has always been relatively easy! To his neighbours Jesus was just an ordinary working man. They thought he should know his place - and they should not be expected to learn anything about God from him. Many of the godliest people I have been privileged to know could be described as ordinary working people. It has been good at times to hare the insight of the Psalmist that within the wonderful and wise order of God's creation the working man toiling

Chapter 5 - Reflections

from dawn to dusk has a legitimate place (Ps.104:19-24). Jesus said, *"My Father is a worker - and I am the same"* (Jn.5:17). Psalm 23 (mentioned above) begins its praise of God by picturing God as a working man embodying God's spirit. It will serve us well to take the insight seriously and gladly.

> *"The LORD does not look at the things man looks at. Man looks at the outward appearance, but the LORD looks at the heart"* (1.Samuel 16:7)
> *"Jesus said to them, "You are the ones who justify yourselves in the eyes of men, but God knows your hearts. What is highly valued among men is detestable in God's sight"* (Lk.16:15)

For any who might undervalue the contribution of uneducated labourers the book of Sirach (38:33f) offers wisdom:

> *These people are not sought out to serve on the public councils, and they never attain positions of great importance. They do not serve as judges, and they do not understand legal matters. They have no education and are not known for their wisdom. You never hear them quoting proverbs. But the work they do holds this world together. When they do their work, it is the same as offering prayer.*

B. A Righteous Man

Only in Luke is Jesus *"A righteous man"* (Lk.23:47). This unique description is given by one of those involved in Jesus' crucifixion - a gentile Centurion. He would be used to suffering and death. Nonetheless, for me the most natural motive for the centurion praising God when he saw Jesus die, and saying Jesus was surely a righteous man, would be that Jesus was comparatively quickly out of his suffering. In that sense God had been merciful and was to be praised – a modicum of justice had prevailed. Whilst the implication that God is only, or more merciful to righteous people might be questionable, the notion of death as a blessing is a comfort in any ministry which is associated with death and dying.

I also find that many people will say they believe Jesus to have been fully human and fully divine, but effectively Jesus is never for them fully human. It can be very difficult to think of the subject of the gospels as such. In Luke's record of the centurion's words the humanity of the centurion and of Jesus are pushed to the fore. One person dies - another watches. They are both naked before God and in need of God's mercy.

Death is not a sign of God's disfavour. Nor does it negate the essential worth of a person. But it does, more perhaps than anything else, confirm our common humanity – and our oneness with one who was crucified.

250

"There is for all humanity one entrance into life and a common departure" (Wisdom of Solomon 7:6).

C. A Stranger

Finally, it is only in Matthew that we read that Jesus is *"a stranger"*:

"I was a stranger ... in need of food, drink and clothes... sick... in prison" (with the corollary) *"Whatever you did - or did not do - for one of these ... you did - or did not do - for me"* (Matt.25:35f, 40, 42f., 45).

This teaching in Matthew is presented as the last, final, or ultimate judgement on people's lives. Significantly in Matthew it is also Jesus' last spoken parable before his own death - and may be seen as a critical comment or judgement on Jesus' own life as well as a mirror for our own. It answers the question, "What in the final analysis makes any human life, any person, acceptable in God's sight?" The answer is to be found not in what anyone believes about Jesus - or even God, certainly not in any religious practices, but in whether or not we follow Jesus' way, live his life; a life serving the needs of others - and not just our friends and family. The example of Jesus calls for a more perfect, "rounded", or inclusive love than that (Matt.5:43-48; Lk.14:13f).

Nonna Harrison in her inspirational work, *God's Many Splendored Image*, says that Christians must *"stretch their spiritual senses to see Christ in their neighbour"*[8]; but as Jesus seems to teach through the parable of the Good Samaritan, a neighbour is one who helps a stranger in need. If I had to choose one title above all others to guide me in my thinking about Jesus and how to respond to him - though I find it at times the most difficult to put into practice - it would have to be that Jesus is *a stranger*.

4. Healing

"Any church that follows Jesus Christ is ipso facto in the healing business" [9].

I must declare that when I first thought about the differences and the similarities which I had recognised from reading all four gospels, healing was not amongst the differences. I had presumed that all four gospels presented Jesus as the great healer; perhaps swayed by comments such as that above by Stephen Ramp; but also that common tendency, which this work tries to avoid, of allowing the witness

---

[8] Nonna Harrison, *God's Many Splendored Image*, Grand Rapids 2007 p.192.
[9] Stephen Ramp TLC p.180

of one gospel writer to override the distinctive voices of the other gospels. It was only when in considering the similarities in the Gospels and I came to prepare a section on Jesus as a healer and set the gospels alongside each other that the really big differences became apparent. I have asked a number of people whether they think that in all four gospels Jesus is perhaps more than anything else a healer. With few exceptions and without reservation the answer has been, "Yes". But it is not so simple.

Matthew is unique. He records a number of healings of individuals by Jesus, but also tells us of Jesus' ministry in Galilee: "*Many who were demon-possessed were brought to him, and he drove out the spirits with a word and healed all who were ill* (Matt.8:16); "*A large crowd followed him, and he healed all who were ill*" (Matt.12:15); "*When Jesus landed and saw a large crowd, he had compassion on them and healed those who were ill*" (Matt.14:14); "*Great crowds came to him, bringing the lame, the blind, the crippled, the mute and many others, and laid them at his feet; and he healed them*" (Matt.15:30). In Judaea by Jordan "*Large crowds followed him, and he healed them there*" (Matt.19:2). In Jerusalem "*The blind and the lame came to him at the temple, and he healed them*" (Matt.21:14). In Matthew Jesus is the consistent and persistent healer wherever he goes.

Mark and Luke offer a rather different picture. Whilst there were crowds who came for healing in the early days of Jesus' ministry (Mk.1:34; 3:10; 5:24; Lk.4:10; 5:15), after his rejection in his home town with the consequent limiting of his ability to heal, Mark records instances only of individuals being healed. One of these, the healing of Bartimaeus, also in Luke, takes place at Jericho on the way to Jerusalem (Mk.10:46ff; Lk.18:35ff). In addition Luke recounts the healing of a group of ten lepers (Lk.17:11ff); but neither Mark nor Luke record great numbers of healings in Judaea, and they record none in Jerusalem.

Baukham says

> "*We should also beware of pouring cold water on the simple eager trust which Mark portrays in so many of those representative people who come to Jesus for help and healing .... Readers of Mark should be able to put themselves among the crowds thronging to Jesus ... carrying their sick friends, relatives and neighbours to him with their prayers, begging his healing compassion for them*"[10].

The confinement of Jesus' healings to a limited period of his ministry in Galilee in Mark does not invalidate Baulkham's comments: though they would be better grounded in Matthew than Mark. Baukham's reference to "*representative people*"

---

[10] TLC p.222

opens the door to reading into Mark and Luke's gospels many more healings, perhaps beyond Galilee; but they are not there in a plain reading of the text.

John's gospel does say, "*A great crowd of people followed him because they saw the signs he had performed by healing those who were ill*" (Jn.6:2), but does not actually say that crowds of, or many people were healed. Nor are there many instances in the fourth gospel of Jesus healing individuals - just three: the royal official's son (Jn.5:46ff), the man by the pool, Bethesda (Jn.5:2ff), and the man born blind (Jn.9). The raising of Lazarus might be added to make a fourth; and John does tell us that there was much more he could have written of what Jesus did (Jn.21:25): but quite clearly John chose not to highlight healing as a major feature of Jesus' ministry. Indeed, Jesus' comment to his critics, "*I did one miracle, and you are all astonished*" (Jn.7:21) would seem to confirm the limited nature of such ministry. John, perhaps, is less interested in physical healing than he is in the need for the healing of people's perceptions and hearts: "*He has blinded their eyes and hardened their hearts, so they can neither see with their eyes, nor understand with their hearts, nor turn – and I would heal them*" (Jn.12:40).

There are many missionary societies. I am most familiar with "BMS - Baptist World Mission". It has been good to see over the last sixty years an increasing recognition amongst Baptist churches that the medical work of BMS is as much part of sharing the gospel as the founding of churches and the encouragement of new believers. For some, in keeping with Matthew's gospel, a healing ministry will be the major focus. For others, like Mark and Luke it will be recognised that such ministry is only possible in some places. And there will be those who, perhaps like John, do not see it as the most important part of serving people in Jesus' name. However, for all their differences Jesus as a healer is to be found in all four gospels. On this basis, but probably with a number of caveats, and a widened understanding of "healing", Stephen Ramp is right: "*Any church that follows Jesus Christ is ipso facto in the healing business*".

Two further comments can be made in respect of healing ministry.

First, it is helpful at times to think of a church as a "community of faith". As such it might have a wider healing function than is commonly recognised. Snyder, reflecting on the paralysed man let down through the roof over Jesus' head (Mk.2:1-12) says this:

"*For those who are more individually oriented, this has to be a puzzling story. Jesus healed the paralytic because of the faith of the four friends. That is, the community of faith (meeting in the house of Jesus) could effect the healing of someone else whether he or she believes or not ... There are other occasions when the faith of one could lead to the healing of another (Mk.5:36;7:24-30; 9:24)"*[11].

Second, Jeffrey John makes the point that the gospel stories of healing, as well as other "miracle" stories, have meanings beyond the level of the individual. *"The gospels mean us to grasp that the healing Jesus brings is as necessary for systems and societies as it is to individuals"*[12]. What the gospel writers sometimes describe in terms of demons and in other instances as sickness or death is couched almost exclusively in individual terms, even within crowds. Jeffrey John is nonetheless in no doubt that the healings (always?) have an essential wider application. Indeed at times it seems as though Jeffrey sees the healings – or at least the gospel writers telling of them - as more motivated by symbolism than compassion. *"Their point is not medical, but spiritual and theological. Whatever history may lie behind the stories of individual healings (Jeffrey John never tells us how much), their meaning and importance in the evangelists' minds is a universal, symbolic one"*[13]. There is good evidence that the gospel writers recognised Jesus' ministry was a challenge to *"principalities and powers"*. They opposed his work and connived in his death. The gospel writers believed any follower of Jesus was likely to experience the same battlefronts. Hence the need to be willing to carry a cross. Costly involvement in issues of justice may be a prerequisite for the healing of societies or a consequence of it; but it may not always be a necessary prerequisite for the compassionate healing of individuals – which seems to me to be the major focus of Jesus' healing ministry and the task for which his disciples were commissioned[14].

5. <u>Four ways to die</u>

Matthew records the death of Jesus in the following way:-

> *From noon until three in the afternoon darkness came over all the land. About three in the afternoon Jesus cried out in a loud voice, 'Eli, Eli, lema sabachthani?' ('My God, my God, why have you forsaken me?'). When some of those standing there heard this, they said, 'He's calling Elijah.' Immediately one of them ran and got a sponge. He filled it with wine vinegar, put it on a staff, and offered it to Jesus to drink. The rest said, 'Now leave him alone. Let's see if Elijah comes to save him.' And when Jesus had cried out again in a loud voice, he gave up his spirit.* (Matt.27:45-50)

---

[11] Graydon Snyder TLC p.186. Possibly the most dramatic example of this is the raising of Lazarus (Jn.11)

[12] Jeffrey John *The Meaning of Miracles* Canterbury Press 2002 p.14

[13] Ibid p.22

[14] Cf. Luke chapters 9-10

Mark's account (Mk.15:33-37) is almost identical, except that it is the man who offered Jesus the drink who said, "*Now leave him alone*" and added, "*Let's see if Elijah comes to take him down*". (Mk.15:36)' rather than "*save him*" (Matt.27:49). And of Jesus' dying moment Mark says, "*With a loud cry, Jesus breathed his last*" (Mk.13:37). The crying out and the dying are of a piece in Mark, not sequential as in Matthew.

Luke's account has a number of differences:
It was now about noon, and darkness came over the whole land until three in the afternoon, for the sun stopped shining. And the curtain of the temple was torn in two. Jesus called out with a loud voice, 'Father, into your hands I commit my spirit.' When he had said this, he breathed his last (Lk.23:44-46)

Luke has no cry of dereliction, nor any mention of Jesus being offered a drink. Luke includes a bisecting of the temple curtain: a symbol which has evoked many interpretations. Only one loud cry is recorded by Luke. Unlike Matthew and Mark it is quite clearly one in which Jesus commits his spirit to his Father.

In John there are more significant differences:
Later, knowing that everything had now been finished, and so that Scripture would be fulfilled, Jesus said, 'I am thirsty.' A jar of wine vinegar was there, so they soaked a sponge in it, put the sponge on a stalk of the hyssop plant, and lifted it to Jesus' lips. When he had received the drink, Jesus said, 'It is finished.' With that, he bowed his head and gave up his spirit (John.19:28-30).

Jesus is in control. His words, "*It is finished*" (Jn.19:30) indicate it is his decision to die because he knows: "*Everything has now been accomplished*" (Jn.19:28). The request for, rather than an offer of a drink is the result of Jesus consciously fulfilling scripture with his words, "*I am thirsty*" (Jn.19:28) - and whereas Matthew and Mark do not tell us if Jesus accepted the drink, John specifically tells us that he did. On the surface Matthew and John have the same words for Jesus' final moment in that Jesus "*gave up his spirit*" (Matt.27:50//Jn.19:30), but what comes before these words gives them a very different nuance. Matthew does not tell us Jesus' words in his last loud cry, but the implication is that they are a repetition of the cry of dereliction, or surely Matthew would have felt it right to say otherwise. The same would be true for Mark. But John has already shared the words of Jesus about his life, "*No one takes it from me, but I lay it down of my own accord. I have authority to lay it down and authority to take it up again*" (Jn.10:18). The manner of Jesus' dying is resonant with Jesus' teaching and living.

There are other differences between the gospels' accounts of Jesus' death, such as John's perhaps surprising lack of any mention of darkness or of specific times of the day. But my deep interest in the differences between the accounts of Jesus' death, and an appreciation of them, is not primarily academic; it is pastoral.

In common with many ministers, over the years I have been involved with people, who have been close to death, or as they died. Some have been my own family members or close friends. Many other people through pastoral and funeral visits have shared with me their experience of seeing people die whom they have loved. The way in which a dying person goes through their final moments can give great comfort to the bereaved, but it can equally occasion deep distress: especially if the person who has died was reckoned to be a person of strong faith, but that was not evident in their dying. I am greatly indebted to the four gospels because they offer not a simple or singular picture of how Jesus met his death, but a collage.

Put succinctly; Matthew, Mark and Luke all have a person who follows Dylan Thomas' dictum and does "*not go gentle into that good night*". In both Matthew and Mark Jesus expresses a sense of being abandoned by God, and they offer little or no relief from that sense. Some might see a crumb of comfort in Matthew's words that Jesus "*gave up his spirit*", but I see no real difference between this and Mark's, "*Jesus breathed his last*". People do die feeling abandoned by God. That is not the same as dying having abandoned God. Nor is it a sign that someone's death is outside of God's loving purposes. According to at least two of the New Testament gospels it is to die in a way that is in keeping with Jesus' experience of dying.

Luke offers a contrasting picture. There is still a loud cry, but it is a cry of surrender to God as Father. In Luke the relationship Jesus has with God as his father (Lk.2:49; 10:21f; 22:29, 42; 23:34) is carried into his dying moment: "*Father, into your hands I commit my spirit*" (Lk.23:46). It has been a privilege to witness such a death on more than one occasion. Almost always the person dying has been supported with the presence and prayers of other people of faith. In Luke, one of those also crucified and dying alongside Jesus put his faith in Jesus, and perhaps even strengthened Jesus' faith (Lk.23:42f). General hospitals are often not a suitable place to die, because in some senses death is a failure for an institution whose major function is to help people avoid death. On the other hand in Hospices it can be the patients who help each other face up to the imminence of death with peace of mind and who inspire the staff. Luke also tells us that the women who had followed Jesus from Galilee "*stood at a distance, watching these things*" (Lk.23:49). Long-time friends who have travelled the journey of life with us can have a significant role, even from a distance, when we come to die. Perhaps their love is the finest possible example of what it means to keep the faith (1.Cor.13:13). To die with a sense of trusting surrender to a loving heavenly Father is to die as Luke tells us Jesus died.

Though I have never witnessed it, there are some members of the Salvation Army who believe the appropriate colour for the funeral of a Christian is white because the person who dies is *promoted to glory*. Whilst the majority of other people still follow a tradition of wearing black[15], wreaths can still be seen at funerals: and there may be a vestige of the symbolic element of "victory" in their use[16]. In John's gospel Jesus said to his disciples, *"Take heart. I have overcome the world"* (Jn.16:33). The life of Jesus in the fourth gospel is one of victorious living - and dying - *"It is finished"* (Jn.19:30). The words are not shouted, but seemingly said calmly as a precursor to Jesus bowing his head and giving up his spirit. Although I have seen heart-felt relief at the cessation of suffering, I do not think I have ever witnessed someone dying where a sense of victory has been evident in that moment. But I have known people who firmly believed their death would be a kind of triumph – the race has been run and the finishing line crossed over. And I have shared in many funeral services where there has been a tangible feeling that victorious living has culminated in death which has not taken away the victory, it has sealed it. To be honest those services are rarely a natural sequence to the manner of the death being marked; but they are often in keeping with the faith that was lived and shared over time. I am sure that only a small minority of those who sing the words of *Abide with me* at funerals are thinking about the words while they sing, or reflect on them at all; but sometimes the hymn is a genuine affirmation of the faith of the deceased person and of those who mourn their passing, who celebrate both their common life in Christ and their death with Christ:-

Where is death's sting? Where grave thy victory?
I triumph still, if Thou abide with me.

Hold Thou thy cross before my closing eyes.
(Henry Francis Lyte)

Of all the reasons for reading each of the gospels as an individual and distinctive witness to what we can learn from Jesus' example, these very different perspectives on the death of Jesus on the cross must be amongst the most compelling. Following Jesus does not mean there is only one "acceptable" way to die!

---

[15] This is changing in England as younger generations increasingly (even if slowly) see no good reason to observe formalities such as dress codes.

[16] It is indicative of the irrelevance of Christianity for many in England that wreaths are much less common than twenty five years ago and are increasingly replaced by other floral tributes - for example, in the shape of a football signifying something which gave some meaning or demonstrated some loyalty in a person's life. Or they may spell out the person's role in a family as mum, dad or grandma, showing the importance of relationships: or their nickname possibly indicating their individuality.

Chapter 5 - Reflections

6. The resurrection

There is no account of Jesus' resurrection in any of the New Testament gospels. There are descriptions of events which relate to his burial and to the beginnings of the realisation that Jesus was no longer in the tomb. Many of the details are similar in Matthew, Mark and Luke; but there are noticeable differences. The fourth gospel has narrative which is unique.

All the gospels may include stories which prepare their readers for Jesus' resurrection. There is no way of knowing for certain whether the Synoptics' story of a man (Mark 5:2ff; Luke 8:27ff) or two men (Matthew 8:28ff) who live in burial caves, but who come out of them, is told in any way to prepare readers for the story of Jesus' leaving the tomb. It is possible that this is a kind of resurrection story. Others are more obviously so. For example, Luke's story of the raising to life of the son of the widow of Nain (Lk.7:11-17), or the story of the raising to life of a little girl (Matt.9:18ff; Mk.5:35ff; Lk.8:49ff). And, of course, it is reasonable to assume John's story of the raising to life of Lazarus, replete with grave clothes from a burial cave with a rock over its entrance, serves as a foretaste of what was to come after Jesus had been wrapped and laid in a rock-covered tomb.

Jesus' reply to John the Baptizer's messengers, *"The dead are raised to life"* (Matt.11:5; Lk.7:22), plus Herod's and others' comments about John the Baptizer having returned from death even after decapitation (Matt.14:2;Mk.14:14, 16; Lk.9:7) suggest a widespread belief in not just the possibility, but the fact of people coming back to life from the dead - though *"rising from death"* was neither a simple nor agreed notion (Mk.9:10; Jn.20:9)[17]. The debate between Jesus and the Sadducees concerned a "general resurrection" rather than an individual event. Martha's comment about Lazarus that she knew he would *"rise again on the last day"* shows the belief was not confined just to the Sadducees' opponents (Jn.11:24). The debate is evidence that belief in resurrection was widespread enough for the Sadducees to feel the need to oppose it. But also very important and worthy of deeper consideration than is given here, Jesus seems not to have seen "the resurrection" as of primary importance: *"But about the resurrection of the dead ... He is not the God of the dead, but the God of the living"* (Matt.22:31f).

---

[17] That there was not universal acceptance of the concept of resurrection is not only evident in the disagreement between the Sadducees and Pharisees on this matter (Matt:22:23//Mk.12:18//Lk.20:27; cf. Acts 23:6-8), but also in other nations (Acts 17:32). There is at least some truth in Braaten's assertion, *"In every age belief in the resurrection of Jesus must overcome a strong a priori prejudice against such a thing happening"* Carl E. Braaten *That they may believe - A theology of the Gospel and the mission of the church* Eerdmans - Grand Rapids 2008 p.95

258

Nonetheless, a wide acceptance in Jesus' day of resurrection as a real possibility throws into question the assumption of some that it was Jesus' resurrection *per se* which brought about the change in his disciples after he had appeared to them. Perhaps it needs to be taken more into account that Jesus predicted (or prophesied) both his death and his resurrection (e.g. Matt.20:19; Mk.10:34; Lk.18:33; Jn.2:19-22; 12:20-33). It is possibly the fulfilment of his prophecy, rooted in his understanding and teaching of the scriptures which moved his disciples to put their trust in him, not the fact of his resurrection. Equally worth consideration is that it was not awe-filled wonder at a unique miracle of resurrection which changed the disciples, but irrepressible joy and gratitude that what had been lost was now found again.

The thought that resurrection is not unique to Jesus is affirmed in Matthew in a way not found in the other New Testament gospels. Matthew tells us that in the immediate aftermath of Jesus' death there was an earthquake, graves opened and "*many of God's people who were dead were raised to life, and after Jesus rose from death they went into the Holy City and were seen by many*" (Matt.27:52f). This insight of Matthew that Jesus' death immediately opened up the possibility of resurrection for others, and Jesus' resurrection triggered a witnessing of this phenomenon is expressed in other parts of the New Testament, but nowhere so dramatically or with such immediacy as in Matthew. In Matthew, through Jesus' death, death no longer holds its sway over *God's people*.

Matthew and Mark seem to be at pains to tell us how the tomb, which in a way symbolises the stronghold of death, was escape-proof. In Matthew it was a tomb meant for Joseph of Arimathea which he had dug out of solid rock himself. A large rock was rolled across the entry and sealed, and a guard posted (Matt.27:60ff) - with Pilate's instruction, "*Go and make the tomb as secure as you know how*" (Matt.27:65). In Mark the tomb does not seem to be meant for Joseph, and there is no guard, but it has been dug out of solid rock and Joseph himself rolled a stone across the entrance - which later we are told was a very large stone (Mk.15:46; 16:4). Luke seems less concerned with security. We hear about the stone only in retrospect (Lk.24:2), but we are told that the unused tomb was dug out of solid rock. John also notes that the tomb was unused, adding that it was conveniently near enough to Golgotha to allow for the fast approaching obligatory Sabbath rest (Jn.19:39ff). As in Luke only retrospectively is a stone mentioned by John (Jn.20:1).

Matthew, having set a picture of total security, describes a second shaking of the earth. The earth shook as Jesus died on the Friday. But at dawn on the morning after Sabbath Matthew tells us:

"Mary Magdalene and the other Mary went to look at the tomb. There was a violent earthquake, for an angel of the Lord came down from heaven and, going to the tomb, rolled back the stone and sat on it. His appearance was like lightning, and his clothes were white as snow." (Matt.28:1-3).

This might be taken as an account of the resurrection moment, but, *"The angel said to the women, 'Do not be afraid, for I know that you are looking for Jesus, who was crucified. He is not here; he has risen, just as he said"* (Matt.28:5f). We do not know from Matthew if the two Marys took up the angel's invitation, *"Come and see the place where he lay"* (Matt.28:6); but we are told, *"The women hurried away from the tomb, afraid yet filled with joy, and ran to tell his disciples. Suddenly Jesus met them, 'Greetings' he said. They came to him clasped his feet and worshipped him"* (Matt.28:8f).

In Mark, there are three women. A woman named Salome is there as well. They do not experience an earthquake, nor see the stone rolled away. *"But when they looked up, they saw that the stone, which was very large, had been rolled away"* (Mk.16:4). It was only:

> *"As they entered the tomb (that) they saw a young man dressed in a white robe sitting on the right side, and they were alarmed. 'Don't be alarmed,' he said. 'You are looking for Jesus the Nazarene, who was crucified. He has risen! He is not here. See the place where they laid him"* (Mk.16:5-7).

Unlike in Matthew, this does not lead to any sense of joy. *"Trembling and bewildered, the women went out and fled from the tomb. They said nothing to anyone, because they were afraid"* (Mk.16:8). It could be tedious to draw out all the differences between Matthew and Mark's accounts one by one, but just this very brief setting of one account alongside the other begins to demonstrate that there are two significantly different stories of what happened, and to whom, on the morning after the Sabbath on which Luke tells us *the women*, having seen where Jesus was entombed and prepared the burial spices, rested as the law commanded (Lk.23:56). These were some of those faithful, devout, obedient-to-the-law people who are found throughout Luke's gospel[18].

If we turn our attention to Luke, the women at the tomb include Joanna as well as two Marys, but there seem to have been a larger group than this (Lk.24:10). Overall Luke's account of that morning is perhaps closer to Mark than to Matthew, but Luke has elements of both as well as departures from both. For instance, as

---

[18] It should be noted that Jesus died on a Friday (the first day) and was "raised on the third day" (Sunday). The second day, Saturday, being the Sabbath which Jesus in accordance with God's "law" observed the Sabbath as a day of rest.

with Mark, the women went into the tomb and did not find Jesus. But *"While they were wondering about this, suddenly two men in clothes that gleamed like lightning stood beside them"*(Lk.24:4). *"Gleamed like lightning"* is an echo of Matthew, but these men are not said to be angels; they are quite possibly inside the tomb not outside of it; and there are two of them. These men in white give no instructions to the women about taking news to Jesus' disciples, but repeat words spoken by Jesus on a number of occasions, and reported in all three Synoptics, *"The Son of Man must be delivered over to the hands of sinners, be crucified and on the third day be raised again"* (Lk.24:7. cp. Lk.9:22; 18:31f; Matt.16:21; Mk.8:31). According to Luke it was the recalling of Jesus' prophecy which led to the women going to the disciples (Lk.24:8f). As in Mark (if we exclude the additional endings of Mk.16:9ff), but in contrast to Matthew (Matt.28:9), Jesus does not appear to the women: but as a preacher one cannot fail to be excited by the words of the two men addressed to the women in or at the tomb, *"Why do you look for the living among the dead?"* (Lk.24:5; cp. Matt.22:31).

Having compared the Synoptic accounts of early Easter morning it may be helpful to set out the account in the Fourth Gospel in full. Some of the differences in John's telling of the story should be immediately obvious.

Early on the first day of the week, while it was still dark, Mary Magdalene went to the tomb and saw that the stone had been removed from the entrance. So she came running to Simon Peter and the other disciple, the one Jesus loved, and said, 'They have taken the Lord out of the tomb, and we don't know where they have put him!' So Peter and the other disciple started for the tomb. Both were running, but the other disciple outran Peter and reached the tomb first. He bent over and looked in at the strips of linen lying there but did not go in. Then Simon Peter came along behind him and went straight into the tomb. He saw the strips of linen lying there, as well as the cloth that had been wrapped round Jesus' head. The cloth was still lying in its place, separate from the linen. Finally the other disciple, who had reached the tomb first, also went inside. He saw and believed. (They still did not understand from Scripture that Jesus had to rise from the dead.) Then the disciples went back to where they were staying.

Now Mary stood outside the tomb crying. As she wept, she bent over to look into the tomb and saw two angels in white, seated where Jesus' body had been, one at the head and the other at the foot. They asked her, 'Woman, why are you crying?' 'They have taken my Lord away,' she said, 'and I don't know where they have put him.' At this, she turned round and saw Jesus standing there, but she did not realise that it was Jesus. He asked her, 'Woman, why are you crying? Who is it you are looking for?' Thinking he was the gardener, she said, 'Sir, if you have carried him away, tell me where you have put him, and I will get him.' Jesus said to her, 'Mary.' She turned towards him and cried out in Aramaic, 'Rabboni!' (Which means 'Teacher'). Jesus said, 'Do not hold on to me, for I have not yet ascended to the Father. Go instead to my brothers and tell them, "I am ascending to my Father and your Father, to my God and your God."' Mary Magdalene went to the disciples with the news: 'I have seen the Lord!' And she told them that he had said these things to her. (Jn.20:1-18)

There is only one woman named: and Mary Magdalene is patently on her own. Her first report to the disciples is not of a resurrection, but of a missing body. The two disciples are the first to go into the tomb, but they see no men in white or angels; and whatever "*the other disciple*" believed was not based on an understanding "*from Scripture that Jesus had to rise from the dead*" (Jn.20:8f). It was after the disciples had left that Mary looked into the tomb and saw "*two angels in white*" strategically seated. In a way these figures in white exemplify the unanswerable questions which arise from looking at all four gospels. Were they angels? Were there one or two? Did they come down from heaven? Were they seated or standing? Were they inside the tomb or outside? Did they roll the stone away? Who saw them? What did they say and to whom? The different answers which can be given to these questions, depending upon which gospel is being read, are all as fascinating as they are perplexing: but they should not be allowed to distract attention from what each gospel writer does convey of an experience which defies precise definition. Does it really matter that Matthew's women hold on to Jesus' feet (Matt.28:9) whereas in John Jesus tells Mary not to hold on to him (Jn.20:17), and in Mark and Luke there is no recorded contact between Jesus and the women and they are not the first witnesses to the resurrection? It only matters if it serves to re-emphasise the need to appreciate each gospel for the witness its particular author has given regarding Jesus' life, death, resurrection and/or coming again, whilst also recognising that they have the common aim of sharing amazing good news.

The story of Mary taken in its own right is a supreme piece of writing. It is a story of bereavement: "*Mary stood outside the tomb crying*" (Jn.20:11). It is a story of overt compassion. The only words John records the angels saying to Mary are, - and Jesus repeats them - "*Woman, why are you crying?*" (Jn.20:13, 15). It is a story of distress and devotion "*They have taken my Lord away - tell me where you have put him and I will get him*" (Jn.20:13, 15). It is all this and so much more, but above all it is a story of one person's encounter with the risen Christ. Perhaps because unlike the other three gospels Mary at the tomb really is the story of an individual, in spite of Matthew's earthquakes, Mary in the garden is for me the most powerful, memorable and inspiring testimony to life in places, and in place of, death.

Chapter 5 - Reflections

One Voice

We have looked at five examples of important differences between the four New Testament gospels; and demonstrated how recognising their distinctive perspectives can be of value. Dealing with differences in detail should not obscure the fact that all four gospels have much in common. All four testify to the preaching and baptizing ministry of John the Baptizer (Matt.3:1-12; Mk.1:1-8; Lk.3:1-18; Jn.1:19-28), though the fourth gospel has no record of John's death at the hands of Herod. All four also tell a story of Jesus and his disciples feeding five thousand people (Matt.14:13-21; Mk.6:30-34; Lk.9:10-17; Jn.6:1-14). As far as I can discern there is no other content which has parallels in all four gospels, with one considerable exception: what are sometimes referred to as "The Passion Narratives".

The differences noted in the gospels' accounts of Jesus' death and resurrection, also acknowledges that all four gospels share accounts of these. Indeed, to a considerable degree all four gospels with regard to the last week of Jesus' life up to and including his appearance to his disciples present a very similar series of events. True, John locates the cleansing of the Jerusalem Temple early in Jesus' ministry (Jn.2:13-17) whereas the Synoptics place it in Jesus final week in Jerusalem (Matt.21:12-17; Mk.11:15-19; Lk.19:45-48). But all of the following are in all four gospels: the triumphal entry (Matt.21:1-11; Mk.11:1-11; Lk.19:28-40; Jn.12:12-19), the plots against Jesus' life in Jerusalem (Matt.26:1-3; Mk.14:1-2; Lk.22:1-2; Jn.11:45-53), the prediction and reality of Peter's denial (Matt.26:31-35, 69-75; Mk.14:27-31, 66-72; Lk.22:31-34, 56-62; Jn.13:36-38; 18:15-27), Jesus' arrest (Matt.26:47-54; Mk.14:43-50; Lk.47-53; Jn.18:3-12) , his arraignment before the Sanhedrin (Matt.26:57-67; Mk.14:53-65; Lk.22:54f, 63-71; Jn.18:13f, 19-24) and before Pilate (Matt.27:11-14; Mk.15:2-5; Lk.23:3-5; Jn.18:33-38); his death sentence (Matt.27:15-26; Mk.15:6-15; Lk.23:13-25; Jn.18:39-19:16), crucifixion (Matt.27:32-44; Mk.15:21-32; Lk.23:26-43; Jn.19:17-29), death (Matt.27:45-56; Mk.15:33-41; Lk.23:44-49; Jn.19:28-30), burial (Matt.27:57-61; Mk.42-47; Lk.23:50-56; Jn.19:38-42), resurrection (Matt.28:1-10; Mk.16:1-10; Lk.24:1-12; Jn.20:1-10) and, if an old additional ending of Mark is taken into account, one or more appearances to his disciples (Matt.28:16-20; Mk.16:14-18; Lk.24:13-53; Jn.20:19-29; 21:1-22).

A quite different work would be needed to deal in depth with just a few of the points of convergence which the four canonical gospels display not only in those passages where there is parallel text, but in the different stories which make the same or similar points, inviting reflection on the demands of faith. The differences highlighted above are not intended to deny such convergence, but they should challenge naive synthesising and show the value of allowing each gospel writer's work to speak for itself. We turn now to some of the areas of agreement - matters in which the four evangelists speak with a common voice, or at least convey the same message. Because there are many of these, and I would like to touch on a number of them, they may not receive as much individual attention as the five differences and in some instances may appear to be almost in note form. But they are of no less importance. My hope is that I or others might in due course explore these further.

1. Self-denying.

> *"Whoever finds their life will lose it, and whoever loses their life for my sake will find it"* (Matt.10:39)
> *"Whoever wants to save their life will lose it, but whoever loses their life for me and for the gospel will save it"* (Mk.8:35; Lk.9:24; 17:33)
> *"Very truly I tell you, unless a grain of wheat falls to the ground and dies, it remains only a single seed. But if it dies, it produces many seeds"* (John 12:24)

As is often the case the fourth gospel expresses a teaching of Jesus in a different way to the Synoptics, but from even the briefest examination it is quite evident that all four evangelists are conveying the same message. Fullness of life, or the greater life, eternal life, kingdom life, life as good news for all is discovered only through dying. The way of the cross, life through death, is not optional for followers of Jesus – nor is it easy.

In the gospel accounts of the twelve men who were first chosen to be with Jesus, to follow him, to share his work and to tell others about him, it is apparent that they are not "leaders" who set a wonderful example to be followed. They consistently fail, and whenever they rely on their own understanding or strength they are shown to be ineffective. Whenever they are looking to serve their own best interests or promote themselves, like James and John in their request for the best seats in the kingdom (Matt.20:23; Mk.10:35), Jesus counsels against such behaviour (Lk.11:43; 14:7). It is only when disciples come to rely on Jesus and follow his example of self-denying service that they will embody and become channels of Jesus' spirit and in this way find the life which is truly blessed.

The basic principle is this: it is in self-sacrificing giving that what really matters can be received. This applies to things like church buildings, which are often primarily designed for the benefit of the people who "own" them. I know from personal experience that those churches who design and/or use their buildings with others' needs as the first priority discover something of the greater life which Jesus wanted his friends to know. Anything or anybody we treat selfishly, firstly or exclusively for our own purposes, we lose. This fundamental teaching of Jesus applies to international relations and national life, to business life, to married or family life, to personal life - to human life in all its manifestations. This is a message which "the world" will often not wish to hear, and may violently oppose or ridicule, but it is a central gospel message as the ONLY way to fullness of life. It needs to be proclaimed with humility and love. Jesus' death, which was his finest hour of glorifying God, is the ultimate proclamation that self-serving or self-promoting attitudes or actions put us outside of the Kingdom of God – dying to such things opens the prospect of Paradise.

"Just when we think we have it all figured out, God reverses our expectations and upsets our careful calculations. Jesus is not only announcing a reversal of values, but a reversal of fortunes. Only one thing is certain: to save our lives we must lose them and to gain the world we must give up everything"[19].

2. Obedience

All four gospels have their own ways of emphasising obedience as integral to Jesus' life, often employing the little word *dei* which is usually translated into English as *must*. In the context of the gospels *dei* carries the sense not of an unavoidable obligation, but the essential requirements for God's will to be done.

"Jesus began to explain to his disciples that he must go to Jerusalem" (Matt.16:21).
"Do you think I cannot call on my Father, and he will at once put at my disposal more than twelve legions of angels? But how then would the Scriptures be fulfilled that say it must happen in this way?" (Matt.26:53f);
"The Son of Man must be delivered over to the hands of sinners, be crucified and on the third day be raised again." (Lk.24:7)
"We must do the will of him who sent me" (Jn.9:4).

Frank Matera uses Mark's gospel to make the point that Jesus' call to self-sacrifice is bound up with the notion of obedience.

"Jesus total submission to the will of the Father reveals that he is utterly obedient and dependent on his Father. Not only does Jesus teach others to save their life by surrendering their life (Mk.8:35). He provides the perfect example of the teaching by refusing to come down from the cross to save himself (Mk.15:27-32)"[20].

Luke tells how discipline and obedience were early features in Jesus' life. Many commentators pick up on the information that Jesus went down to Nazareth with

---

[19] PGM p.179
[20] Frank J. Matera *New Testament Theology* Westminster John Knox 2007 p.21

265

his parents "*and was obedient to them*" (Lk.2:51); but of equal, if not greater significance are the boy Jesus' words "*I must (dei - δει) be in my Father's house*" (Lk.2:49)[21]. At the age of twelve Jesus believed there was a primary imperative for him to be obedient to "his Father's" will. This is not an obedience necessarily nurtured by a discipline which makes a great deal of saying prayers at set hours, or daily readings of scripture passages. These may be helpful, but on balance may actually be distractions from truly sensing the response or actions I MUST do in obedience to what my heavenly Father requires.

Should anyone ask, "How I can know what God requires of me?" there is no set answer. But if the obedient example of Jesus and his teaching are our guides it will not be unconnected to becoming like a little child again, vulnerable, trusting and self-giving. Little children who live in a trusting relationship with their parents seldom need to ask what their parents want them to do or not to do. The loving relationship itself is the essential guide. Without such a relationship of trust in God there is little chance of being God's obedient child (Matt.18:3).

3. Compassion

> "*When Jesus saw her* (Mary) *weeping, and the Jews who came with her also weeping, he was greatly disturbed in spirit, and deeply moved ... Jesus began to weep*" (Jn.11:33, 35).

John's story of Jesus' involvement with Lazarus and his sisters is possibly the most moving demonstrations of Jesus' compassion, but his righteous love for people is an obvious constant in all four Gospel narratives. Both Matthew and Mark tell us that the motive for Jesus feeding a great crowd was compassion, using the same Greek word - Σπλαγχνίζομαι (splanknizomai - Matt.15:32; Mk.8:2). In a variant form the same word is used for the feelings evoked in Jesus by a crowd whom he compared to a flock of sheep without a shepherd (Matt.9:36; Mk.6:34), or when large numbers of people came in need of healing (Matt.14:14). For a Synoptic story to rival the raising of Lazarus as a demonstration of Jesus' compassion in John, perhaps Luke's account of the raising of a widow's son is a contender. The NIV puts it, "*When the Lord saw her, his heart went out to her and he said, 'Don't cry'*" (Lk.7:13); but the clause, *his heart went out to her*, is a rendering of that same Greek word elsewhere translated as compassion. Although English translations do not always make it apparent, Luke uses the same word in two of Jesus' parables, describing the motives of both the Good Samaritan and the father of the Prodigal Son (Lk.10:33; 15:20).

---

[21] Marty TLC p.307

Mullins says of Jesus, "*He shows great compassion towards the sick, the possessed and the outcast and towards the crowds who come to hear him or to seek healing. He is moved to tears by the refusal of Jerusalem to respond to the message of peace*"[22]. Mullins also notes that in Zechariah's Benedictus the motive for what God has done and what God is doing now is the compassion (or mercy) of God[23].

The word "compassion" is not found in John's gospel, and Jesus' encounters with people in need are perhaps even marked by a sense of distance. For instance, the man healed by the pool near the Sheep Gate does not know who has healed him (Jn.5:13); and the crowd who are fed have not related to him in any way he would desire (Jn.6:15). It is probably true that John wishes to make broader points through the telling of these stories rather than focus on the personal implications or individual motives. But Jesus' invitation at the feast "*Whoever is thirsty should come to me, and whoever believes in me should drink. As the scripture says, 'Streams of life-giving water will pour out from his side*" (Jn.7:37f); Jesus' description of himself as the Good Shepherd (Jn.10:11), his dealings with Martha and Mary (Jn.11; 12:1-7), the washing of his disciples' feet, and Jesus' post-resurrection dealings with Mary Magdalene (Jn.20:15ff), Thomas (Jn.20:24ff) and Peter (Jn.21:15ff) provide ample support for saying that in all four gospels Jesus shows abundant compassion. The parable of the unmerciful servant (Matt.18:21-35), told to Peter in answer to a question about forgiveness, suggests Jesus expected the same attitude to be displayed by his disciples. "*This is how my heavenly Father will treat each one of you unless you forgive your brother from your heart*" (Mat.18:35). Put bluntly, to "follow Jesus" means to follow his example - including his compassion - or it means nothing at all.

4. Sex and Marriage

Churches often appear to be obsessed with people's sexual activity and associated morality, along with "correct" doctrine. None of this preoccupies Jesus. If Jesus can be said to have been obsessed with anything, it was with the dangers and misuse of wealth, money and possessions. Wilhelm says, "*Of the 38 parables in the New Testament 17 pertain to possessions and giving, and over 2,100 verses touch on the subject. More than right beliefs Christ is concerned with the right use of resources*"[24]. Similarly Ernest Marvin:

[22] TGL p.50
[23] Ibid. p.136
[24] PGM p.180

Chapter 5 - Reflections

"Fully one sixth of Jesus' teachings are about money. Do you know how much Jesus has to say about sex? Nothing, except for one word in passing about lustful thoughts. Yet "lust" and "sex" are model religious sins in the popular mind. It is a fixation not of the Bible, but of conservative and evangelical religion, both Catholic and Protestant"[25].

Perhaps Marvin slightly overstates his case. It is not a case of "anything goes". Jesus' stood in the tradition of John the Baptizer. John's public condemnation of Herod's "unlawful" marriage to his sister-in-law brought about his imprisonment and cost him his life (Mat.14:3-12; Mk.6:16-29; Lk.3:19f; 9:9). Jesus also gave more than just' *"one passing word about lustful thoughts"*. In Matthew Jesus said: *"I tell you that anyone who looks at a woman lustfully has already committed adultery with her in his heart"* (5:28). But there are a few more words of Jesus on sexual behaviour in the gospels. For example, Mark's record of Jesus reference to *sexual immorality* (Mk.7:21), and there are implications of an unacceptable sexual conduct in Jesus' words to the woman taken in adultery, *"Go and sin no more"* (Jn.8:11). However, Marvin and Wilhelm are both essentially right with regard to the imbalance between Jesus' priorities and those of many churches. It is self-evidently more comfortable for me to focus on someone else's questionable sexual behaviour rather than on my own or other church members' failures in generosity of spirit and money. The words "mote" and "beam" come to mind (Matt.7:3).

Some of Jesus' words relate to marriage and divorce. Teaching about divorce does not feature in John, and the Synoptics vary in their accounts of what Jesus said on the subject. According to Luke and Mark, divorce followed by re-marriage is adultery (Lk.16:18; Mk.10:11f). The words of Jesus, *"Anyone who divorces his wife and marries another woman commits adultery, and the man who marries a divorced woman commits adultery"* (Lk.16:18//Mk.10:11f) come as a stand-alone, uncompromising piece of teaching in Luke. In Mark, these words are set in the broader context of a conversation in which a first principle of faithfulness and unity in marriage is seen by Jesus as God's intention *in the beginning*; but Moses' law allowed divorce because, as Jesus said, *"Your hearts were hard"* (Mk.10:5). Matthew is similar to Mark in the content of the conversation surrounding the teaching on divorce, but gives an exceptional ground on which he believed divorce was acceptable: namely the marital unfaithfulness of a wife. Matthew also adds the almost comedic comment of Jesus' disciples which might be paraphrased thus: *"If marriage is for life, with no escape, it is better not to marry"* (Matt.19:10): and Jesus perhaps ironic reply, *"Not everyone can hack it. If you can, fine. If not, do not get into it. The Kingdom of Heaven is more important"* (Matt.19:11f). In fact, no one can be sure that they will be capable of a life-long commitment to marriage,

---

[25] Ernest Marvin on Luke 16:19-31 Expository Times Vol.11 Aug.2010 p.564

but if it is regarded as something from which there needs to be the proviso of an "escape" it is definitely better avoided.

Both Matthew and Mark make reference to the "*hardness of heart*" which made necessary the Mosaic permission to divorce. Both also include Jesus' teaching, "*Out of the heart come evil thoughts – murder, adultery, sexual immorality, theft, false testimony, slander*" (Matt:15:19; Mk.7:21f). This potentially broadens the consideration of sexual behaviour beyond the question of marriage. Mark does not offer further teaching, but what the other gospels and Jesus have to say, and his example, are very challenging.

Matthew not only quite deliberately includes Rahab, the Jericho prostitute, in the list of both David and Jesus' ancestors, but tells us that Jesus said to the religious of his day, "*Truly I tell you, the tax collectors and the prostitutes are entering the kingdom of God ahead of you*" (Matt.21:31). In John Jesus has an extended conversation with a Samaritan woman who seems to be a serial-divorcee, and/or a permanent relationship disaster, currently "*living in sin*". Yet this woman became an effective witness to Jesus, the first woman missionary. Furthermore, if John 8:1-11 are accepted as part of the gospel record, in dealing directly with a woman "*taken in adultery*" Jesus offered no condemnation. Although, as already mentioned, the obvious inference of Jesus' words, "*Go, and sin no more*" is that he regarded adultery as sin, the story in Luke of a woman described as "*Leading a sinful life*" (Lk.7:37) puts that into perspective. Simon the Pharisee's inhospitable and judgemental attitudes provoke Jesus lament, "*Whoever has been forgiven little shows only a little love*" (Lk.7:47). In contrast Jesus identifies the woman as an exemplar of great love and devotion. It is probably not putting it too strongly to say that in all four gospels inhospitable and judgemental attitudes were much more anathema to Jesus than sexual misdemeanours. But how many Christians and churches are prepared to believe that, say so, and act accordingly?

5. Baptism and the Holy Spirit

W. J. Abraham says:

> "..... *Baptism in the Holy Spirit. This is so crucial that it is found as the single agreed purpose of the work of Jesus in all three synoptic Gospels.... The language of Baptism speaks of immersion, of being saturated and snowed under in the life of God*"[26].

---

[26] W. J. Abraham *TLC* pp.163 & 166

269

Chapter 5 - Reflections

All my upbringing and sympathy makes me want to say "Amen" to this without reservation. In all honesty the evidence of the gospels themselves means that I cannot. Nonetheless, Abraham's statement serves as a useful starting point for reflecting upon Baptism and the Holy Spirit.

Baptism and the Holy Spirit are not completely separable subjects, but let us at least try to consider Baptism in its own right. All four gospels agree that John the Baptizer administered a baptism in water (Matt.3:11; Mk.1:8; Lk.3:16; Jn.1:26). The Synoptics give the Jordon as a general area for John's ministry, whilst the fourth gospel locates his ministry precisely at Bethany (Jn.1:28) and at "*Aenon near Salim - because there was plenty of water there!*" (Jn.3:23). The Synoptics also agree that John's baptism was, "*a baptism of repentance for the forgiveness of sins*" (Matt.3:6; Mk.1:4; Lk.3:3). The fourth gospel makes no mention of this, but it is in keeping with John the Baptizer's self-identified role as "*the voice of one crying in the desert, 'Make straight the way for the Lord'*" (Jn.1:23). To *make straight* might be interpreted as a parallel to the Synoptics' call for repentance. More important for a consideration of baptism, John the Baptizer says of his ministry," *the reason I came baptising with water was that he might be revealed to Israel* " (Jn.1:31). John knows his ministry is not an end in itself: "*He must become greater. I must become less*" (Jn.3:30): and all four gospels record John's testimony that the one who is to come will *baptise with the Holy Spirit* (Mk.1:8; Jn.1:33), Luke and Matthew adding "*and fire*" (Matt.3:11; Lk.3:16).

Because Matthew and Mark tell us about Jesus "*coming up out of the water*" (Matt.3:16; Mk.1:10) it is easy to accept Abraham's view that baptism *speaks of immersion*, but this is baptism in water as practised by John the Baptizer[27]. The baptism which John the Baptizer forecast for his "successor" would not be of this kind. There is no record in the New Testament of Jesus ever baptizing anyone in water. The Synoptics never mention Jesus exercising a ministry of baptism, and John's gospel categorically states in response to rumours that Jesus was baptising more people than John the Baptizer, "*In fact it was not Jesus who baptised, but his disciples*" (Jn.4:1f)[28]. Having no further evidence, we can only (idly?) speculate what exactly was the nature and purpose of baptism by Jesus' disciples.

---

[27] cf. Romans 6:3-9 for a passage on baptism "*into Christ*" which lends itself to interpreting baptism as immersion/burial leading to new life/resurrection - but which does not seem to see Baptism as in the name of the Father, Son and Holy Spirit

[28] Sadly we are told neither the nature nor purpose of baptism by Jesus' disciples: but it would seem from the Book of Acts that post-Jesus' ascension they administer water baptism.

It is necessary to set alongside the preparatory and perhaps intentionally transient nature of water baptism as offered by John, the fact that according to Matthew Jesus himself asked John for baptism in water, saying, "*It is proper for us to do this to fulfil all righteousness*" (Matt.3:15). Of course, if the emphasis in Jesus' words is on "*us*" this could be interpreted as specific to John and Jesus; but it is equally legitimate to see this as a principle or example having a wider or general application. This kind of baptism, however, is clearly not "*the single agreed purpose of the work of Jesus in all three synoptic Gospels*". In fairness to Abrahams, his claim is that it is "*baptism in the Holy Spirit*" which is "*so crucial*". So let us consider whether this is so.

The Synoptic gospels agree that following Jesus' water baptism "*the Spirit*" (Mk.1:10; Jn.1:32), "*the Spirit of God ... like a dove*" (Matt.3:16), or the "*Holy Spirit in bodily form*" (Lk.3:22) descended upon Jesus. It is reasonable to suggest, though I am one who does not choose to follow the reasoning, that in effect Jesus having been baptised with water then received a second baptism in or of the Holy Spirit[29]. My main reason for not accepting this "second baptism" theory as satisfactory is as follows. The Synoptics all add that the descent of the Spirit was accompanied by a heavenly voice which declared Jesus to be God's beloved Son. John's gospel in similar vein, although it does not record Jesus baptism in water, presents us with John the Baptizer as the one who saw the "*Spirit come down and remain*" and who on this basis testified, "*This is the Son of God*" (Jn.1:34). But this apparently visible descent of the Holy Spirit cannot be to establish Jesus as God's Son, but to confirm what is already true. I would contend that "*the spirit coming down*" is not best understood as a second baptism, but as the anointing of the anointed one - the Messiah (Lk.4:18 cf. Matt.12:18). Put crudely, baptism is "going down into - and coming up out of". That is, water baptism symbolises a new beginning, repentance and conversion - a kind of death and new life. Anointing has a different dynamic. It is "coming down upon from above" and confirms blessings already promised or received.

As the gospels between them make plain, Jesus was God from the beginning (Jn.1:1), was conceived by the Holy Spirit (Matt.1:18), would therefore be *The Son of God* (Lk.1:35), and knew his son-ship as a twelve-year-old (Lk.2:49). If it could be said of John the Baptizer, "*He will be filled with the Holy Spirit even before he is born*" (Lk.1:15), how much more so would this be true of Jesus. Though Luke encourages us to ask for the Holy Spirit with confidence (Lk.11:13. cp. Jn.3:34),

---

[29] Acts 19 gives an account of people who had received the baptism of John who were subsequently baptised into the name of Jesus (not the Trinity). Following their second baptism Paul laid his hands on them and "*the Holy Spirit came on them*" (Acts 19:1-6). But Paul's initial question was, "*Did you receive the Holy Spirit when you believed?*" - Not "*when you were baptised*". A definitive order of Baptism and receipt of the Spirit is not available in the New Testament.

the Holy Spirit is not a "one-off-fix". It is the active presence of God working through people's lives and confirming in them their high calling. For Mary it meant she would have a son (Lk.1:35). Elizabeth and Zechariah, both *"filled with the Holy Spirit"*, were inspired to offer praise (Lk.1:41, 67). Luke says of the old man Simeon, *"The Holy Spirit was on him. It had been revealed to him by the Holy Spirit that he would not die before he had seen the Lord's Messiah. Moved by the Spirit, he went into the temple courts"* (Lk.2:26f). These exemplary people's lives were constantly touched, moved and shaped by God's Spirit.

For Jesus the post-baptismal continuing movement of the Spirit meant he *"was led by the Spirit into the wilderness to be tempted by the Devil"* (Matt.4:1; Mk.1:12; Lk.4:1); but it was also literally the inspiration for his works of exorcism which testified to the coming of the Kingdom of God (Matt.12:28). The denigration of the nature of his inspiration (Mk.4:30) was unforgivable: *"Anyone who speaks against the Holy Spirit will not be forgiven, either in this age or in the age to come"* (Mk.3:29//Lk.12:10//Matt.12:32). This had to be so, because the Spirit was not only the inspiration for Jesus' ministry of exorcism, but legitimization for his entire ministry:

> *"The Spirit of the Lord is on me, because he has anointed me to proclaim good news to the poor. He has sent me to proclaim freedom for the prisoners and recovery of sight for the blind, to set the oppressed free"* (Lk.4:18 cf. Matt.12:18)

Although the very direct reference in the early chapters of Luke's gospel to the activity of the Holy Spirit is not maintained throughout the rest of the gospel, the Holy Spirit is obviously present. As we have already noted Luke speaks of the Holy Spirit's role in exorcisms, and tells us that Jesus, in common with Elizabeth and Zechariah, was led to give praise to his Father because he was *"full of joy through the Holy Spirit"* (Lk.10:21). More than this, the many stories of Jesus dealing with spirits which were impure (Lk.4:33, 36 etc), evil (Lk.7:21; 8:2. etc), disabling or crippling (9:42; 13:11) testify by way of contrast to the "Holy" Spirit in Jesus who challenges and nullifies their power. Certainly in Luke, and by inference in Matthew and Mark, the work of the Holy Spirit could be said to be ever-present in Jesus' life. But to move from this to say with Abrahams that, *"baptism in the Holy Spirit ... is found as the single agreed purpose of the work of Jesus in all three synoptic Gospels"* is a considerable step too far.

Indeed, at least in Mark and Luke, baptism for Jesus is not ultimately a baptism by the Holy Spirit, but a baptism of death by crucifixion. This is a particular challenge to those of a Pentecostal persuasion, and any within the Charismatic movement who might legitimately be called "happy clappy". But it is equally difficult for most mainstream churches, and for all Christians. The repeated call of Jesus to his disciples in the Synoptics is not to receive the Holy Spirit, but to follow the way of the cross, which Jesus himself felt constrained to follow: "*I have a baptism to undergo, and what constraint I am under until it is completed*" (Lk.12:50). He would set an example which he prophesied his disciples James and John would follow, "*You will drink the cup I drink and be baptised with the baptism I am baptised with*" (Mk.10:39). For many who undergo baptism by immersion there is an encouragement to think of it as symbolising or prefiguring the time of our natural deaths when we shall be somehow translated to heaven. This has little if anything to do with the baptism Jesus underwent and expected his friends to share. Baptism is not some kind of guarantee that when we die everything will be alright, but the call and commitment to a discipleship prepared to pay the ultimate price.

Matthew pictures the risen Christ saying to his disciples, "*Therefore go and make disciples of all nations, baptising them in the name of the Father and of the Son and of the Holy Spirit*" (Matt.28:19). If all that has gone before in the Synoptic gospels is taken into account this possibly, but not necessarily refers to immersion of believers in water (cf.Mk.16:16), following Jesus' example with John the Baptizer. But as Jesus said to Nicodemus, "*No one can enter the kingdom of God unless they are born of water ... and the Spirit*" (Jn.3:5). Not two baptisms, but one immersion of new birth into the will of God. The water ritual of baptism will be a symbol of the ongoing work and companionship of God's Spirit in our lives (Jn.4:24; 14:17). If this is so, we will be in the business of confronting and combating the evil spirits which bedevil so many. We will be acknowledging that the way of the cross is the only legitimate path for Christ-followers to travel.

The ongoing active companionship and inspiration of the Spirit for disciples is promised in various ways in all four gospels:-

> "*The Advocate, the Holy Spirit, whom the Father will send in my name, will teach you all things and will remind you of everything I have said to you*" (Jn.14:26)
> "*When the Advocate comes, whom I will send to you from the Father – the Spirit of truth who goes out from the Father – he will testify about me*" (Jn.15:26)
> "*It will not be you speaking, but the Spirit of your Father speaking through you*" (Matt.10:20//Mk.13:11//Lk.12:12. cp. Jn.16:13).

John tells us, "*Up to that time the Spirit had not been given, since Jesus had not yet been glorified*" (Jn.7:39). But after Jesus' death and resurrection, when Jesus met with his disciples, "*He breathed on them and said, 'Receive the Holy Spirit'*" (Jn.20:22). According to the fourth gospel, it is only through Jesus' ghastly yet glorious death, his second baptism, that his gift of the Holy Spirit to his disciples becomes possible. Only in like fashion can the gift find its fulfilment in us and flow through us.

In John's gospel there are a number of possible indicators that water baptism for followers of Jesus might not be a requirement. The man by the pool in John 5 did not need to get into the pool to be healed. When Jesus washed his disciples' feet and Peter wanted to be fully washed Jesus' reply might suggest that water immersion was not necessary. And there is no compelling reason to accept that Matthew 28:19 refers to water baptism, though the Book of the Acts of the Apostles records such an activity. Whatever stance we take with regard to the gospel evidence on water baptism, we will surely take fully into account that whereas John the Baptizer's work was to baptize in water in preparation for the work of Jesus, in none of the gospels does Jesus baptise anyone in water, nor seem to state unequivocally its desirability as an essential ingredient in following his way.

6. The Kingdom of God/Heaven and eternal life

I looked at the subject "*The Kingdom of God*" in some depth in the chapter on Luke's gospel (Magnificat). In these reflections it is appropriate to simply note some of the things on which, at least in some measure, the gospels agree or diverge on the matter.

Matthew calls it the "*Kingdom of Heaven*", but quite clearly this can be taken to be the same thing as *The Kingdom of God* since a number of Jesus' sayings are repeated word for word in other gospels except that "heaven" is replaced by "God". It should be acknowledged, however, that the words "God" and "heaven" have quite different connotations for most twenty-first century Western people. They do not necessarily evoke the same response; especially in those for whom "heaven" is a place where people go after they die! The kingdom of God easily has a "now" connotation, whereas the kingdom of heaven perhaps more readily produces a sense of "not yet". Whether or not Matthew and Luke recognised the alternative meanings they offered by their choice of words is a matter for speculation, but it is possible, and fits well with some of the observations made in reflections previously made on the two gospels.

Matera says, "*The starting point of the synoptic tradition is Jesus' proclamation of the kingdom of God*"[30]. This is correct in as much as the kingdom of God forms part of Jesus' initial preaching ministry in all three Synoptics. Luke alone, however, indicates that Jesus' preaching of the kingdom was "the" purpose of his work: "*I must proclaim the good news of the kingdom of God to the other towns also,*

---

[30] Frank J. Matera *New Testament Theology* Westminster John Knox 2007 p.43

because that is why I was sent" (Lk.4:43). Matthew's inclusion of so many parables by Jesus about the kingdom may indicate the priority he believed Jesus gave to the kingdom, as witnessed by words of Jesus found only in Matthew, "*Be concerned above everything else with the Kingdom of God and with what he requires of you*" (Matt.6:33). In Mark Jesus says, "*If your eye causes you to stumble, pluck it out. It is better for you to enter the kingdom of God with one eye than to have two eyes and be thrown into hell*" (Mk.9:47; cp. Matt.18:8). The kingdom is clearly very important. Just how important it is for Mark might be indicated by the fact that in six of Mark's sixteen chapters the Kingdom of God receives no mention. Mark also has only one obvious parable of the Kingdom - the mustard seed (Mk.4:30-32). But it should also be taken into consideration that Mark informs his readers, "*With many similar parables Jesus spoke the word to them, as much as they could understand. He did not say anything to them without using a parable. But when he was alone with his own disciples, he explained everything*" (Mk.4:33f). Mark also tells us, "*When he was alone, the Twelve and the others around him asked him about the parables. He told them, 'The secret of the kingdom of God has been given to you. But to those on the outside everything is said in parables*'" (Mk.4:10f; cf.Lk.8:10). They may express it in quite different ways, and allocate different amounts of space to it, but in all three Synoptics the kingdom was a significant subject in Jesus' preaching and teaching.

Whatever the kingdom is, Jesus himself said it had come near (Matthew 3:2; 4:17; Mark 1:15; Luke 4:43). He also instructed his disciples to give others this same message, "*The Kingdom of God is near you*" (Matt.10:7; Lk.9:2; 10:9). Luke prefaces this instruction with information that when giving this message the disciples were visiting those towns where Jesus intended to go (Lk.10:1). Possible inferences from this are either that Jesus was the kingdom of God, or the kingdom of God was "in Jesus". He and the kingdom were literally "*near*". Furthermore, Luke tells us Jesus said the kingdom of heaven is "*in your midst*"(Lk.17:20f). But since he also said it is "*not something that can be observed*" any simplistic equation of Jesus with the Kingdom will not stand up to close scrutiny. Jesus and the kingdom are inextricably linked, but they are not one and the same. For the most part the kingdom would seem to be an entity in its own right with a compass surpassing that of the pre-resurrection / ascension Jesus of Nazareth.

There are some who will enter or inherit the kingdom, whilst others will not. Taking all four gospels into account, amongst those who are or will be accepted are the poor or "poor in spirit" (Matt.5:3; Lk.6:20); those persecuted for righteousness (Matt.5:10); those who practise and teach the Law in a way which surpasses the Scribes and Pharisees (Matt.5:19f), who do the will of the Father in heaven (Matt.7:21) and produce fruit fit for the kingdom (Matt.21:43); those who welcome and become like little children (Matt,19:14, 23; Mk.10:14, 23; Lk.18:16, 24); many from the east and the west (Matt.8:11; Lk.13:29); those who are born again of water and the spirit (Jn.3:3, 5); repentant tax collectors and prostitutes (Matt.21:31f); those who meet the needs of *"one of the least of these brothers of mine"* (Matt.25:34, 40). The people who will not enter the Kingdom, or will be ejected from it, are the opposites of those who will. So they are the unrepentant (Matt.21:31f, 43); those who are not poor and whose riches are an obstacle to following Jesus or receiving the life he offers (Matt.19:23; Mk.10:23ff; Lk.18:25); those who do not produce fruit fit for the kingdom (Matt.21:43); and so on. I expand on this a little in a separate section below ("In and Out"), but clearly according to Jesus' teaching not everyone will enter the kingdom. So however it may be understood it is something which can be entered, but only according to certain strict criteria.

Matthew and Luke tell us Jesus was *"teaching in their synagogues, proclaiming the good news of the kingdom"* (Matt.4:23; 9:35; Lk.4:43; 8:1). Jesus said to his detractors, *"If it is by the Spirit of God that I drive out demons, then the kingdom of God has come upon you"* (Matt.12:28; Lk.11:20): and to those teachers of the law who were favourable to him; *"Every teacher of the law who has become a disciple in the kingdom of heaven is like the owner of a house who brings out of his storeroom new treasures as well as old"* (Matt.13:52). If Jesus' initial message was kingdom focussed, then it continued to form part of his message.

In all of the above the kingdom seems to be something which is present in the here and now. When Jesus said to a teacher of the Law, *"You are not far from the kingdom of God"* (Mk.12:34), there is no apparent sense of needing to wait for the passage of time in the words *"not far from"*. But elsewhere there are many sayings which suggest the kingdom is yet to come: it belongs in the future. The disciples were taught by Jesus to pray, *"Thy kingdom come"* (Matt.6:10; Lk.11:2) with the most natural inference that it was not already here – certainly not already complete. There are some *"who will not taste death before they see that the kingdom of God has come with power"* (Matt.16:28; Mk.9:1; Lk.9:27 - cf. Matt.10:23). It is tied up with the future coming of the Son of Man in judgement: *"Then the righteous will shine like the sun in the kingdom of their Father"* (Matt.13:41ff). None of these sayings rule out a partial realisation of the kingdom in the present, but all suggest there is at least a future dimension to it, or it is yet to be completed. However, in Luke there is a saying which most naturally means the kingdom is not yet present: *"When you see these things happening, you know that the kingdom of God is near"* (Lk.21:31). In this instance the word *"near"* does carry a sense of "time". When Jesus was approaching Jerusalem we are told *"the people thought that the kingdom of God was going to appear at once"*. So Jesus told them a parable of a man who went away to be made a king, and whose subjects failed to wait with due respect and patience (Lk.19:11). The kingdom is something for which people like Joseph of Arimathea wait (Mk.15:43; Lk.23:51). Jesus *"will not drink again from the fruit of the vine until that day when I drink it new in the kingdom of God"*

(Mk.14:25; Lk.22:18) - or, in Luke *"eat of the bread"* (Lk.22:16). And when the dying thief asked Jesus, *"Lord, remember me when you come in your kingdom"* Jesus reply suggests that he would be in the kingdom that very day (Lk.23:42f) - but not right now!

I am not the first to ask, "Is the kingdom a present reality or a future hope?" Nor I guess am I the first to relate the answer to two things.

The first, Jesus' words to Peter,

> *"I will give you the keys of the kingdom of heaven; whatever you bind on earth will be bound in heaven, and whatever you loose on earth will be loosed in heaven"* (Matt.16:19).

This is not the place to discuss how others have institutionalised these words - although it is worth making the point that the binding element of these words is addressed to all the disciples as well as Peter (Matt.18:18). What I take from these words with regard to the kingdom is this. In the life of the kingdom what happens *on earth*, in the zone of time and place, as a consequence of people putting their faith in Jesus as *"the Christ, the Son of the living God"* (Matt.16:16) has ramifications *in heaven* - that "home" or "realm" of God in which past, present and future are as one. Perhaps this was so evidently true for the Synoptic gospel writers that they felt no need to spell it out; and to Jesus that he never said it in a direct way. But the presence of Moses and Elijah at the transfiguration (Matt.17:1-13; Mk.9:2-13; Lk.9:28-36), the telling remark that God is the God of Abraham, Isaac and Jacob - the living, not the dead (Mk.12:26f), and the picture of people from the East and the West sitting down at a table in the kingdom with Abraham, Isaac and Jacob, are all indicators that the hard and fast dividing lines many would draw between earth and heaven or "now" and "then" are not ones Jesus saw as paramount. Any saying which relates to the kingdom and at a surface level seems to confine it to either "here and now" or "there and then" should be read as part of a wider understanding which encompasses both.   There are elements of Braaten's work with which I strongly disagree, but not his discernment that, *"heavenly and earthly levels of reality ... are interconnected. The spiritual and material realms are intertwined in the biblical drama of salvation"*[31]. Rob Bell offers an intriguing perspective when he suggests that Jesus *"drags the future into the present"*[32]. Hope is an attitude as well as a spur.

My second point of reference is John's gospel.

---

[31] Carl E. Braaten *That they may believe - A theology of the Gospel and the mission of the church* Eerdmans - Grand Rapids 2008 p.125
[32] Rob Bell "Love Wins" p.41 Collins 2011

As we recognised earlier, John was aware of "*the kingdom*" (Jn.3:3, 5). He mentions it before his much more common, "*eternal life*". But John opts for the latter phrase, using it seventeen times. This is in marked contrast to the Synoptics. They also know about "*eternal life*", but only use that term two or three times. For example, in the story of the man who asked "*What must I do to inherit eternal life?*" (Matt.19:16; Mk.10:17; Lk.18:18).

Why did John make his particular choice? Of course, a definitive answer to this question is not possible, but this is one theory. I believe John's gospel was written some time after the Synoptics, when the "here and now", that kind of "nearness" of the kingdom which Jesus embodied and proclaimed was no longer the "here and now". Yet for John what the Kingdom of God was about was as real as ever. That life which "kingdom language" conveyed and which Jesus exemplified was still available to be lived. John wanted to share his belief that God, and God's kingdom is an ever-present possibility. John's use of "eternal life", with John's given explanation and overall context, is a way of transmitting his belief in the continuing reality of the kingdom Jesus proclaimed – it is literally through Jesus *life for the age* (η αιωνιος ζωη).

In Matthew, Jesus told his disciples, "*This gospel of the kingdom will be preached in the whole world as a testimony to all nations, and then the end will come*" (Matt.24:14). It is commonly understood, and some of Paul's writings seem to confirm, that "*the end*" was believed by Jesus' first followers to be imminent. The kingdom of God on earth would be established quickly, closely followed by its consummation. John was old enough, or belonged to a generation who had to come to terms with the non-fulfilment of this time-frame - as have all right thinking Christians ever since. The gospel was as important as ever, but it needed terms of reference which could speak to those who were not Jesus' contemporaries. So for example, if in Luke Jesus can say to his contemporaries, "*The kingdom of heaven is in your midst*" (Lk.17:21); in John Jesus speaks in ways which address not just his own generation, but are timeless. For example, "*Whoever believes in me, streams of life-giving water will pour out from his heart*" (Jn.7:38; cp.Jn.4:14).

For those who might criticise the above reflections for failing to offer a clear definition of the kingdom, I can only repeat Mullin's very sensible words:

It is very difficult to give a clear definition of the kingdom of God (or kingdom of heaven)...which is not a state or system brought about by good, religious, God-fearing people. It is "God's project", a divine plan to which one must respond. The mysteries of the kingdom are a gift of revelation of what is partly seen and partly hidden, partly present and partly future.... (in the, yet beyond) here and now.

This calls for a paradoxical outlook on life and a world with its established assessments and values[33].

Whatever words are chosen to share news of that kingdom or eternal life which is present in all four gospels, the essential element for participating in the life which Jesus offers is trust. In John; *"Whoever believes in him shall not perish but have eternal life"* (Jn.3:16 - see also Jn.3:15, 36; 6:40, 47; 17:3). In the Synoptics perhaps a more practical expression of this trust is given in Jesus' declaration: *"Everyone who has left houses or brothers or sisters or father or mother or wife or children or fields for my sake will receive a hundred times as much and will inherit eternal life* (Matt.19:29; Lk.18:30) - or as Mark ends the saying, *".. and in the age to come eternal life"* (Mk.10:29f). In John, *"Anyone who loves their life will lose it, while anyone who hates their life in this world will keep it for eternal life"* (Jn.12:25). In Matthew we read, *"Whoever practises and teaches these commands will be called great in the kingdom of heaven"* (Matt.5:19): in John, *"I know that his command leads to eternal life"* (Jn.12:50). The parallels could continue; but all four evangelists want to convey that life "in Christ", eternal life, kingdom life, is on offer, everyone should have a chance to hear about it and by putting their trust in God as seen in Jesus anyone can have a part in it.

7. **In or Out**

This section takes up and expands the thoughts shared above in relation to the kingdom of heaven that, to put it crudely, some people are acceptable to God others are not. This is related to, though not identical with being accepted as a disciple, one who followed and was with Jesus. Most people who encountered Jesus were not told to follow him, nor is there any hint that they were expected to become disciples. Some were specifically told to go home (Matt.9:6//Mk.2:11//Lk.5:24; Mk.5:19), or given other instructions (Matt.8:4; Lk.9:60; 10:37; 17:14). The disciples, at least in the Synoptics, often failed to live up to the standards which Jesus set (e.g. Matt.8:26); but they made the essential commitment by giving Jesus priority in their lives (Matt.19:27). Nonetheless it would be hard to make a case from the main body of the gospels that being accepted as a disciple is the same thing as being "in" or "out" of the kingdom - Judas Iscariot being an obvious even if extreme example. In due course, when Jesus was no longer physically present, following his "commands" would be the pattern for discipleship. It is on this basis Matthew can record Jesus' post-resurrection instruction, *"Go, then, to all peoples everywhere and make them my disciples"* which derives from Jesus' claim to *"have been given all authority in heaven and on earth"* - his kingdom has to be made known. But it is manifestly

---

[33] TGL p.180

apparent that those who would invite others to be disciples of Jesus are themselves to be obedient to "*everything I have commanded you*" (Matt.28:18-20).

The essential ingredient for discipleship, according Jesus ultimate authority, putting trust in him, having faith in him, being absolutely committed to his way, is captured in the Synoptics in such words as "*Whoever does not take up their cross and follow me is not worthy of me*" (Matt.10:38; Lk.14:27); or, "*Whoever wants to be my disciple must deny themselves and take up their cross and follow me*" (Matt.16:24; Mk.8:34; Lk.9:23). John does not have this "cross language" for discipleship, but, when Jesus says, "*Greater love hath no man than this, that one lay down his life for his friends*" (Jn.15:13), he is expressing a closely related if not the same truth. And Peter's, "*Lord, to whom shall we go? You have the words of eternal life*" (Jn.6:68) expresses that kind of trust, and the need and call to have trust, which is an oft repeated theme in John (Jn.3:16, 18, 36; 5:24; 8:24; 11:25; 12:46; 14:11).

The call to "take up a cross" or "lay down one's life" indicate how challenging is Jesus' call to discipleship for anyone who considers being "in" his company. The cross, of course, is not to be identified with the sufferings and trials which one encounters as a normal part of being human, it consists of those trials and tribulations which we take upon ourselves in the service of others in Jesus' name, or which are the consequence of "owning" his name. Indeed, there is a view that the suffering involved in crucifixion should not be the major focus in what Jesus endured. The greater sacrifice was receiving the abuse and ridicule and bearing the shame. Being branded and treated like a criminal; mocked; scourged as a form of humiliation; stripped of his clothing; hung on a post; all of these were shockingly shameful for Jesus' contemporaries[34]. Of course, it was in some ways a logical outworking of Jesus' teaching that obedience to God meant self-abasement; but it was not easy to understand or to endure in a world within which shame and honour were such powerful determinants of behaviour and attitudes. Contemporary Western society finds it difficult to comprehend how some Moslems can want to kill someone for insulting the prophet Mohammed. The difficulty in understanding may well be because, albeit subconsciously, we have accepted that the author of Christianity not only willingly accepted insults and shame, but in doing so in a spirit of forgiveness and love for his persecutors he believed he truly honoured God. This is a mode of thinking which I believe most Moslems today would find extremely difficult to appreciate; which most Christians find equally difficult to put into practice; and which few of Jesus' contemporaries could really fathom, much less embrace. In all honour-based societies a dishonouring of oneself, family or friends, much more one's god, requires retribution. It cannot be overstressed how

---

[34] The intense humiliation Jesus endured is perhaps best expressed in Matthew's account of Jesus' trial, subsequent treatment and execution – Matt.27:27-44

radical Jesus' teaching and example were and remain. Sadly in twenty-first century England we still have a very worldly honours system as part of our national culture, and it is the exception rather than the rule that people who do menial tasks are given honour - and never the highest worldly honours! That Jesus advocated the role of humble servant for all his followers and willingly accepted the shame of the cross remains for the most part a creed not a way of life. Jesus rightly discerned that to be honoured in this world probably means we are not "in" in his kingdom - the values are so different – diametrically opposed.

I was raised singing the chorus, *Trust and obey* [35]. The two go hand in hand in all four gospels. The positive initial responses of some who were called by Jesus to "*follow me*" (e.g. Mk.1:18, 20) is indicative of a trustful obedience which would be asked from then on: "*Whoever practises and teaches these commands will be called great in the kingdom of heaven*" (Matt.5:19). John puts the call to obedience as a direct challenge by Jesus to his disciples: "*If you love me, you will keep my commandments*" (Jn.14:15); which leads to the promise, "*If you keep my commandments, you will abide in my love - just as I have kept my Father's commandments and abide in his love*" (Jn.15:10). To be "in", in the relationship of love which Jesus knew with his Father, is to manifest trust and obedience akin to that of Jesus.

Where there is a lack of trust and obedience, people are often described as being "outside". Sometimes this is in parable form. John the Baptizer imagines people as chaff "*burning with unquenchable fire*" (Matt.3:12). Both he and Jesus compare unfruitful people with trees being chopped down and consigned to the flames (Matt.3:10; 9:19; 25:41). For John the Baptizer being fruitful is the result of repentance (Matt.3:8; Lk.3:8). In Jesus' teaching it is directly related to doing his or his Father's will (Jn.14:12). Jesus' birth family who wished to take him away from his work are described as "*standing outside*" (Matt.12:46; Mk.3:31f; Lk.8:19f). They are contrasted with those who do the will of Jesus' Father and who are spiritually as well as physically "inside" with Jesus (cf. Matt.12:48-50; Mk.3:33-35; Lk.8:21).

Some people begin inside, or at least with the potential for being inside, but they are either thrown out like tasteless, useless salt (Matt.5:13), locked out, as with the foolish virgins in the parable (Matt.25:11), or discover they are on the outside with apparently no way in (Lk.13:25). The rebellious subjects of the kingdom in Jesus' parable, "*will be thrown outside, into the darkness, where there will be weeping and gnashing of teeth*" (Matt.8:12). The same fate of expulsion awaits the "*worthless servant*" (Matt.25:30; Lk.19:22), the pitiable late arrival who failed to dress properly (Matt.22:13), and those who are generally described as "*evil*"

---
[35] *When we walk with the Lord in the light of his word* J. H. Sammis 1846-1919

(Matt.13:42, 50). Those who fail to use the narrow door (Lk.13:25; Matt.7:13) "*will stand outside knocking and pleading* (in vain)". Peter denied Jesus: "*And he went outside and wept bitterly*" (Matt.26:75; Lk.22:62). Judas who betrayed Jesus' trust "*went out. And it was night*". The importance of this real and constant danger of being thrown outside or locked outside is portrayed by these and other very strong images,

There were those who thought they had an automatic right to be "in". Some thought it was their birthright. Our equivalent might be coming from a Christian family ("*My uncle was a vicar!*"), or a Christian country[36]. There were Jews in Jesus' day living in Judaea who claimed the birthrights of, "*children of Abraham*". Jesus did not see this as an insignificant matter, saying, for example, that a woman with a crippling spinal curvature was a "*daughter of Abraham*"(Lk.13:16 - see also Lk.19:9). But though it should have been a help, physically being Abraham's offspring was not what really mattered. John the Baptizer said, "*God can raise up children of Abraham from these stones*" (Matt.3:9; Lk.3:8). The determining factor for legitimately claiming descent from Abraham is this: - "*If you were Abraham's children,' said Jesus, 'then you would do what Abraham did*" (Jn.8:39). Being "in" is by spiritual generation and orientation, not physical (Jn.1:13; 3:5).

Others believed their position in society made them acceptable to God. They came from "good families", or were honoured members of their society. But Jesus' kingdom is not of this world (Jn.8:23; 14:22; 18:36), his followers were not to copy the authority and privileged structures of this world (Matt.20:25; Mk.10:42), for as Mary sang, "*The rulers will be brought down, but the humble will be lifted up*" (Lk.1:52). Put succinctly: "*The last will be first and the first will be last*" (Matt.19:30; 20:16; Mk.10:31; Lk.13:30). Those who thought they were "in" would discover it not to be the case - and vice-versa.

Jesus seemed to reserve a special application of "Woe" for the religious of his day (Matt.23:13-32). For example, the Pharisees who loved "*the most important seats in the synagogues and respectful greetings in the market-places*" (Lk.11:43 - see also Matt.6:1; 23:1-7; Mk.12:39f; Lk.11:43; 20:45-47). As for the chief priests and elders, members of the Jerusalem "establishment", who challenged his authority (Matt.21:23) who plotted against him (Matt.27:1), and who ultimately professed that they had no king but the Caesar of this world (Jn.19:15), Jesus prophesied of them: "*There will be weeping there, and gnashing of teeth, when you see Abraham, Isaac and Jacob and all the prophets in the kingdom of God, but you yourselves thrown out*" (Lk.13:28). People from all four corners of the earth, presumably Gentiles like the centurion whose faith surpassed anything Jesus has

---

[36] As, for instance, claimed by Eric Pickles. Guardian newspaper 6th April 2014.

seen in Israel, would find acceptance in their stead (Lk.13:29)[37]. Furthermore, Jesus told them, "*tax collectors and prostitutes are entering the Kingdom of God before you*" (Matt.21:31). Though often unacknowledged and unmet, this teaching of Jesus stands as one of the biggest, , challenges to the privileged and powerful positions and postures of many "dignitaries" or "proud office holders" in the life of churches as well as wider society today.

There are many instances in the gospels, many of which we have touched on before, where contrasts are made or choices given which signify inclusion or exclusion. A selection of these, each of which could be elaborated, are: prioritising God or money (Matt.6:24; Lk.16:13); the forgiving or the unforgiving (Matt.6:14f. cp.Mk.11:25-26) - the disastrous consequences of being unforgiving are reinforced by the parable of the unmerciful servant (Matt.18:23-35); acceptance and succour for disciples as opposed to their rejection which leads to a fate worse than Sodom and Gomorrah (Matt.10:12-14, 40-42; Mk.9:41; Lk.10:12. see also Matt. 11:20-24); and, "*Whoever acknowledges me before others, I will also acknowledge before my Father in heaven. But whoever disowns me before others, I will disown before my Father in heaven*" (Matt.10:32f; Lk.9:26; 12:8f). These Synoptic "opposites" are in a way summarised in Jesus' words comparing the blessed (Matt.5:3-11; cp.Lk.6:20-23) and the woeful (Matt.23:13-32. cp.Lk.6:24-26). To these could be added a considerable number of others from the Fourth Gospel; e.g. - "*His own received him not, but to those who did ...*" (Jn.1:11f); those who do good or those who do evil (Jn.5:29); light or darkness (Jn.12:35f), sight or blindness (Jn.9:39-41), night or day (Jn.9:4); life or death (Jn.11:25); and many more. Each conflicting doublet invites a personal, and sometimes a corporate, consideration as to where we stand, and an appropriate response.

One saying, and its variants, which relates to being "in" or "out", acceptable or not to Jesus, and which has caused considerable debate is, "*For whoever is not against us, is for us*" (Mk.9:40). In Luke "us" is replaced by "you" (Lk.9:50), but both sayings are Jesus' response to his disciples' condemnation of an exorcist who "*is not one of us*" (Mk.9:38). Mathew and Luke have an unconnected saying by Jesus, "*Whoever is not with me is against me*" (Matt.12:30; Lk.11:23). Tucket says that Mark 9:38-40 is diametrically opposed to Luke 11:23 - and presumably, though Tucket does not mention it, also to Luke 9:50. I cannot see why there has to be a conflict between the two sayings. The assertion of the disciples that the exorcist is "*not one of us*", is clearly rejected by Jesus, with the inference that his words and his works show he is "with Jesus", at least in spirit. The words about those "*who

---

[37] The supposed superiority, or religious purity of Judah in contrast to the rest of the world is perhaps illustrated by the description of its neighbour as "*Galilee of the Gentiles*" (Matt.4:15) - and the sarcastic remark of the Pharisees, "*No prophet ever came form Galilee*" (Jn.7:52)

are not with me" are spoken in a quite different and significantly contrasting context. In both Matthew and Luke this latter saying follows the accusations of the Pharisees that Jesus cast out demons by Beelzebub (Matt.12:27; Lk.11:19). We have, therefore, a man who casts out demons in Jesus' name, and Pharisees who accuse Jesus of casting out demons in the name of Satan. Tucket says, referring to Mark 9:40, if this episode is given as teaching for the early church, then for Mark allegiance to Jesus is more important than membership of a church; *factionalism and triumphalism* are outlawed. *"Mark thus has a much more open-ended ecclesiology than, say, Matthew does"*[38]. I would contend that the teaching of Mark 9:40 is given in various forms in all the Synoptics. Tucket may be justified in interpreting Jesus' rejection of *factionalism and triumphalism*, but not to set one saying or one gospel as contrary to another.

Jesus said to his disciples, *"The secret of the kingdom of God has been given to you. But to those on the outside everything is said in parables"* (Matt.13:11; Mk.4:11; Lk.8:10). Yes, the disciples are privileged, not to have knowledge which gives them status setting them above or against others, but to be shown by Jesus himself how the way of humble, faithful service of others in the spirit or name of Jesus and his Father is a way that everyone must travel if they are to be part of Jesus' "in-crowd".

8. The final judgement

This subject has probably been harder for me to examine that any other part of this work on the gospels. I have preached on the subject in the past, but rarely, if ever, looking at more than one saying or parable at a time. As a result I have probably over-simplified Jesus' teaching and avoided some issues with which I have been uncomfortable. I have tried not to do that here.

It would seem from a consideration of those things which determine whether or not a person is "in" or "out" of God's grace, is part of the kingdom, or merits a blessing or a woe, that there are innumerable factors to take into account. So many, in fact, that it would be reasonable to say that no one could fulfil all the requirements. The fact that Jesus did not reject his disciples when they so obviously failed to live according to the teaching Jesus gave them is an encouragement for all who share their lack of faith and charity, but it does not take away the obligation to try.

Are there some crucial things, or is there some most important thing, which "must" be true of us, in order for us to be "in"? If we say there is, what are the criteria for a final judgement on our lives?

---

[38] Tucket: OBC p. 905

There are good reasons to focus on 'what' is the basis for a final judgement rather than 'when' such a judgement will be; but a word about when is not without value given that contrary to Jesus' clear teaching so many over the span of Christian history have believed and persuaded others that they could offer a specific date, or a specific marker in human experience (e.g. physical death). Jesus related the moment of ultimate judgement to his coming or return as the Son of Man, but offered no date and imprecise, seemingly unfulfilled time-frames (Matt.16:28; Mk.9:1; Lk.9:27). Moreover, Jesus warned that anyone who came predicting, "*The time is at hand*" (Lk.21:8), or, "*Look, here is the Christ*" would probably be a deceiver (Mk.13:5f; Matt.24:4f, 23). No one, not even the Son or the angels in heaven, knows "when" (Matt.24:36; Mk.13:32). What we learn from the Synoptic gospels is that like the flood in Noah's day, or the destruction in Lot's time, the signs will be there, and the coming of the Son of Man when it happens will be as obvious to all as lightening which covers the whole sky. The immediate response will be one of mourning by everyone (Matt.24:27, 30f; Mk.13:24-27), though it will be the "*Day of redemption*" for some (Lk.21:25-28) as well as a day when the fate of the unfaithful will be: "*Cut him to pieces and assign him a place with the hypocrites, where there will be weeping and gnashing of teeth*" (Matt.24:48-51. cf.Lk.12:36, 43-46). But the final act of separation will come "out of the blue":

> *That is how it will be at the coming of the Son of Man. Two men will be in the field; one will be taken and the other left. Two women will be grinding with a hand mill; one will be taken and the other left* (Matt.24:39b-41).
> *I tell you, on that night two people will be in one bed; one will be taken and the other left. Two women will be grinding corn together; one will be taken and the other left* (Lk.17:34f).
> "*Be careful, or your hearts will be weighed down with carousing, drunkenness and the anxieties of life, and that day will close on you suddenly like a trap*" (Lk.21:34)

Whether "*that day*" in Luke and the other Synoptics' (four times in Matthew, three in both Mark and Luke) is quite the same thing as John's "*last day*" (six times in John - 6:39, 40, 44, 54; 11:24; 12:48) is open to question, but all four gospels report sayings of Jesus which indicate a "day" which is coming when people will be judged, or perhaps "separated" might be a better word. According to the parable of dividing fish (Matt.13:47f), and the parable of the wheat and tares and its explanation, until that day comes there is to some extent delayed judgement:

> "*Let both grow together until the harvest* (Matt.13:30). But, "*at the end of the age ... the Son of Man will send out his angels, and they will weed out of his kingdom everything that causes sin and all who do evil. They will throw them into the blazing furnace, where there will be weeping and gnashing of*

teeth. Then the righteous will shine like the sun in the kingdom of their Father" (Matt.13:40-43, 47-50)

John the Baptizer, whose own call to repentance divided his hearers, realised that Jesus' work in the world would also separate or divide people. He said of Jesus, "*His winnowing fork is in his hand and he will clear his threshing floor, gathering his wheat into the barn and burning up the chaff with unquenchable fire*" (Matt.3:12; Lk.3:17). Then Matthew tells us, "*Jesus began to preach 'Repent for the kingdom of heaven is at hand'*" (Matt.4:17). People had to make a choice, as John's gospel also affirms:-

"*For God so loved the world that he gave his one and only Son, that whoever believes in him shall not perish but have eternal life. For God did not send his Son into the world to condemn the world, but to save the world through him. Whoever believes in him is not condemned, but whoever does not believe stands condemned already because they have not believed in the name of God's one and only Son. This is the verdict: light has come into the world, but people loved darkness instead of light because their deeds were evil*" (Jn.3:16-19).

The benefits of belief are remarkable: "*The one who believes has eternal life*" (Jn.6:47); "*Whoever lives by believing in me will never die*" (Jn.11:26); "*Everyone will hate you because of me. But not a single hair from your heads will perish*" (Lk.21:17f); "*For my Father's will is that everyone who looks to the Son and believes in him shall have eternal life, and I will raise them up at the last day*" (Jn.6:40). But those who benefit are starkly contrasted to those from whom they are separated: "*You do not believe because you are not my sheep. My sheep listen to my voice; I know them, and they follow me* " (Jn.10:26-28)."*Whoever believes in the Son has eternal life, but whoever rejects the Son will not see life, for God's wrath remains on them*" (Jn.3:36).

"*Whoever rejects the Son will not see life.*" These words suggest that it is not doubting, or failing, or lacking in some other respect with regard to Jesus which incurs God's continuing wrath, but consciously rejecting Jesus. In this sense people bring a particular verdict upon themselves, a verdict the consequences of which have been seen before, but the lessons of which have not been learned. So, of any town which rejected his messengers Jesus said it would be, "*more tolerable for Sodom and Gomorrah on the day of judgement than for that town*" (Matt.10:16; Lk.10:12). And of Chorazin, Bethsaida and Capernaum - the towns "*in which most of his miracles had been performed ...It will be more bearable for Tyre and Sidon on the day of judgement than for you*" (Matt.11:20, 24), "*The men of Nineveh will stand up at the judgement with this generation and condemn it; for they repented at the preaching of Jonah, and now something greater than Jonah is here*"

(Matt.12:41; Lk.11:32). The rejection of Jesus by some was occasioned by a wilful failure to learn from the scriptures: *"But do not think I will accuse you before the Father. Your accuser is Moses, on whom your hopes are set. If you believed Moses, you would believe me, for he wrote about me"* (Jn.5:45f. see also Jn.5:39f).

However, even more important than ignoring Moses' writings, and life-affirming or self-damning, was the acceptance or rejection of Jesus' words:

> *"Very truly I tell you, whoever hears my word and believes him who sent me has eternal life and will not be judged but has crossed over from death to life"* (Jn.5:24).

> *"If anyone hears my words but does not keep them, I do not judge that person. For I did not come to judge the world, but to save the world. There is a judge for the one who rejects me and does not accept my words; the very words I have spoken will condemn them at the last day. For I did not speak on my own, but the Father who sent me commanded me to say all that I have spoken. I know that his command leads to eternal life. So whatever I say is just what the Father has told me to say"* (Jn.12:47-50).

Jesus says, *"I do not judge that person. For I did not come to judge the world "* (Jn.12:47). This sounds definitive, but other sayings in John cloud the picture. For example, the caveat in Jesus' words, *"I pass judgment on no one. But if I do judge, my decisions are true, because I am not alone. I stand with the Father, who sent me"* (Jn.8:15f): or in similar vein, *"Moreover, the Father judges no one, but has entrusted all judgment to the Son ... And he has given him authority to judge because he is the Son of Man"* (Jn.5:22, 27). Even more of an apparent contradiction to Jesus' claim, *"I did not come to judge the world"* (Jn.12:47) is this: *"Jesus said, 'For judgment I have come into this world, so that the blind will see and those who see will become blind. '"* (Jn.9:39). My own opinion is that Jesus did make judgements. Prime examples of this are the seven woes in Matthew and six in Luke against the Scribes and Pharisees (Matt. 23:13-38; Lk.11:37-52) which lead to *"You snakes! You brood of vipers! How will you escape being condemned to hell?"* (Matt.23:33); and culminate in, *"So upon you will come all the righteous blood that has been shed on earth"* (Matt.23:35; Lk.11:50-52). It might seem that this is not only judgement, but condemnation. However, it can be reasonably argued that Jesus was only making plain the verdict which the subjects of his woes were bringing upon themselves, and that in fact his judgement was woe-producing discernment rather than prescription or sentencing.

It is in keeping with this that Jesus cautioned his disciples, *"Do not judge, or you too will be judged. For in the same way you judge others, you will be judged"* (Matt.7:1f). Jesus set judgement and condemnation alongside the desirable quality of mercy or forgiveness: "*Do not judge, and you will not be judged. Do not condemn, and you will not be condemned. Forgive, and you will be forgiven*" (Lk.6:37). In Matthew's version of The Lord's Prayer he includes, "*Forgive us our debts, as we also have forgiven our debtors*" (Matt.6:12). Luke has "sins" (Lk.11:4) not debts (a different Greek word), but both agree that if we forgive others, our Father will forgive us. If we do not forgive others, nor will our Father forgive us (Matt.6:14f; Lk.6:36f). Matthew reinforces this message with the lesson from the parable of the unforgiving servant: "*This is how my heavenly Father will treat each of you unless you forgive your brother or sister from your heart*" (Matt.18:35). If we are looking for those things which count in any final judgement which God might make on our lives, then forgiveness for others or a lack of it would seem to be one of them.

Another, and closely related determining factor of God's judgement, would seem to be "charity". It might seem odd to begin thinking about charity with Jesus' words to his followers, "*Unless your righteousness surpasses that of the Pharisees and teachers of the law, you will certainly not enter the Kingdom of Heaven*" (Matt.5:20); but surely Jesus was not talking about a more meticulous keeping of rules and regulations (Matt.23:23) or better offerings at the altar (cf. Matt.9:13; 12:7). He was referring to the kind of Godly behaviour which the Pharisees and teachers of the Law neglected: "*You have neglected the more important matters of the law – justice, mercy and faithfulness*" (Matt.23:23). Our behaviour and attitudes need to reflect the nature of God: "*Be merciful, just as your Father is merciful*" (Lk.6:36 - see also Matt.5:7). Indeed, Jesus asked his disciples to "*Be perfect, therefore, as your heavenly Father is perfect*" (Matt.5:48) - which sounds impossible, but Jesus explained to a rich young ruler who seemingly had kept all the commandments from his youth what he meant by perfection: "*If you want to be perfect, go, sell your possessions and give to the poor, and you will have treasures in heaven. Then come, follow me*" (Matt.19:21). A practical demonstration of charity was needed before any possibility of perfection could be countenanced. The story of the rich young ruler offers a test-case of what is needed to show righteousness which "*surpasses that of the Pharisees and teachers of the law*"; and which, of course, meets the requirements of love of God and neighbour as identified by Jesus in answer to the question, "*Which is the greatest commandment in the Law?*" (Matt.22:36). As we have noted before, Jesus does not come to abolish the Law, but to perfect it. We will never be perfected by our unfailing obedience. We can be perfected by emulating to the best of our ability God's unfailing, merciful and redeeming love.

Nonetheless, Jesus as fulfiller of the Law means that the things which the Law prescribes or proscribes must be taken seriously into account. Jesus, confronted by a woman taken in adultery does not condemn her, but he does say, "*Go and sin no more*" (Jn.8:11). If an eye or hand is causing anyone to offend they must take the radical action necessary to eliminate the cause of offending (Matt.18:9; Mk.9:47). People who do not follow a righteous path, even if Jesus walked in their streets, and even if they performed miracles in his name will be told, "*I don't know you or where you are coming from. Away from me, all you evildoers!*" (Lk.13:24-28; Matt.7:22). The rich young ruler was not an evildoer, but he was unwilling to do those things which would have materially impoverished him and in the eyes of the world probably humiliated him. A lack of charity is often accompanied by a lack of genuine humility. This makes "belief", active trust in God, impossible. Jesus said, "*How can you believe since you accept glory from one another but do not seek the glory that comes from the only God?*" (Jn.5:44). "*Life does not consist in an abundance of possessions*" (Lk.12:15).

Other things are important in determining by what criteria we are judged. The words we speak matter. In the parable of the gold coins the master says, "*I will judge you by your own words, you wicked servant!*" (Lk.19:22). Matthew gives Jesus' direct teaching: "*But I tell you that everyone will have to give account on the Day of Judgment for every empty word they have spoken. For by your words you will be acquitted, and by your words you will be condemned*" (Matt.12:36f).

Our attitude to life itself is also important, "*For whoever wants to save their life will lose it, but whoever loses their life for me will find it*" (Matt.16:25; Mk.8:35; Lk.9:24; cf.Matt.10:39); "*Very truly I tell you, unless a grain of wheat falls to the ground and dies, it remains only a single seed. But if it dies, it produces many seeds*" (Jn.12:24).

But I want to draw these thoughts about judgement to a close principally using a section of Matthew's gospel. I believe it has much to teach about the subject of judgement. However, I begin with a verse from the Fourth gospel: "*Now is the time for judgment on this world; now the prince of this world will be driven out*" (Jn.12:31). These words are spoken shortly after the account of Jesus' entry to Jerusalem and just before Jesus went to the upper room with his disciples, on to Gethsemane and thence to his death. There may be a day of reckoning to come when the Son of Man comes in his glory for the second time, but there is also judgement intimately connected with and demonstrated in the closing days of Jesus' life prior to Golgotha. The way of the cross is offered in contrast to the way of the world: "*Now is the time for judgment*"!

In the way Matthew constructs the four chapters (Matt.23-26) which precede the story of Jesus' passion and death in his gospel the reality of judgement "*now*" is made explicit. The seven woes in Matthew (23:13-32) are followed by prophecies and descriptions of traumatic events to come and the signs of the *end of the age* (23:33-44), but the woes are indicative that what will happen "then", at the end of the age, is rooted in what people are doing "now" - repentance is never for tomorrow. Matthew follows the woes and signs with four parables. They all involve judgements or decisions by people who in this way seal their own fate: the wise and the wicked servant (Matt.24:45-51); five wise and five foolish virgins (Matt.25:1-13); two profitable and one wicked and lazy steward (Matt.25:14-30); the sheep and the goats (Matt.25:31-46). All four parables portray a kind of final judgement about individuals. The first three raise questions about people's service of God, who is portrayed as a master and a bridegroom. Have they been faithful? Have they taken the necessary steps to be ready to serve? Have they been profitable servants? These are important questions. But I believe that Matthew's placing of the parable of the sheep and the goats where it comes is quite deliberate and raises the most important question of all. In Matthew this is the last parable told by Jesus. It is clearly a parable of the ultimate ground for judgement, or separation.

The ultimate criterion is how people have responded to Jesus when he presented himself to them as a stranger in need. To repeat the point: how people have responded to Jesus when he presented himself to them in a stranger in need is the basis for ultimate judgement. As though to confirm this, in Matthew the parable of the sheep and goats leads into three real life examples of what people did in response to Jesus. The chief priests and the elders, in keeping with their constant rejection of him, plotted to kill Jesus (Matt.26:1-5). Judas, who John tells us was a persistent betrayer of trust, a thief (Jn.12:6), agreed to betray Jesus for money (Matt.26:14-16). But sandwiched in between these negative scenarios comes the commendable, amazingly generous and beautiful anointing of Jesus' head with expensive perfume - giving without regard to cost (Matt.26:6-13) - exactly what the rich young ruler could not do, and the opposite of Judas' motivation of greed and the chief priests' desire to destroy. Some people were already poles apart, separated, condemned or commended by their own words and deeds; others through their generous love were already sharing in Jesus' life and death and greater life. That is how judgement works.

9. The greatest commandment.

If I was asked what is the greatest commandment, on the basis of life as part of the Baptist Union for the past ten years or more, I would have to respond with Matthew 28:19-20 "*Therefore go and make disciples of all nations, baptising them in the name of the Father and of the Son and of the Holy Spirit, and teaching them to obey everything I have commanded you. And surely I am with you always, to the very end of the age*". Mission, mission, mission, has been the dominating rhetoric of our denominational life, accompanied with urges for more church growth and church planting. One department of the Baptist Union tried to reshape this, or at least provide a balance, by an initiative called "Crossing Places". This encouraged people to recognise and use opportunities to show God's love where they live and work or play without ulterior motives or hidden agenda. The department has been closed as part of a cost cutting exercise. The Baptist Union has not been alone in seeming to believe that a gospel imperative (as well as a financial one!) is "grow or die". Whereas, perhaps naively, it seems to me that the genuine gospel demand is "be prepared to die in order to find new life". Matthew 28:19-20 is a great commission, it is not the greatest commandment.

In some senses it should be easy for any Christian to answer the question, "What is the greatest commandment?" The question was put directly to Jesus and he gave a direct answer. It is not found in Matthew chapter 28, but in Matthew 22:25-40, Mark.12:28-31 and Luke.10:25-27 (the text of these if given below):

Those who espouse and prioritise missionary enterprises perhaps need to take to heart the many cautions about mission or evangelism found in the gospels. In Mark it is not only demons who are told to keep to themselves their knowledge of Jesus (Mk.1:34; 3:12), so are people who have experienced the healing power of Jesus: a leper (Mk.1:44), the parents of a little girl (Mk.5:43), and the friends of a deaf mute (Mk.7:36). Jesus even cautioned his disciples not to speak about him (Mk.8:30), or at least not until after his resurrection (Mk.9:9). But probably the strongest admonition against unbridled and misplaced missionary zeal comes in Matthew. It is in a text which I have never heard used as the basis of a sermon. Jesus said, "*Woe to you, teachers of the law and Pharisees, you hypocrites! You travel over land and sea to win a single convert, and when you have succeeded, you make them twice as much a child of hell as you are*" (Matt.23:15). Missionary work is not *per se* good. It is to our shame that mission "in the name of Jesus" has at times effectively been aimed at cloning ourselves, or perhaps even worse instituting a form of imperialism. That is a cause for woe.

When Jesus sent his disciples out, it was to places "*where he himself would come*" (Lk.10:1, cp. Matt.11:10). They were not sent to create more disciples in their own image; they were sent to heal and preach so as to prepare the ground for Jesus to be received. It is inconceivable that they would have imagined they could determine the results of Jesus' presence in any place or in any life. One highly commendable, but apparently unwanted, feature of "Crossing Places" was that it had no pre-determined or measurable outcomes. However, this open-ended approach is in a context in which some pastors are "paid by results", and models, handbooks, videos and endless other materials are available to produce a purpose-driven church with goals or targets, leaders and management teams rather than encouraging churches to be dedicated to losing their lives in the service of others assisted by servants (ministers and deacons). There are clearly choices to be made.

Chapter 5 - Reflections

I am not against missionary activity. Jesus did commission his disciples, the first thing Andrew did after listening to Jesus was to go and tell his brother (Jn.1:41), and the fields were ready for harvest (Jn.4:35). But my firm belief is that a proper response (that is, one Jesus would commend) to the commission in Matthew 28:19-20 can only be made if the greatest commandment is the motive force and guiding light of any missionary endeavour. It is a delight to know many missionaries for whom it is.

Mark does not record the great commission as given in Matthew, but in Mark Jesus envisages the gospel being *"preached throughout the world"* (Mk.14:9). According to Jesus, when it is preached the story of the woman with the alabaster jar of very expensive perfume will be part of it. Why? Because the love and devotion shown by her actions is precisely in keeping with the greatest commandment as identified by Jesus in Matthew 22:25-40, Mark.12:28-31 and Luke.10:25-27:

> *"One of them, an expert in the law, tested him with this question: 'Teacher, which is the greatest commandment in the Law?' Jesus replied: '"Love the Lord your God with all your heart and with all your soul and with all your mind." This is the first and greatest commandment. And the second is like it: "Love your neighbour as yourself." All the Law and the Prophets hang on these two commandments"* (Matt.22:35-40).

> *"One of the teachers of the law .... asked him, 'Of all the commandments, which is the most important?' 'The most important one,' answered Jesus, 'is this: "Hear, O Israel: the Lord our God, the Lord is one. Love the Lord your God with all your heart and with all your soul and with all your mind and with all your strength". The second is this: "Love your neighbour as yourself. There is no commandment greater than these"* " (Mk.12:28-31).

> *"On one occasion an expert in the law stood up to test Jesus. 'Teacher,' he asked, 'what must I do to inherit eternal life?' 'What is written in the Law?' he replied. 'How do you read it?' He answered, '"Love the Lord your God with all your heart and with all your soul and with all your strength and with all your mind"; and, "Love your neighbour as yourself."' 'You have answered correctly,' Jesus replied, 'Do this and you will live.'"* (Lk.10:25-27).

The differences between these three accounts merit attention, and reflect much of what has been said in this work about the different emphases of the Synoptic gospel writers. In Matthew the commands to love God and neighbour are seen as the basis from which the whole of the rest of the law is derived, *"All the Law and the Prophets hang on these two commandments"* (Matt 22:40). In Luke's version, it is the lawyer who identifies the crucial law; and all attention becomes focussed on the command to love one's neighbour, since in Luke it is followed and interpreted by the parable of the Good Samaritan (Lk.10:29-37). In Mark Jesus includes the beginning of the Shema - a call to listen obediently: " *Hear, O Israel: the Lord our God, the Lord is one*" (Mk.12:29; Deuteronomy 6:4).

Whatever the differences in the Synoptic accounts of the greatest commandment, the variations are minor in comparison with their unanimity in the combination of Leviticus 19:18 and Deuteronomy 6:5 to identify the essential kernel of the greatest commandment as "Love God - Love your neighbour". To anyone who effectively prioritizes Matthew 28:19-20 by saying that the greatest love that can be shown to anyone is to introduce them to Jesus, it should be pointed out that such a sleight of hand has scant justification in the stories of Jesus or his teaching.

In Luke, the greatest commandment is part of a conversation which begins with what was meant to be a trap-question, "*What must I do to inherit eternal life?*" (Lk.10:25). Luke, in common with Matthew and Mark records the same question being asked by a rich man (Matt.19:16ff. Mk.10:17ff. Lk.18:18ff). But there are effectively only two other references in the Synoptics to *eternal life* (Matt.19:29 // Mk.10:30 //Lk.18:30. & Matt.25:46). In contrast the fourth gospel has seventeen instances where the term *eternal life* is used. With one exception, Peter (Jn.6:6), the words are used by Jesus. Predominantly the basis for eternal life is belief in Jesus as the one whom God has sent, and eternal life is his gift. But John also records Jesus' saying, "*I did not speak on my own, but the Father who sent me commanded me to say all that I have spoken. I know that his command leads to eternal life. So whatever I say is just what the Father has told me to say*" (Jn.12:49f). The words, "*I know that his command leads to eternal life*" are not obviously synonymous with the Synoptics "greatest commandment", but in John's Gospel any authority Jesus claims is derived from his Father (Jn.10:18; 12:49; 14:31), and belief or trust in Jesus derives from trust in God (Jn.14:1). This trust is shown by obedience to what is commanded; and what is commanded is love (Jn.13:34; 15:17). Love is the intended outcome of obedience to the commandments (Jn.14:21; 15:10); but it is also the motivation for obedience (Jn.14:15). The Synoptics identify love as the "greatest commandment": in John's gospel it is Jesus' "only commandment".

10. *The Eucharist or the Lord's Supper.*

I have singled out the Eucharist for special consideration because of the particularly strong impact I felt when reading the gospels and laying them alongside the practices of churches in this matter. It has left me with many questions and practical issues for consideration. But as with most important matters, whatever legitimate answers there may be will only come by wrestling with the subject (cf. Genesis 32:22ff). What follows is certainly not an end result, a final statement, more of a progress report on a work-in-hand.

In offering thoughts on almost any subject one's background is inevitably influential. For the first twenty years of my life I neither heard nor knew of the word "Eucharist". I was raised in the 1940s and 50s in a Baptist Church which "observed the Lord's Supper" at "The Lord's Table". The tradition of my home church was that this "observance" came after a service of public worship had been formally ended and was by invitation for baptised church members only – what was known as "the closed table". Only in my later teens was it integrated into the main service and the more general invitation given along the lines: "*All those who love the Lord and accept him as their Saviour are welcome to share in this meal*". The Lord's Supper was also regularly referred to as "Communion" or "Holy Communion". People received it. They did not, as in some traditions, "*make their communion*". In theory, though not entirely in reality, morning and evening services served two different congregations, so The Lord's Supper was shared once a month both morning and evening. I still do not know a rational explanation for once a month; nor why for certain expressions of the church it has been an annual ritual, at least for the laity[39], whereas for many in "High Churches" it is a daily requirement[40].

When I went to Rawdon College in Yorkshire to train for the Baptist Ministry in the early 1960s, I entered a slightly more ecumenical world; although I can still remember the shock waves caused in the college because an ex-student had "defected to the Anglicans". At Rawdon I was positively encouraged to question my beliefs and my previous experience of church; but it was in Manchester with the influence of Michael Taylor that such questioning really began to have an ecumenical context. On leaving college I was further educated and blessed. In my first full-time pastorate the local Roman Catholic priests, and one of the three local Church of England priests, welcomed me into their fraternal along with those few Free Church colleagues who were open-hearted and open-minded enough to participate. There was a small Council of Churches of which I became secretary, a role I have also enjoyed in Northampton. Over the years Councils of Churches which consisted predominantly of representatives of the major traditional English denominations have evolved into "Churches Together". They now typically embrace a multi-national variety of traditions as well as many independent and newer manifestations of "church" - with an ever increasing diversity of views about sharing bread and wine.

---

[39] e.g. a widespread phenomenon in 16th century Europe. see D. MacCulloch *A history of Christianity* Penguin 2010]
[40] This practice is possibly justified from Acts 2:46 which records a "daily breaking of bread". But see more on this below.

Chapter 5 - Reflections

Many of us have been privileged to sense, and sometimes to draw upon the deep spirituality of men and women of faith from a very wide variety of traditions. Anything I say or write about churches, including the Eucharist, is in no way meant to demean what someone else believes and practices. The Eucharist is possibly the most sensitive subject in inter-church dialogue. The Rt. Rev. Lindsey Urwin, commending a newly installed Anglican priest-in-charge to celebrate a daily Eucharist, said, "*The Eucharist is not just something we do; it is that which makes us who we are, the Body of Christ*"[41]. This echoed the response of a former Roman Catholic Bishop of Northampton at a Theological Society meeting. When asked why his church would not welcome all Christians to share in the Mass, he declared his conviction that the sacrament of the Mass is in effect what the church is. To effectively secularise the Mass would be to deny or destroy the church's identity as the body of Christ. As early as the second century C.E. Irenaeus noted an intimate connection for him between the Eucharist and the role of a bishop as well as its anti-Gnostic stress on the real physical presence of Christ[42].

Nonetheless, however much we may wish to respect each other's praxis, an honest appraisal of what the New Testament says on the subject of the Lord's Supper, or Eucharist, raises difficult questions for "Sacramentalists" as well as for me.

On leaving college more than forty years ago the Baptist church where I first ministered full-time agreed with my suggestion that we observe the Lord's Supper every Sunday. At that time the grounds I gave for this were that it was Biblical. I believed then that according to the Acts of the Apostles this is what the early church did. I have since realised that these were not solid grounds. There is little if any New Testament evidence for such practice; and probably none in the Book of Acts. In fact new converts met daily (Acts 2:46). They shared fellowship meals, but these were unlikely to have been sacramental: probably more to do with the initial aim of the apostles to "hold all things in common" (Acts 2:44). Moreover, the only possible example in the entire New Testament of a Sunday meeting for worship could actually have been on Saturday (Acts 20:7) and was probably arranged because Paul was leaving the next day rather than in accordance with a set day for sharing word or sacrament[43]. In addition to this absence of Biblical warrant for Sunday worship, I think that many Christians would be amazed to learn that apart from the Synoptic gospel accounts of the last supper, and Paul's account

---

[41] All Saints, Northampton 28-4-12

[42] MacCulloch *A History of Christianity* p.143

[43] TEV, NEB and the Jerusalem Bible all suggest translating the verse as "Saturday" in keeping with the Jewish way of reckoning the week: but scholarly opinion is divided. See the Trinitarian Societies article
http://www.holybible.com/resources/Trinitarian/article_448.htm for a well balanced review

Chapter 5 - Reflections

in 1 Corinthians 11, nowhere else in the New Testament is there a reference to the
disciples or others of the earliest Christians sharing bread and wine[44], just as there
are no references to Christians meeting on the first or any other specified day of the
week.

I am not alone in believing that some churches subsequently read into the
scriptures their practices, including the celebration of the Eucharist.   Paul
Bradshaw questions the assumption that Jesus instituted the Eucharist at the Last
Supper[45]. Michaels reflecting on John 6:41-59 remarks on the way references in
the fourth gospel to eating Jesus' flesh and drinking his blood have been interpreted
as having Eucharistic connotations. But Michaels tellingly says the following:

> *"'The Jews' are confused by Jesus' reference to 'eating' him, and their
> confusion is hardly likely to be allayed by referring to a Christian ritual that
> did not yet exist. More likely, the sacramental or Eucharistic interpretation
> of the text belongs to 'reception history' of the text rather than to the gospel
> writer's intention (much less the intention of Jesus within the story)"*[46].

Michael's is surely correct. The Eucharist is not in the text, it is in the mindset of
later commentators. There is no mention in John of a last supper in which bread
and wine are shared. If we take into account that John's gospel has no record of
Jesus' baptism and specifically states that Jesus himself did not baptise, then this
"omission" with regard to the sharing of bread and wine by John possibly
represents a non-sacramental (even anti-sacramental) school of thought which is to
be found not only in subsequent expressions of Christianity[47], but in the New
Testament itself. One possible inference from the story in John 5 where a man does
not need to get into a pool to be made whole is that the ritual of baptism/immersion
is not necessary. Furthermore, there would seem to be a firmly stated injunction in
the New Testament against the sharing of bread and wine in any kind of
"ceremony", or involving an altar, or even a building! Consider line-by-line the
implications of the following from Hebrews:-

> *"It is good for our hearts to be strengthened by grace,
> not by eating ceremonial foods, which is of no benefit to those who do so.*
>
> *We have an altar from which those who minister at the tabernacle have no
> right to eat.*

---

[44] MacCulloch *A History of Christianity* p.159
[45] Paul F. Bradshaw *Reconstructing Early Christian Worship* SPCK 2009 reviewed by Erin
Evans Expository Times Aug.2010 Vol.11 p565
[46] TGJ p.396
[47] e.g. in the 16-17th century. See MacCulloch *A History of Christianity* p.665

Chapter 5 - Reflections

Jesus suffered outside the city gate to make the people holy through his own blood.
Let us, then, go to him outside the camp, bearing the disgrace he bore.

Through Jesus, therefore, let us continually offer to God a sacrifice of praise – the fruit of lips that openly profess his name.

And do not forget to do good and to share with others, for with such sacrifices God is pleased" (Hebrews 13:9-16 abridged) [48].

The plain meaning of these words is that the ritual we call the Eucharist is not what God requires. Sacramental practice even suggests that the once-for-all sacrifice of Jesus was insufficient and detracts from the call for Jesus' followers to share in his "disgrace".

Yet, knowing all of this, and keeping it in mind, I have continued to encourage a weekly observance of the Lord's Supper within a service which is intentionally the sharing of Word and Sacrament, sometimes including grapes and matzos in addition to bread and wine as a means of encouraging everyone to share. Why? Because, although terms such as "Eucharist", "Holy Communion" and "The Sacred Mass" may unhelpfully institutionalise what Jesus did, sharing in the Lord's Supper is Biblical, though the manner in which it is done may not be; and I have done my best not to see it as a ritual. Furthermore, the Lord's Supper is also at its best essentially non-cerebral, providing an opportunity for us to *"feed on him in our hearts by faith with thanksgiving"*. MacCulloch says of this sharing of bread and wine:-

"From the earliest times of its institution, it involved a recital of the words of Jesus which ordered his followers to do it in remembrance of him, and it was done as a re-enactment of that 'last supper' which Jesus shared with his Twelve before his arrest. The power and mystery of the Eucharist, linking the crucified to those who break bread and drink wine ever afterwards, has provoked intense devotion, gratitude and joy among Christians ...."[49]

Churches in which I have been involved have acknowledged that others call the sharing of bread and wine "The Eucharist", but it is not our preferred term. Because the Eucharistic rite is commonly the practice of churches wherein for them it is the most important thing they do, it has ossified into a more-or-less set

[48] This is totally in keeping with the words of the prophets who denounced the sacrifices being made in their day as a distraction from doing what God really wanted cf. Isaiah 1:11-14; Amos 5:21. See also Ps.50:5-15
[49] MacCulloch *A History of Christianity* p.92

297

ritual, for which a church sets rules for participation or exclusion. Contrariwise, in keeping with Paul's terminology (1 Cor.11:20) we participate in *"The Lord's Supper"*, shared at the Lord's Table. It is not for us to decide who the Lord will accept at his table. Judas Iscariot was not barred from the last supper. If the gospel stories about the company Jesus kept have any credence at all, those of us who are "religious" are probably the least well qualified to determine the guest list for the *Lord's* Supper[50]. "We" (religious people) were not only for Jesus, but also for many of the prophets, the chief targets for the harshest criticism. Furthermore, in keeping with Hebrews 13:16 and the general tenor of Jesus' teaching, it is not the most important thing we do. Whilst respecting the viewpoint of the two Bishops mentioned above, our love for one another and the world, not an observance of a ritual, gives us our true identity as the body of Christ.

I should also declare two reasons why sharing in the Lord's Supper has been of great benefit to me. First, I have usually followed the Baptist tradition in which deacons take the bread and wine to the congregation. This seems a much closer reflection of Jesus' way both in feeding the crowds and his instructions at the last supper (Luke 22:17), as well as a better embodiment of the idea of "Communion", than people going to a priest to "make their communion". But this pattern has also meant that as the minister/celebrant there have been a few moments in the midst of worship in which I could find space for my soul to rest, and feed on him in my heart. Engagement in the activity of conducting worship may be serving God with all my heart and mind and strength and soul, but I have valued the brief opportunity within worship to stop being active in order to be more consciously receptive and contemplative, to offer my personal devotions and to be one with the whole congregation in a common act.

Second: many years ago in the 1960's John Robinson, the then rather controversial Bishop of Woolwich wrote *Liturgy Coming to Life*[51]. In this book he pointed out that the word "remember" used in the Eucharist is a translation of the Greek *anamnesin* with the root verb *mneuo* which includes the idea of bringing the past into the present. Robinson believed that is what Jesus was inviting his disciples to do – was not to remember him in the sense of "he is now preserved in history", but to re-member him in the same sense that he asked them to believe that wherever two or three of them came together in his name he would be there with them, a real presence. I have not only felt that when the bread and wine are shared Jesus of Nazareth is somehow present, but also all those saints who have been a blessing in my life but who walk this earth no more - what I sometimes call *"the whole company of God's people on earth and in heaven"*. If I am honest, apart from sharing the Lord's Prayer at funeral services, there is no other moment in worship

---

[50] see MacCulloch p.6 for a closely related point.

[51] John A. T. Robinson *Liturgy Coming to Life* Westminster Press 1960

when I feel this so strongly. Rob Bell's notion that the Kingdom of Heaven drags the future into the present is paralleled by Robinson's dragging the past into the present, and it all evokes such a sense of wonder and blessing[52].

MacCulloch rightly says that as well as the benefits, arguments amongst Christians about the meaning of the sharing of bread and wine have provoked deep anger and bitterness, not to mention divisions and mutual destruction[53]. I can only hope that in a developing atmosphere of genuine and mutual ecumenical respect such times are past - though not all my experience supports the hope. However, as part of a Baptist Church I am not only heir to that tradition which gave pride of place in its worship as well as its architecture to the pulpit rather than the altar[54]. It is also a tradition which replaced the altar with its notions of repeated sacrifice by the table which recalls the once-and-one-for-all sacrifice made by Jesus which the bread and wine symbolise. Martin Luther may not have actually said, "*Here I stand. I can do no other*", but the words capture the reality for many Christians, including myself, and those who have grown in other traditions.

But let us to turn to what the gospels say. It was not practicable to "unpack" the strong messages of Hebrews 13:9-16 above as I would have loved to do. For the same reasons many of the gospels' important references to bread or wine will not receive a mention here, let alone be followed up. I have tried to limit the basis for the following discourse to those passages which many would see as a gospel justification for the sharing of bread and wine in a sacramental act.

The three synoptic accounts of "the last supper" include significant variations as well as commonalities.

> "*While they were eating, Jesus took bread, and when he had given thanks, he broke it and gave it to his disciples, saying, "Take and eat; this is my body."*
>
> *Then he took a cup, and when he had given thanks, he gave it to them, saying, "Drink from it, all of you. This is my blood of the covenant, which is poured out for many for the forgiveness of sins. I tell you, I will not drink from this fruit of the vine from now on until that day when I drink it new with you in my Father's kingdom." When they had sung a hymn, they went out to the Mount of Olives.* (Matt.26:26-30).

---

[52] Rob Bell "Love Wins" p.41 Collins 2011

[53] Examples of this abound throughout MacCulloch's history of the Church; but Zwingli v Luther would be a classic example p.620

[54] cf. MacCulloch p.681

Chapter 5 - Reflections

"While they were eating, Jesus took bread, and when he had given thanks, he broke it and gave it to his disciples, saying, 'Take it; this is my body.'
Then he took a cup, and when he had given thanks, he gave it to them, and they all drank from it. 'This is my blood of the covenant, which is poured out for many,' he said to them. 'Truly I tell you, I will not drink again from the fruit of the vine until that day when I drink it new in the kingdom of God'
When they had sung a hymn, they went out to the Mount of Olives." (Mk.14:22-26).

"After taking the cup, he gave thanks and said, 'Take this and divide it among you. For I tell you I will not drink again from the fruit of the vine until the kingdom of God comes.'
And he took bread, gave thanks and broke it, and gave it to them, saying, 'This is my body given for you; do this in remembrance of me.'
In the same way, after the supper he took the cup, saying, 'This cup is the new covenant in my blood, which is poured out for you. But the hand of him who is going to betray me is with mine on the table'" (Lk.22:17-21).

Matthew and Mark end the supper with a hymn; which might suggest a formal ritual. But Luke ends it with Jesus' prophecy of betrayal. This in turn leads to an argument amongst the disciples about which of them was the greatest and Jesus' comment, *"I am among you as one who serves"* (Lk.22:24-27), reminiscent of John's story of Jesus washing his disciples' feet (Jn.13:3-17). In Luke, the last supper is but one part of a wider teaching session.

There are other differences. In Matthew the cup which is offered to all of the disciples is Jesus' blood of the covenant poured out for many for the forgiveness of sins; whereas in Mark it is Jesus' blood of the (new?) covenant poured out for many with no specified purpose. In Luke there are two cups - or one cup is used twice - with different accompanying words. The cup before the meal is to be divided amongst the disciples: the one taken at the end of the meal is the new covenant in Jesus' blood and it is poured out for "you". In none of the gospel accounts does Jesus say of the cup, *"Do this in remembrance of me"*. The testimony of Paul in his letter to the church at Corinth is that these words were part of the tradition he had received *"from the Lord"* (1 Cor.11:23, 25); but as we have noted Paul's account is an isolated and unique justification in the New Testament for sharing both bread and wine *"in remembrance"*.

But Paul with regard to the bread is in accord with the gospel writers in that Jesus is nowhere reported to have said the words which I have often heard, and which I have used in the past, *"This is my body which is broken for you"*. The brokenness of the bread, like the suffering involved in his crucifixion, does not seem to have been of major significance to Jesus. The bread was the gift of his own body to his disciples and it was receiving, remembering, sharing and embodying him which was being encouraged, not commemorating his brokenness (Matt. 26:26; Mk. 14:22; Lk.22:19). Indeed, bread was traditionally an offering which accompanied sacrifice not part of the sacrifice itself (cf. Leviticus 7:13). The cup represents the sacrifice, and according to Matthew and Mark it is not to be drunk in remembrance, but will be shared in the post sacrificial "kingdom". This perhaps raises some serious questions for those who have prioritized the cup over the bread in the regular celebration of the Eucharist.

There are those who regard John's account of the feeding of five thousand (Jn.6:1-15) as a parallel to the Synoptics' Last Supper, in spite of the complete absence of wine and the inclusion of fish (see also Jn.21:13). They will need to include the manner and setting of the miraculous feeding, as well as the accompanying excursus on Jesus as the Bread of Life in considering how the bread might be best appreciated. However, for bread (and cup) there is no single irrefutable "explanation". Rather we are invited into a world of symbols which can constantly enrich us, and even to some extent satisfy us; but in every gospel account the *living bread* is tasted in a Passover context. It is food for a journey, not a meal to make us content with where we are.

In John's Gospel Jesus does not give himself at the last (supper) to his disciples in the elements of bread and wine - although Jesus does offer himself earlier in the gospel as *the bread of life* to all who were listening, not just his disciples (Jn.6:35). Perhaps less obviously Jesus offers himself as wine through his first sign in Cana of Galilee, water into wine (Jn.2:9, 11), or in Jesus declaring his blood to be the *true drink* (Jn.6:55), the ramifications of which are taken up at his last supper when Jesus speaks of himself as *the true vine* (Jn.15:1-11). But in John, at his last supper Jesus gave himself to his disciples in service, not sacramental elements. He washed their feet (Jn.13:3ff). The conjunction of the first sign, in which the obedience of the servants produces the best wine, and the foot washing sign in which Jesus takes the role of a servant is easily lost by a non-Johannine over-concentration on the wine. Wine as a symbol or sign used by Jesus does not feature very much in any of the four gospels. I would suggest that churches by calling some things sacraments and ritualising them have to some degree privatised and severely limited the availability of the many signs and symbols which in the ministry of Jesus were offered freely to all as ways to receive him.

It is important to me that within the company of the Christians who are an encouragement and challenge to my faith are members of the Society of Friends and the Salvation Army whose worship for quite different reasons seldom if ever includes the Eucharist. There are Black Pentecostals who break bread when the spirit moves them, and many Free Church people who still "observe the Lord's Supper" once a month. There are low Anglicans who try to attend Holy

Communion once a week; Catholics who celebrate the Eucharist every day. The priority or otherwise given to the Eucharistic tradition seems to bear no direct relationship to the depth and evident devotion to following the example of Jesus in loving, sacrificial living. When viewed improperly the Eucharist has been something to die, or even kill for: we are better without it. But when the sharing of bread and wine is appreciated as a commission to follow Jesus' example and to live sacrificially in "holy communion" with God and all our neighbours, it has the potential to change us and the world.

Chapter Six.

Using the differences: - An example - A sermon based on Mark 1:16-20; Matt 4:18-22; Luke 5:1-11; John 1:35-42.

"The Calling of Jesus' First Disciples"

The four New Testament gospels offer three quite distinct stories of how the first people who chose to follow Jesus made their start on what was to be a demanding physical and spiritual journey. The calling of the first four of the twelve disciples is an example of how the gospels often tell the same basic story, but have differences which mean that each is worth reading. Each has something special to teach us.

Mark 1:16-20, which is word for word the same as Matt 4:18-22, is probably the story that most church people think of as the call of the first four of the 12 disciples whom Jesus selected *"to be with him, to learn from him and through him, and to share his ministry of spreading good news in word and action"*. These (italicised) words might be seen as a description of a "Christian" or Jesus-follower in any age. But in thinking about how the first followers of Jesus began their following it is helpful to consider more than the account in Mark and Matthew; for Luke and John also have something to tell us. If we conflate the stories, or prioritise one story in particular, we will lose the distinctive yet equally valuable messages which each have to offer.

Let us first consider the call of Jesus' first disciples in Mark. In the way in which Mark recounts the calling of the first four disciples (Simon and Andrew, then James and John) their encounters with Jesus and his calling of them appears to be completely "out of the blue". (Mk.1:16-18) Jesus is just walking along when he sees two fishermen about their business, Simon and his brother Andrew. Jesus says, "Follow me - and I'll make you fishers of men" - and "at once" they leave everything and follow Jesus. The fact that they are casting their nets from the shore has suggested to some people that these were poor fishermen who could not afford a boat, but had to rely on fishing in the shallows for smaller fish. Perhaps their nets are all these poor fishermen have to leave - but that would almost certainly be a big sacrifice for them - the nets were their living. Having called Simon and Andrew, Jesus going a little further sees James & John (& Zebedee their father) in a boat preparing their nets. "Without delay" he calls James & John. These men, apparently quite unconnected to Peter and Andrew, have a boat, a father and hired men. They have rather more to leave behind, but they also follow there and then. I don't know for sure whether we can make the social distinction, because the same Greek word is used for the nets being used by all four fishermen [44], but I like to think they were not in the same working conditions when Jesus called them. What is possibly more important, however, is that there is an immediacy about Mark's record of the call of the disciples. They follow "immediately" or "at once". I can remember a group laughing at a Bible study when they learned to look out for the word "immediately" or synonyms when we were studying Mark's gospel. The word keeps on appearing, because there is an urgency which runs right through Mark's Gospel and gives it a unique flavour. For Jesus in Mark's gospel the way of the cross calls, and the passion must be entered into in less than a year; so you need to get on board at once for the journey. Instant decisions are needed and made. Watch, pray and be ready to act now, because you never know when it might be too late. That is how it has always seemed to some people, and how it is for some today. I have a good friend, a pastor of a multi-national church. He tells his story of being down and out and literally destined for the gutter. But he went into a chapel for a bit of shelter and warmth. He was sitting at the back trying not to be noticed when the words of the preacher spoke to him and were a call for him to follow Jesus. There and then he accepted the call, and in that moment his life was changed. He has always felt that had he not made the decision at that specific moment it would have been too late.

Mark's Gospel tells a story which rings true for many. Sadly there are those who make this the one and only template for responding to the call of Jesus to follow him. This may be because they only know this story, or because it has been their experience and they believe everyone must share their experience. But it is not the only story on offer in the gospels.   Let's look at Luke's story.

Luke has a story of the call of just three disciples, Simon (Peter), James & John. This story is very different in some ways from Mark. The context is not the same as in Mark. You will remember that in Mark the call of the disciples is "out of the blue". Luke (5:1-11) places the call of Peter, James and John within a story which concerns the catch of a large number of fish, and a confession by Peter of his unworthiness. Prior to Peter's call, Jesus had already engaged in an extensive preaching and healing ministry, and had healed Peter's mother-in-law of a high fever (4:38-39). This is no stranger on the shore.   In Luke (5:2-3), Jesus gets into Simon's (empty!) boat and uses it as a pulpit to preach to the people who are crowding in on him. I often wonder if Jesus preached the parable of the sower. (Although Luke has it in chapter 8:5-8.) If he did, then the spoken farming parable was followed by an acted fishing parable. After Simon's unsuccessful whole night of fishing Jesus provides more appropriate teaching in the form of a symbol for Simon the fisherman of a "successful" ministry (many fish are caught) - which provokes Simon's response of "*Go away, I'm not good enough for this*", and Jesus' wonderful and thoroughly biblical rejoinder, "*Don't be afraid, from now on...*". Like most good marriages, the coming together of Jesus and his first disciple in Luke was preceded by a time of preparation: then "*From this day forward, for better or worse, richer or poorer, etc.*"

In Luke, James & John are Simon's partners (Lk.5:10a), and unlike in Mark's account, they are not called separately. Andrew, Simon's brother, receives no mention in this story. In fact this is really the story of the call of Simon - only Simon is specifically called (Lk.5:10b-11). But here is the big difference. In Luke, Simon's response follows on from teaching, guidance and reassurance by Jesus. Indeed, as we have already noted, if we look a little earlier in Luke we find that Jesus had already been in Simon's house and had restored Simon's mother-in-law to health. This is no out of the blue response.

Can you see already how the two stories (Mark contra Luke) provide different templates for how the call of Jesus may be given and received? In Mark four people are called, two by two. The call is unexpected and the response is immediate and positive. In Luke, a number of people are clearly involved, but the call comes particularly to one person who needs nurturing - even if with shock treatment - into a positive response to Jesus. Beware of churches and Christians who only know Mark's story, and who only know about instant conversions and instant decisions. It's not the only valid story - not the only story which should be told. Some people need a lot more work, a lot more patience, a lot more love - even a lot more evidence! I can testify from my personal experience, and from lives I have seen changed that the call to follow sometimes takes a while to register, and then perhaps more even time to begin to accept the call in a life-changing way.

Also worth our attention in Luke's story is that the partnership of Simon with James and John and his ownership of a boat puts Simon in the category of a small businessman, not the poor fisherman in Mark. Simon has to leave a business in order to follow the call of Jesus. At an induction of a minister in Northampton, the newly ordained minister spoke of how he had left his small but moderately successful business, handing it over to his partners in order that he might follow what he believed to be the call of Jesus on his life - but it had taken a lot of encouragement for him to take such a step. Luke's story of the call of Simon also resonates for some.

But there's yet another story!! The story in John's Gospel - and this is even further away from the story in Mark, because this story has nothing about fishermen; and James and John are never mentioned in John's Gospel. In fact you have to get to the end of John's Gospel (Jn.21:3) before you learn that some of Jesus' disciples can fish, and only at the end of the story did Jesus' instructions lead to the large haul! John's gospel story of the call of the first disciples of Jesus begins with the fact that John the Baptist had disciples (Jn.1:35 - See also Acts 19:3-4). It was John the Baptist's testimony to Jesus as "The Lamb of God" that led to two of John's disciples leaving him to literally "follow" Jesus. This following, however, was without any invitation from Jesus to follow him. And after they had started to follow Jesus he invited them not to follow, but rather to begin to learn about him and from him - to spend a day with Jesus. In John's gospel these two were the first followers of Jesus - but they were neither called nor chosen. In John's gospel the first disciple to have a clear call to follow is Phillip.

It intrigues me as to who the other, unnamed first disciple in John was (Andrew's wife?). But one of the first two is named as Andrew. Andrew doesn't feature at all in Luke's story and is marginal in Matthew and Mark, but in John's Gospel Andrew learns something about Jesus, and the first thing he does is to go and tell his brother - who is Simon – also known, of course, as Peter. Most unlike Matthew, Mark and Luke's stories, Peter in John's gospel receives no initial call from Jesus to follow him, but he is recognised by Jesus. Jesus already knows who he is - and Jesus recognises what this man will be in his company, no longer Simon, but Peter, the rock. In spite of all his wobbling (!!) he was still the rock.

Toward the end of John's Gospel it becomes very clear that Peter had become a man of great influence amongst the disciples, and is especially earmarked by Jesus for a pastoral ministry. BUT the main point from the story about Simon Peter becoming a follower of Jesus is that John's Gospel tells us that Simon Peter came to Jesus in the first place because someone else told him about Jesus, and told him enough so that he wanted to find out for himself (Just like the Samaritan woman's co-villagers later). When Peter came to Jesus it began the process which would turn him into a new person. If, once Peter had met Jesus, the following was instant, the conversion took a long time! Andrew may not have been the best disciple ever, and in fact, according to Mark, Andrew didn't share in some of Jesus' greatest moments like the transfiguration, the raising up of Jairus' daughter, or even watching with Jesus in the garden of Gethsemane. BUT Andrew brought Simon, his brother, to Jesus though he could never have known what a wonderful thing that was to do. There are countless examples of people who did great things for God, but who were initially invited to learn about Jesus by someone whose name has long been forgotten.

I hope it is abundantly obvious from the Gospel stories of the call of Jesus' first disciples that there is no one specified, predetermined way for people to encounter Jesus for the first time, nor a single and correct way for people to respond. But what we can say is that some people still need to hear Jesus' call to follow him for the first time; or to be invited to come and learn about him. And some may be here right now!! Some may be your colleagues at work, your partners or your neighbours. And some may be your brother or your sister or your child - or your parent! If you, or we, invite them to learn about Jesus their response is in God's hands, but God has often put the opportunity of invitation into ours. Will we take it?

Please allow me one little footnote: As we've seen, in John's Gospel the direct invitation to Peter to follow Jesus is not given at the beginning of the Gospel. In fact, "*You must follow me*" are the very last words Jesus speaks to Peter in John's Gospel (Jn.21:19, 22). Jesus said, "*If anyone want to be my disciple they must take up their cross every day and follow me*". Responding to the call to be a disciple is not a one-off decision, but a day by day journey of faith made secure by the love of Jesus. You'll know this if you are following Jesus, and you'll want to invite others to join the journey. AMEN

Note: I have shared the thoughts above within two services as an itinerant preacher. On both occasions I ensured that every member of the congregation had copies of all three gospel texts. This is in keeping with my belief that whenever possible people should have a Bible passage available. In this way the Bible can speak directly to them, but it also provides the opportunity to check whether or not the expositor/preacher is being true to the word.

Index

Index

Index

Index